THE JOURNEY OF

ONE HUNDRED YEARS

A Historical Novel

BY SAM PAWLAK

ISBN 978-0-9700513-5-6

Acknowledgments

When a literary work has taken the greater part of twenty years, from idea to publication, the words of thanks and appreciation could become another volume in itself. However, to recognize the primary contributors to this historical novel, I can only say thanks to all whose encouragements, suggestions and critique have made this book a dream accomplished.

First and foremost I need to acknowledge my wonderful wife Patricia, whom I not only was bestowed the joy of sharing fifty-two years of marriage, but she read, reviewed, and listened to me personally read aloud the nearly 1,200 pages of original text. I am most grateful that she was part of every page before her promotion to her heavenly home just six months before the book went to print.

Equally, I am grateful beyond adequate expression to my son Sammy, and my daughter April for the untold hours of research, review, suggestions, laughter and tears as they treated each story within the story with attention, interest and emotional consumption. They acted as if they had never heard these stories, in spite of the hundreds of times they had heard them while growing up.

Thanks to Hannah's Voice International Publishers, and the administrative staff for the enormous undertaking that caused this script to evolve into a sensible, readable and desired presentation, allowing readers to make this journey side by side with each character.

A word about location is so vital to the understanding of this effort. I give a special thanks to the two main locations where this book was given life. Due to the wonderfully courteous management of the Sunrise Bread Company in Titusville, Florida, almost three years and often eight house per day, the upstairs, far northeast, corner table provided atmosphere and welcome for this writer. The final four years of incessant lap-top clicking took place on the silent mezzanine of one of the most beautiful libraries in America, The Cerritos, California Public Library. The grandeur, modern magnificence, and demanded silence provided someone of my generation the necessary focus to accomplish what my younger counterparts could do with ear buds blasting music in each ear.

Inasmuch as this is a historical work (I have always possessed an immense passion for history), several resources must be given due credit. Among the top were three of the greatest works ever written about the nation of Poland: James A Michener's "Poland" and Norman Davies' "God's Playground." And no serious writing about Poland could be accomplished without reading Henryk Sienkiewicz's "The Trilogy."

I also want to mention the many writings researched on the Pullman Box Car Factory of Michigan City, Indiana, the Bedford, Indiana Limestone Quarries, the Monon Railroad, the Chicago Stockyards, and the wonderful "Chronology of Michigan City, Indiana. Of course, my favorite resource "Google Search."

Because this historical novel is based on one family's story, I am obligated to say, although the author has taken literary license as necessary, the real thanks goes to the many family members who have contributed by relating their stories of the past, or having lived out many illustrations before my very eyes. The final acknowledgment must be expressed to the wonderful friends and citizens of my two favorite countries in the world, Poland and the United States of America.

Contents

Foreward

The stories recorded in these pages have been shared through the years around living rooms, dining tables, and family gatherings. They include tales of trials, challenges, triumphs, deaths, and life at its very best. This gripping chronicle does not simply record the account of one family, but it is the greater telling of a familiar history. It is the history of European immigrants, the history of a Midwest industrial town, the history of a thriving new nation, the history of a family like millions of others facing the struggles of poverty, sickness, social obstacles, armed with only an unwavering love for each other, and sometimes wavering faith. This journey of one hundred years for one family may prove to be the journey of your family as well.

Sammy Pawlak Jr. - Son of the the author

If you could envision a timeline stretched across your path and you could catch a snippet of 100 years, you would discover in that splice of history: stories - stories of people, of changes, of struggles, of victories. You would see individuals finding themselves and sometimes losing themselves. You would see how the circumstances and environments and societies pulled and sought to shape those people. Though their wardrobe may be different and their accents unfamiliar, you might even find yourself identifying with a character or two. This 100-year snippet is a historical novel based on the journey of my family: immigrants arriving to the shores of America with baggage and hope, eventually making it back to their homeland to share the treasure they had found. My hope is that you will also find treasure among the pages, even as you read the tragic parts, and you will find courage from the telling of my father's family's story to make your own journey with courage and purpose.

April Dawn (Pawlak) Goodner - Daughter of the author

CHAPTER 1 - 1893-1903

"Cool...cool...cool...ah!"

Kaz said the words over and over as he gently cupped his little, chubby, eight-year-old hands. He guided every drop to his sunburned and hurting face. He was too young to know what a gold discovery was, yet the same excitement filled his being. The water was not only comforting, it was invigorating. For almost two weeks, he had been running the deck of the cattle-hauling sea vessel. This had taken its toll on his normally white cheeks. Salt water and sun over the unseasonably warm Baltic was no match for the wonderfully cool basin of water. He may have been the only person to have found this little storage closet. The amazing, metal bowl-shaped container gave the water an aesthetic shimmering effect that was pure delight. Then the thought came crashing into his active mind, he'd better get back to mother before she gathers a search party. Someone else might intrude on his secret discovery.

"Matka! Matka! Here I am." he bellowed, seeing her panicked expression. Her eyes were darting from side to side like two search lanterns from a rescue party.

"Kaz, where have you been? I've looked everywhere!" He ran to her welcoming arms and slid his face against hers. She firmly grasped his shoulders, pushed him a focus-length away, and began her dreaded interrogation.

"Why is your face wet? Your cheeks are cold! Where have you been? What were you doing?"

"Just putting water on my face," he replied. "My face, on my face." pointing to his red, blistered cheeks.

"Where did you find water?"

"I don't know." he said with head dropped in unavoidable guilt.

"You show me, and you'll show me now, Boy. You understand?"

Like a criminal taking the jury back to the location where bodies were buried, Kaz began the deck long journey. He knew he must reveal his hidden stash. Nothing in him would allow him to be dishonest, not with this loving, wonderful, and tyrannical dictator of his little heart. As the narrow, unpainted, wooden door squeaked open, she could see it.

"What is this?" she thought to herself. The brilliant sunshine streaming through the fully ajar door. It looked somewhat like one of her deep rounded soup pans. Much more luminous than the cast iron pots she left behind. Though not clear, the liquid did seem somewhat fresh.

"Excuse me Madam, but are you looking for something?" Queried the deep, raspy voice behind her.

Startled, she answered, "My son was showing me this place. He said he found cool water for his face here."

"He said, what?" bellowed the old salt of the sea. Then laughter, uncontrolled laughter followed by coughing fits, and more laughter. He placed his large thumb beside a nostril. The most sickening explosion of nasal release was blown over the ship's edge and into the Baltic wind. Gasping for air between broken laughter, the ship's first mate sputtered, "That's a first, Lady. A boy washing his face in the fancy new toilet-bowl commode. Do you know what people have been doing in that thing?" He wheezed through more intermittent chokes of laughter.

Suddenly, the shock hit her. This was a toilet. It was not anything like the outhouses she had known all her life. Then the ugly, mocking man calmed her a bit when he said,

"It's alright lady, the water in that thing is pretty clean. Won't hurt the boy. I don't think." Then he staggered up the side deck of the ship still laughing and shaking his head.

She realized this entire event was delivering an exciting but sobering announcement. Nothing would ever be the same again in the lives of the Pawlak family of Poznan, Poland.

The cattle stalls, bedded with fresh hay, were getting more stuffy and pungent each day. They had provided shelter from the heat of the day and somewhat bearable temperatures at night. The latrine system on the ship was a little more familiar. That was before the amazing discovery in the little closet. At the end of the stalls were a long row of metal fire buckets. A shoulder-high wall served as the only level of privacy. The buckets were emptied each morning, tied to a long rope, thrown overboard for a good sea water cleaning, and returned to their insensitive location.

As Anna Rose reclined on her side, Kaz lay in her lap. She stroked his head, as only a mother's touch could perform. She tried again to push what she had left behind, somewhere in the lower region of her fearful heart. Maybe she could thrust to the surface of her thinking the new life that lay ahead. One way to do this was to arouse the imaginative young mind beneath the hair flowing through her heavily worked fingers.

"Can you imagine America, Kaz?" She whispered.

"Oh tell me, Mama." He excitedly pleaded. He rolled over on his back to look up into the safe eyes hovering over him.

"Uncle told your father that the cities are alive with people everywhere. The country is so green it will hurt your eyes."

"Are there lots of children there like me, Mama?" he inquired.

"Well," she said, using more of a teacher's voice, "They may dress differently than you, and certainly will not speak Polish. They will mostly be speaking English but you will soon learn this too."

"How about toys?" He asked.

"Toys are made in factories, Kaz." She lightly pinched his sunburned nose. New vision began flowing through them both like the Vistula River at flood stage. She raised her voice to a girlish squeal. "Food, Kaz! Food almost everywhere you look, and some already cooked for you." She rapidly continued. "Money. Yes, money Kaz, more in one month than we would see in a year back in Poznan."

"Where will we get money?" he asked. His young mind felt a little confused.

"Well, Papa said that Uncle will get him a job in a big factory that makes trains. They hire many people from Poland, and Germany, and other countries too. Papa will make enough money for us to have our own house. For now we will have to stay with Uncle, but maybe only one year or so..." Caught up in her own fantasy, she burst out the most amazing declaration his little ears could imagine.

"Kaz, I have even heard that money grows on the streets in America!"

Her arms pulled him up from his comfortable, and somewhat lazy posture to a full bear hug. His face buried into her neck, with a near smothering strangle-hold. She excitedly swayed him back and forth, threw back her head, and burst into laughter; laughter she had not known or felt in months. The laughter slowed and descended into a contemplative hum. She took a deep, slow, cleansing breath and soon, unexpectedly tears started to flow. A painful, inner moan and a quiet whisper slipping across her trembling lips whispered, "Poznan...Poznan...Poznan..." As she drifted off to sleep, a shaky unheard word formed on her lips,

"America."

The Loud piercing scream of the ship's whistle, powered by the same hissing steam that has propelled this huge vessel, penetrated her body like a blood curdling scream. She rolled Kaz's head, rather abruptly, off her lap, and he awakened with the thud of his head on the not-so-hay-padded-floor. Now, fully awake and clear eyed, she saw the shadows of her fellow passengers scurrying toward the narrow stairway leading topside. A wave of fear flushed through her face. Perhaps there is a fire somewhere on the boat. Maybe they have sprung a leak or struck another sea going vessel. She thinks, Why else would that awful whistle be blowing and why else would everyone be scampering for the deck?

"Kaz!" she cried out. "Come, Boy! Something has happened." Seeing the sleepy panic in his young eyes, she attempted to settle herself in order to keep her son from a nightmarish reaction to her tone. Much more subdued, she urged

"Let's just go up top and see what all the excitement is about."

Their progress was impeded as the bodies congested at the bottom of the steps. Moments later they were close enough to the stairway to see the early morning light in the hazy blue sky above. One of the problems with staying in the steerage below was never being sure if it was day or night. Just then they heard the almost hilarious rumble of voices above. It did not sound like fear or panic. No, they heard cheers, laughter, some screams but not dreadful. Anna reached the topside first, and placed her foot firmly on the deck at the top of the stairs. She attempted to pull Kaz up with her, but the spring in his young legs propelled him a good step ahead of her. To her amazement, everyone was crowded around the outside rail of the ship. They were not looking overboard. All eyes seemed to be on the horizon. Kaz spotted it first.

"Land Mama! Land!"

She gazed upon what her young boy could not yet recognize. She saw smoke, haze, towering formations. In the midst of the mirage-like vision, she could clearly see the outline of buildings

"This is it." She thinks. "This must be a large city, bigger than even Poznan."

Then the declaration she had waited for attacked her ears. Many voices began calling out, from bow to stern,

"America, it's America!"

Someone began to Sing, "O say can you see?"

They didn't know any more words, or at least didn't know them in English so they sang again,

"O say can you see? O say can you see?"

Others joined in and sang those few words over, and over, and over until riotous laughter broke out, followed by hugs, tears, and cheers. At least for the moment, their eyes firmly set on their adopted new land, what they could see pushed their old country out of their minds.

There would be no Statue of Liberty to welcome them as so many Italian, German, Polish and Slavic immigrants before them. They were not coming into the famed New York City at all. These more crude, animal hauling ships had been run by a more questionable enterprise. The U.S. immigrations department felt it better to bring them into a more quiet setting where they could be processed at a slower and more investigative approach. So they chose the less combustive port city of Baltimore, Maryland.

The Whistle sounded three more long blasts. Everyone on board had been instructed when hearing that signal to move to the center front of the deck. It was there the Captain could easily step from his wheelhouse and address the passengers. Not being accustomed to making speeches to his cargo of bovine, he spoke slowly and loudly. Using his native German language, which all of his Central European sailing guests sufficiently understood, he explained the disembarking strategy that lay before them. Anna would later explain to her naturally inattentive eight year old the procedure they would have to follow. He would have plenty of time to play his last four hours on the ship. Each family would exit the ship by the same gang-plank. They would be permitted egress just a few at a time due to the fact the immigration offices in Baltimore were much smaller than those at Ellis Island in New York.

It would not take Anna and Kaz much time to gather their personal belongings. One large sheepskin-lined carry-all with a firm leather strap would be the entirety of their luggage. At that moment she began to feel lonely. She thought about her husband, and the way he had assured her that after he had settled the last few details of this move, he would quickly follow. Still, it would be a bit uncomfortable without him.

She knew Marek Kawolski but not well. Marek had been a life-time friend of her husband's family, thus they called him Uncle, as would be the custom of their people. Kaz was excited about meeting Uncle. So many times Papa had told him about this brave man who made it all the way to America. The way Papa made it sound, Uncle was as brilliant as Tadeusz Kosciuszko, who created the first American Cavalry for President Washington or Kazimiersz Pulaski who came from Poland to fight in the American Revolution, only to die of his severe wounds on his way home to Poland. In Kaz's little mind Uncle was all of these, as well as other famous Poles like Copernicus and Chopin all wrapped into one.

"Careful Kaz." Anna instructed as he took one small step at a time down the rather narrow gang-plank leading from the tired, old, smelly home they had known for months.

"Just don't look down, Son" she encouraged, speaking as much to herself as to the boy at the end of the little hand she was clutching. As they lighted off the last unstable end of the walk, they both noticed some travelers on knees kissing the new soil that felt so firm beneath them. Others were offering prayers to their beloved Holy Mother for the safe journey. Anna thought it proper to kneel and cross herself but in her mind she said, "I'm saving my kisses for when my husband Jan and little son Stephen are in my arms at last." She did say, under her breath, a quick prayer of thankfulness, knowing that prayer would be something she would not do often once Jan arrived. It was not likely that prayers, candles, or rosary would be tolerated by her husband's detestment of the church now that it had boiled over to complete and total hatred.

Watching Kaz, the pride of her life, the little son who would hardly ever leave her side, and the reason they were chosen to travel together first, made her truly thankful to God. He ran around in circles, rolled on the grass and turned summer salts. He was like a small puppy that had been caged for days. He was free. It was grass, not ship boards and smelly hay. Even as the rain began to lightly fall on Baltimore that late morning he was a new boy in a new world.

"Oh, Thank you God" she said aloud, "We have a new life. We will live again. We will live again."

After a few more minutes of letting Kaz exhaust himself with running, they began to follow the cobblestone street in the direction of the immigration office. Police on horses lined the two-block trek to make sure all from the ship were not tempted to try a side street on their own. Having lived most of their lives under tight government control, not many of these persons would ever consider entering this country in any other way than under the complete approval of this new authority.

The rain was falling steadily and the winds had picked up sharply. Kaz was pulling his cap down almost over his ears to keep his mop of hair covered and dry. The sudden sharp nip in the air seemed a relief from the salt spray and sun of the ship.

"You're getting too far ahead Kaz" Anna called, "Come on back here by me" she implored.

With an "Aw shucks" look, he slowed his pace, and turned to take that obedient walk back to his mother. The gusts of wind were growing stronger. Some dirt flew into the corner of his eye. He stopped in his tracks and pushed his finger toward the pain in the corner of his eye, and began to rub out the particle lodged there. As he dropped his head to perform this extraction, his good eye saw it. "What can it be?" he thought. Green and flat, it stuck to the top of his grass-moistened shoe. Quickly squatting like a baseball catcher he would come to know in this new place, his hand thrust to his shoe. He grabbed it just before the next huge gust of wind could carry it away. As he pulled it to his face, both eyes now clear and focused, he examined it closely. In the corner of the green and white rectangular paper a number 20.

"It is! It is!" he screamed.

The object, firmly clutched in his right hand, he went running at full speed toward Anna.

"Mama! Oh Mama, you were right, you were right!"

She dropped the heavy bag carrying their entire life's belongings as he pushed the paper so close to her face she had to back her head to focus.

"You were right Mama!," he affirmed again. "Money does grow on the streets of America!"

As Anna amazingly held the document known as Legal Tender between her two hands on that gusty Eighth day of May, 1893, neither of them could imagine in their unspeakable fortune how long it would be before they would ever see a twenty dollar bill again.

As they approached the front of the immigration office they met with something pleasant but odd. There were three ladies and two gentlemen all with different musical instruments in their hands. As the quintet played, the music was not so different from the Polka band that used to play in front of the church in Poznan. The oom-pah-pah rhythm had a familiar style. The ladies began to sing a lovely song. Neither Anna nor Kaz could understand the lyrics, yet it seemed welcoming. Unexpectedly, from behind the ensemble came a tall and rather thin man with a small box under his arm. Quickly the man reached into the box and pulled out a small item. He smiled, extended his hand toward Kaz and said,

"Welcome to America, son, and may God Bless you."

The only word Kaz really understood was God. It sounded much like the German word for the divine being. Kaz looked up at his mother as if to ask, "Can I have this?" at which Anna simply guided his hand, holding a little leather bound book, toward his coat pocket.

"It is your first present you have received in America," Anna said, smiling softly.

"Oh! A present?" he said with his voice and eyebrows rising at the end of the word.

"Please step this way." interrupted a strong and deep voice. "Come, come, come on folks" he urged as the uniformed officer waved his hand vigorously, motioning them into the immigration queue. As they stepped to the window, Anna quickly handed the paper work to this rather firm faced official.

"Oh! Poland." He said, "Moment...wait." he said slowly then he left his post and disappeared for a few minutes. When he returned, he had a young woman in a similar uniform, except for the skirt. She came to Anna and Kaz directly and said, "Dzien Dobre Pani." Anna felt relief, and Kaz immediately felt at home. The young immigrant translator explained to them that their papers were all in order but they were to be boarding a train for Chicago right away. Due to the ship's late arrival, they would have to hurry to get to their approved location. After a few signatures and ink blotted stamps by the officer, the young woman hurried them to a horse-drawn carriage near the rear of the building. As they sped off Anna called out,

"What is your name?" to which the young woman yelled back,

"They just call me Hattie."

"Hattie" Anna repeated. "Oh! I love that name."

Kaz stared out the window as the train moved rather swiftly through the countryside. Mile after mile of farmland was all there was for the boy to see. He had seen some trains in Poland and was enamored by these steel giants. Never had he seen so many trains as in this new land. They were all going in different directions. The black smoke rising from the stack at the front of the engine was particularly intriguing to a little eight year old. Kaz mused to himself, "When Papa comes he will build those trains with Uncle.

"Mama?" Kaz said while patting Anna's shoulder, "When Papa makes trains do you think I can help?"

Little did he know those words would take on a lifetime of meaning one day.

"Chicago, next stop Chicago" the conductor announced as he moved swiftly through each passenger car. Anna could not believe her eyes. The buildings were so tall. There were people everywhere, and smoke. The window at their increasingly uncomfortable seat was opened slightly. She questioned in her mind, "What is that putrid odor?" As she reached over Kaz to close the window with one hand and hold her above-average-size nose with the other, the conductor caught her eye.

"Sorry Mum, the slaughterhouses. It's Chicago lady." He caught her unknowing confused look and said, "Cows, lady, and pigs, and sheep." Then he made a dramatic sweep of his thumb across his throat from ear to ear while pushing a strangling noise between his teeth and tongue. She had a most dreadful thought: was he telling her that is where they kill people? Then she saw at the end of the large building the explanation. Never had she seen so many animals at one time. She saw thousands of large cattle. Oh, she thought about watching farmers slaughter animals back home and realized it was burning animal innards pouring from the smokestacks with their offensive odors.

As they stood before the station's information window, the news was devastating; they were not yet at their final destination. They would still have to take their tired, weary bodies yet down the busy street outside of the train depot, and walk better than two miles to the next ocean. Well, not really an ocean but it sure looked like the Baltic. They would come to know the strange name Michigan. In time they would find that this body of water, over three hundred miles long and one hundred miles wide, was not an ocean but a freshwater lake. Little did either Anna or Kaz know that day that this Great Lake would become the centerpiece of their lives for generations.

"No Mama, not another ship" whined Kaz.

"But it is a small boat and we will only be on this for a few hours Kaz" she assured.

The double deck sightseeing boat would carry them the short thirty-two miles east from Chicago. They would actually cross an invisible state line on their five-hour trip from Illinois to a place called Indiana. Late in the day the boat would make a sharp southerly turn toward a harbor and land. This place looked different than the dark and busy Chicago yet had every reminder of the Polish Sea Shore along the Baltic, so much like the tri-cities of Gdansk, Gdynia, and Sopot. At first sight they saw the beautiful, white and tall sand dunes. The harbor was bordered on both east and west sides by huge wooden cargo piers. Before their arrival the eastern most pier had held a tall wooden lighthouse, but a recent autumn storm, like only Lake Michigan could produce, had destroyed it. It would be another ten years before a new powerful steel lighthouse would be erected. The future lighthouse's white color and crimson red rooftop, cast against the blue/green foaming surf below, would become the symbol of this bustling commercial port city for decades to follow.

As they passed the long wooden pier, Kaz noticed men and boys with long fishing poles extended across the water in the direction of their passing boat.

"Maybe Papa will take me fishing there when he comes!" shouted Kaz.

"I can promise you, Boy; the way Jan Pawlak loves to fish he will take you at every opportunity."

Traditions were only beginning to form in their minds, but both would come to know this pier-fishing tradition would never pass away.

"What is this place?" Kaz enquired.

"Otis, Kaz. This is where Uncle lives and they call it Otis."

Little did Anna know that she was still not at the assigned little village where they would start a new life. This was a town about 10 miles yet from little Otis. Legend would say that this port city at the southernmost tip of the Great Lake had acquired its name because it was the closest town to the next State. So the place they were once again coming ashore, beautifully placed between Illinois and Michigan, would carry the unique name, Michigan City, Indiana. For more than the next century the family of Jan and Anna, and a vast multitude of Polish immigrants would become the ingredient, personality, and fiber of this beautiful city by the lake.

Instead of fearfully walking the narrow gang-plank of a steamer ship, they passengers would make a dreadful climb up a walkway of narrow boards to the high wooden dock above. This much smaller boat was moving up and down in the turbulent water. The amazing number of ships kept the harbor water as tumultuous as a pot of Anna's boiling Rosół z kurczaka (Sunday chicken soup), a regular Polish custom. Chicago may have become a major sprawling city of America, but the harbor at Michigan City seemed even busier. Barrels of Whiskey, barrels of cider, vinegar, apples, bushels of salt, and bulk goods along with literally tons of merchandise made this place a maddening scene. Corn, barley, oats, rye, pork, lard, flour, and butter by the ship load declared that behind this port must have been the most fertile land their eyes would ever see. Even with all the massive accumulation of product, nothing could begin to match the mountains of fish, piled on the remaining boats traversing the harbor at the end of this significant tributary known as Trail Creek.

Finally atop of the wooden studded structure, and breathing heavily from the climb, mother and son stood with a bit of a lost look on their faces.

"Anna, Anna over here!" came a deep but youthful sounding voice. As they both pivoted their heads to the voice from their right they saw the tall, thin figure.

"Oh, Marek!" Anna squealed, then grabbing Kaz's coat sleeve, they bolted toward those two hands waving in the sunset. In the most proper Polish custom they grasped each other's hands, waist high and extended their faces ahead of their shoulders to kiss each side of their faces. Not just one kiss per cheek but several times. Both Marek and Anna were comforted with the sense that they were grasping family again. Without waiting for any formality, Kaz quickly threw his arms around Marek's waist and began to repeat one word,

"Uncle, Uncle, Uncle!"

As Marek quickly unburdened Anna from the heavy bag she had carried to the new world, he led them to his rather large farm wagon nearby. All three could sit together on the wooden bench seat. The horse attached to the wagon was huge, bigger than any horse Kaz had ever seen.

"It's a Belgian horse." Uncle explained, and then went on to tell them it belonged to his neighbor Zibiegnew. "I could never afford such a horse with the money I make at the factory."

As they began the final leg of this journey, they crossed a rather rickety bridge over the busy harbor and began a downward trek through a pleasant town. It was growing darker, and Kaz noticed the uniformed men on each side of the street with a long implement in their hands. At the end of the pole-shaped item was a small burning flame. As the wagon passed, Kaz twisted his body to look back. With fascination he saw them push up a glass cover on top of a large post, and reach the small flame within the globe. Then the entire top of the large pole burst into light, and the entire street was illuminated.

Kaz began to realize that this was not a very smooth ride. The street, he would later learn, had the name of Franklin Street. Named after a famous father of American History, the street was built from flat, round pieces of wood. This wooden answer to cobblestone, like he had seen in Baltimore, was hewn from a combination of cedar and plentiful sycamore trees that grew along the banks of Trail Creek.

The quiet of the dark of night was diametrically opposite from the bustle of the busy harbor and clamoring town behind them. They rode the wagon into what appeared to be a black abyss. After what felt to both Anna and Kaz like a night long trip, their tired eyes finally saw shapes of small buildings with minimal light. Any moonlight would have helped but there was none to be found that night. Then they saw a beautiful sight, a fairly large church building with some candlelight pushing amazing color through the tall stained glass windows.

"Well we are finally here," Uncle announced as he brought the huge, sweaty beast to a halt.

Uncle helped Anna from the wagon, then Kaz. He led the way up the little path and onto a small wooden porch of a fittingly small house. He soon lighted two kerosene lanterns, and Kaz got his first glimpse of his new American home.

"Your room is here to the right" Marek said, as he quickly went to light the small lantern on the old bureau."

"Oh look, Kaz." Anna said with admiration. "A bed, a real bed." She questioned in her nearly exhausted mind, how long had it been since she actually had laid her body on a bed.

"You get changed and I will make some warm soup and bread for
your poor empty stomachs before we sleep," Marek said. Then turning to Anna he said, "It is so good to have you here safely. You must go across the street to the church in the morning and light a candle, and say a prayer of thanks for this safe journey."

Anna softly touched his hand, rather firmly holding her upper arm, and replied, "Yes I will, but remember you must not let Jan know I went to the church, and offered prayers."

Marek dropped his head a bit sadly and removed his hand from her arm to say, "Yes Anna, I understand, but this is a new life and a new place. Maybe Jan will change his mind in time."

Kaz removed his coat. Suddenly he felt the weight of the object in his coat pocket. He remembered the little book given to him in Baltimore. As he quickly pulled it from its secure hold, he said excitedly to his uncle,

"Look Uncle. This was my first present given to me in America. It's a little book, see."

Kaz pushed the little book upward toward Marek's face. Marek rather quickly snatched it from the boy's hand. He looked at the front cover, slightly opened the pages and ran his big thumb from front cover to back. Then Marek, clutching the book between thumb and forefinger, rather harshly pounded the book several times on the palm of his other hand. Finally, he looked down at Kaz and spoke in a bit of an aggravated voice,

"Listen boy. You must throw this book away. Don't keep this book!" he then began to rapidly fire off his vocal explanation. "This is a holy book and you are a wicked little boy." In the same breath he continued, "You will never be holy enough to read and understand this book, and if you want to know what is in this book, we will go across the street to the priest and he will tell us what we need to know from the holy book."

Just as firmly, Marek turned and walked out of the room. Anna, followed quickly behind him to assure him that the boy meant no wrong.

As Kaz stood dumbfounded in the dimly lighted, little bedroom, tears began to gather in his sleepy eyes. What had he done? Why was Uncle upset with him? Uncle was his hero. Kaz knew he never wanted to disappoint this great man. But there was another problem. This had been his first present in America. Mama said it was a present. Now Uncle Marek said to throw it away. Both his mother's and Uncle's phrases rang in his little ears. He would make a difficult decision. He would not throw the little book away. He looked around the room for a place to hide it. There was a small closet. It was empty. As he took the lantern in hand and examined the little place where they would hang their few clothing items, he saw it. There was a small hole in a board on the back of the closet, right at floor level. The little book fit longwise into the hole. There, Kaz would safely keep the little gift with the thought, maybe someday I will be able to read and understand the strange words on those thin onion skin pages.

****

Several months had passed since Papa had been reunited with the family. Kaz slept on the straw-filled mats at the end of the bed where Jan and Anna held each other late into the night, and dreamed of the opportunities that lie before them.

Kaz had been in his new school just a few weeks. It was certainly convenient to simply walk across the street from Uncle's house to the school housed in the large Polish Catholic church. Regardless of the fact that the school was taught by Polish nuns, and it was necessary to use the Polish language, most of the time Kaz really looked forward to the English language class. It was the last class of the day, and being fresh on his mind he could run home quickly, pull the little book from its hiding place in the wall, and try to find an English word he recognized. This covert proceeding was as much a daily game of intrigue as it was a desire to learn English.

Although Otis was a small village in America, it certainly held many similarities to the small villages in rural Poland. Perhaps the fact that most of its one hundred or so residents were Polish emigrants, primarily from Poznan, gave it this atmosphere. You could smell the Polish dishes late in the afternoon from each house. This was the time of the day when the largest meal was prepared and served.

Papa was not often at those meals. Jan, Marek, and several other men would rise each day before the Sun was up. They would walk as a group through the little town to a nearby railroad stop. They would board a particular passenger car on what would become an historic rail line. The Monon line was its name. The railroad line from Chicago to Louisville, had many smaller branches throughout the state of Indiana.

The name Monon came from a Potawatomi tribal word meaning "to haul or tote." Twenty-eight years earlier this railroad had carried the body of what would become perhaps America's most honored and beloved president, Abraham Lincoln. The Monon would only carry the body of the assassinated leader 90 miles from Lafayette to Michigan City, but it would nonetheless be part of the 1660 mile train memorial to the man who would save the nation. Otis was not one of the scheduled stops for the Lincoln Funeral train, but so many people gathered at the train stop that the engineer stopped the train, and the memorial director allowed the residents of little Otis to view the body of the great emancipator.

The Monon Line would carry the famed and beautiful Southern Indiana limestone to construct the great Empire State Building in New York City as well as the Pentagon, National Cathedral, and Washington Monument in the nation's capital. For years to come the proud persons of what would become known as the Hoosier State, would remind others that each new slab of Indiana limestone rode a Monon flat-bed railcar first, wherever its destination.

There was no honorable fanfare this day as the small band of newly arrived immigrants would huddle tightly in the not-so-clean or pleasant passenger car. They would take the same journey North as Anna and Kaz had taken southward to Otis. The train would stop near the southwestern corner of the lakefront town of Michigan City. From there the foreigners, as they would be referred to by many, would walk briskly in the cool, fall morning toward the large smokestacks just visible in the rising Sun.

The buildings were huge, mostly one story, but built extremely tall. Long dark windows, covered with metal rib-work ran from roof edge to just above the ground. Large, dark, smoky, and harsh would be the words that best describe the block after block of industrial mass. The complex at its peak would comprise nearly 100 buildings. It looked like a city of its own, minus homes, comforts, laughter, or hospitality. The name was molded into a large iron sign, and affixed to the huge arch leading onto the premises. Haskell & Barker were the words. It was within these walls that Jan, eventually Kaz, brothers, in-laws, cousins, grandsons, and a large segment of the Pawlaks would spend most of their working lives, sometimes under the most horrid conditions, trying to squeeze out a living for their families. They would all find it far from the dreams of prosperity, health, or happiness that they heard would be theirs in this land of plenty.

Most of the newer workers would begin in the foundry department. Without a doubt, this was the hottest and dirtiest work in the entire plant. The huge heating furnaces and the horrid smoking pollutants excreted into the non-ventilated surroundings. The strongest of men were only able to stay in these conditions for short periods of time. Jan and the others there would stagger intermittently into the nearby lumber yard gasping for fresh air and then wiping the sweat from their nearly sightless eyes. After a few gasps the familiar voice of their foreman would be hollering to the top of his voice,

"Come on, you bunch of dumb Polaks! Get back to work. These trains won't build themselves."

Jan would always look the Foreman straight in his eyes and firmly reply, "The name is Pawlak, not Polak."

The men were given thirty minutes for lunch. The small sandwich, piece of fruit, and cup of water Anna had prepared for Jan was certainly not filling but, knowing her hands had prepared it gave him a small mental retreat from this filthy inferno. Part of the motivation to sustain these days was the fact that if he worked hard, and could get recognized by a boss, he might be able to move up to another department. The wheel assembly line was heavy and hard work, but he knew he could do it. The best place to work would have been in the paint barn. The conditions had to be kept very clean for the paint to look perfect before the box cars left the plant.

Jan was amazed to see how many young boys, some not older than Kaz, were among the workers. Their primary job was to carry water to the workers. Their little faces were always so dirty. The new box cars were brought in and out of the different buildings, depending on their stage of assembly. As the fall weather on Lake Michigan was getting colder each day, the huge sliding doors, that allowed the boxcars entrance and exit, were being closed. The large train engines that would pull the box cars belched dark, black, coal smoke from their stacks as they entered the buildings. The massive doors would be closed behind them. The building would immediately fill with so much smoke that you could not see the worker next to you. By the time the doors were reopened, and the engines retreated, every face was black. Coughing would ensue for the next half hour.

The most unpleasant job the grimy faced young boys were required to do involved sanitation work. Should a worker need to relieve his bladder they would just find a place between the boxcars and urinate on the floor. Most of the floors were just dirt and gravel but some areas were wooden blocks similar to those that paved nearby Franklin Street.

Along each back wall of the multiple buildings ran a long wooden platform. This assemblage of thin wooden planks started about four feet high, and descended along a twenty-foot path until it touched the shop floor. This platform was about four feet wide, and served at the only latrine system in the series of buildings. Should a worker need to have a bowel movement, he would simply find an unused place on the platform. No privacy and only stacks of old newspaper for necessary purposes.

Before the end of the day the young boys, mostly brought there by their fathers, had the unpleasant task of carrying water buckets to wash down the putrid platforms. After shoveling the waste at the end of the platform into wooden boxes, they would then haul the boxes on a cart to a back field to throw them into a huge crater made for this purpose. The boys would then return to the work areas with buckets of powdered lye, and spread it along the platforms in preparation for the next day's use. They also would traverse the plant, seeking out the urination places, using their sense of smell as detectors, and spread more lye on those spots. Many of the youngsters would become victims of tuberculosis and many other conditions yet to be named by the medical system.

As the long twelve hour day would draw to an end, Jan and the company of Otis men would retrace the steps they had sojourned before day break. Once aboard the crowded passenger car, Jan would try to position himself in a way so he could close his tired eyes, ignore his aching body in hopes he would have strength to be gracious to his loving Anna and playful son. This did not feel like paradise, yet he would feed his family, and they would be sheltered. There was still a sense of freedom. The future may still be, to some measure, his to control.

It was not long before Jan and Anna would see their family grow.
A second son, Stephen, would now be their first American-born child. In just a few short years these boys would be the joy of their father's life.

"Kaz. Stephen. Wake up, Boys." Jan whispered. "It's Saturday, Boys. Let's go fishing." Kaz jumped from the little mat on the floor. Why was it, he thought, so hard to wake up when Mama calls me for school, but when Papa says "fishing," I am wide awake?

That winter cold in Otis had been extremely long. The calendar said April but the final visages of the deep snow had just melted over the last couple of days. They had not been fishing for almost six months, and today meant summer was just around the corner.

As the boys jumped off the train ahead of their father, he called out,

"Hey, you little wild horses, get back here and help me with these fishing poles!"

The boys looked at each other and broke into laughter before running back to the rail platform. As they each took a long cane pole from their father's hand, they quickly returned to a slow trot up the street.

"Wait, wait for Papa." Jan called. "We must stop at the market for bait."

A bit frustrated that they could not get their eyes on the lake and the long fishing pier yet, they slowly turned around and watched Jan enter the front of the familiar store. When he came out he had that large bucket. They had to see for themselves. Yes, sure enough there was enough little minnows scurrying about that container to catch a week's supply of delicious Lake Michigan perch.

Looking down the long wooden pier, Kaz was enthralled by the kaleidoscope of color and movement before him. He could see so many long, bamboo-cane, fishing poles. Each pole was extended level across the water. One by one they would rise and lower slowly. This coaxing method, moving the little minnow attached to the end of the line was a fool proof method of tempting the passing schools of undisciplined fish. From where Kaz stood, the view was like witnessing the largest Japanese fan, moving as if to cool the entire lake before it.

First it was Papa, then Stephen, and finally Kaz would feel the tug of the little, tasty fish. With first-time excitement on each catch, they would pull the trophy to the pier, wait for the thrashing to slow a bit, and unhook the victim, always declaring their fish was the biggest yet.

As the sun began to set in the westerly direction of Chicago, papa would let the boys catch a few more while he would begin to clean their catch of the day, wrap the fish in some newspaper, and prepare the draught of fishes for their homeward trip. Once home, Anna would make a fuss over their success, and proceed to roll each morsel in corn meal and gently drop them into the hot oil that filled the bottom of her large Iron skillet. Cautioned to watch for the bones, the family would gently peel the beautiful white meat from the sides of each perch and groan approving sounds about the table. This was a true testimony from each family member, as to the succulent perfection of this day's catch.

Reaching across the table to touch her husband's arm, Anna spoke softly,

"Jan, thank you for such a wonderful dinner."

"Well," he replied, "I don't mind providing food when it was that much fun." They laughed.

"Besides," he continued, "Seeing the boys have that much fun makes me feel like a good father."

"O Jan, you are the best father." she responded. Jan quickly pulled his hand from under hers, dropped his head and rather distantly uttered,

"If only that were true."

She arose quickly from the table and turned away to deal with the wood cooking stove. Then she walked around the table and stopped behind Jan. Placing both hands on his strong shoulders she said to her boys,

"If you're done eating, go prepare for bed and I will come say prayers with you soon." She began softly to rub her hands across his back in a comforting way.

"Jan Pawlak, my beloved, I have something to tell you. Not only are you a great father, but you will soon get the opportunity to prove it again."

"What must I do now," he asked.

"Nothing Jan, you've done enough." she said, and then continued, "you are going to be a father again, Jan."

He stood and turned toward her, then placed his arms around her tightly and whispered in her ear,

"Maybe it's time for a girl."

She began to weep. In her mind she began to recount her blessings. She reasoned, a new land, a new life, another American child, and perhaps a daughter. What if it was a girl? What would they name her? Anna began to think of the beautiful baptismal dress she would make for a daughter. Then the cold, awakening thought came to her mind. It was so difficult having Stephen baptized without Jan's knowledge. Could she do anything that important behind his back a second time, but he had made his declaration, and sworn a personal oath.

"By whatever gods there might be, I will never step foot into church again!"

As Jan drank one last cup of strong coffee, Anna removed herself to the bedroom to see that the boys were ready for their ritual before going down for the night. As she entered the room she saw that Stephen had already collapsed on his mat, and was sound asleep, exhausted from his day of vigorous fishing. To her surprise, Kaz was sitting on the edge of their bed near the lantern. Even more shocking was that in his hands was that little book Uncle had told him to throw away almost a year ago.

When he saw Anna enter the room, startled, he stood quickly from the bed and turned his back. It was too late. She had seen the book. What she did not expect was the look on his face when he turned to her. His eyes were moist and his demeanor a bit confused.

"What are you doing, Kaz?" she questioned firmly.

"I was trying to read this book." he sheepishly replied.

"But can you read the English words, Kaz?" she inquired.

"Today I did read a few..." as he opened the pages softly.

"Did you understand them, Son?" she quizzed.

"I think so, Mama." Kaz said.

"Then read them to me." she urged.

His little voice slowly stammered out each word from the page,

"For God...so loved the world that...He gave His only begotten...Son that who...so...ever believeth in Him...should not perish but...have...ever...lasting life."

"Do you know what it means, Kaz?" she said even more softly.

"Yes Mama," he said. "It means that God loves everybody, even me, Mama."

Anna took the little book from Kaz's hands and looked at the pages. She felt a little strange. Her nine year old would be able to read and understand this new language when even she could only manage a few local phrases. She laid the little book on the bed and then gently directed her son to his sleeping place for the night. After he laid down, and she covered him, she reached back to the bed and handed him the little book, which she now knew was a Bible. Kaz held it to his chest, and stared at the ceiling above him. Anna kissed his cheek, and she quietly returned to the kitchen to join her husband.

Kaz laid there for some time without any feeling of tiredness. This was a day he would never forget. A thought began to move about in his amazing little mind. If God really loved him, what was he to do about this? He then replayed Uncle's admonition the night he arrived in this room.

"If you need to know anything from that holy book we will go to the priest and he will tell us what we need to know."

Yes that was the answer! He would go to the priest, and see what he should do about this God that loved him.

Kaz often saw the same people going into the church each day when he would enter the school. He already understood that they must be what his catechism class had called devout. Though his young mind did not understand the word "religious" he knew he must do something about this new discovery from this holy book.

Over the next few years, Kaz would act on this truth in every way he could. His love for music would lead him to become a choir boy, and his serious dedication to the church would qualify him to be a dedicated altar boy. These duties he would perform diligently, without the knowledge of his father, until the day Jan would announce they were moving from Uncle's house to a new house in Michigan City.

From the small village of Otis to the busy port city by the lake, their lives would become an even more remarkable adventure than any they had experienced since leaving Poland those seven years earlier.

Kaz would remember well the evening his father explained to him, at the small dinner table, the new direction for his life. Jan would use wonderful logic to help Kaz understand that 8 years of attending school was well sufficient for a young man his age. Being fifteen, fluent in the English language, and stronger than a young bull was reason enough for him to take advantage of the position his father had secured for him at the factory. Kaz would not have to work in the foundry, like his father had. His father's work ethic and dedication had been rewarded by many promotions. Kaz could now start directly in the Wheel Assembly Department.

This first stage of the process was the foundational beginning of what would become a beautiful railroad box car in just a matter of a few days. The wheels weighed over seven hundred pounds each. The early, crude tools for lifting were, at best, a slow and cumbersome way of manipulating these spherical masses of Mr. Carnegie's steel. It was faster and less complicated to gather three or four strapping young men to one side of the wheel and force the wheel to stand on its edge. Then, with two workers on each side of the wheel they would lift it upward until it could sit upon a rail. The second wheel would be handled exactly the same way while the huge axle would be put in place between the wheels, and passed to the next group of waiting assemblers.

In Kaz's first few days at Haskell and Barker he had little thought that he would give the next thirty-six years of his life and, literally, the strength of his strong, Polish back to this industry. He was proud that his chosen profession would open the door way to this entire, blossoming, nation he now called home.

****

"Emil, Emil. Come on! We are going to be late." Kaz bellowed from his huge and powerful chest. Pounding on the door with impatient rapidity, he continued. "Come on, Man! 1900 will be here and gone before we can catch it if you get any slower."

Suddenly in the midst of Kaz's, big fisted knuckles pummeling the outside surface of the door like a sledgehammer, the door swung open. Kaz nearly fell inside the little hallway where his newfound friend, and workmate at the factory was slipping on his rubber boots.

"Easy, Kaz." Emil Pohl urged, "It is only 11:00. We have plenty of time to get to the lake and see the fireworks."

"Yes, I know Emil" Kaz assured, "But I want to stop by the Polish club and get some hot beer first. It is free tonight and Stanley Nowak, from the factory, is serving it. He won't even ask our age, he will just wink and give us some."

Emil shot back his rebuttal,

"Yeah unless Father Wrobel sees you. He doesn't like his altar boys drinking beer you know."

"That's not a problem anymore, Kaz argued, "I'm not going to be an altar boy any longer. No time with the work at the factory now. I'm sure not using my Saturday and Sunday free time for that stuff anymore."

Kaz was even a little surprised at his own attitude and new found independence. He could not quite understand why his church activities, that once seemed so important and rewarding, had become a cold, meaningless, ritualistic bore. With his folks never darkening the door of the church, and his brother and sister being totally uninterested as well, he thought, why should he continue to pretend the church was an important facet of his life?

Soon Kaz and Emil had trudged the fairly deep snow all the way up Franklin Street, stopped by the Polish hall, and stayed out of Father Wrobel's sight long enough to consume two hot beers. Feeling warm on the inside and heavily bundled on the outside, they made it all the way to the lake, and the snow covered park to welcome, not only a new year, but a new decade. Exactly at the midnight hour, the sky across Lake Michigan burst into an array of glorious light. Sparkling devices flared from every direction. There were more Chinese firecrackers in one location, than anyone had ever heard. These explosions pounded against Kaz's ear drums even more furiously than the noise of the box car factory. What caught his eye above all were the huge, arched signs. Each sign burned with blazing pyrotechnics a numbered message: 1900.

Kaz remembered from school that when time changed its measuring technique, from BC to AD, the years of 1-100 would be called the First Century. As odd as it seemed in his mind, he quickly understood that this formula would mean this new decade of 1900-2000 would be considered the Twentieth Century.

"Emil!" Kaz shouted above the fireworks and screaming crowds "Do you realize, not only is our old country gone, but we are now in a brand new century?" Emil shouted back, nose to nose with Kaz,

"I wonder what changes we will see in our life, Kaz."

Even though Emil would eventually outlive Kaz by many years, this friendship would grow into amazing proportions, like that of King David and Jonathan in the Bible. That night neither Kaz nor Emil had any idea they would face very few triumphs or disasters without the voice, hands, and companionship of one another. Over the next four decades Kaz would watch his world change rapidly. Nothing would impact the lives of Kaz and Emil like the events of the dawning century, but this night they were just two young men with stars in their eyes, snow beneath their feet, good beer in their stomachs, ringing in their ears, and a glorious feeling. Their world was good and only going to get better. Maybe they would even stop by the Polish club for one more beer on their way home. After all, they would soon become American Citizens, but for now they were still Polish men.

That same New Year a company named Eastman Kodak would introduce a one dollar mechanism called a Brownie Camera. Now anyone could capture history.

CHAPTER 2 - 1903-1913

Between the time Kaz grew from 8 to 28 years of age he would witness the first transatlantic radio signal, a president's assassination, the birth of the teddy bear, and the invention of a license plate for the ever growing number of automobiles. Kaz and Emil would actually go to a theater in Chicago and see the first silent movie, "The Great Train Robbery." He would learn of baseball, and read about the first-ever World Series. Perhaps the most astounding event that would capture his imagination was when two brothers, named Wright, accomplished the first flight of man. In that first decade of this twentieth century, New York City would build a train system underground and call it the "Subway." Einstein would propose his "Theory of Relativity." Kellogg's would start selling Corn Flakes. San Francisco would suffer a devastating earthquake. The first electric washing machine would be produced. Ford would invent the Model T automobile. Near the end of that first decade of this new century something called plastic would be created. For the remaining fifty years of this new Twentieth Century nothing would stay the same. People would dance wild dances like the Tango. Ernest Rutherford would discover the structure of an Atom, which only sounded interesting and innocent at the time. Parachutes would be invented so men could now jump from those amazing flying machines, and an unsinkable ship named the Titanic would sink. Henry Ford would create a moving assembly line. Income tax would be introduced to the American worker. Automobiles would be so prominent the invention of the traffic light would be necessitated. The world would become smaller as the Atlantic and Pacific oceans would be opened to each other via something called The Panama Canal.

For the next few years life would be a combination of new ventures, and the excruciatingly mundane. Jan and Anna Pawlak were able to purchase the modest, two-story house along the side of the street. For some reason, the predominantly Polish immigrants referred to this region of town as Snake Town. What made it so advantageous for these families was that each plot was large enough for a sizable vegetable garden. A small, fenced yard could hold a few chickens, geese, a turkey or two, and some rabbits. Some more brave souls would even retain a goat and a couple pigs.

Most of the summer, Kaz accompanied his brother Stephen, sister Hattie, (whom Anna had named after the kind lady that helped them in Baltimore) and both parents to that wonderful garden. The onions and potatoes were his favorite. He would unearth them, press them to his large Polish nose, and smell them deeply. He could almost taste how wonderful they would be in Mama's big pot of Hunter's Stew or Bigos, as they were called in Polish. These garden goods would be preserved in the small cellar out behind the house and would provide a table of delight for the next winter.

The work weeks were long in the factory and the evenings were both relaxing and back breaking. But then came Saturday. Before the Sun could reveal its first ray of light, Papa, Kaz, and Stephen were peddling their bicycles northward to the long pier at the lakefront.

Summer Sundays meant a little extra sleep, a wonderful lunch of Chicken soup and Polish Pierogies. Then Kaz, and sometimes the whole family would hike to one of the nearby forests. They were simply called "The Woods." Each wooded area was given a name to match its owner, or the closest farmer. These missions had but one goal, find and capture the biggest and best mushrooms the woods could produce. There were many varieties to be discovered and it took an experienced hunter to know the best tasting ones, while avoiding the poisonous imposters. The greatest prize would be the large mass of mushrooms clustered into the shape of a large beard, named in the Polish language, Kosi Broda (goat's beard). They were rare, but definitely the tastiest.

Once home with their harvest the fun work began. Each mushroom would be sliced into small flat pieces. Mama would take a sewing needle and long piece of thread, and would begin to prepare a garland of fungi delight. The long strings of mushrooms would be hung across each room of the house and left to dry appropriately. The next few days the aroma was simply a prophetic broadcast to the senses, inviting each family member to imagine the scrumptious taste when added to Mama's soup, or smothering her unmatched cutlets.

Sunday evenings in the summer were Kaz's favorite time. He and Emil would often walk again to the beautiful park at the lake. Kaz had a natural love for music. So much so that he would learn to play the guitar and mandolin. He even tried his hand at constructing a few stringed instruments. His favorite was what was called, the Potato Bug. It was similar to the old European instruments a strolling balladeer would play.

He also appreciated talented musicians. The park proudly boasted one of the finest bandstands in the country. The covered concert platform was round, white, lighted with new electric bulbs. Completely around the band stand, placed intentionally on the grass were several hundred dark green benches, which provided the extremely gifted conductor a fantastic venue to showcase his gifted symphony orchestra.

Not a great number of twenty-four year-old, single men would find themselves at the Sunday concert with so many other summer attractions nearby, but both Kaz and Emil felt peaceful when listening to this wonderful music. Besides, the setting sun and the lake breezes were a welcome relief to the late August heat.

"Let's sit on the back row tonight Kaz" Emil suggested as he had already spied a couple seats near the end of the row.

"Why so far back?" Kaz questioned. As Emil looked back over his shoulder, Kaz noticed a rather sly little grin on Emil's face. Placing his big index finger to his lips, Emil shushed Kaz and nodded his head toward the row of seats in front of them.

"Oh," replied Kaz, "Emil Pohl you rascal" and they both covered their mouths to help hold inside what would have been an explosive laugh. As they removed their hats in a gentlemanly bow, they remained standing while a long line of heavenly looking beings filed into the row ahead of them. As the last two beautiful, young women took their seats, Emil looked at Kaz, winked, and with cap covering his mouth he whispered,

"The best ones are sitting right in front of us, how lucky can a couple old bums like us be?"

Kaz never responded. His eyes would not blink, nor could he seem to move his head away from the direction their eyes were staring. What beautiful hair, he thought. What a pleasant way she sits, he mused. She seems like a princess, properly seated on her throne. That beautiful soft, summer dress seemed to be protecting shoulders made of pure diamonds. Then Kaz came up with a brilliant way to see her face. He had not really gotten a good look at her as she had moved to her seat. Emil said the two in front of them were the best, but this required a little closer examination. Kaz noticed that none of these ladies had picked up a copy of the concert program.

"Move Emil," Kaz quietly commanded. "Let me get past you." As he forced his legs past Emil's huge knees, he ran full speed toward the finely dressed man holding the programs.

"Twelve, please." requested the somewhat breathless Kaz.

"Why would you need twelve now, Chap?" asked the Irish bloke.

Kaz knew by the sound of his accent and his inquisition that he must have been a retired Cop.

"Sorry I have a group of friends who forgot to get a program when they entered," he explained quickly as he put out his hand to the distributor.

"Your group would not happen to be that row of pretty young ladies sitting in front of you, now would it?" the man asked as he laughingly counted out the programs and handed them to Kaz.

Kaz never responded to his embarrassing interrogation, but moved quickly back to the audience. After stopping to gather himself, and pressing down any uncomely hair atop his head, he proceeded to the end of the row of classy ladies. Clearing his throat he spoke firmly,

"Excuse me ladies, but I noticed you were without programs. Can I be so kind as to offer you these?"

Slowly, and one at a time he passed the programs, waiting for each to be passed on to the next. He became even more deliberate with each piece of paper so he could fix his gaze on the second girl from the end of the row. This was the strangest feeling he had ever known. He was spell-bound. There was no longer any attempt, on his part, to act nonchalant. He hoped his mind was not speaking so loud as to be audible. His mind was passionately declaring, what a beautiful face. Those blue eyes are breathtaking. That hair is even more beautiful from the front. He then went somewhere he had not expected to go, those lips. Never had he seen a more magnificent pair of lips. Not even on one of Michelangelo's greatest works of art. They were not ordinary lips, but full, shaped by God's own hands. He thought, this is what Eve's lips must have looked like. Little did he know that decades from this night women would pay good money to have chemicals injected into their lips in hope of displaying what this beauty came by so naturally.

After some time she could not help but notice his fixation and stare. Though naturally flattered, she turned her head and lowered her eyes in the most demure attempt to pretend she was studying the program this rather handsome man had so kindly given her.

The rest of the evening they would act as if they were engrossed with the beautiful medley of Beethoven, Mozart, and Chopin, while sensing each other's presence as thick as the heat and humidity of this late summer night. As the last notes of the finale blended with the great applause of the approving audience, Emil could not restrain himself. He gently tapped the soft shoulder of the woman sitting in front of him, and boldly asked as she turned about to look in his direction,

"Do you and your friend come each week to the Symphony?"

This is not the way Kaz would have attempted to dialogue with the lady in front of him, but before he could be embarrassed, Emil's interest responded,

"Why yes, we do. And how about you?" Emil was nearly stricken dumb. The fact that she spoke to him at all surprised him, but to think she may have noticed him as well amazed him.

"Yes, Yes, both of us come each Sunday night of the summer." He announced, shaking his head in a matter of fact way.

Kaz felt some of Emil's boldness. The beauty In front of him was now facing them both.

"Please excuse us ladies." Kaz confidently interrupted, "This is my best friend Emil, and we are so honored to meet you both. If you don't mind us asking, what might your names be?"

With that Emil's newfound friend said, "My name is Mamie, and this is my friend, Mary."

"So nice to meet you both." Kaz said as all four extended their hands toward each other for a proper handshake.

"I don't want to be too forward," Kaz said as he twisted his cap in his hand so tight that the wool was strained to the point of permanent damage, "But we would be so honored if we could escort you ladies to next week's concert, and ask you to be our guests for some ice cream afterward."

Mary was the first to respond. "We normally come with our sisters, cousins and friends here." gesturing in the direction of the wide-eyed companions, listening to these arrangements with intense interest. "However, if our fathers give permission, we would gladly join you."

"How will we know?" asked Emil.

"Stop by the Merchant's Bank on Friday." Mamie instructed. "I work late, and will be able to confirm these arrangements if all are approved."

"Ok then." Kaz responded with a beaming smile across his face, "I hope it all works out."

After some more formal words of farewell the men started one direction, and the ladies, another. Suddenly, Mary called back toward them,

"I'm sorry but we never got the other name."

"She's talking to you, Kaz." Emil clarified. Spontaneously Kaz placed one hand aside his mouth and hollered back, "They call me Ed, just plain old Ed."

"Are you crazy Kaz" Emil growled, "Why did you use Ed instead of Kaz?"

"It just came out without thinking," he said. "You know, ever since that foreman hired me at the shop he started calling me Ed. I am so used to hearing it every day from everybody. It just popped out before I could think. Besides Emil, that face would make any man forget his name."

They burst into uncontrolled laughter, threw an arm around each other's shoulders, and staggered down the street, totally intoxicated on the lingering effects of two beautiful creatures, and drunken with the amazement of their unbelievable night at the symphony.

****

Kaz and Emil walked to Mamie's home first. Mamie's father was a huge man but very soft spoken. After a little tea and some basic information gathering, he laid out the boundaries they would be expected to travel that evening; directly to the park and directly home. The trio then walked across the street and up four houses, until they arrived at Mary's. Mary's father was an even more massive hulk than Mamie's. They actually never made it into the house, but sat face to face with both Mary's parents on a rather small porch. Mary's parents' questions were not as much about the evening before the young quartet, but more about Kaz's future plans. Questions like,

"Is your job secure?"
"Do you plan to make Michigan City your home?" and

"Are both of your Parents from Poland?"

Mary's Father, George, explained to the young men that their family had just recently come to town. A little family history soon made them aware that they were a large family with seven children already, and a new one on the way. Although Mary was born in Chicago, the family had immigrated from Poland, or more accurately, the portion which was actually considered Austria at the time. This was only one of the many times Poland had been occupied by her neighbors. George talked a bit of politics, and excitedly assured the young men that things were underway back in the homeland, that would lead to a free Poland.

Both Kaz and Emil were getting a little fidgety as Mary's father was beginning to drone on. Suddenly George stopped, mid-sentence, and said,

"But listen to me go on. You have to make it to the concert on time, and I am keeping you from that." He continued, "It must be true about us Chicago people, we can sure talk."

Although they had just recently moved from what was known in those days as South Chicago, a distinct community of its own, George explained that Chicago had gotten its reputation as "The Windy City," not from its above average wind velocity, but from its politicians' famed and wordy speeches.

Finally, Kaz and Mary were walking as a couple behind Emil and Mamie. They began their journey toward the park. For Kaz this was like a dream coming true. The evening was perfectly warm. The sun was still a good distance above the horizon. The swish of both ladies', full-skirted dresses were a most pleasant and feminine sound, and made a hypnotic rhythm. As they reached the summit of the main thoroughfare through town, Mamie saw it first. There was a strange and dark cloud in the distance. She turned to look back in Kaz and Mary's direction and asked,

"What in heaven's name is that in the sky?"

Both men removed their billed caps, placed a palm-down hand over the westernmost sides of their faces, and uttered in unison,

"That is smoke." Kaz continued with the obvious, "Something is on fire up there."

The dreadful thought then crossed the fish-loving mind of both Kaz and Emil. What if it were the pier? If it were colder they could imagine a fisherman building a small fire to keep warm, and something going wrong. But it was much too hot for anyone to have a fire on the pier. As they picked up their walking pace, they could not believe their eyes. The cloud of smoke was getting larger and darker. The nearer the park they walked, the more clear it became that the fire was not in the direction of the pier, but perhaps in the park itself. Once they reached the base of the bridge crossing the harbor, they were joined by a growing number of people. Even before they got clear sight of the fire, voices from running boys coming from the park began to herald the shocking news.

"The Band stand is on fire."

Another breathless news boy shouted to all an even sadder note, "The thing is completely on fire and burning to the ground."

Just then, they saw the first fire trucks. They knew it must be bad because the nearby firehouse at the north end of the city had even hitched a set of horses to the seldom used, old fire wagon. A bucket brigade had begun to form, but it was already obvious the only good they could do was to water the ground and wooden seats in hope of preventing the fire from spreading. Just a few minutes earlier Kaz had been experiencing a dream come true. Now he was a part of what he could only believe at the time was a pure nightmare. As the two couples stood at a safe distance, they watched one of the most beautiful places in their world become as black and ugly as the inside of the Haskell & Barker box car factory.

It was dark and Emil broke the hypnotic spell that held their stare at the unbelievable event.

"If we don't start for home now, we will be later than we promised the girls' dads.

"We still have time to stop for some ice cream." Mary said, to their surprise.

"Our Fathers have probably heard by now what happened and will know we did not get to enjoy a concert." Mamie interjected an assuring note, "I am sure it will be alright."

"Well if you say so" Kaz responded, "I just could not endure the thought your parents would think us undependable to our word and disallow us another date."

"Date?" Mary questioned,

"I know it's a rather new phrase among young people, but are you sure this is your idea of a date?"

It really broke the heaviness of the evening's event and they all allowed themselves to break into hardy laughter. Kaz seized the momentary light-heartedness when he said,

"My mother has a new cylinder for her Victrola, and she was playing a new song the other day, it was called 'It'll be a hot time in the old town tonight."

The four of them could contain themselves no longer. They howled like the few remaining wolves that roamed the sand dunes of the area. Then it happened,

"Oh Ed," Mary cried, "You are so silly, and we should really be more respectful at a time like this." Then she burst into laughter again and did the unthinkable. She clasped her hands firmly around both of Kaz's wrist and held them in front of her like someone playing with a child. In a moment she saw the awestruck look in Kaz's eyes. She composed herself and slowly released her grip. With a little embarrassed smile, she cleared her throat, dropped her gaze, and turned to Mamie with a look that said,
"Say something and get me out of this uncomfortable situation."

For the rest of the summer and into the late autumn Kaz and Mary would see each other almost every evening. Long walks would eventually turn into long conversations. They would learn each other's likes, dislikes and dreams. Kaz soon began to realize what a special girl Mary was. Her family's Polish/Austrian influence, on the southern borders of Poland, had created an insatiable appetite for classical music. She would spend the rest of her life spending hours listening to the masters. Especially her fellow Pole, Chopin. She would explain to Kaz how impressed she was when she learned that even though the great conductor, famous for his happy Mazurkas, tunes from the lakes region of northwest Poland, Chopin would be buried in Paris. He left written instructions that his heart was to be removed from his remains, and entombed in the Cathedral in Warsaw.

Perhaps the most intriguing part of Mary was her religious dedication. She was so faithful to Sunday Mass. Mary would become like a little, excited girl when she would tell Kaz how much she loved the beautiful St. Stanislaus Church and its stained glass windows, marble floors, artistic Stations of the Cross, and magnificent altar. Her father told her that this church was so much like the cathedrals he knew in Poland and Austria. She was not sure if she liked the Latin masses more than the Polish language mass, but the Latin made her think more deeply. Mary's discussions about God made Kaz revisit his own feelings, and he wondered what had happened to that time when he knew God loved him. All he knew for certain was he felt like a better person when he spent time with Mary. The long walks often ended with long embraces and even some tender kisses. It was hard for him to grasp how he was now holding this beauty, who had once even considered becoming a nun.

Snow was again falling as they left the midnight Christmas mass, beginning the cold trudge back toward Snake Town. As they approached Mary's house, Kaz stopped in his tracks, and reaching to take hold of Mary's arm, he slowly turned her face toward his. He pulled her petite body tenderly against his. Looking into her sparkling eyes he said,

"The church was so beautiful tonight. The only thing more beautiful was you, and not just you, but you being with me."

Mary knew even for this kind man she called Ed, this was an unexpected speech. Kaz continued,

" I can only imagine one time St. Stan's," as they commonly called it, "would be more beautiful. That would be the day you would stand with me at that altar, and become my wife."

Then he said the unimaginable, "Mary, I am in love with you. I want to spend the rest of my life with you. Won't you please become my wife?"

After a long pause, she spoke,

"Well. . . you know we have this custom. You would have to ask my father's permission." "Then you are saying you would marry me if your father would give his blessing?" Kaz exuberantly questioned.

"Of course, Ed." she said softly, "I have known you were the man for me since you handed me that program last summer at the symphony concert."

"Then let's ask him tonight!" Kaz urged impatiently.

"Oh no, Mary objected kindly while placing her fingers on Kaz's gaping mouth, "My father would have gone to bed immediately after getting home from Mass. Besides," she continued, "It would be better for me to invite you for Sunday Dinner, and have us properly deliver this announcement, and ask for their blessing after we eat." She put on a little, impish smile, and said, "That way my Papa will not want to talk so long as he will be looking forward to his Sunday afternoon nap."

With that Kaz kissed Mary again, this time longer and more firmly than he had ever attempted. Pushing her softly to arms-length, and holding her hands he said,

"Mary, you have made me the happiest man in the world tonight!" to which she replied,

"Ed, don't get overcome with your happiness yet. We have a lot of things to think about. After all, nothing will be the same for us again."

Feeling warm on their faces, warm in their hearts, and frozen on their feet, they quickly moved to Mary's front door, and quietly whispered good night. It was fortunate Mary could not feel her feet after their lengthy stand in the snow, because she was sure they were floating across the room once inside the house.
Kaz, for some unknown reason, decided it would be best to run home that night. The only thing stranger than the heavy steam pouring from his mouth with each breath, and the difficult balancing act on the icy street was his occasional bellow in the night.

"Yes! Oh Yes! She said `Yes!" then he realized more than an hour had passed since midnight. Like a crazy man released on the sleeping city, he began to yell at the top of his voice, "Merry Christmas to all!"

He began to run out of breath, and his vociferous song began to quiet, the word changed from "Merry...Merry...Merry..." to "Mary...Mary...Mary."

He felt like the little eight-year-old boy that rolled on the grassy hills of Baltimore a lifetime ago.

Time passed quickly, and the plans for their wedding were all in place. The only hitch that would confront the soon to be married couple took place just a few days before the ceremony. Kaz and Mary arrived at the courthouse building in plenty of time to acquire the marriage license before the office would close for the day. Soon a rather stern looking lady was asking them all the required questions. Date of birth, place of birth, immigration dates, and citizenship status. Then she turned to Kaz and said,

"Please give me your first, middle, or Christian name, Sir."

He spoke without a thought, "Paul" giving the English equivalent to the old-world Polish name, Kazimierz Paweł.

Suddenly a ghastly squeal burst from his right,
"What did you say?" It was Mary, and she looked like she had seen a ghost.

"Did you say Casimir?" she balked.

"Well, yes." Kaz responded quickly.

"No this can't be!" Mary wailed. "Your name is Ed. You said your name was Ed."

"Yes," he tried to quietly explain, "most people know me as Ed, but my real name has always been Casimir, and my family and old friends know me as 'Kaz.' Why does it matter anyway?" he asked with slight agitation.

"I was engaged once to a guy named Casimir. He was so terrible my father ran him out of town, and I promised my parents I would never get involved again with any man named Casimir."

"Oh, for love of Mike!" Kaz said with a roll of his eyes, "You know me as Ed. Do you think I am different from the man you have fallen in love with because you find out my real name is Casimir, or because some know me as Kaz?"

She calmed down a bit and then talked to herself,

"Well, Shakespeare did say, 'a rose by any other word would smell as sweet.'"

As she slowly turned her attention to the rather impatient clerk of the court, she resolved her own question, signed the necessary documents, and shook her head in disbelief at this newly gained knowledge. With license in hand, they descended the old courthouse steps. Amid the impending blizzard building across the lake, she declared one of many oaths yet to come,

"I will tell you one thing Ed, or Kaz, or whatever your name is, we will never name one of our sons Casimir."

With that she stretched both her fisted hands at each side and firmly stomped one foot on the bottom step of the courthouse entrance.

"So," Kaz said grinning from ear to ear, "It sounds like you plan on having more than one son, if I hear you right."

"Oh, you are such a silly man." She said, while pinching the end of his nose teasingly. She then grasped his arm and started the brisk walk into their future.

They began to plan for a June wedding in another American tradition. In Poland, August was the most popular month for weddings, probably because it was the warmest month of the year. They were very fortunate to have chosen June. Many of the long, cold, winter nights of their courtship led to even longer embraces and longer kisses. Because Mary was so thinly framed June would have been the last possible month she could have disguised the baby growing within her. Four months after their beautiful wedding Mary would deliver into this world Jan and Anna's Pawlak's first grandson. In 1910, and under these circumstances, a girl would normally have been put in asylum far from home. To the credit of her family Mary would not be an outcast, even though her premarital condition would never be spoken of again. Anna would deliver a baby weighing over 10 pounds. Kaz would gently hold the above average size boy in his big hands. An awesome sense of responsibility would overwhelm Kaz. Mary would softly reach from her bed to her husband's arm and add to the awesomeness of the moment.

"He is American Ed, truly an American." Kaz smiled and sheepishly asked,

"Shall we name him Kazimiersz?"

Mary's eyes filled with tears and she replied,

"The man you love the most is called Jan, Let's name him John after your father."

"A fine boy he is," Anna added, "and a fine man he will become, like his father."

As Kaz closed his eyes in contemplation of this hour, his full heart entertained an unexpected question. Does his Heavenly Father love him in any proportion to how he loves this warm and beautiful son now sleeping calmly in his arms?

Two months later Mary was pregnant with their second child. Their little rented house, just a few blocks away from Snake Town, would have a comfortable small garden. Mary took some relief from the unusually hot, July afternoon by watching Johnny crawl across the soft grass, and try already to pull himself up on the fence post in an attempt to stand. She hoped he would take his first steps before the new baby arrived. She knew this would be unusually young for an infant to walk, but this child seemed to be amazingly strong than for his age.

Kaz came home from the factory that day with an exciting announcement.

"I am taking you and the baby to the park this evening."

"Why the park tonight," she asked, "We have not been to the park this entire summer, with the baby and all."

Kaz reasoned, "It will be good for you both, and I have a little surprise for you."

"I don't know Ed, I am so big with this baby I'm carrying, I am not sure I can walk that far."

"Well you sure won't go any later this summer so this could be our last chance."

As she lifted Johnny from the grass and handed him to his father, she murmured to the growing boy, "Oh, your father is such a silly man, but we will appease his crazy ideas today."

Once John was secured in the large, shaded baby buggy, they moved slowly through the streets. Occasionally, Kaz would stop and allow Mary to catch her breath and massage her side where the active little creature in her was kicking its legs like the great athlete he was destined to become. They entered the park and first gazed upon the tall statue that welcomed each entrant. Though Roman in design, the monument was erected to honor all soldiers who had ever fought for the freedom or preservation of the nation. Once past the sight-line of the monument Mary saw it. She could not believe her eyes. There before her stood the beautiful Bandstand where she first met Kaz. She was taken back to that warm August night when the symphony was merely background music to the romantic overtures being sent to her from the seat directly behind her.

Her mind's eye was suddenly filled with the flames and smoke of their first official date. She shuddered at the thought of the loss of the place that produced the magical, musical journeys she so missed that summer.

"Oh, Kaz," she uttered, "Did you know about this?"

"Yes, my love. I have known for some time it was being rebuilt. It has been the talk of the factory. You see, Mr. Barker has donated the money for its reconstruction."

This was the same Mr. Barker of Haskell and Barker, the owners of the box car factory.

"But this is the best part of the surprise yet..." Kaz continued, "Tonight they are dedicating the new bandstand, and the Mr. Ames's Municipal Band is going to entertain with an evening of marches, many by John Phillip Sousa."

"Ed, why did you keep this a secret from me?" Mary quietly asked.

"I wanted to surprise you and make this occasion a special celebration for the soon arrival of our second child."

Mary touched his arm and said, "You may be even more sentimental than silly, my beloved husband, but thank you for the wonderful surprise."

"Oh, there is more." Kaz exclaimed, "Just turn around, Mary." He insisted.

To her amazement, there stood Emil and Mamie. She had not seen them since their wedding, shortly after Johnny's arrival. She threw her arms around them both, and burst into tears. This was something she seemed to do the closer in came to her next delivery.

"Oh, I have missed you both so much. With the new bandstand and all, this feels like our first time here again."

Just then, she felt her abdomen against Mamie and said, with a little laugh, "Well, I don't look the same as then."

Just then Mamie stood erect, placed her hands over her own stomach, and revealed to Mary the obvious increase in her midriff, and declared,

"Well, you're not going to be the only mama from the old Snake Town girls. We could have our own little Christmas gift this year. See?"

The girls hugged again. Kaz extended his hand toward his dear friend Emil. Those two massive hands, not unlike a couple of ham hocks, slapped together and began a pumping motion that could have struck oil if attached to a Texas drilling pipe. Emil had stopped earlier at Dingler's meat market. As they all found a soft, grassy place to sit down, Emil unsheathed from the thick red butcher paper several beautiful, golden-colored, smoked fish. Kaz took from one pocket his bone-handled knife, and from the other a large chunk of strong smelling, limburger cheese. To top off this feast fit for a king, Emil pulled from a cloth sack a large fruit jar filled with his latest production of succulent elderberry wine.

"...From my own berry bushes." Emil proudly proclaimed.

They had just begun to feast on the delicacies when the conductor struck his baton several times on the side of his wooden music stand, raised his arms high above his head, and with one powerful, downward motion of his arms the band began to play that familiar tune that would be named a few years later, The National Anthem of the United States of America. The people were familiar with words that Francis Scott Key had penned at Ft. McHenry during the battle of 1812. As the attendees each stood to their feet like a magnificent choir, many with broken English accents, they began to sing,

"O Say, Can you see by the dawn's early light?"

Tears began to fill Kaz's eyes and a huge lump in his throat made a swallow of his first piece of smoked fish nearly impossible. His mind was carried back almost two decades earlier. He could feel his little skinny waist pressed against a ship's rail, and instead of a square block of cheese in his thick palm, he felt the tender, loving grip of his mother's hand. Through his blurry eyes he no longer saw the newly designed bandstand, but a distant shore. The voices around him mysteriously faded into a discordant, memory-recording of enthusiastic echoes,

"O say can you see..........O say can you see......O say can you see."

Perhaps the most courageous adventure's proclamations, "America! it's America! Oh, America at last."

Kaz's mind withdrew from the memory at the song's fermata ending. Soon after the appreciative crowd took their seats, Kaz and Emil excused themselves from the ladies, and said perhaps they would slip over to the nearby basin to see if anyone was catching fish this evening.

Johnny was sleeping on Anna's lap, in spite of the vigorous marches and crashing cymbals exploding from the new Bandstand. As the girls talked of marriage, houses, and babies Anna quizzed Mamie,

"Have you thought about names yet?"

"Well boys are prominent in both our families, so I have given more thought to a boy name than a girl name."

"Then what have you come up with?" pressed Mary.

"There is a new name I've heard lately. I really like it."

"Well, what is it?" asked Mary

"Don't think it is odd. It is not one of the old names we are used to."

"Please Mamie, you are killing me with suspense. As Ed would say, 'for love of Mike.' Mamie, tell me."

"OK Mary, but don't scoff. I want to name a son Kenneth,"

Mamie watched Mary absorb the idea as her head tilted slightly to the side.

"Hmm, Kenneth." Mary repeated, "Yes. I think I like it. It is different for our culture, but sounds strong and yet kind. Do you know what it means?"

"I was told by an American girl that it means 'wise' or 'to know.'

Mary then said, "Then, it would be a great name and you have my approval." at which they both laughed at the thought either would need anyone else's approval for what they would name their child.

"But wait, Mary" Mamie suddenly interjected, "You have not yet told me what you will name your new child."

"Well," Mary said, lowering her voice, "I know we should probably think about a family name like my father's name, George, or Ed's dear friend Uncle Marek, but I had a cousin back in Poland they called Franek. I have learned that the English equivalent is Frank." She continued, "I know many good Catholics name their sons Francis, but I really don't care so much for that name, and it is often used in America for girls. So maybe I will use Francis if it is a girl, but I like the sound of Frank for a boy."

"I like it, Mary." Mamie said approvingly. "You know, in this Country, with them being less than a year apart, many will call your two, Johnny and Franky." She smiled a sympathetic little smile and said, "It sounds like a couple of energetic, little rascals to me."

CHAPTER 3 - 1913-1923

Nostradamus, the famous sixteenth-century pill pusher turned prophet, who was accredited with some 6,338 predictions, would have been amazed at the accuracy of Mamie Pohl's prophetic words a decade earlier. Johnny and Franky looked for any excuse to escape the chores of home to run the neighborhood, skinny dip the Monon Ditch, pick up a baseball game in a nearby field, or act out a battlefield scene from stories they heard from someplace called the Western Front. The parents were grateful that their boys were only imagining partaking in the "War to end all wars," especially as the flag-draped coffins were being shipped home by the thousands.

The little house was getting quite crowded since four children now sat at the dinner table each evening. Kaz and Mary's third and fourth child were girls to match the set of boys. Lilly was becoming a strong, confident, young girl with a tremendous tendency toward humor, a trait that would come to carry her through many challenges that lay ahead. Little Sophie was Mama's little helper. It was obvious she was going to be the worker bee of the family.

Sophie began to develop a significant self-consciousness. Perhaps this was the product of teasing from her brothers, or some of the abstract behavior Mary was beginning to display. There were the times each month when the life insurance man would come to the house to collect the few dollars set aside for the policy Kaz had secured due to the horrible Spanish flu pandemic spreading across America. When the rap would sound from the front door, Mary would go into a pure panic. She would order the children to hide so the collector would not see them. She would even say,

"Don't let this man see how poorly you are dressed or how bad your hair looks today."

To the boys it was a fun game of hiding behind the curtains. To Lilly it was just a normal visit of the insurance man. But for Sophie, she felt shame at being asked to hide.

"There must be something really ugly about me." she thought each time.

While many Jewish children in town were infused with the prophetic affirmations of their prominent parents, and confidence building statements like, "You can own this town one day," the Pawlak children were caught in the tension of their mother's aspirations and doubts. Mary consciously voiced her desire to see her children fully Americanized, but her behavior didn't always portray her hope for the "American dream" to be realized. She felt the need to constantly remind them of their inabilities. If any of her children were to voice a future dream, like being a teacher or doctor someday, they would be reminded they were not American, but Polish.

So, it was of little surprise that for many decades to come, the majority of the Polish descendants would spend their lives working for the companies owned by the minority Jewish proprietors and business owners of the city. Yet the Poles would make the city a remarkable place to live and raise a family.

Energetic was the most placid word possible to describe the overly active, amazingly adventurous, uncontrollable packages of perpetual mischief of Johnny and Franky. At age 8 and 7, respectively, the duo was like twin tornados, so familiar in the midwest States. The boys were just ten months apart in age and nearly identical in size, due to the fact that Frank was said to be twelve pounds at birth. The validity of this fact always remained difficult to document. Like most children born in 1911, Frank was born at home with the aid of a Midwife. Some said this lady also worked in the fish market, and may have just held Frank up by his feet and announced a weight of 12 pounds, as if estimating a sizable Lake Michigan carp. The other possibility was that they had no scale, and had to wait for Mr. Winski, the Polish-Jewish immigrant to bring his rag cart by the house. He would use the scale on the back of his cart. This left the very believable possibility that Frank, although truly a large baby, could have been a month old before actually being weighed for the first time. Whatever the truth of his birth size, nothing outweighed the daily challenge he and his brother presented to their tiny little mother, Mary. They were not cruel, rebellious, or hurtful boys. They simply were a moving catastrophe waiting to happen.

In the winter months it was just too cold to use the outhouse toilet at the end of the back yard. One of the daily chores expected of Johnny and Franky was to carry the large bucket used for that purpose to the sewer ditch each evening. It would require both of them to hold the pale's handle from each side. The daily power struggle for command was always present for these twentieth-century, twin-like siblings. They were neither suckled by a she wolf, nor fed by a woodpecker, and neither would build a city like Rome, but they were, in many ways, America's answer to Roman Mythology's Remus and Romulus.

"Frank," John commanded, "Pull the bucket this way."

Frank snapped back, "No, I want to go this way with it this time."

One would begin to pull the bucket in his direction while the other would swing the bucket nearly out of the other's grip. Then the arguing would soon be followed by threats, and eventually laughter.

"Stop, Frank," John would holler, giggling breathlessly, "You're going to make me drop this thing."

Frank was laughing so hard he would plead with his brother,

"Johnny Please, I'm about to pee my pants."

Finally, they became so weak with giggles that they would invariably drop and spill the entire contents.
On the few occasions they made it all the way to the ditch, and began the final pitching motion, Frank would instruct John in no kindly tone,

"Sit the bucket down." Then John would take over the leadership of this chaos.

"Put one hand on the handle, Frank and the other under the bottom of the bucket."

He slowly detailed his words in an insulting staccato. Frank screamed back in John's face.

"Just make sure you lift the bucket high and away from your body this time before we throw it in the ditch."

John recoiled with "When you've done this as many times as I have then I will listen to you."

As to be expected, the results often ended in both being drenched from the horrid contents falling from the sky above them. After some spitting and sputtering, and a great deal of consternation, they started back to the house still reminding each other,

"This was your fault!"

There were the times when their sibling rivalry slipped over into the near fatal. One such occasion was the day they were chopping firewood out back for the upcoming winter season.

"Frank," said Johnny, "You're stacking that wood upside down. Pa wants it with the bark side down, and you're putting it with the bark-side up."

At that point Frank responded with, what would years later become his favorite response to his teenage sisters,

"Aw, just shut up."

No sooner were those words out of Frank's mouth, Johnny fired back, "You shut up."

Both boys had become well-versed in the offensive side of the English language. The most natural volley was quickly out of Frank's mouth,

"Why don't you make me shut up?" But this time Frank added an element of sincerity to his verbal posturing. Faster than his hero, Jack Dempsey, the reigning Heavyweight Champion of the World could throw a right hook, Frank brought his wide-open hand across the left side of John's meaty cheek. As Johnny reached up to his burning face, he bellowed,

"Are you crazy?"

Frank seeing the fury in John's eyes bolted for the back door of the house. Up to this point Frank had been pretty calculated in this uproar. He just made one, nearly disastrous, mistake. He left the wood-chopping hatchet in John's possession. Just as Frank reached the archway of the rear entrance to the house, Johnny let fly the hatchet. The weapon of early Native American fame rotated vertically as perfectly as if it had been a tomahawk thrown by Geronimo himself. Frank, running at his top speed, placed his front foot into the doorway when, precisely at head-height, the hatchet's sharp side struck the door facing, sunk into the wood a good quarter inch, and remained there with its handle making a loud vibrating noise. The result of this fracas would have been unthinkable if the weapon had arrived one inch to the left, or if Frank had been one step slower. The events of that day would remain John's and Frank's secret until long after their parents were gone.

Mary was not one to "spare the rod" but her efforts to distribute this kind of discipline were of little avail. When she would catch the boys in some absolute disobedient behavior she would take after them with a broom. Holding the sweeping section with both hands, she began her hot pursuit. To her anguish, both boys could outrun her. Several laps around the house would weaken her before they were even breathing heavily. When she could corner them in the house they would simply run to their room, put their backs to the bed and wedge their feet, suspended in air, against the inside of the door. She had not near enough strength to force the door open. While she would cry her threats, they would simply have more fun and laughter at the cost of her frailty. When she was crafty enough to get in the room before they could close the door, they just rolled under the bed, grabbed the bed's springs' pulled their bodies upward off the floor, while she attempted to swing the broom at them with no more success than baseball players trying to make contact with the famous Walter Johnson's fastballs of that day.

When all her efforts failed, she would simply surrender the battle and declare the ultimate warning,

"When your father gets home he will spank you good."

As soon as Kaz arrived home on one of those battle days, Mary welcomed him with the announcement every father loves to come home to:

"You must give those boys a good whipping tonight. They have been terrible, and disobeyed me all day." Kaz just bit the corner of his bottom lip, as he often did, shook his head in disbelief, and cover the entire subject with one phrase:

"Them Dahg-Gahn (Dog gone) Kids!"

Nothing more would happen until a week or two later. The boys were simply walking through the house, and the next thing they felt was that huge, wide hand strike their buttocks with the same effect of 1,000 bee stings.

"What was that for?" they cried out. Kaz snapped back,

"Two weeks ago, when you drove your mother crazy all day."

The timing seemed strange but as they both would walk away rubbing their bottoms, hoping for some relief, they came to realize a great lesson: Judgment isn't always immediate, but it is inevitable.

With the eight and seven year old, wild boys, a three year old, little girl getting into everything, and a one year old baby girl not even walking yet, Mary wondered how she would break the news to Kaz that the family was not finished growing yet. That evening after dinner, Mary made an odd suggestion.

"Ed, she offered, "Let the boys keep their eyes on the little ones, and walk with me to the dairy for an ice cream cone.

This was an unexpected surprise. Often, Kaz would stop the ice-cream truck, buy two cones with the hope of surprising Mary. He wished these little gestures would help her with her increasing depression and less amiable behavior. Mostly she would refuse his show of kindness and say,

"Ed, you are being a silly man, spending good money on treats when it could go so many other places."

More than once he went back to the front porch, sat down on the top step, and with rotating licks, finished both of the cones.
Her uncharacteristic suggestion of a walk and an ice cream cone just about took his breath.

After finishing their dessert, and walking toward home for a while, Mary spoke.

"I have something to tell you Ed, but I wanted to wait for the perfect moment."

"What is wrong Mary," he asked with obvious concern. "Why would you need a perfect moment to tell me something? Are you sick? Is there something wrong with one of them ? What, What is it?"
His voice rose anxiously.

"Oh Ed, listen to yourself," she said, bringing the walk to a full halt. As she took him by the arm, turning him to face her, she half smiled, and said softly but firmly,

"We are going to have another baby, Ed; another child."

Kaz quickly pulled the old wool cap off his head and began to twist it as he had years before while garnering the courage to ask Mary to the Symphony.

"A fifth child!" came bursting from his mouth. Kaz instantly began to suppress the vision of what one more mouth to feed would look like at that time. "Oh, that is wonderful

Mary, just wonderful!" were the words spewing out, but a wave of fear and concern could not be hidden in those, ever deepening crevasses at the corner of his eyes. "Well, what do you think?" Kaz asked, softening his voice and his furrowed brow. "Think we'll be lucky enough to have three girls in a row?"

"After those two sons of yours, I think I could deserve that!" Mary replied. They both began to laugh as Kaz shook his head in sympathetic understanding. Then she became very serious, to the point of sullenness. She continued, "Ed, I have been thinking about something else."

"Please don't tell me it may be twins." He teased.

"No, you silly man, just listen to me a minute." She continued looking deeply into Kaz's eyes, like she had not done in years. "If it is a boy again, I have already decided on a name." He knew better than to ask the fateful question by now. She continued, "I want to name him after his father." He felt enough leeway to say it,

"Casimir? Surely not." his voice dropped.

Rather smugly, she retorted, "No, No, No. I made a promise years ago about that, and I plan on keeping my word."

"What then?" Kaz inquired. He saw a small tear well up in the corner of both her eyes.

"I want to name him Edward," she said softly. "That was the name of the man I fell in love with, and still love."

"Wow," Kaz said, "For the first time you just made Ed sound really nice. I think it would be a fine name. I feel it will be a son." he then added, "You know, the boys are a lot like me, but I feel this boy may be a lot like his mother. We will see that he loves the things his mother loves."

So, as the second decade of the new century was drawn to a close, Mary would bring forth her fifth child, a son. He was not nearly as big as her first two boys, but he was beautiful. This boy had a head full of natural blond curls and a strong voice. With each hour of late-night screaming, due to the colic, Mary would walk the floor, hum a tune and think,

"With those tenor notes, perhaps he would become a great virtuoso like her beloved Caruso."

This would be her last child, but in time, this child would come to epitomize what would be known as true "Americana."

Before long Johnny was spending more time with his grandparents, Jan and Anna, than the other children. In the old Polish tradition, the eldest son was the favored son. Johnny loved being with his grandparents. Neither Jan nor Anna had become fully fluent in the English language. Anna was even less fluent than Jan. It was a great comfort to her that Johnny picked up the Polish language so well, at least, enough to communicate with her more comfortably than her other grandkids. While fishing one Saturday with both the older boys, Kaz moved into the same discussion his father had with him many years ago. He would carefully point out to both, the greater value of finding gainful employment, rather than spending unnecessary years in school.

Their catch of fish that day was astounding. They knew they had more fish than they wanted to clean. Kaz suggested,

"Hey boys, let's take about half of these fish to your Grandpa Jan." The boys agreed, more thankful they would not spend the rest of the afternoon cleaning all those fish. It was Frank who posed the question first,

"Pa," as they had come to refer to their father, "Why doesn't Grandpa Jan care to join us on the fishing days anymore?" Kaz replied,

"I think the heat of the factory is just taking a toll on your Grandpa these days." Kaz had noticed that even on Saturdays Jan would make excuses for not going fishing. Often he would say,

"My garden needs tending." Jan loved to put a little parental guilt on Kaz by reminding him, "You know son, I don't have kids at home to help me anymore, and my grandsons like to play a little too much."

After taking turns carrying the long stringer of fish, Kaz stepped on the front porch of the old homestead. Johnny and Franky were close behind when they heard a disturbing sound.

"It is Grandma crying in there," said Johnny.

"What is she saying" asked Frank, "I don't understand Polish like you do. John, What is she saying?" he demanded.

Frank placed the stringer of fish on the front yard, and the three rushed into the house. Johnny quickly switched to his familiar Polish asking,

"What has happened Baba?" This was normally a small child's way of saying Grandmother. In her familiar Polish she said to Kaz,

"Jan fell in the Garden. When I got there he was unconscious." She continued in a sobbing voice, "By the time I got to him he looked extremely bad." She further explained, "I screamed for someone to help me. Mr. Kazmucha heard me, and brought his car. He took us to that new St. Anthony Hospital on Wabash Street."

"Matka, I will go there now." Kaz said, turning quickly to run out the door.

"No, No" Anna yelled to the top of her voice, grabbing Kaz's arm to turn him toward her. She wailed,

"It is too late, son!" then she cried out, "He is already gone."

Anna slid downward from Kaz's arms and from a kneeling position placed her face in her hands, and began to sob like Kaz had never seen his mother cry before.

It was quite a different experience to have a funeral service in a funeral home, as opposed to a church. With Jan's disenchantment with the church, Anna thought it best to use this available alternative. Ott Funeral chapel had been there for almost a half a century so it was not a strange way to proceed. Jan Pawlak's body would be the first of this immigrant family to be buried in American soil. Because of Anna's love for St. Stanislaus Church, they graciously allowed Jan to be buried in their Catholic cemetery. Like scores of other immigrants, this brave adventurer, who would make a way to bring his family to a new land of opportunity, would in time, be forgotten. It would be almost eighty years before an aged grandchild would finally place a headstone upon that grave.

Within a year of the passing of Jan Pawlak, Uncle Marek would also die, and be buried in the Catholic cemetery in Otis. As Kaz attended Uncle's mass, he was fully aware that the two men who made it all happen were forever gone.

CHAPTER 4 - 1923-1933

Frank started working in the local grocery market, and John took on the unpleasant task of following his grandfather's footsteps into the foundry at Haskell and Barker. Not long after John entered employment in the box car factory it was taken over in a major industrial buy-out, by the famous passenger car manufacturer Pullman Standard Company. From then on everyone would come to simply refer to this life-blood source of Michigan City as Pullman's.

The grocery business required long hours, and significantly interfered with Frank's real love, Baseball. Although he was rather lean, his body was strong and fast. He had an uncanny flexibility which made him an excellent first baseman. His ability to stretch into full splits like a gymnast, meant few throws in his direction ever got by him. To round out the package of the perfect baseball player of that day, he was a pure contact hitter. It was said by other teammates and several scouts,

"It was easier to get the sunrise past a rooster than a fastball past Frank Pawlak." Later, Franky Miller, one of his teammates with the Michigan City Orioles, said,

"Frank may not have been the best player to live, but he was among the best to ever put on the uniform."

As he was now in his upper teens, an ideal situation opened up for Frank. Mr. Parry needed an extra man to work the night shift at his bakery. He was even willing to teach the baking trade to a willing worker. This was a heaven-sent idea to Frank. He could arrive at the bakery in the early evening, work until sunrise, get home and sleep a few hours, get to the pier for an hour of his other love, fishing, and make it to baseball practice before he had to be back to work in the bakery the next evening. Since all their games were played on Sunday, and the Bakery was closed that day, this was the fulfillment of all Frank could want in his life.

Older brother John became a bit envious of Frank's new found fortunes, and when a second opening came at the Bakery John decided it would be better making breads, rolls, cakes and good Polish Donuts, called Paczki. But after a few nights working in the bakery, John could not sleep, nor could anyone else in the house, as the flour dust of the bakery bothered John even more than the pollution of the foundry. Night after night John would go into coughing fits, beat his massive chest, and proclaim,

"Dat lousy flour dust is chokin' me to death." In the broken accent of a pure immigrant, he would continue his agonizing refrain, "I can't get no breeze in my lungs."

After several nights of sleeplessness, Kaz finally pleaded with John,

"For love of Mike, John, please quit that bakery and get back to Pullman's so someone can get some sleep around here."

John was back in the Factory the next morning. With the boys working, and gone most of the time, Sophie and Lilly were being beckoned to spend time with their Babcia (grandmother) Anna. Anna was an amazing lady to these girls. She seemed more peaceful and less demanding than their mother had become. She was rather rotund, and even jolly as compared to the more serious and thin Mary. They loved to sit on Anna's front porch and watch her peel apples for an American delight called apple pie. Anna always used a sharp paring knife, and she could peel an entire apple in seconds without ever breaking the descending strip of peel. The whole apple was ready for dissecting. On one such occasion a newspaper reporter happened by and saw this handy work in progress.

"Excuse me, madam," he said as he approached the front porch,

"Oh sorry, mister," interrupted Sophie, "My grandmother does not understand English very well." Turning quickly towards Sophie and Lilly the reporter doffed his straw hat and continued,

"Well ladies, perhaps you could explain to your dear grandmother that I have been watching her for some time, and I am utterly amazed at her skill and technique in apple peeling."

Both girls giggled at this rather emboldened character as he was standing, intrusively on the top step. He continued without missing a beat or taking a breath,

"Would you be so kind as to ask your dear grandmother if I could have the privilege of taking her picture, and writing a little article about her skills in the gazette of my employment?"

Though the girls were not completely comprehensive of the reporter's phraseology, they did explain the gentleman's intent to Anna. With a mixture of limited Polish language and some helpful hand gesturing, Anna agreed to the photo. Using her young translators, Anna also gave the reporter enough of her personal portfolio and baking purposes to enable him to write a quite accomplished personal-interest story. The family and neighbors were all abuzz when that week's newspaper had Anna's picture on the front page with a story about the amazing apple-peeling exploits of this Snake Town Grandmother.

Not unlike her daughter-in-law Mary, Anna mostly wore a clean, pressed, full apron over her dress throughout the day. However, there was something different about the way Anna's apron hung on one side. Sophie and Lilly even talked about it. It was as if there was something kind of bulging a bit at the right front corner of their grandmother's apron. One day, Helena, their Aunt Hattie's daughter asked outright,

"What do you think that bulge in the front of Grandma's apron is?"

"Oh! It must be some strange growth on her stomach." Sophie quickly responded. Lilly rapidly injected,

"Maybe it is a pistol. Maybe she uses it to make Johnny and Franky behave." All three girls burst into laughter. Each had a different physical reaction to this incident. One quickly held her hand over her mouth as to speak no evil. The other placed her index finger vertically in front of her lips with a silent "Shush." Lilly just waved her hands at the other girls as if to say,

"Go away and don't talk about this anymore."

They all understood that behind their Grandma Anna's amiable personality and memorable Grandmotherly ways, laid a deep secret that, to their knowledge, had been entrusted to only these girls. Lilly, being the eldest of the three, would be called at least once a week to Anna's bedroom.

"Lilly, my beloved," Anna would say softly, "I am attaching this money inside your jacket; I need you to run this little errand again for me."

After affixing the money safely she would repeat the familiar instructions.

"Dear, go for me to the Polish Pharmacy. Remember the back door in the alley, behind the store?"

Lilly nodded her head in response with each detail Anna would restate.

"Remember how you tap three times, pause and tap four times, and then wait?"

Lilly was much too respectful to interrupt, but wanted to say each time,

"I know, I know how to do this Grandmother." Anna would then say,

"You can take the other girls with you but you must handle this transaction for me."

After she had followed the specific door knocking formula, a tall man would appear, crack the door a bit, and say In Polish,

"Dzień Dobrej, little one."

As per Anna's instructions, Lilly would thrust the money through the narrowly opened door, and in just seconds a paper bag with a hard object would be rapidly handed out. Lilly would place it in her jacket pocket, and the three giggling girls would run nonstop back to their grandmother's home. After Anna quickly retrieved the package from the girls, she would always say the same thing,

"It is time to get home before your mothers start to worry."

The girls seemed to know this was Anna's private matter. They just knew by instinct they were never to investigate the package, or even tell anyone of this regular excursion. Once out of sight, Anna would close her bedroom door, slip the bottle of illegal elixir out of its package, open the lid as tenderly as a safe-cracker would romance a bank vault, and place to her lips what no virtuous woman of her day would ever be seen consuming publicly. After several long draws from the forbidden drink, she would lay herself back on the bed, safely place the bottle in her dress pocket under her apron, and reestablish the little questionable bulge with her deep secret intact. In a few minutes hot tears would begin to slide across her temples and gather in the ear lobes under her hair. Across her lips would begin to whisper again the words,

"Poznan...Poznan...Poznan..."

She would wonder at the pain in her heart and say to God above,

"Will this ever go from me, or must I bear this to my final breath?"

****

Not since the biblical relationship of Jacob and Rebekah had a mother and son seemed so naturally connected. Eddie, as he was now called by all the family, was truly an amazing child. Johnny was working hard in the box car factory, and becoming a faddish bodybuilding specimen. Frank was honing his skills as a master baker and cake decorator, while using his every free moment on the baseball field. Lilly was finishing her level of education to soon affix herself as a highly esteemed, and hard worker in the Arno Tape Factory.

Nearby, on the banks of the very harbor that brought her father and grandmother into this city some thirty six years earlier stood the tall plant known as The Smith Brothers building. Ever present in the minds and nostrils of the residents, the famous cough drop company was known for their boxes with the recognizable black silhouettes of the founding brothers, and the powerful fragrance of liquorish emanating from its smoke stacks.

Sophie was preparing for her teen years. Though a very quiet and timid girl, it was obvious she was going to be a rare beauty. She was still lanky and at that gangly, awkward stage. Sophie had already given herself to what would become an unending and impossible responsibility; serving and pleasing her mother. She had also developed an eye for something thought unnecessary in most poor, first-generation immigrants; fashion. Sophie saw clothing styles making amazing changes as the roaring Twenties were evolving into the plush and stylish Thirties. She could not wait for the next mannequin to display the latest Parisian, or at least Hollywood design. What made her new found love for clothing a rather cruel joke was that she honestly believed she would never have the kind of money required to wrap herself in that breathtaking beauty. Compounding this resolute station of life, at least in her mind, was the fact that she honestly believed she was some ugly freak of nature. Her large European nose was not considered a statement of dignity in America's growing visual vanity. She was physically developing in what she considered, "Top Heavy" for her slim and above-average height. Her regular and painful self critique would soon become a personal disdain that would translate into a genuine belief. She would accept the saddest restrictions any beautiful young woman could place upon themselves. Sophie believed it to be pure selfishness to enjoy fulfillment or happiness.

Mary was only in her late thirties, but already taking on the posture and behavior of a much older woman. It was not without some understandable cause. She seemed to be bothered by some continuous intestinal malady. She was not one to suffer in silence. Behind her back the family often rolled their eyes and laughed when asking each other,

"Has mother given you her regularity report today?"

They were not intending to be unsympathetic or uncaring; it was just that the continuous verbal bulletins, followed by the dramatic grimaces had become so common. Mary's other affliction was the one that now restricted her mobility and placed more of the day to day responsibilities on the girls. Mary's parents, believing it unseemly for girls to have large feet, kept her in binding shoes, too small for her growing feet, for many of her childhood years. Just as many Asian parents of the past would bind their girl's feet so they would not grow, the effect on Mary's feet would be an adult lifetime of excruciating pain. She would spend hours daily with her feet in soaking basins. For the next four decades the vast volume of her medical care would come from an army of podiatrists. There were only three things that brought some measure of relief to her and the family, her learned prayers from her childhood prayer book, her classical musical records, and her youngest child Eddie.

Eddie would spend time with her while she was pursuing some level of relief in the foot soaking basins. As the music would waft through the living room, he would hum the familiar orchestrations. Should a vocalist be singing a particular aria from a renowned opera, his young tenor voice would join. This was as sweet to Mary's ears as any voice projecting from the famed Vienna Boys Choir. Kaz's namesake, Eddie, was not only a talented and sensitive boy, but just as active as any boy in the neighborhood the same age. One day he was climbing one of the rather large trees on the street. One of his favorite adventures was to climb just as high as possible. He loved the sensation of being at the narrowest and highest limb near the top of the tree. If it were a windy day the adventure was even greater. Eddie wrapped his arms tightly around the narrow tree, felt it sway several feet each way in the wind, and imagined he was at the top of the mast of a pirate ship under attack. It was not long until his bravado transformed into terror. As his imagination increased, so did his fear. Questions would come flooding his mind.

"What if the limb should break? What if I should fall? How will I ever get down?"

When he realized no one was coming to his rescue, and he did not want to hear another lecture on the danger of climbing to those heights, he began to loosen his grip, and step-by-step, slide his way back to safer levels and eventually solid ground.

On one particular day it all would change.

"Help, please help me! Won't someone help me please?" came the pitiful and blood curdling cry that particular cold autumn day.

"Wait, did you hear that?" said Janek Nowak to his mother. Janek was a neighbor boy who was raking leaves in the next yard.

"It sounds like the Pawlak boy from up the street," replied Mrs. Nowak. "He probably has himself stuck up that tree again." she declared as she motioned her son to drop the rake and follow her to the rescue. Upon her arrival at the large elm tree she was amazed to see that Eddie was far from the top of the tree but lying prostrate on the pile of golden brown leaves that had gathered below the lowest limb. He was holding his left arm, and howling like a young wolf.

"Oh my goodness boy, what have you done to yourself?" Janek's breathless mother asked.

"I fell, I fell from the very top!" cried Eddie.

"Well let me look at that arm boy," she ordered, while forcibly pulling Eddie's other hand away.

"Oh! Joseph, Mary and baby Jesus" She bellowed forth, "You have broken it like one of those shaky limbs you were climbing, son." Turning to her own son she instructed, "Janek, hurry to tell Mrs. Pawlak that her fool-hardy boy has hurt himself, and she needs to come here right away."

Janek's frozen stare at the horrible sight of a human bone protruding through skin and jacket sleeve was suddenly broken by his mother's powerful voice,

"Are you deaf young man? Move now, Son!"

Within minutes Mary was on her knees, stroking her Eddie's hair, and assuring him that help was on the way. Johnny had just arrived home from work as the Nowak boy was beckoning Mary to the accident scene.

"Come on Eddie" John kindly said, as he gathered his little brother up into his powerful arms. Mary tried to hold the fractured limb as still and level as possible, but Eddie would scream out in agony with each step Johnny would take toward home.

"Just lay him there on the bed Johnny," Mary said.

"I'm sorry, Ma!" Eddie whined, only to have his near panicked mother respond,

"Shush now, Eddie, and let me put this pillow under your arm."

She seemed rather calm considering the gravity of the situation. As she prepared to go to the kitchen for two cool clothes, one for the arm, and one for the brow, Kaz burst into the room like a raging Bull.

"What the heck happened to Eddie? The neighbors said he was hurt or something."

Just then he saw the grotesque result of Eddie's rapid descent from the tree top.

"Oh for the love of Mike, Eddie, you need to start wearing a parachute Son if you're going to keep climbing those trees." Kaz mused, trying to bring some verbal relief to the moment. Little did Kaz know that those words, intended to lighten the severity of the moment, would settle deeply into the mind and heart of an adventurous young lad. Neither would that be the last time Eddie would be comforted by this particular suggestion of his Father.

As darkness fell, and a cold rain began to fall, Kaz and Mary were struck with an overwhelming frustration.

"Mary," Kaz softly said as he placed the last few pieces of cut wood on the newly built fire in the stone hearth. "The boy needs to be taken to the hospital. That arm could get infection or blood poison if we don't do something."

"You think I don't know that Ed?" She snapped rather harshly. "We have no money Ed," she continued. "I sent Lilly to get that young Dr. Bernoski, but he said he could not do what Eddie would need, and that we must take him to the hospital."

Kaz, still brushing the fire wood and ash from his hands, turned to Johnny and said,

"I will get a blanket to put around Eddie. Mary you get the umbrella, and Johnny, let's carry Eddie to the hospital."

As a trio of father, mother, and son served as the human ambulance that night, they moved Eddie through the driving rain toward the tall grey building, barely visible up the street ahead of them. When they reached the corner of Wabash and Ann Streets, Mary said,

"Ed, you go on, I have something to do."

"What could you possibly have to do but get this boy to the hospital Mary?" He asked, utterly confused by this strange behavior in his wife.

"Just go Ed, Johnny, get him out of this rain and to the hospital."

Johnny was far too engrossed in his little brother's degenerating condition, being evidenced by the feverish face pushing into Johnny's huge chest muscles. He gave no attention to his mother's strange departure into the night.

Mary was walking rapidly and sobbing even harder. She seemed like a pitiful soul lost out in the darkest night of her life. It was not long until she raised her head, peered through the torrent, and fixed her eyes on the lighted porch and accompanying number beside the amazing beveled glass doors. The large, beautiful, and exotic Ben Franklin Stove stood intentionally stationed in the center of the massive room behind those doors. The mother of pearl windows at the front of the sculptured, silver masterpiece allowed the flickering fire to make a picturesque declaration, "The warm and the wealthy abide within these confines." Mary's body was shaking uncontrollably as her cold and tiny knuckles struck the heavy wooden frame of the monstrous front doors. Mary knew that she would need to call on all her gracious manners and proper training. Because she had not been privileged economically to know the life-style of the upper crust and well educated, she still knew she must not behave or communicate as an illiterate street dweller.

"May I help you madam?" slowly drawled the words from the large round face of a southern and properly-attired house maid.

"I am sorry for the intrusion," Mary's shaking voice responded, "But my son has had a terrible accident and I need to speak with Mr. Barker at once."

The maid straightened her back and declared, "I am sorry about your son, but Mr. Barker is deceased, and Mr. Spaulding is traveling out of State at this time and is not available."

Mary felt embarrassment rise flush her face, but the mother on a mission persisted in spite of her faux pas. With desperation in her voice, Mary pleaded,

"Perhaps Mrs. Barker-Spaulding is home, and could help me?"

Then with a very kind gesture the maid said to Mary, "Please, Madam, won't you step into the foyer and out of that terrible rain?" She proceeded to explain, "Mrs. Spaulding is receiving dinner with a few guests at this time, and just cannot be pulled away, you understand?"

Suddenly, like a ghost appearing behind the maid, there was a most impressive lady. She stood next to the centerpiece of the room, the heating stove.

"Lena, what is going on there?" Came the voice from within the warm room.

The lady of the house was a striking beauty. Catherine was the heiress of John H. Barker's fortune, which she had the misfortune of gaining when her parents had died in her youth. Turbulently married to Howard Spaulding in New Yore, the wealthy young woman rarely spent time in the Michigan City mansion.

"Sorry Mrs. Spaulding," the maid expounded, "I tried to explain to this dear lady that you were unavailable at this time."

"Well, that doesn't seem to be exactly the case, now does it dear?" She said while moving cautiously toward the somewhat ghastly figure in the doorway.

"What has brought you to my door on such a stormy night, my dear?" she asked.

"Oh, Mrs. Barker...I mean...Spaulding, I am ashamed to have even come, I must be out of my mind," said Mary.

"Well you are here, right mind or not so why don't you quickly tell me why." Urged this lady from a world Mary could only imagine.

Mary quickly lost no time in rehearsing the events of that late afternoon and evening. Feeling she had gone this far, she may as well declare the full purpose of her intrusion.

"Mrs. Spaulding," she said with utmost respect, "My husband has worked for your family's company for almost twenty-five years, and his father, over thirty years before that. Now, my oldest son has followed their footsteps for over five years already." She continued, "That means our family has survived, and lived from the benefits of your father's industrial brilliance, but Mrs. Spaulding you cannot deny that my family as well as thousands of others like us have also provided an outstanding lifestyle for you."

Mrs. Spaulding interrupted, "I'm sorry dear, what did you say your name was?"

A bit startled, Mary dropped her head and said, "Pawlak, I am Mary Rose Pawlak."

"May I call you Mary?" the lady asked properly.

"Well...yes of course. Yes, you may." Mary said, while slowing her heaving breath and shaking.

"Now Mary," Mrs. Spaulding replied, "What can I do about your son tonight?"

Mary slowly gathered her thoughts and finally spoke with boldness, "Mrs. Barker, whatever they do to save my son's arm at that hospital will cost more money than we could garner in months of work at the box car factory. I was just hoping that perhaps the dedication of the Pawlak family to your company could acquire us some assistance in this terrible thing that has come upon us."

With a kind hand placed on Mary's arm Mrs. Spaulding explained that even though she had sold the factory years before to the Pullman-Standard Company, there may still be something she could do.

"Lena," Mrs. Barker speaking directly to her maid ordered, "Take care of my guests, and explain that I've had to run out for a moment, and I will rejoin them for after dinner drinks." Then, she turned her attention to Mary and instructed, "Wait at the bottom of the steps and I will have William, my driver, bring the car around. He will take us to the Hospital."

Mary had never even sat inside an automobile like this. As they burst through the front doors of the St. Anthony's Hospital each nurse, nun, and worker jumped to their feet with the same sputtering greetings,

"Mrs. Spaulding, how may we help you?"

Mary was fully in shock when Catherine Barker Spaulding simply said,

"This is my friend Mary Rose. Her son is already here with a badly broken arm. I want him to be treated with the best of care. I will take care of any expenses incurred now or in the future until this boy is completely recovered from his injuries."

As quickly as they entered, Mrs. Spaulding, the epitome of industrial might and all its benefits, was out the door and out of sight, with not as much as a goodbye to Mary. The elderly nun guided the stunned, factory worker's wife down the long, dimly lit hallway toward the room where Kaz and Johnny would be waiting for Eddie's procedure to be finished. Midway down the hall Mary noticed a small chapel on the right.

"May I stop here for a moment?" she asked the Sister.

"Take as long as you please," was the gentle response.

Mary did not have her book of prayers, nor did she even have the family heirloom of her mother's rosary. But without any formality she fell into a corner of the chapel and cried out passionately the following words,

"Oh God, thank you, thank you, thank you. You sent to me another good Samaritan." Sobbing openly, she repeated over and over again, "Thank you, dear Jesus, Thank you, dear Jesus, thank you, dear Jesus." After composing herself she rejoined the kind nun in the hallway and began to wonder how she would ever explain to her Ed and Johnny where her strange abandonment of them had led her this amazing night.

After several weeks Eddie was fully recovered, and Mary would never again see the Spauldings. Kaz had only ever seen the late Mr. Barker on those election days when he would gather the immigrant citizens in the work yard, and instruct them as to the candidate they were to vote for when they got to the polling booths. Kaz was well known as that employee that got to the factory earlier than necessary. He just loved to have a pot of coffee made in his work area, and to spend a little quiet time with last night's newspaper. His primary reading was the front page headlines, the weather reports, and quickly the sports page. The latter section for only two items, the fishing report (ice fishing in the winter), and a few baseball scores. The stock market pages toward the end were simply a non-understandable grid work of abbreviations and numbers that only held an interest to the much wealthier than himself. As the other workers arrived in his section of the boxcar plant, he was the up-beat, rather happy voice of welcome each day. It was never clear if his desire for early arrival and happy attitude was his love for his work, or just the fact it was a bit warmer and more positive than the first hour of the day with his beloved Mary Rose.

It was a cold, October, Friday morning when Kaz opened up his paper to read a big, bold headline, which he honestly did not even understand. He had already consumed his first cup of coffee, and moved to the sports page when Walter Duda interrupted by snapping his thumb and middle finger against the backside of Kaz's paper.

"Pawlak, you old coot!" Walter bellowed, "Are you hiding behind that paper, and crying over the million bucks you lost yesterday?"

Without making any sense out of Duda's inquiry, Kaz questioned, "What the heck you blabbing about this early anyway?"

Walter replied in a rather heckling manner, "Well I never see ya with no different clothes or new hat so I figures you must be sticking all that money away on that Stock Market stuff, you old miser!" at which the morning tormentor wheezed a friendly cough and hocked up a large bronchial excretion, and blew it through his rounded lips to noisily smack against a nearby boxcar.

"Oh yeah," Kaz sighed, "I got so much bucks I buy that stuff everyday."

By that time several of the other workers had gathered and began to clamor with each other about what would happen now, and how much longer would they even have a job? Finally when Kaz realized that he did not understand what all the fuss was about, he spoke up,

"For love of Mike, what are you guys talking about? Losing our job, over what?"

About that time Walter Duda shouted, "Come on, Pawlak. You're the one with the paper, there, right on your front page, read it! 'STOCK MARKET CRASHES,' and right there, under that. Look, 'BLACK THURSDAY.' That means we could all become beggars before this is over." For a final effect he angrily stated, "That's what us poor, old, bunch of boxcar builders are talking about, friend!"

Over the next day or two Kaz came to understand that the "land of milk and honey" was soon to become for many the "land of stale bread and lard." The stock market crash of October 24, 1929 would burst the largest prosperity bubble America had ever known. In one day 12.9 million shares of stock would be sold off, and five days later another 16 million shares gone. Making this even more devastating to America's economy was the fact that most of those stocks had been bought on "margin." Simply put, investors had purchased stocks with borrowed money. When the lenders demanded their full monies owed, because the stocks were of no value, the investors had nothing to pay with. The only result was the lenders lost everything they had. The stock market crash would mean the decline in industrial output, failing companies, and ultimately, unemployment. The residual effect was over half of the nation's banks would fail. Wages would fall, building power decreased, foreclosures and repossessions would become the norm. The only things that would rise in numbers over the next three to four years would be bread lines, soup kitchens, and homelessness. Cardboard communities would scatter the landscape of many large cities. As a place to attach the blame these homeless villages would be called, "Hoovervilles" identifying President Herbert Hoover as the easiest one to hold responsible. By 1931 and into early 1932 those few individuals who still had any money in banks would demand all of that in hand, and bank runs would be the final death knell to many of those institutions. In 1932 most American voters went to the polls believing that the only answer was a totally new shift in the political landscape. A wealthy man, and profound orator would become the longest serving President in the history of the United States. Franklin Delano Roosevelt
would use his first inauguration to comfort the populous with what would become perhaps the most famous words in American history,

"The only thing we have to fear is fear itself."

He closed every bank in America, opened every bar by abolishing prohibition, and making the sale of drinkable alcohol again legal, and creating a government sponsored work program like had never been heard of in all of history. Roosevelt would label this approach to recovery his "NEW DEAL." The overwhelming result was a sense of hope for a better future whether it would work or not. The Great Depression, as it became known, would not actually loosen its horrible grip on the citizenry until the dark cloud of WWII began to take its shape, far from the shores of America. With war on the horizon, the demand for industrial output became the best antidote to a near fatally afflicted American economy.

Kaz was fortunate to hold on to his job at the box car factory for a couple of years. Johnny only worked for a few more months as the layoffs came according to seniority. Lilly still worked for some time into the depression before even cough drops would be considered a luxury, and home remedies would leave her factory surviving with just a skeletal crew. After several months, the only thing the bakery could sell was some loaves of bread, and most of the former customers were baking what they needed at home, if they could acquire the ingredients.

Frank knew quite a lot of folks in the surrounding area because of his nearby baseball travels. He was able to find some work in the apple orchards and nearby farms. Those opportunities provided, at best, two or three days of work per week and fifty cents per day was the average wage one could hope for. But it did keep you off the bread lines, and out of the soup kitchens.

Mary and the girls were able to take in some washing and ironing from the Edgewood and Long Beach neighborhoods adjacent to the city. Due to the fact that most of the Professional launderers were already out of business, some of those families were still financially stable enough to have their clothing cleaned by others, especially at the measly prices they could get by paying under these survival circumstances.

Perhaps Frank had the greatest relief and diversion for these most miserable and depressive days, baseball. Yes with the players mostly unemployed, time was in abundance. Hitchhiking was a common practice and the few motorists, who could still afford the fuel, were more than willing to help folks get to their destination. Going to a baseball game, organized in one of the regional towns, provided not only a great break from the reality of everyone's miserable existence, but helped the young and talented athletes keep their skills intact, and their dreams alive with the ever present hope of making the "Bigs," as the players called the Major Leagues. Almost every Sunday Frank would try to hitch a ride, or jump a flatbed trailer to participate in the greatest game ever created. It was the game with no clock, the game of one-on-one skills, throwing, running, catching, sliding and hitting. It was not truly a game, it was America's pastime. This came to be the only sport you could watch, and hold a conversation with the person beside you, at the same time. America was baseball, and baseball was America.

For Early June, the weather was unseasonably hot and dry when Frank and a few of his team mates jumped off the farm truck at Heston Corners. Today they were playing the best team in the area. Better than Otis, New Carlisle, Saugany Lake or any of those teams across the Michigan line, like Three Rivers, St. Joe, or Benton Harbor. One fact remained; there was not a more heated rivalry than Heston Corners and Frank's beloved Michigan City Orioles. Perhaps it was the natural prejudices of Big ole Swedish farm boys, and the predominantly Polish immigrant City lads, but they really despised each other with the same animosity you would have for some bully that made your life miserable in the past. Making the challenge even greater was that Heston possessed the best pitcher in the region. The big, blond, powerhouse Swede named Swanson. His name was probably really Swanstrom, but the best the immigrant kids could do was Swanson. The big Swede had already been scouted by the Cleveland Indians, and having a blinding fastball and a round house curve made him nearly unhittable. However, it was not that combination of pitches that made him hated by every opponent. It was the, then allowable, Spitball.

As Frank stepped into the batter's box for his first attempt at the big guy, he moved his hands up the neck of the baseball bat even a little more than his usual "choke up" hold. He bent his knees a little deeper on this day. He had studied the science of batting, and though he had power to put the ball over the fence, it was not his favorite approach to batting. To Frank, effectiveness as a hitter meant you "hit them where they ain't." Frank's goal was to be one of four or five hitters in succession that would spray the ball around the field, advancing runners in a flurry of dust and speed, he referred to as "the merry-go-round."

Swanson would hold the ball in his glove and then began to cover one side of the ball with several spewing layers of tobacco juice produced by the huge wad of Bull Durham's finest. The Physics involved in the spitball was that as the ball would travel toward the home plate it would be fractionally slowed every time the heavier and wetted side met the resistance of the air. This made the ball erratically jump slightly, and as it would lose speed, the ball would move in a downward motion, not unlike one rolling off a table. Frank, on the other hand, proposed a challenge to spit-ballers, as they were called then. With his shortened grip, lowered body position, and uncanny eye to follow the rotation of the ball, he could make contact where most other batters would embarrass themselves with their feeble attempt of a swing. One other factor aided Frank. He was one of the few batters who preferred the low pitch. He was quick enough with the bat, and strong enough with his swing that he could drive the low pitch in an upward motion that resembled much more a Bobby Jones iron shot in golf than a baseball batter's level swing. Frank would swing at Swanson's first pitch, driving it into left field, and smiled a rather teasing smile toward the pitcher's mound while standing safely on first base. His second time at bat he would foul off several tobacco soaked pitches until he finally lifted one high over the right fielders head. It would not clear the wooden fence, but it would hit at the top and skip over the wall like a flat stone being skipped near the Lake Michigan shoreline. By rule, Frank would have to stop at second base this time with what the rule book called "a ground rule double." Later in the game Frank would drive another first pitch far down the right field line, and the ball would ricochet off the fence. Before the other team could return the ball into the infield, Frank would be sliding head first into third base. By the time Frank would get his final shot at Swanson he was looking squarely at a batter's most coveted prize, "hitting for the cycle." This meant one batter was able to make a single, double, triple and Home run in one game. Hitting for the cycle was as good as it would ever get for a baseball player. So, as Frank strode to the plate on this late, hot, summer afternoon, he did something that was even a stretch for him. He stood outside of the batter's box and called out to the future Major League pitcher,

"Hey you big ugly Swede! If you're as good as they say, why don't you throw me a dry one for a change?"

Swanson, infuriated at being verbally accosted, hollered back,

"Just get in the batter's box, you dumb Polak, and I'll show you something."

The big farm boy held the ball in his glove directly in front of his mouth. He began to spit the nasty concoction of saliva so hard and loud that everyone in both dugouts could hear it. He wound his arm like an airplane propeller, lifted his huge leg well over his head, and unleashed an evil pitch. It would never come near the plate but make a direct path to the intended target on any right handed batter, Frank's left ear. Only the cat-like quickness of an exceptional athlete would allow Frank to drop to the ground as the death ball's wind moved so close to Frank's huge head that a few of those long black hairs were moved out of their normal location. Frank produced an expression of anger that even his team mates had never seen on his face before. After picking himself up, and brushing off the dirt he again shouted at his challenger sixty feet away,

"The plate's over here in front of me, you gutless bum. I dare you to throw one that hard in there."

Frank often reminded his team mates of a scientific fact in baseball, the harder they come in, the harder they go out! What had been a rather interesting game that found the teams knotted in a 3-3 battle held the attention of everyone. The question circled: could Frank, not only hit for the cycle, but win the game against the best pitcher around? Swanson picked up a new ball, reached to the ground for some dry dirt, and visibly began to grind the dirt into the ball for two purposes; one, a better grip on the ball, and two, to let this nobody, Polak, City boy know he was going to abandon the spit ball, and throw so hard that even this bloke, that had touched him for three hits already, would never get his choked-up bat anywhere near this blazing pitch. As the ball screamed toward the center of the plate at knee high level, Frank extended those powerful arms and hands, his head steady, his eyes widening a bit until he recognized the speed and rotation of the ball. He swung with every muscle of his body releasing all the energy it could muster. The cracking sound of wood meeting leather sounded more like an axe cutting into a solid oak tree. The ball launched off the fat part of Frank's bat and began an upward trajectory toward the clear, blue, Heston Corner's sky. It would not drop from that sky until it had cleared the fence well beyond the deepest part of the ballpark.

As Frank rounded the bases he waved heckling motions at the huge figure standing on the pitcher's mound with his shoulders slumped, and his head hung in total defeat. When Frank rounded third base, there at home plate was the smiling face of Franky Miller and the rest of the team, waiting to welcome home the day's hero.
Suddenly, Frank's elation and sense of accomplishment hit a huge wall of realism as he remembered something that his delirious teammates were totally unaware of, this would be the last time Frank would round the bases of any baseball field for a long time to come.

Frank was rather late getting home that night. He was sure happy to see that plate of fried liver that his mother, Mary, had kept atop the wood burning kitchen stove, just for him. It had been months since he had any kind of beef to eat. As he savored each bite slowly his mind traveled from the day's excitement to the unclear future that awaited him. Kaz entered the back door, just off the kitchen with a few vegetables he had stored on the back porch for tomorrow's soup.

"Hey Franky, you're pretty late tonight boy." his father declared. "Did you have trouble hitching a ride home?" he asked.

Before Frank could clear his mouth to answer, his Pa continued,
"How did the ball game go today? Did you do ok against that Swanson guy?"

Frank finally finished chewing, slightly straightened up in his chair and said, "Yeah you might say I did alright, I hit that big ugly for the cycle and won the game with a homer."

"Wow," Kaz responded, "You're becoming a real Tom Cobb out there!"

"That's Ty Cobb, Pa."

"Yeah, him too." Kaz quickly answered, while waving his hand in a motion that said, It doesn't matter what the heck his name is. "Anyway I'm glad you did good today." Kaz said as he began to cut up the vegetables on the table.

Frank took a long drink of water that Mary had poured him as she sat down at the table, and he snatched the vegetables from Kaz with a disgusted look at how he was cutting them.

"Hey I got something to tell you since we're here together." Frank said to both parents. "You know I've been getting a little work on the farms, but it just is not enough money to do any good. So, I went down to the WPA office today. You know they are building that observation tower at the park, and some other stuff around town, but the guy said he has more workers than he can use now."

With this Frank turned his head away from his parents at the table, lowered his voice, and began to speak slowly as he stared at the kitchen sink, and continued, "My friend, Peo, told me about another one of these Works Programs that Roosevelt has started." He then shared what he had learned recently, "That TVA program has put a lot of people to work, but they are pretty well full, and that is permanent employment." He continued, "and WPA is overflowing with guys seeking work, but this other thing is different." His voice rose excitedly. "They call it the CC's." Then, he spelled it out with his finger on the table. "It is actually three C's. 'CCC' stands for Civilian Conservation Corp."

Kaz interrupted, "What do they do?"

Quickly Frank answered back, "Well they do stuff about nature and the land, like Peo says. They cut down trees in California, in the mountains somewhere so if there's a big forest fire there they'll have these openings that help stop the fire." He went on to explain. "They call them fire breaks, or something like that."

"California?" Mary shouted with a panic in her voice, "That is on the other side of America Frank!"

"Yeah Ma, I know." Frank replied, "But listen, they pay about twelve bucks a month, and they provide all your food, and they even house you, but the best part is they send eight bucks home to the parents each month." He went on to explain, "It is for single guys my age, and it would only be for six months, then you have to come back home and wait another six months before you can go back again, so more guys can work and help their families during this depression thing."

It fell quiet for a moment at the table when Frank saw his mother's confused look. He continued speaking,

"Look, eight bucks a month would cover the rent on this place, and even buy a little food. I'd still make four bucks a month, and that's more than I'm making now." Then he reasoned audibly, "Pa and Johnny could take the farm work I get, and with the stuff you and the girls do you would be able to get along until the Box car factory gets back to work."

"When would you go?" Mary inquired.

"Me and Peo would leave tomorrow if we're gonna get in on this next six months group. Then he dropped the real bomb. "I already signed up, it's a done deal Ma."

Kaz asked quickly, "How are you going to get to California?"

"Well we catch the train in the morning. The big guy will be there, and it won't cost nothing. We go to some fort in Kentucky first. Oh yeah, Fort Knox, they call it." Frank continued to explain, "The Army guys will put us through some camp, like soldiers, so we will be in shape to do the tree cutting stuff, then we will take another train out to some place called Mountain Home in California. The mountains out there are named after some Saint, I think." Frank stood up at the table and began to carry his plate to the sink. In an attempt to ease the shock of the night he said, "Awe, I should be back here by Christmas anyway."

By now the conversation had awakened Sophie, and as she staggered, half asleep, into the kitchen she inquired as to what all the talk was about. Mary, half crying announced to Sophie,

"Your Brother Frank is leaving for California in the morning." She quickly explained most of what she understood the situation to be, wrapped her robe around her, and moved quickly to the bedroom. Sophie, somewhat stunned simply said,

"Wake me up, Frank, and I will go with you to the train station."

"Sure." said Frank, knowing he would slip out in the dark of the morning by himself to avoid the uncomfortable searching for words and gestures that this family seldom expressed in emotion filled times.

Mary laid facing one wall while Kaz, wide eyed stared at the window in the adjacent wall of their bedroom. Neither of them spoke, but the room was filled with the heaviness of the fact that this would be the first Pawlak to travel beyond this little region of Northwest Indiana since Kaz and his mother Anna had been welcomed into the arms of Uncle Marek almost 40 years earlier.

As Frank gathered an extra set of clothes for his journey, the wide-eyed, contemplative parents could hear his rustling noises. The three of them were well aware that Kaz, Mary, Johnny, Frank, Lilly, Sophie, and Eddie Pawlak would never be the same as a family again. What none of them could know was that Frank was not the only one preparing for a life changing journey, but the entire family was on the precipice of a new life that would forever alter the priorities, directions, and purpose of the Pawlak family.

Kaz, Mary, Eddie and the girls loved the letters Frank sent home from far away California. The Pictures were beyond their imagination. The images of mountains, sunsets, and sunrises were unlike anything they had ever seen. Even the nearby cities of Redlands and Ontario seemed like a paradise. Wide boulevards, centered by beautiful medians, lined with gorgeous pepper trees. Each community seemed surrounded by acre upon acre of orange trees. They were most amazed with the photos Frank sent home of his train trip to California, especially the part where the train actually stopped on the massive trestle and allowed the westbound boys to disembark from the passenger cars, and take photos of the magnificent Royal Gorge, high in the Colorado Rocky Mountains. Mary felt so proud when Frank sent the Redlands news clippings about the welcome ceremony at the Mentone, California CCC Camp, known as MOUNTAIN HOME.

It was a hot July day when the Indiana boys stood to attention under a perfect blue and cloudless afternoon. A local soprano welcomed the Hoosier young men with a beautiful rendition of "On the Banks of the Wabash Far Away." The melancholy song painted pictures of the beautiful, little river in Indiana that would a few years later, be the inspiration for the great songwriter, Hoagie Carmichael's bluesy tune, "Up a Lazy River," made famous by the Mills Brothers. After a local pastor would bring a stirring sermon of welcome and hope, a young girl performer would close the event with a lovely welcome song about California. The irony of that little girl was her name. Even though she would never become famous, a few years later, everyone of those CCC boys would secretly admire a voluptuous, bombshell, poster starlet, who would change her given name from Norma Jean to the same as that little, unknown girl in that CCC camp in the San Bernardino Mountains. The name was Marilyn Monroe. Although there seemed to be no viable evidence or connection, Frank would always wonder if Norma Jean had ever known the little girl from Redlands, California, or could she have seen the name somewhere near her Southern California home, and decided it would be the perfect stage name. Frank would become even more enamored with the famous Miss Monroe when she would become the wife of one of America's greatest baseball players, Joe DiMaggio.

Frank did not have to cut the fire trails very long. As soon as the company commander found out he was an experienced baker, he was put to work in the camp bakery. He loved it. Once again he could work all night, sleep a few hours, and then search out the wonderful trout streams and mountain lakes in the area to pursue his beloved pastime of fishing. The money sent home was just what Frank said it would be. The extra cash kept the family from living on the street, and with the four dollars Frank retained, he loved his shopping days in the men's stores of Redlands. By the time Frank would return home he had used his four dollars per month to become the proud owner of two new sport jackets, three fine pairs of slacks, and five or six of the most stylish shirts. When dressed out with that raven hair, slightly parted in the middle, and slicked back with some good pomade hair grease, Frank could rival Errol Flynn, or a young Clark Gable on any summer stroll down Hollywood Blvd.

Back at home, everything continued as before, except for one little deep secret that Kaz had been keeping from the family for some time, almost 7 years to be precise. Mary had no idea that for all this time Kaz had attempted privately to revisit those early passions he once knew as a boy and teenager; that was this whole spiritual search. Kaz knew at a young age that there was a God, and more importantly that God loved him. It is what the little book said. He felt it with every catechism class. God seemed near to him when he was faithfully serving as an altar boy. He knew God was pleased with him when he sang those ancient songs and chants as a choir boy. He often posed the question to his own mind, "What happened?" Why did he abandon something so important to him? Perhaps the religious part had become, simply unfulfilling. The traditional and repetitive aspects of church life had become nothing more than some ancient ritual. Meaningfulness seemed to have been replaced by form and memorized tradition. Then there was the overshadowing rules, guilt, and impossible pursuit of pleasing that God. But this rather happy, jovial, and non-driven little fellow was deeper than anyone would have thought. So much so that he began his own quest to answer these nagging questions about his greater purpose in this existence. The secret manifested itself in Kaz's evening walks, twice a week. While the family thought he just preferred to be alone with his thoughts, they never imagined where his walks took him.

This night would be different, as Mary decided to take her hurting and sore feet for a little walk. Just as she crossed the railroad tracks, she saw him.

"Ed!" she cried out, "What on earth are you doing? Come out of that place."

Kaz stopped in his tracks, frozen. "It's too late." he thought. There was no way he could make it look like her conclusion was a misunderstanding.

"I might ask what you're doing out here tonight, also." He stammered, knowing this would never serve Mary as a satisfactory explanation.

Mary's eyes were focused like a laser beam at an angle about two feet above Kaz's head. One fairly bright light bulb attached to the upper wall of the building behind Kaz cast a shadowy but clear enough illumination on those two words, "KINGDOM HALL."

"Good night, Kaz." a few voices kindly uttered as they passed by his still frozen position in the yard.

"Evening Ma'am." came a soft greeting in Mary's direction, as more of the rather small gathering headed for the street lights and their way home.

"Well?" Mary continued with her first few steps toward Kaz. "Ed, please explain why you would come to this place?" Then
Without waiting for any such explanation she began her rant. "I have heard about this place and these people. They're not Catholics, Ed. They are some strange cult. They don't believe what we believe, Ed." Before she could continue to build her list of objections Kaz interrupted,

"But they are nice, Mary." his soft voice conveying the idea she might lower her voice a bit. Kaz motioned her to turn around and begin walking toward home with him.

"How often do you come here?" she snapped out at him.

"A couple times a week." he forcefully spat back at her

"Ed, pray tell me, how long have you been doing this behind my back?"

"Oh for love of Mike, Mary!" Kaz moaned, as he rolled his head in a big circle, "I was not doing anything behind your back, I was doing something I wanted to do for a change." To emphasize his rare boldness, he stopped her by grasping her arm, looked her in the eye, and slowly turned his head and spit hard upon the ground. As he dropped Mary's arm, and began walking again he softly explained, "All they really do is read. They just sit and read these different books that their leader has written. In all honesty, I don't understand a lot of it, and I don't even agree with much of what they say, but I like the people, and it is quiet. I don't know if it has helped me or not."

Mary asked quickly, "Helped you do what?"

"Find out where God is, Mary," He blurted out loudly, "I don't know where he went, or where I went but this crazy life is making no sense to me."

Finally Mary asked with a bit of sarcasm, "Well, how long have you been looking for him in this KINGDOM HALL place?"

Kaz paused, then dropped his head, and almost whispering said,

"About seven years I guess."

At which Mary burst into laughter, and soon Kaz joined her in the humor of the moment. Mary slipped her arm into his and said again those most familiar words,

"Oh! You are such a silly man" and they slowly rambled toward home, occasionally laughing like a couple of courting lovebirds.

Now that Kaz's personal pilgrimage toward spiritual truth was no longer a secret, he felt it safe to venture further. The next part of the sojourn would be to invite his family along. To his great surprise, Mary agreed to make a visit to the Hall with him. Johnny, Lilly, and Sophie found the people to be just as kind and friendly as their Pa had assured them. They found most of the reading and teaching a bit confusing, which would be understandable for young people who had not been privy to a regular, religious church experience. Their mother, Mary, had made sure that they were not, by definition, "heathen." She had required her children to read a scripture and pray before bed each night, as long as they could remember. However, this practice was to them just as much a part of nightly retirement as turning down the bedding, and lowering the lights. They believed they were good people for doing such a thing regularly.

For Eddie, the meetings at the Kingdom Hall were exactly what any such activity would be to a super-active boy of a young age; boring beyond words. He also knew that his mother still considered this a religious thing of some kind, and she would never tolerate his wiggles, nor his stretching out over a couple chairs to doze off. The only thing left for him was his daydreams. He would get lost in the high flying adventures of his always active young mind until he heard the wonderful words. "You are dismissed. Go in peace."

As Kaz and Eddie were walking from the pier one particular Saturday afternoon, Kaz heard a familiar voice,

"Hey Pawlak, slow down there, you old man."

Kaz put down the stringer of perch, and slowly rotated at the waist, he saw a most pleasant sight. It was his old buddy, Emil Pohl.

"Emil, my old friend!" Kaz shouted, as he ran back to grasp that huge hand, and throw his other arm around Emil's shoulders. With the plant closed, and everybody going so many directions to scratch out a little pay, they had not seen each other in over a year.

"Kaz you remember my boy here, Kenneth, don't you?" reaching behind him and pulling the tall, handsome, young fellow toward Kaz.

"Wow, he's bigger than you now, Emil," Kaz said with a combination snort and laugh.

"You should talk!" Emil replied, "Kenny tells me your boy Johnny has become a mountain of a man, and may be the strongest guy in town."

"Oh, he's a strong one, but not quite like that Bagula Kid."

They both laughed just thinking about the young man from town who was being touted as the next strongest man in the world.

"Hey," Kaz responded, "We should get together soon."

"Good idea, Kaz," Emil replied, "How about now, here, right now."

"What do you mean?" Kaz asked,

"Kenny here will see your boy home safe, and we can stop by that new tavern that opened last week." Emil continued, "I worked all week last week for old man McKinney at his coal yard and I got enough money to buy us a couple cold beers."

It took no deep pleading when considering this invitation with his old pal. In only ten minutes Kaz and Emil were bellied up to the brass rail at the new "Town Tavern" as it would be called for years to come. After the, now legal cold beer, and catching up on both family activities of late, the two old pals headed back toward the south end of town. As they talked, and laughed, and bemoaned this cursed Depression, they hardly noticed the figure walking behind them. Suddenly, they crossed the railroad tracks, and heard the distinct chime of a metal heel protector on a shoe strike the steel rail of the track. Simultaneously, both heads spun to look backward and see what made the noise. When they saw the young priest walking rather closely behind them, they remembered how often they had heard those metal heel protectors strike fear into their juvenile hearts back in the Catholic School days. In as much as a priest's vow of poverty meant the Parrish would take the responsibility of housing, feeding, and clothing their clergy, some frugal mind made sure all the priests had the metal on their shoe to help sustain the life of the footwear.

Neither Kaz nor Emil recognized this young priest, although they still knew most every priest at both Saint Stanislaus and St. Mary's. Being customarily appropriate in such circumstances, both men stopped at the far side of the intersection, waited for the priest, and greeted him with the traditional, "Bless you, Father," They made a passage for him to proceed his walk ahead of them. After a few more steps the young priest stopped in his tracks, turned again to Kaz and Emil, and softly said,

"And bless you both, my sons."

Putting out his hand in the direction of Emil's big chest as if to say, "Stop right here, fellas," he moved uncomfortably close to their faces. For a moment both the old friends looked at each other wondering, "Did we do something wrong?" Their attention refocused as the young priest moved even closer to them.

"Are you men fully employed these days?" queried the priest, in what was a distinctly definable Irish accent.

"No, not fully, Father." Kaz stammered while Emil chimed in,

"You know, father. An odd job here and there."

"Hmm." said the priest, while rubbing his chin in contemplation. "Odd jobs, aye?" The priest replied, and then bursting into explosive laughter the priest made a rather strange comment, "Well me sirs, since I seem to have the good fortune today of meeting a couple masters at the odd jobs, I may have a proposition that could well be the oddest job you blokes have ever been party to." The young Irishman of the cloth continued, "But let us settle on the remuneration involved first." He had their attention and took full advantage, not stopping even for a good breath. "I have four American dollars to be divided betwixt ye in whatever manner you find fair amongst yourselves should ye perform the mission-task I have in mind."

Emil could not help himself, and interrupted the priest in mid- speech.

"We would split it evenly Father, and be very grateful for two dollars at any time, sir."

Kaz stood quietly with a little smile that was either suspicious or mischievous.

"The money sounds amazing." said Kaz softly, "but that kind of payoff would suggest no easy task. Am I right, Father?"

The young priest began to run his thumb and forefinger along the lapel of Emil's light summer jacket.

"You men appear to be Polish immigrants to me." Looking deeply into Emil's eyes he moved his hand from the jacket and touched Kaz's arm with his index finger and said to Emil,

"But I fear this one might have a little Jewish blood in him. Sounds like your friend here is looking for some further negotiation."

"Father, I meant no offense," Kaz quickly responded,

"I simply can't think what kind of work would bring that kind of money today."

"But ye are interested, Yes?" the priest questioned, thickening his Irish brogue, and elevating his final tone to that of a talented tenor.

Kaz and Emil slowly nodded their heads up and down, and finally both uttered,

"Yes, sure we are."

"You gentlemen know where the old Parish House is, behind the school, over that direction?" The priest questioned while pointing in a westerly direction. Kaz replied,

"Sure, Father we know it well."

"Then, meet me at the side door about 8:00 pm tonight and you will be given your instructions."

The priest abruptly spun about, and rapidly marched off ahead of the old friends. Kaz and Emil just stood and watched for a few moments. The piercing sound of those metal heel protectors sparking off the cobblestone street ahead of them somehow sounded more like a commanding general heading to war than a handsome, young Irish holy man bringing his message of hope and peace.

It was a slow, gentle rain on a very warm, summer evening when Kaz and Emil turned the corner toward the old Parish house. This was the place that housed the holy men. Although neither of them had ever been privy to the inside of this strong, brick, two-storied house, they had heard that the atmosphere there was second only to the throne of God in Heaven. This was the obvious byproduct of the vast assemblage of pure, spotless, sinless priests who abode within. Of course, as they became older they heard many other stories, quite to the contrary, to the activities and life-style of the unquestioned and privileged church hierarchy. They left those stories to being, most likely, the product of the godless and pessimistic heathenism outside the church world. The eeriness of the night was even more enhanced when the large wooden door began to screech on its hinges as it was opened slowly from the inside. Even stranger was the fact that whoever was opening the door was not visible to the big-eyed duo stepping inside. Once the door was closed, both the men were somewhat relieved to see it was the young, Irish priest at the backside of the door. They were also somewhat disappointed to find themselves not in the Holy of Holies itself, but only in an entrance lobby, and that not very large but well lighted.

"So you're ready for your odd job, I see." Said the priest with a singing type cadence in his voice.

Kaz and Emil would never see this priest again after this evening but would argue for years to come that his name was either, O'brian, O'Leary, or O'Houlahan. To their amazement, the priest quickly handed each of them two, crisp dollar bills.

"Now it's not often that ye get your pay before ye even work for it, but you must understand something very clearly, my dear sirs." the priest explained in a quiet and almost conspiratorial voice. Turning to the corner of the entrance hall, he quickly bent over to grasp what appeared to be a new bushel basket. It was obviously heavy and covered with a large cloth. Kaz and Emil, looking thoroughly confused stared at the basket at their feet.

The priest spoke a little louder and much slower. "These are leftover tomatoes from the Italian vegetable stand out there on Chicago Street." He continued, "They are old, soft and on the verge of rotten. Do you understand men?" he asked.

Kaz, beginning to wonder if were they were a part of some strange hoax, shook his head slowly, and responded to the priest,

"We have no idea what you are talking about."

"Ok, then listen carefully." Instructed the holy man.

"There is a large circus tent that has been erected over there on 2nd Street. I don't know if you men have seen it or not."

"Yes." said Emil, "I saw it going up yesterday."

"Sure, sure" Kaz chimed in, "I thought maybe some magic show or animal thing was going to be in there."

"Ah, you're not so far off my friend, but something much more dangerous." explained the priest. He continued telling the pals,
"There is a band of evil, cultish heretics invading this town like a Czarist invasion. But worse than conquering persons lives for self-gain, they are coming to conquer the souls of men by means of unbiblical brainwashing." He was almost preaching with fist clenched

and waving about the air. He passionately continued. "They desire to destroy Christianity and the Holy Roman Church by using the godless reformation teachings that a person does not need the church or its traditions to be righteous or even forgiven of sin." The priest seemed to compose himself a bit, and again quietly explained what he needed these men to do. "We must drive such as these from our city. The authorities say that the legal protection of religion here prohibits them from exercising them as long as they abide by the local laws." The young priest got to the assignment at hand when he said, "Now men, these evil doers will not stay where the public rejects them. This is where you come in. I need you to take this basket of rotten tomatoes in a manner no one will see you. Their assembly will sing some strange songs, not legitimate approvals of the church, and then their leader will stand and begin to speak his rhetoric of hellish teaching. When he begins, I want you to move close enough to his position to begin pelting him with these tomatoes, and don't stop until every one of them has been hurled and met their target." He explained that the chaos, hilarity, and humiliating attack would send the crowd running away for fear of some domestic disturbance, if not a pure riot. The speaker would be such a disgusting display of nastiness that he would have no other choice but to ashamedly recognize his ineffectiveness, close down his crusade, and choose another city for his godless diatribe. It sounded strange, but it did sound agreeable to both Kaz and Emil. The fact that they so seldom had two dollars each in their pocket also made them feel it was only right to fulfill their part of the agreement. Kaz and Emil could hardly keep from giggling like Johnny and Franky used to do when carrying the old "honey bucket" out to the ditch as boys. They moved slowly in the dark each grasping one handle of the bushel basket full of soft, slimy, rotten tomatoes. After some time and much struggle, they set the heavy basket beside the huge chestnut tree, just to the side of the tent of meeting. Gasping for air and sweating profusely, they hid in the shadows, awaiting the proper time, as they had been so clearly instructed, to launch their attack. In their minds they were boys again, pulling a prank on their neighborhood rivals, but in their spirit they saw themselves like two valiant, Polish warriors of the past, poised to charge with King Jan Sobieski, and drive out the evil Mustafa at the battle of Vienna. Neither friend could have imagined that the events of the next few minutes would not only change their lives forever, but in time they would come to fully understand that it was not a coincidental meeting with an unknown priest that had them under that tree tonight.

Perspiration ran down Kaz's sideburns and across his jaw line, soaking the collar of his shirt gathering into an actual pool, at the deep indentation below his protruding Adam's apple. Leaning his head back on the gnarled tree trunk, and trying to silence his heaving chest, which was begging for more air, Kaz rolled his eyes in the direction of the tent service. He had to look through Emil's profile to focus on the activities at a distance. Silhouetted in the forefront of his vision was Emil's huge nose and the steady stream of moisture pouring from its tip.

"Hot night, isn't it Emil?" whispered Kaz.

"Sure is, friend." Emil responded by silently nodding his head.

Kaz gestured with his hand in a downward motion as if to say, "Let's just sit a moment and catch our breath."

Both men sat motionless in the darkness of the night. The only sound they could hear was the preacher on the small stage at the front of the meeting tent. To their surprise, the speech maker did not act or speak like the power-crazed dictator the Irish priest had so passionately described. The gentlemen's voice was more instructional and soft, almost to the point of kind. Before Kaz realized, he was no longer breathing heavy. For a moment he stopped strategizing his planned invasion. Now he was actually hearing the voice of the supposed master proselyte, and even more amazing, Kaz was a bit intrigued by the content of the oration.

"I have a question I would like to pose to you, my listeners on this beautiful summer night." declared the rather slight build man at the podium.

Kaz could see, even from his distanced position under the tree, that the man was neatly dressed in a white, dress shirt and decent looking, charcoal suit. His receding and tightly slicked-back dark hair, accompanied by the studious, wire-rimmed glasses, gave him a rather impressive look of academia, in contrast to the more emotional, and Bible-thumping itinerantes who were becoming popular across the southern States in recent years.

"Have you always had this big empty place in your heart that nothing seems to satisfy?" the preacher questioned the crowd. He paused for what seemed like an uncomfortable time of silence. He then stepped to the very front of the stage, leaned forward at the waist, and raising his voice in a slightly inquisitional manner, asked again, "Have you always had this big empty place in your heart that nothing seems to satisfy?" As dramatically as John Barrymore would have moved across a theater stage to deliver his most effective line, the little clergyman took two large steps backward, positioned himself squarely in the middle of the stage, and bellowed to the top of his voice one last and most effective rhetorical assault on the, self-examining consciences of the spellbound audience.

"Have you always had this big empty place in your heart that nothing seems to satisfy?"

Heads began to nod affirmatively, and a few voices audibly cried out,

"Yes, yes I have."

"Well," responded the speaker, "If you will allow me the privilege of sharing with you for a few moments tonight, I would love to tell you why you admit that, and what will fill that empty void in your life."

"Hey Emil, Kaz spoke in a normal voice, as the affirming shouts of "Amen" and "Yes, tell us" filled the tent, to the point that Kaz knew he was not going to be discovered by speaking at a normal volume.

"Let's go in and listen for a little while. This guy sounds kind of interesting. We can always slip out and get the tomatoes a little later."

"Are you sure we will have time Kaz?" asked Emil.

"Sure, he is going to be speaking for a while." assured Kaz. "I would like to hear his answer to that question he posed, Emil, wouldn't you?"
Emil shrugged his shoulders and waved his hand laterally for Kaz to lead the way. They both took a handkerchief out of their pockets, almost simultaneously, wiped the last sparkles of sweat from their foreheads, straightened their jackets, brushed the fronts and seats of their trousers, and began their trek into the side of the tent as if they were only interested attendees. No one would have suspected in any way they were insurgent terrorists on an assignment to wreak absolute havoc on this night's event. Where they entered the tent, they knew the most inconspicuous location to place themselves was at the end of the unimpressively constructed bench nearest the side of the tent. They made sure they were located toward the back of the assemblage. This also would serve as the quickest way to slip out, access their vegetative armament, and perform their planned sortie attack at the optimal hour. Kaz slipped his cap from his head as he would have respectively done when entering any religious gathering place. Emil noticed and quickly did the same. Both men lifted their gaze toward the front with more interest than either of them even noticed. To Kaz's surprise, even at the distance he had placed himself, the kindly little orator seemed to fix his eyes squarely on one person alone. Kaz knew it was him. To his absolute shock, Kaz felt that the entire congregation had vanished from the facility. He did not even sense that his buddy and partner in mischief was sitting close to his side. It was just

he and that set of deep-set eyes from a distance. At that moment the friendly voice turned powerfully direct, and his words cut through the air of the night. The man at the front leaned across the speaker's podium, transforming the crude piece of furniture into a magnificent pulpit. The following declaration sped straight to Kaz's ears, exploded in his head, and drove itself downward at the speed of a Kentucky coal-miners elevator, landing, with a screeching thud somewhere in Kaz's inmost feelings.

"My Friend, I will tell you what that empty void in your life has always been, and why you have never been able to fill it, and what will fill it for the first time in your life, tonight. One word, one name, one person is the answer to that void in your life." He then said it, "That word, that name, that person is none other than JESUS CHRIST."

As if Kaz were not already spellbound his eyes were unblinking and fixed at the direct stare of this amazing messenger from another world. His mouth gaped open and extremely dry, his mind not believing what his ears were hearing. He gasped in unbelief at the next words that were personally ushered in his direction.

"For the Bible clearly tells you," the speaker softly and tenderly continued, "For God so loved the world that he gave his only begotten son, that whosoever believeth in him, shall not perish, but have everlasting life."

Emil likewise, sensed the man up front speaking directly to Kaz. He turned his gaze from the preacher to his old friend at his side. Emil could hardly believe his eyes. Just where the sweat had been streaming down Kaz's face earlier, he saw a virtual flood of tears pouring from Kaz's eyes. Emil thought to himself, "Kaz is not a crying man," and he questioned in his mind what had moved his friend to such a place and reaction. Then another rather strange question seized Emil's thoughts, "What is that strange feeling I'm feeling when the man was quoting that part about God loving the world and sending His own son?"

Both of their focus returned to the speaker as he continued,

"Money has never filled that empty place. Friends have never completely filled that place. Your house, car, and clothes have never given you complete satisfaction. There has always been something missing, and you were looking in all the temporary places."

Kaz was, for a moment, carried back in his mind to a much earlier time. He had a bit of a contradictory moment in regard to what the preacher had just said. He remembered a time where he did feel like everything was good, and he was satisfied in his life. Those early days in Polish school were his happiest. Then he admitted to himself it was not just school but the religion classes, the altar work for the priest, singing in the choir as a boy. Then like a bolt from the sky came the true memory and he said loud enough that Emil almost could hear his voice,

"When I read that book. It was those same words the preacher just said. That, 'God so loved the world' part. That was when I felt whole.

Kaz then turned to Emil and said, "I thought it was because I could understand English. No, no, that was not it. God was wanting to live in me."

Emil had no idea what Kaz was saying but he knew something was happening to his friend, and just maybe it was happening to him, as well. When Kaz broke from his deep thoughts his attention was again guided by his eyes back to the front of the gathering. A young man had slipped from the crowd to the stage and positioned himself at the upright piano on one side of the stage. The rather accomplished pianist began to softly play a pleasant melody that was unfamiliar to Kaz and many other onlookers that night. Kaz heard the speaker make another rather alarming statement.

"You may have even tried religion to fill the empty place in your life. You may have been very devout at one time. You could have been an altar boy for the church, or a choir boy, but in time, even those honorable pursuits did not satisfy, and something is still missing."

For a moment Kaz began to think to himself, "Is this guy some kind of witch? How does he know my story, my life, everything I have done and thought?"

Just then the speaker answered Kaz's questions,

"My friends," he said, "I don't know you, and have never met any of you before, but I can assure you, God knows you. He has watched every step of your life, and it is really God, not me, who is talking to your heart at this moment."

After a few more amazing statements the preacher reasoned,

"My friends, to bring this truth to your awareness, and not give you an opportunity to resolve these issues of need in a personal way, would be like offering a starving man a life-saving meal, but give him no place or time to consume it."

Music softly continued, while a few singers, gathered near the piano, began to sing a compelling lyric announcing in the song that Jesus was passing that way. The preacher presented a personal proposition to those under his voice, when he said,

"If tonight, you will believe, by faith, that this Jesus died on that cross for you, was buried, and on the third day rose from the grave alive as promised, and has ascended back to Heaven returning for you one day, as He said in his word, and you will simply ask Him, in prayer, to come into your heart and fill that empty place He has been waiting to fill, He will forgive you for every sin. He will come live inside of you. He will give you a new life, and you will never be the same again."

The preacher invited anyone who would like to pray, and start a new life to simply step from their seat, and meet him at the front of the stage. He offered something that he said Jesus called "born again," and asked if they wanted to receive something called "Salvation."

Kaz was not surprised how quickly his body weight shifted to his legs and feet, but he was a bit surprised to feel Emil's large shoulder slide against his in an attempt to beat Kaz to his feet. Kaz was as surprised as Emil had been when he saw Emil's eyes filled with tears, and saw Emil motion his head toward the front with these words,

"Let's go up there, Kaz."

Two men who came there with a united mission to bring fear, calamity, embarrassment, and destruction knelt in the sawdust of an unimpressive tent meeting, and experienced the epiphany of their lives. These two men talked directly to God, and they recognized their own self-acclaimed virtues were as rotten as the abandoned basket of tomatoes near the huge chestnut tree. An unspeakable sense of joy and peace seemed to settle on them.

Within a few moments total strangers began to gather around them. Some were audibly voicing phrases like, "Thank you Jesus." and even a few "Hallelujahs" were heard over Kaz and Emil's heads. Kaz knew something was truly different. He was so joyful and peaceful. These feelings seemed more than just emotions. He wondered if it was even proper to think that this encounter with God was even more powerful than the best and favorite experiences he could recount. He thought the night Mary said she would marry him could never be exceeded. Even holding his newborn children in his arms had always seemed the greatest feeling he would ever know in his heart. Not even a stringer full of Lake Michigan perch made him as giddy as this night. He felt a little out of control. He would have little out-bursts of laughter followed by another unexpected session of inward weeping. Never had he breathed so deeply. He felt so young, so clean, so fresh. Not sure of all that had just transpired on this summer evening, one thing was an absolute reality; he was not the same man, nor would his life and purpose ever be the same. He did not think it right to voice it, but he knew he was loved by God. He had begun a personal relationship with his Savior that would be the most important facet of his life. As Kaz and Emil shook the last hands and were congratulated by the last crusade workers on the decision they had made that night, they exited the tent in the same direction they had entered. When walking past the tree, they spied the basket, both laughed out loud.

Then Kaz said, "Maybe we should get rid of that thing."

It felt as if they were contemplating destroying the evidence of their past life. But when they reached for the basket, to their surprise, someone had taken all of its contents. Emil would then utter the most powerful conclusion to what he would call the greatest night of his life.

"Kaz, those tomatoes are as gone as my Sins."

Kaz knew one thing for sure; that night, he and Emil had moved from a couple of barely existing immigrant men with no great plans for a successful future, to brand new men with totally different lives ahead of them.

Even though it took a little while, and a lot of conversation, Kaz was able to convince Mary to attend the next evening meeting at the tent. He was a little disappointed that Mary did not seem to have the same emotional draw to the speaker's enlistment procedure as he and Emil had experienced.

"Mary," Kaz softly whispered as the soft music played again at the conclusion of the preacher's invitation, "Don't you want to go up there and pray that prayer with him?"

"Shush" Mary softly ordered Kaz, as she placed her delicate little hand on his wide and thick hand and continued, "I did this a long time ago, Ed. I prayed with a pastor on the radio one day, and, I already received Jesus into my heart."

"But you never told me that, Mary." Kaz said, with a questioning look on his face. Mary replied,

"I thought you would think I was crazy, and make fun of me."

She lowered her head, and softly dabbed a little tear from her eye with a clean, white, decorative handkerchief she had been holding in her lap. Once again, Kaz leaned to her ear and softly said,

"I think we are beginning a new life, Mary, a brand new life."

"We're not the only ones, Ed." Mary whispered, as she motioned her head toward the distant front of the tent meeting place. There she and Kaz observed their first child standing at the front of the stage, head bowed and being prayed over by the minister that night. Mary took Kaz's hand and gently pulled him from the aisle where they had been seated.

"We should stand with him, Ed."

On the far side of the audience another couple watched in amazement as Kaz, Mary, and Johnny started a new chapter in this family's journey. The other couple soon moved to the front to stand with these dear friends. After the closing benediction was prayed, Emil and Mamie Pohl would enfold their arms around Kaz, Mary, and Johnny.

"We are all family now, the family of God." Emil declared.

After a few nights, the tent folded, and the evangelizers returned to their personal homes and church family some miles away. Before they left Michigan City, the minister introduced several of these new converts to a small group of Christians who were meeting on Sundays and a couple nights of the week. They were gathering in an auto repair garage over on Barker Ave, the street named, of course, for the famed Barker family that impacted such a large part of their lives.

As the summer passed and winter approached, both Lilly and Sophie would join the family in those meetings in the auto repair garage. Both girls quickly came to have their own encounters with their spiritual need, and fully accept this personal relationship with Jesus Christ as fervently as their parents and brother. As the winter hardened and the Lake effect snow mounted, the meetings became as much a battle of determination to the body as it was an inspiration to the soul.

The cars to be repaired would be moved out of the garage each time the group would meet for services. In the middle of the room was one small wood and coal burning, pot-bellied stove. The fifteen to twenty faithfuls who gathered sat as close to the stove as possible. Each attendee heavily weighted in all the clothes, coats, scarves, and boots they could acquire. The one thing that helped fight off the horrid cold and winds sweeping through the gaps in the wooden building was their new found fervency in their style of worship. It was not long after Kaz and the family began to worship with these new found friends that the Bible teacher and group's leader explained to them,

"We are not just believers, we are Pentecostal believers."

Kaz and Mary were very familiar with the word "Pentecost." After all, it was one of the biggest Sundays of celebration and special masses in the Catholic Church where they had grown up. But somehow they figured this leader was indicating something more or at least different than they were acquainted with. They would soon learn that this group was an off-shoot of a somewhat new phenomenon that had been growing in size and popularity since the turn of the century. They came to learn that several newly organized denominations had sprung up across the nation, as well as several European nations.

Kaz intently grilled the group leader, "What do you mean when you say you are Pentecostal?"

"Well, Kaz, we really believe that we are becoming the church that Christ meant to establish here on Earth. Like the church you read about in the Book of Acts."

Kaz kindly but firmly fired back, "How would that church be different than the church now?" using the term, "The Church," meaning the only church he had ever known or really was aware ever existed, the Catholic church. The answer came back in a kind and instructional manner,

"You see Kaz," the leader said. "There are things that the First Century followers of Christ practiced and experienced that we may have let slip away over the past, nineteen hundred years. These were blessings and gifts that the Lord left us to enjoy and use for His work."

"How did 'we' lose them? What are they? What good would they do?" began Kaz's rapid-fire inquisition.

With his hand lifted up as a policeman stopping oncoming traffic, the patient leader simply said,

"Kaz we will take some time to look at the scripture together, and answer from God's word each of these questions. But for now, let me tell you some very exciting facts."

Kaz set back in his chair a little more subdued as the teacher continued,

"For now, Kaz, let me just assure you that you have only begun your journey with God, and he has some additional blessings for you to experience in your life."

"Blessings?," cried Kaz, "I can't take any more blessings! Since I have found God I feel like I am going to explode already."

Kaz slowly dropped his head and placed his gloved fingers to his temples and said while shaking his head,

"What else could God possibly give me?"

Over the next few months, Kaz would come to understand that the "more" God had for him was what the church defined as a filling of power, to the individual, through the Holy Spirit. He would be taught that this was an experience similar to his baptism in water, which in this case was done to adults who confessed Christ as their Savior and was actuated by the full immersion of their body into water. This Holy Spirit filling, or baptism, as many would call it, would be defined as an immersion of a person's spirit into the Holy Spirit (often referred to in Pentecostal circles as "the baptism of the Holy Ghost"). What would make it both controversial to some, and supernatural to others was that this experience would be accompanied, to the individual being filled, with the audible speaking of unknown or unlearned languages. This was most commonly referred to as simply, "speaking in tongues." These Pentecostals believed this was all scripturally supported by the Book of Acts, particularly the second chapter, and St. Paul's teachings in his letters to the Corinthians as well as many other New Testament references. Accompanying these teachings and experiences was also the overriding fact that with this newfound truth came newfound freedom and expression of worship. The services themselves were highly spirited, hand clapping, foot tapping, amen shouting, hand raising, vibrant singing, and on occasion, even some innovative aisle dancing. It was evident that restraint, ritual, and rigidity were not a requirement to people who have been "set free from sin and guilt," and enabled them to enjoy the present presence of God Almighty and His Holy Spirit.

These highly charged believers had two major objectives to their mission, which they believed to be their calling: First, they must do all to bring people to this "Born Again" experience and Second, perhaps, if truth were known, more parallel than secondary, was their mission to get all of those believers to be, "baptized in the Holy ghost and speaking in other tongues." They believed literally the words of Jesus, that this would give them the power to be His witnesses.

"Hurry, sister! We must get home quickly," said Norma, as she ran with her winter coat tail flying in the wind. "Mama will have the cookies and milk waiting!" she reminded her little sister so excitedly.

Her mother, Ruth had made this ritual the one thing these girls could count on more than anything. Running home from school, the warmth of the kitchen when bursting through the back door of the little frame house, and seeing that treasure, warm cookies right from the oven and two tall glasses of cold milk. But this day would be different. "Noni," as they called Naomi in the family, had actually bolted past her older sister Norma, and was the first to swing open the heavy, winter, storm door and then the inner door to their stomach's Fort Knox treasury. Once inside the door, Noni stopped so quickly that Norma nearly knocked her over as they entered the kitchen. Then came a high-pitched scream from both girls, followed by a duet of perfect voices in unison,

"What happened? Oh no, where are the cookies?"

"Hush, hush, stop! Quiet, girls!" Bursting through the swinging door at the other side of the kitchen with a half shout-half whisper came their mother, Ruth.

In hushed tones, Norma began to whine, "Mama, where are our cookies and milk?"

Noni's eyes were filled with tears like some great tragedy had befallen her young life. They were home from school, but no cookies and milk. This had never happened to these newly dejected princesses of Queen Ruth's Castle.

"You girls will just have to wait today. Several of the church people are here, and we are praying for Mr. Pawlak."

Ruth partially cracked the swinging door toward the living room to show the girls the seriousness of the moment. As Norma could get on tip toes and see over her little sister, they squeezed their still cold cheeks against the narrow opening of the door. Their mother controlled the size of the crevasse, and made sure they observed quietly.

"Why is he laying on the floor?" asked Noni, "Is he sick?"

"No, No, honey." Ruth whispered down at her, "He is being filled with the Holy Ghost. We have been praying with him all afternoon, and he has been filled and has been speaking in tongues." She continued, "You know, girls, Mr. Pawlak now speaks three languages, Polish, English, and his new heavenly language." Then Ruth instructed, "Now, you girls, take off your coats, and be real quiet in here until we finish up out there."

The girls may have not fully understood all that had transpired that day in their mother's living room, but they did acknowledge two things, this must have been wonderful for Mr. Pawlak, and it sure seemed to make their mother happy. But many years later Norma would tell one of Kaz's grandsons,

"I resented your grandfather for many years, because he beat me out of my cookies and milk that day, but I think I told him later I forgave him."

Soon each of the family members would come to their own personal experience, and find this new empowerment in their lives very fulfilling.

Eddie was still a young boy and not yet too interested as to what had happened to his parents and siblings. And with Christmas just around the corner there was some new excitement; Franky would soon be home from California. It was Johnny who said one evening to Kaz,

"Hey Pa, maybe I should write Frank before he comes home and explain all the changes that have happened to us since he has been in California." At which Kaz simply replied,

"No, just let him see for himself when he gets home."

Then Kaz put his Bible on his lap, and stared out the westward window of the living room. He listened to the contradiction of sounds between the strong winter wind and the warm crackling fire. With a rather sad sound in his voice said,

"You know, Johnny, Franky has never cared much about this God thing. He will be a hard one to reach."

CHAPTER 5 - 1933-1943

Sophie was not nearly as hurt as peeved, but she made herself a promise. Franky might have slipped off in the dark, without her to begin his California adventure that warm morning six months ago, but there was no way she would let him simply slip back into town unnoticed. Since her parents had received a document from the government stating that Franky would be arriving back into Michigan City on the New York Central Railroad, she not only knew the date, but the exact time and station. There she stood, a striking figure of a woman appearing more mature than her sixteen years of age. She was dressed warm against the December wind, while outfitted in the fashion and style she loved so much. The long, dark, wool coat was eye popping with the grey fox collar high around her long neck. The long, leather boots might have been seen on any major fashion magazine cover of that day. The egg-shell colored silk scarf was obviously a piece she had studied long the day she paid a good portion of her hard-earned money to add to her sizable collection of accessorized wardrobe. The matching, tan, ear muffs and leather gloves were her favorite, having come from the Marshall Field department store on Chicago's famed State Street. As the dark smoke wafted above the huge, black, engine broiler's, smoke stack, the screeching, steel wheels made their last few rotations. She looked through the windows at the standing passengers waiting to disembark. She spotted him in seconds. That was Franky's mackinaw coat. She would know it anywhere. As he bent slightly at the waist to pick up his military style, duffel bag, she saw the top of his big brimmed hat. Sophie snickered a bit thinking it was the same kind of hat that Al Capone was often seen wearing. She saw the brim of the hat raise a bit, and then she saw his face.

"Why was Frank always the most handsome of the family?" she thought to herself. She could already imagine that thick black frock of hair, slicked back under his hat, and that stately nose with the big hump on it, so like the nose engraved on the face that adorned the "Indian Head Nickel." Then, she saw the answer to her previous question. "Oh! those baby blue eyes." She literally whispered out loud, "and the same thick lips as our mother." Her disdain for her own image was only outdone by her admiration for Frank's.

Just as the excitement of the awaited reunion peaked in her emotions, Franky's eyes made direct contact with hers as her gloved hand rose to enthusiastically proclaim her presence. Frank quickly elbowed the little guy beside him, pointed his own gloved finger in Sophie's direction and said,

"Look Peo, that's my Sister Soph, the nickname he would call her for many years to come. "She came to meet me."

He stepped off the train and walked several steps. Sophie grasped both sides of his face, kissed him on the cheek, then wrapped her arms around him and, half crying, said,

"Welcome home Franky, we have really missed you."

"Good, ah, Yeah good." seemed to be the only response Frank could muster due to the fact that to his memory this may have been the first time his sister had ever hugged or kissed him. He had been so mean spirited toward his sisters that he didn't quite know what to do with this strange and new level of affection that seemed to befall him. It was just too cold to walk home all the way from the north end of town so they began their trek toward the nearest street car station. It wasn't until they got to the station that Frank remembered the electric street car service had gone bankrupt a few months before he left for California.

"For love of Mike." Frank sighed, "I forgot about the street cars. Well, we will just have to walk a little faster to stay warm I guess."

"Oh! Frank," Sophie said beginning the post greeting conversation, "We all can't wait to hear the stories about California and all you did out there."

"Well," Frank replied, "There are some pretty good stories to tell, and I can't wait to get back there again."

"Back there again?" Sophie snapped, "Hey, you're not even fully home yet and you're talking about going back again?"

"Oh yeah." Frank said as he pointed Sophie to avoid the large snow pile just ahead of them. "I just meant..." he said with a little pause, "I might think about it later, you see the way this CCC thing works is, after you come home for six months, allowing some others to work and make a little money to send home, you can sign up for another six months. I might look into that," making it sound less absolute and somewhat less important. "But you're right, I just got home. We will see how things work out." he said while looking for a way to transition away from his rather premature announcement.

The first few days home were exciting for Frank as well as the family. The evenings building the fire with Johnny, and telling about the San Bernardino Mountains gave his parents and siblings their own imaginative travel log experience. Frank even felt some comfort at tolerating Johnny's snoring in the bed they shared. Some nights, Frank would lay awake and laugh to himself how Pa's snoring in the next room could even outdo Johnny's right beside him. For the first few mornings home he would awaken to a mixed emotion of comfortable familiarity and missed sounds of the old CCC camp at Mountain Home, in the foothills of the only range of mountains that ran east and west in America. Within days, Frank would have to find whatever work he could. It was still the thick of the Great Depression. It was winter and there would be no farm work available. The bakery was forced completely out of business soon after Frank had left for California. Fortunately, while looking for some work one afternoon, an old acquaintance of Frank's saw him on the street and abruptly asked,

"Franky, are you able to travel a few miles to work?"

"I'd find a way to make it happen." was Frank's answer. The old pal continued,

"If you can make it over to Porter, there is a New York Central office. Ask for a Mr. Elmer Young." The man paused and continued, "Actually, he is Reverend Young. He preaches at some little church over there, but I guess they must not pay him anything because he is a foreman on the railroad. I hear he is looking for a guy to work in the railroad yard. I don't know exactly what the work is, but he said it is long and hard, but it pays $8.00 bucks a week."

"Wow," Frank responded, "That is more money than I have heard anyone paying these days. Yea, sure," Frank said emphatically, "It's only about nine miles away. I will get over there right away."

Frank wasted no time in getting there. He was employed on the spot, and began work that very afternoon. One thing was true, it was hard work. Loading coal into coal cars, cutting wood, and stacking it behind the engines preparing to head out, helping the brakeman with heavy repairs, and anything else necessary to keep the trains moving. The long, twelve-hour days were certainly physically taxing on him, but the eight, one dollar bills in Frank's pocket every Friday felt great. It also meant he could still help with the overall costs of the house, and have a few dollars for himself. Some things were certainly different around the house since he came home. Not only was his mother still reading her Bible everyday but in the evenings he would see his father, Kaz, often reading the Bible. Many evenings when he would arrive home late, the house was empty. This continued for a couple weeks before he was finally informed that most of those evenings, the family was going to special services in some different kind of church. Nobody really talked about it, and it was a little frustrating to Frank when on Sunday, his only free day of the week, the whole family would go to this meeting place on both Sunday Morning and Sunday night. To make his world feel a little more strange, was the fact that when he would arrive at work each morning his foreman, Rev. Young, was always reading a Bible. Some mornings he would be talking religious sounding stuff to another worker there. On one such occasion, Rev. Young looked up from his reading and directly asked Frank,

"Hey Franky, do you go to church anywhere?"

Frank answered in a not so soft manner, "Naw Elmer, I don't have no time for that religious stuff, got a lot of better things to do with my time and my money than that stuff."

Seeing a rather startled look on the Reverend's face, Frank quickly added, "No offense. If that's important to you, well, go for it but it's just not my cup of soup."

Frank quickly headed to the work yard like he remembered something important that could not wait.

As the winter faded, and the spring began to renew the spirits, Frank began to feel that old baseball feel again. He wondered if he could pick back up in the summer with the Orioles. But then again, with the long work hours, how would he even have the time to practice and play? After calling the old coach he was delighted to hear they would love to have him back again if he could work out the schedule. They would only let him play on weekends if they could get that sweet swing of his back in their lineup. Frank convinced Elmer Young to let him work from 4:00am to 4:00 pm each day so his evening would be free to play ball again. It meant Frank was up by 2:00 a.m. each day. He would be on the road hitchhiking by 3:00 a.m., working by 4:00 a.m. and hitchhiking home by 4:00 p.m. each afternoon. Then he would head to practice until dark, eat a late supper, and fall into bed, only to repeat the same schedule the next day. The money in his pocket was nice, but the greater reward was to smell the leather of that five-fingered baseball glove as he hovered over first base, and once again drive those laser-like singles, doubles, and triples to the places where the other team's players were not located. As long as Frank could find time for baseball, there would be no sacrifice of time or effort too great.

Frank was so busy that he seldom saw the family at all. Kaz's hope that Frank would observe the spiritual changes in his parents and siblings, creating an interest was really
nowhere to be found with their separate lives. Kaz, Mary, and the rest of the family had
become so entrenched in their new lifestyle and family of faith, that each of their com-
mitments was even more intensified than they had ever expected. Some major new
progress was taking place among that small group of people meeting in the old auto repair
shop. For one thing, they were gaining new converts on a regular basis, and had almost
tripled in size. It became evident that the congregation would soon have to try to find a
larger gathering place. Secondly, it was also apparent that these new believers needed more
than just the inspiration of their regular gatherings, but also some true guidance in their
personal lives. What was needed most was a true pastor to help negotiate the future direction of what could possibly be a strong and effective new church congregation for this
growing community.

Meanwhile, in a small town about thirty miles east of Michigan City, named Mishawaka,
lived a transplanted family. The family was originally from Southeastern Kentucky, and
later Southern Indiana. After an early life of Coal-mining, the head of this family found
himself, wife, and six children completely entrenched in their new city, the father's new
profession as a minister, and the very exciting and rather large, for that day, church congregation. Although James Rice was not the pastor of the church, he was serving the pastor by directing music, teaching Bible classes, and honing his public speaking skills by
conducting religious services on the street corners of Mishawaka and adjoining communities like the much larger city of South Bend. On some occasions James would be invited to
join a consortium of church enthusiasts, and conduct larger, outdoor, crusades. These
meetings served one purpose, and one purpose only: to proclaim the Gospel, or as they
called it, "The Good News." The ultimate goal was to make new converts of the non-reli-
gious and especially the unchurched. The part James loved the most was that both the
little modest street meetings and the larger campaigns involved his wife and older
children.

The screen door banged its familiar announcement that hot afternoon, Daddy was home.
The young daughter and even younger son quickly abandoned their play toys and both
leapt toward their father's rather thin frame, only to be swept up, each into an awaiting
arm.

"Daddy, you smell like paint," wailed Estella June, as her whitish-blonde pigtails swung
about her head.

"I like that smell!" declared James' and Martha's youngest child, Freddy.

It was not often that their father would still be wearing his white, house painter's overalls. As he finished the multiple cheek kisses, he lowered his admiring cargo, and began to un-button the overalls at the collar. As usual, what was seen underneath the amazingly un-stained work outfit was the white dress shirt, sapphire blue necktie, and dark, perfectly pressed, dress slacks. He was a painter on the outside and preacher on the inside. Always ready for whichever need would beckon his call.

James and Martha's oldest daughter and son were already married and living nearby, leaving only daughter, Opal and mother, Martha positioned dutifully at the stove and sink preparing the evening meal. The timing seemed perfect as James hung his work gar-ment on the nearby coat rack, and moved into the rather large kitchen. He first patted Opal on the back as if to say, "Good work," and then stepped behind his Martha, wrap-ping his arms around her waist. She turned her head around far enough to meet his lips with a tender kiss. She had married this little man when she was only fifteen years old, and she left her beloved Kentucky hills. He was truly everything to her from that day forward.

"Ladies," James softly spoke, "I need to tell you something very important."

Both Martha, so stately and tall, and Opal, the rather serious eighteen year old woman, stopped their tasks, and turned toward him immediately.

"I have really been praying about something, and I believe I have received a clear directive from the Lord." He stated firmly with head up and eyes attempting to look as directly as possible at both attentive women in front of him.

"What are you talking about Daddy?" Martha questioned, using the endearing term she began using with their first child, who died at eighteen months from the pandemic spread of Spanish Flu in America. She continued to use this term to her dying day.

"Well," James lowered his voice, while raising an index finger toward his temple, "I know the time has come for me to step out in faith and give myself completely to God's work."

"What does that mean?" Martha wiped her hands on her apron as she raised another question, "Are you talking about becoming a pastor of your own church?" Rapid-fire came the questions, "You mean moving somewhere else?" she continued, "Another town? Leaving our home? Our friends?"

James raised his hand as if to stop the onslaught of questions,

"Listen, He softly said, "I will explain if you give me a minute." Directing them both toward two chairs at the round, oaken table in the kitchen, he began to explain. "There is a group of fairly new believers that have contacted me, and they've asked me to consider becoming their pastor."

Martha interrupted, "When did that happen and why did you not mention this before?"

James' manner became a bit stern as he would make a rather shocking and firm declaration.

"Marthy," he would slowly utter with the pronunciation that identified his deep hills, Kentucky, upbringing. "I would have not said anything to anyone about this, including even you, until I heard from God as to this matter," then leaning into her face a little closer his voice took on that of a classroom instructor as he continued, "After all it is Him I will stand before someday and give an account, in regard to my willingness and obedience."

She did respect that and knew better than to presume any superiority to his position or calling. However, the shock of this news could not totally constrain her, so, in an apparent disinterest she raised the most important question,

"Where do you believe God is calling you to go?"

Quickly he responded, "Michigan City. I am to start a new church with these few people in Michigan City."

"Michigan City?" she cried, "Have you lost your mind?" She stood to her feet. All five feet and nine inches of her body bristled like an Arizona cactus. She stomped one foot on the wood floor, then slapped one long hand on the table at her side. Towering over her very short and frail-looking husband, she began her following declaration and intention as to this, so-called, divine direction.

"My home is in Mishawaka," her voice boomed until the younger children came running, but they quickly halted at the door to the kitchen only to hear their enraged mother fire another volley across the bow. "My Friends are here, my women's society is here, my Bible class is here, my house is here, my married children are here, and I will not step one foot into that prison town of fish-smelling, sand-embedded people, whatever you think their need is." To make clear her firmly established intentions, she finalized her diatribe with tears streaming down both cheeks, and dropped the heaviest bomb in her armament. "You can go there if you want, but you will go alone! Me and your children plan to live the rest of our lives right here in the "Princess City" of Mishawaka, Indiana!" With those words she stormed from the kitchen, out the door, and down the sidewalk until she was completely out of view of her shocked husband, and mouth-gaping children, staring through the same screen door that, just a few minutes earlier, had echoed such a welcome home sound. The first to brave a word was the eldest daughter still at home.

"Daddy," she softly said, "What are you talking about? Moving?"

With that James broke his stunned gaze from the doorway where Martha was growing smaller in his cone of vision, but not slower in her ferocious march, already a good block or two down the street.

"Yes Daughter." James said decidedly, "As sure as I have ever known anything, I know I have heard the Lord in this matter." He walked across the room and placed one gentle hand on her thin shoulder, continuing, "Opal, surely you will go with me. I know how much you love the Lord and His work. I will desperately need you to play your guitar, especially in the street corner meetings we must do several days a week."

Quickly yet respectfully she began her verbal response to this unexpected surprise of the day,

"You know, Daddy, that I want to do anything the Lord would call me to do." James began to speak further when his daughter quickly moved a hand toward his lips and continued, "And there is nothing I love more than doing street services with you, but Mishawaka is my home since we left Jasonville when I was just nine years old. I am now eighteen. This is my church. My friends are here. My youth group at the church, what would they do? I am their leader, they need me." With tears beginning to well up in the corner of her eyes and her lower lip initiating an unintended quiver, her voice became whiney and pleading, not unlike the nine year old she had just referenced.

James knew he must seize the opportunity to appeal to his daughter's sense of maturity and accomplishment when he responded,

"Opal, listen for a moment." Then in a pleading voice he insisted, "Listen to your father. This is an amazing opportunity to build something good, and a great opportunity to build something for God." Then attempting to reach a more practical level of reasoning while still peaking the emotional opportunity of time, James verbally offered the biggest piece of candy when he said, "Besides, this group already has a few handsome young men attending their gatherings." Quickly turning the highly spiritual argument to a fanciful realm James projected, "Who knows, daughter of mine? You might even meet your husband over there."

But James never expected the immediate, firm, and hopelessly exasperated retort that flew from between his daughter's beautiful, firmly clenched teeth,

"Oh Daddy, are you kidding me? There is nothing in Michigan City but a bunch of dumb Polaks! No, I am with my mother on this one, Dad. If you go to Michigan City, you will be going on your own." At which she hurled her body in the direction of the same door her mother had so dramatically escaped the maddening idea.

The screen door produced an even more explosive closure as the daughter headed in obvious pursuit of her mother, combining the fury of two Kentucky thoroughbred women, fanning each other's flame of opposition in such a maniacal disruption of one man's idea. By the time Opal found her mother, sitting quietly on the park bench near the St. Joe River, which meandered its way through their city, she was surprised to see a much more peaceful view than she had expected. After chiding Opal for following her there, Martha asked,

"So, what happened?"

Opal's walk had only added energy to her fury.

"Daddy is really serious about this!" She almost screamed.

"Settle down, Opal Marie." her mother quickly injected.

"He wants me to go help with music and street meetings, and you won't believe what else he came up with." With her head rotating as wildly as the water crashing over the nearby dam she announced, "He said I might even meet my future husband there. Oh, Mother! This could not be the worst timing in the world. Dad does not know that George is going to give me a ring, and ask me to marry him this week." As she threw her head over on

Martha's lap she was utterly shocked with the words that proceeded from her extremely calm mother.

"Opal, I left my home and family with that man when I was only fifteen years old. He has never led me or this family wrong yet, and he never will." Martha softly continued, "If you need to stay and begin a new life here with George, your father and I will understand, but when I walk back into that house I will first ask God's forgiveness for my actions today, and then I will ask your father to forgive me. Then, I will assure him that I would go with him to the gates of Hell if he believed that is where God is sending us." Then she chuckled a bit and added, "Maybe that is exactly where he is leading us." They both exchanged their tears for a few minutes of mind-cleansing laughter."

Forty years earlier, Anna Pawlak had laid back on the straw in the bottom of a cattle-hauling vessel, and tearfully whispered the words, "Poznan, Poznan, Poznan." Martha Rice laid back on the banks of the river, and fearfully repeated the words, raising her voice in question each time, Michigan City? Michigan City? Michigan City?

Within a few weeks Rev. James Rice, with Martha at his side, began to gather with the small congregation of people in Michigan City. James was able to help secure employment for himself again as a painter and wallpaper hanger. The biggest move he made was to rent a two story building on the West side of town, right on the corner of 10th Street and Ohio Street, only one block from a passenger rail line that ran from South Bend to Chicago.

Opal stayed behind, and was engaged to George as they planned for a future in her beloved Mishawaka. It was not very long after Opal's engagement that she became uncomfortable with the prospect of a future life with George. There could not have been a finer young man of character and religious devotion, but it did not take long to see that George's life was deeply entwined with that of his mother. Opal began to see an inevitable future where she would always be a secondary priority to her betrothed. She began to look for more and more opportunities to absent herself from the long evenings with George... and his mother. Many of those evenings found her boarding the South Shore Train to Michigan City to be with her parents, and assist her dad in his services both in the newly acquired building, and on the street corners in open-air crusades. It was, however, a Sunday evening service, back in her Mishawaka Church, where Opal found herself kneeling at an altar prayer bench in the front of the sanctuary. Her concerns about her future plans had reached a place of inward conflict.

"Oh God," she muttered through her tearful voice, "I desire Your perfect will for both my life and George's life. I need guidance, relief from this anguish, or at least peace as to know if I am on the right path."

She did not have a supernatural visitation from some heavenly messenger, but she felt a sense of well-being, and an honest perspective on the inevitable reality she was facing. After gathering her emotions, dabbing away the few tears in the corners of her eyes, she stood and began the slow but steady return to her seat. As she sat down beside George she placed one hand on his forearm and said,

"George, I need to share my heart with you tonight."

Just as kindly, George slightly turned his body toward her and placed one hand upon hers and interrupted,

"Opal, I already know what you are going to say, and I have known for some time this was coming."

Opal felt a mixture of relief and pain, as she would not have injured this good man in any intentional way.

"I have been doing some praying too," George continued, "And I don't really feel I am ready for this step in our lives."

With that, Opal pulled her hand out from under his, slipped the lovely engagement ring from her finger, and softly folded it back into George's kind, soft hand. George excused himself to a few people sitting in the pew, as he stepped over them and into the middle aisle. Opal watched him walk, upright and assured out the back doors of the church. She listened to his steps rings off the concrete stairs, and heard the heavy wooden doors thump closed behind him. She looked toward the ceiling of the sanctuary and whispered in prayer,

"Ok, Lord. I guess I will go to Michigan City after all to help my folks, and see just what it is you really have in store.

The advantage of the new location for the church group was that the building had an upstairs apartment. James and Martha lived above it. By the time Opal joined with her three younger siblings, it was pretty crowded for a family of six. Furthermore, some of their living space had to serve double duty for the church's needs, like Sunday School classes and department meeting rooms.

Soon, James was able to make enough money on his side jobs to move the family to a nice, two story, brick house on Spring Street, a couple blocks off of the main, downtown, business district. For Opal it was much closer to where they set up the street meetings. This meant less distance to carry the instruments and equipment for the open air presentations. For little Junie and Freddy this meant much more window shopping at the big stores so close to home. This was great fun for the little kids, and for Junior it opened an entire world of exciting, if not worthwhile adventure.

James Junior was only thirteen years old, but could easily be mistaken for a twenty year old man. Mischief seemed to be a tasty delicacy to Junior. Trouble just seemed to locate him everywhere he went. He had two favorite pastimes, guitar, at which he became quite accomplished, and fighting, which he seemed to enjoy more than breathing. He was already six feet tall. He could grow a Clark Gable mustache already and wore a Bogart gangster hat pulled over his face, a cigarette dangling precariously from a corner of his lip, jacket collar turned up in the back, a pair of black, leather gloves turned down at each wrist. He was a visual billboard for tough guys and fun lovers that caught the eye of every young girl. He was also the same advertisement for any nefarious enterprise that created the legends of that era.

James and Martha became so concerned for the direction they saw their son headed, they decided to send him to a relative of high religious and spiritual repute. The problem with this arrangement was that this husband and wife lived in the heart of Chicago. After only two weeks, four fights, three visits from the police, and the guardians finding him playing music in one of the toughest bar rooms in the city, they quickly returned him to Michigan City. They found out the hard way that sending James Rice Jr. into Chicago was the proverbial placement of a fox in the henhouse.
Use of tobacco in any form, as well as the consumption of alcohol of any type was strictly forbidden in the home of this pastor and his wife. These, among many other indulgences, were some of the most basic, doctrinal topics found within the new congregations of Pentecostalism.

Imagine the explosive reaction in James' and Martha's home, the afternoon that Junior came through the front door, greeted both parents with a hug, only to exhale a pungent breath of beer upon both parents.

"James Junior," bellowed his father, "You have been drinking AL-KEE-HAUL!" James' Kentucky accent nasally whined out each syllable.

"I thought I smelled that Devil brew!" Martha chimed in.

Even though James was half the size of this overgrown boy, James grasped him by the shirt, and quickly dragged him to the back porch where sat a number 10, galvanized, washtub full of water. Martha had been preparing to wash several of James' white shirts. She had not yet put the lye soap into the tub, so the timing was perfect. Junior, being half dragged to the porch, could not believe what happened next. His father firmly grabbed him by the back of the neck, pulled his face toward the tub, and immediately shoved Junior's head beneath the water. Junior was adept at fighting, and he was strong too. Had this been some rival or stranger that held him beneath the water, he would have used everything at his command to overtake this attack, but this was his dad, and respect alone would not allow him to take that route. Junior wondered if his father would ever let him up. He was quickly running out of air. At the last possible moment, James pulled Junior's head out of the water. Junior was choking, and spitting, and gasping for air. James loudly proclaimed,

"Look, Marthy, he's so drunk, he can't even talk!" and James thrust the young rebel's head again into the tub of water, this time firmly holding Junior's nose and face to the bottom of the old galvanized tub.

This non-requested, and totally unappreciated form of baptism did change one certain habit of Junior's. No, he did not give up fighting, drinking, girl chasing, and trouble, but he made sure to never come near his parents if he thought the slightest smell of "Devil's brew" was anywhere on him.

In spite of challenges at home, James was absolutely enthralled with the advances the church was making. Things were shaping up so well that he felt it was time for a radical advancement in the life and spiritual health of the church. He heard that many churches were adding intensity to their church endeavors with something called "extended meetings." The church would now be open seven days a week. Sundays would conduct both morning and evening meetings, then each night of the week the church would have another service. They often brought in guest speakers from the area, or if none were available James would do the preaching himself. These meetings were high-spirited events. Music would be a major factor with long successions of congregational singing, and special numbers by soloists or any combination of persons who wanted to participate. The services each night were targeted for primarily three areas of concentration. First, was the conversion of the sinner. Second, was this infusion of the Holy Spirit that would empower believers to a level of boldness for reaching others. The third area was one that caught the attention of the unchurched, and produced the largest numbers of interested and inquisitive onlookers. This was the practice and belief that human sickness and disease could be miraculously, and even instantaneously healed by the simple act of placing oil on someone's forehead, and believing in faith that God would divinely heal them. They followed examples recorded in the Biblical accounts. These meetings were a powerful blend of sincere, yet emotionally charged enthusiasm. The music was loud, and at times forceful. The congregation displayed little reserve and would often become audible in their exuberance and affirmation. Many would testify to their own physical improvements. Some would bring back to future services confirmation from medical experts that their incurable diagnoses had been reversed, and there was now, no evidence of the previous condition.

One family in the congregation could not have been more entrenched and enamored with these events. Kaz Pawlak, his wife Mary, eldest son John, daughters Sophie and Lilly, and even young Eddie seemed to enjoy the excitement, and of course the music. The only member of the family that did not participate was Frank.

As truth would have it, Frank was really unaware of any of the things of this nature going on in the family. It was work, a little fishing and baseball, baseball, and more baseball.

If there was one immediate goal of the growing congregation of Pentecostals, it was to recruit as many people as possible into this newfound joy that had come to these members through their newfound faith. Both Kaz and Johnny were often tempted to try to win Frank into the fold, yet there never seemed to be the right time, or even the available opportunity.

One particular night the service had run quite late. Every time the excitement, or what some might even call hilarity of the service, would subside enough to bring the evening to a conclusion, someone else would request special prayer. With each reemphasis of need the intensity of the activities would seem to rekindle the fervor. Sophie began to feel a heaviness come over her heart. She slipped from her seat, and found a place in the front corner of the church where she knelt and prayed. It was like a cloud of sorrow had fallen over her, and she could not understand these feelings. She had not realized that almost three hours had passed since she found herself on her knees. Most of the people had left for their homes, and only the pastor and a couple others remained in the building. It was well after 1:00 a.m. Even Kaz and the rest of the family had returned home some time ago, and they were soundly sleeping in the darkness of their home.

Suddenly Sophie began to weep, almost uncontrollably. To her own amazement she heard the words coming from her mouth. They also were coming from somewhere deep within her soul.

"Frank, Frank. Oh, God. it's Frank!" She cried out loud enough for the others to hear. " My brother, Frank. My brother, Frank."
Her outburst turned into a heartbreaking prayer to her God,

"Dear Lord, my brother will never come to you! All he thinks about is baseball, baseball, baseball. Oh, God! You will have to go to him, or he will never come to you."

As she lay face down on the floor, she buried her face in the bend of her arm, wept violently, and continued her plea, "Save my brother. Go to him, God. Save my brother, Frank! Please God, go to him!"

"John! Johnny, something is wrong with me! Look, look, what's wrong?" Frank was trying to raise his body to a sitting position but the violent shaking of his arms, legs, torso, and head would not allow it. "Look at me, John! Something is wrong. I can't stop shaking. It's my legs, my arms, wait I can't stop shaking. What is going on John?"

John bolted from his side of the bed. He was quickly and fully awake, and standing in awe. Never had he seen his brother like this. It was like some kind of convulsion, yet he was not afraid. There was no feeling of panic for John. Instead, he felt a strangely, unexplainable warm feeling. John thought to himself, "This cannot be right. My brother looks like he is dying, yet I feel so peaceful, even calm and joyful."

As understanding dawned, John exclaimed, "Franky, listen to me, I know what is happening." John came around to Frank's side of the bed and placed his hand on his brother's shaking chest, and to his own surprise said,

"Frank, it is God. It is God. He is trying to get a hold of you. He is touching you, Frank. I feel God in this room, Frank."

"Then what do I do? I can't stand this John! What do I do?"

John quickly replied as he took hold of Frank's shaking arm,

"Get on your knees, Frank! Here, I will help. You must call out to God! Just ask Christ to come into your heart. Ask him to be your Savior.

Frank attempted to throw his legs off the side of the bed, while still in a somewhat convulsive spell. Johnny reached across Frank's body and placed his huge hand firmly in the middle of Frank's back to assist his slither from the bed to the floor. As Frank's knees struck the wooden floor with a thud, he forced his upper body forward, mid-thrash, and forced his face toward the place he had just been laying.

"O God, Please God help me," Frank began to plead in a rather pitiful and fearful voice. "If you're there God, if you're real, if you hear me, don't let me die, please."

"What is that noise?" Mary shouted, while grasping Kaz's arms beside her.

"For love of Mike." Kaz growled from his heavy, snore-filled sleep. "What are they doing in there, wrestling?"

As Kaz staggered toward the boys' room, Mary pulled her blankets under her chin, sitting like a frightened child, as she waited for her husband to discover and still this mid night uproar. The door swung open with the same ferocity Kaz would have used some years before to separate the clamorous hooligans he had sired. When the door slammed back against the wall, Kaz could not believe his eyes. There were not two fighting little boys, but two sizable grown men. One had his body half laid across the bed, weeping and literally wailing for a merciful deity, somewhere in the heavenlies, to rescue him from certain disaster and affliction. To Frank's side, also on his knees, was Kaz's superhuman mass of man. John was weeping sincerely, and calling out commands to Frank in the most desperate voice,

"Call on Jesus, Frank. Tell him you're sorry for your sins! Ask Him to come into your heart! Beg him to save you now! He wants you, Frank. He died for you, Frank. He is the only thing that matters now!"

"I do want God," Frank shouted out loudly. "If this is you, God, I want you now, take my life. I will give you everything. I want you more than anything in my life." These declarations were coming faster than any fastball Frank had ever faced down.

As Kaz stepped toward his sons an amazing phenomenon took place. Just as suddenly as Frank was awakened with his body uncontrollably shaking, Kaz's body began to shake. His legs first, then his arms, and quickly his hands began to shake like someone who had just plunged both hands into hot water. As Kaz stood in the room, trembling and slinging both hands rapidly, Frank's body began to calm at the voice of his father.

"The Holy Spirit is in this room, boys," Kaz shouted! He is right here, now! Frank, he is coming into your heart. You are being saved, right now." Then Kaz used that new phrase that had been explained to him in that tent meeting. "You are being BORN AGAIN Franky."

The physical gyrations began to subside for both father and son when Frank began to describe what he was feeling.

"I feel so light. It is like a huge weight has just rolled off my back. I am happy. Yes, really happy." Then he spoke with a most serious and sober voice. This was unlike anything Kaz or Johnny had ever heard in Frank's voice.

"Something is really different. I don't feel like the same person.
I am not the same person. I feel love. I feel safe. I am so light. I feel like I could float. I feel clean, really clean."

Kaz and John began to laugh hilariously. Partially because Frank had never spoken like this, and partially because they recognized this amazing description of Frank's epiphany. What became known as Frank's conversion to Christ, was the exact description of everything they had experienced when they had surrendered their lives to their Savior. After the temperament of the rooms calmed, and the three conversed about the entire evening for some time, Mary felt it safe enough to find her way to the room's doorway and asked,

"Is what happened here tonight what I think happened here?"

Kaz quickly affirmed that Frank had an incredible encounter with God, and was now in the fold.

Mary smiled and said, "I am so glad the whole family belongs to Jesus now. I just don't know why all this had to happen so loudly."

Their rapturous laughter was only broken by the sound of the front door opening. With the door being locked securely from the inside, Sophie would turn around to see Kaz, Mary, Johnny, and Franky standing in their night clothes, like birds on a telephone line. Being startled at the lighted house and the characters before her she simply asked one question,

"What happened here tonight?"

Almost simultaneously she heard,

"Sit down, you won't believe this!"

It was an unexplainable feeling, and what would have been an unthinkable event, just a few months earlier. Kaz held the front door of the wooden storefront building on Chicago Street, and proudly observed every member of his family file into the Sunday morning service as a human reenactment of the noisy passenger train rattling around the curve just one short block away. After a few greetings and introduction of their second eldest son, Frank, the family took up the entire fourth row of the clean and well decorated, humble, little sanctuary.

This place felt very different to Frank from the massive, ornate Catholic churches he had very seldom attended. Mostly, it took a wedding, funeral, or special holiday event to see Frank in a church. In a matter of a few minutes an elderly lady stepped to the front of the church and rapidly pounded the desktop bell she held on her non-striking hand. It was the kind of bell you would see at a window of a bank or telegraph office, designed to announce to someone that a customer was waiting for service.
Suddenly, from three different doors people began to enter the chapel.

"What is going on?" whispered Frank in the general direction of his brother, John.

"It means Sunday School is over and they are coming from the classes to join us for the regular worship service."

Frank quickly inquired, "Is it like a regular school?"

"No, no." John quickly answered, "It is a school where they study the Bible, different stuff for different age groups. Kind of like Catechism classes back in the Polish school, I think."

Then the lady who rang the bell walked to the speaker's podium with a book in her hand and began to read,

"The nursery class had four in attendance and two absent. The beginner class had three present, and three absent today. The junior boys had seven today and nobody was absent."

At this, the crowd, in one voice, shouted "Amen!" while two or three individuals bellowed,

"Praise the Lord!"

After the lady had finished a couple more class reports, she announced that all should stand for prayer as they dismiss the Sunday school hour, and prepare for the service. She then asked, what Frank would later learn was one of the many rhetorical questions in this form of church service,

"How many believe God is going to meet us here today?"

The audience hollered back the expected answers in the affirmative forms of "Amen," "Praise the Lord," or "Hallelujah," and a couple bass voice declarations of "Glory." Frank sat as erect and still as if he were posing for an exploding powder photograph. All he heard was, "God is going to meet us here today." Frank's mind went back to a few nights before when his father had bellowed in that bedroom, "God is in this room." Frank began to reason that if God shows up here again today he would begin that freakish shaking and convulsive thrashing. That would be the most horrible thing to have happened to him right here in front of all these strangers, the first time he ever saw them. John could sense his brother's nervousness, seeing Frank's frozen body and clenched fists next to him. He was pale as the white sheets his mother would hang in the summer wind.

"Frank, what is wrong with you? Are you sick or something?"

Without moving one muscle of his rigid body, and keeping his head straight forward, Frank attempted to whisper from the corner of his mouth,

"Is God showing up here again? I don't think I can take that again, John."

John, now much more familiar with the mode of operation and the typical church jargon, threw both hands over his face and thrust his upper body toward his lap in an attempt to hide the hilarious, and what he hoped would be, unnoticed laughter. As soon as he had gathered his composure, John leaned into Frank's shoulder and quickly replied,

"God doesn't show up here Himself. It means we will feel His presence like He will be watching us, and happy that we are worshiping Him. He will give us blessings today, and we can feel that. Like, you know Pa is with you even when he can't come to your ball-game. Ok?"

Frank relaxed a little and his body seemed to lower a few inches in his seat. Just then, Frank's attention was completely diverted. Up the side aisle, against the wall, he saw an amazing sight. There walked an attractive young woman, wearing a very nice, white dress, with sleeves gracefully falling all the way to her wrists. At her neck was a sky blue collar and a fashionable, large bow made with that same shade of Frank's favorite color. As she approached the stage or, "platform," as this church world would come to call the elevated section at the front, Frank noticed, clutched in her right hand, a dark brown guitar case. His eyes continued to follow her every step as she ascended the two steps, and walked confidently to the back of the platform. Her long, brown hair flowed around her shoulders and wafted all the way to her small waistline. As she gracefully bent at the knees, and opened the guitar case from a modest side-way approach, she abruptly stood erect and in one attractive turn, swung the guitar upward, using her right hand to rapidly position the guitar strap over her head and about her neck and shoulders. Frank certainly knew a pretty girl when he saw one. He had caught the eye of many young ladies who had hung around the baseball fields who wanted to express how well they thought he played that day. He had even had a pretty steady interest in a girl named Rose before she moved way off to San Antonio, Texas. It was then that he learned the hard lesson that although, "Distance makes the heart grow fonder" it is often for "Someone a whole lot closer!"

But this, this was different. Never had he seen a girl quite like this gal. Frank's mind gave her the ultimate compliment of the day, she was, "Swell." He became even more spellbound when she pulled the pick from the strings at the top of the guitar neck, placed her fingers solidly on the strings to form what Frank knew from his time with some guitars as a C-chord. She strummed down the strings from E to E, and adjured the waiting congregation to rise to their feet, and join her in singing everyone's favorite hymn. Frank reached his feet a little slower than most of the programmed congregants, but he suddenly realized that he had heard this familiar tune on one of his mother's recordings. Enthusiastically, the crowd sang,

"Amazing Grace,
How sweet the sound that saved a wretch like me.
I once was lost but now I'm found,
Was blind but now I see."

It was not the familiar tune, nor even the warm feeling that Frank felt about the words he is applying to his own recent experience. It was this girl, no, woman. Her eyes were closed as her voice changed to sing a deep, clear, and rich, alto harmony. But it stood out in some way, still audible above the entire congregation. At the end of the song there is a spontaneous outburst of voices that began to individually, yet corporately, fill the room with phrases like,

"Thank you, Jesus," and "I Love you, Lord." Others speak out loud, "Wonderful Lord!" and "Thank You, God." as their faces looked heavenward. As the mixture of vocalization began to subside, the guitar began strumming a much faster rhythm, and the young, female song leader raised her voice to an exciting level with a very different song,

"Wonderful, Wonderful Jesus is to me,
Counselor, Prince of Peace, mighty God is He,
Saving me, keeping me from all sin and shame.
Wonderful is my redeemer, praise His Name."

All hands were clapping vigorously to the beat of the song. What had been solemn reflections a few moments ago had transpired into a happy, exciting, high-spirited escapade that rivaled any Saturday night ballroom dance with the hottest big band leader of the day. After several of these musical adventures, the young songstress set her guitar to one side and descended the platform steps to take a place on the front row beside a tall distinguished woman.

"Perhaps, her mother." Thought Frank, as a small man with wire-rimmed glasses walked to the speaker's lectern. Frank would learn another church term, and that would be that the speaker's podium was called the preacher's pulpit. It was considered a "sacred desk," because on this item of furniture would be laid the one item that carried more worth and respect than anything else in the building, "The Holy Bible."

Prior to Rev. James Rice's sermon that day he made, what seemed to Frank, one more strange request.

"Before I speak to you this fine Lord's Day, I would like to know
If perhaps there would be someone in this congregation for whom God answered a
prayer, or performed a mighty work on their behalf this week?"

Frank saw a movement out of the corner of his eye. It was his sister, Sophie, who had been
sitting next to his mother at the far left end of the row.

"Yes, Pastor." Sophie began, "One night this week, I was late at the front, praying when I
became overwhelmed that my brother did not know Jesus as his savior. I stayed for several
hours praying for his salvation, and when I got home late, he was awake, and he had experienced an encounter with God, and has become a true Christian." Sophie stretched her
long arm to her right and pointed her index finger directly at Frank's embarrassed face and
gaping mouth. She continued with an excited squeal,

"And he is right here ready to live for Jesus the rest of his life!"

The crowd burst into shouts again using their favorite vocal expressions for several minutes, since applause would have never been an acceptable expression in this church. Applause was considered by these folks as something "worldly people" did to praise men and
their accomplishments, rather than give God His rightful recognition. When the shouting
subsided, the pastor looked kindly at Frank, lowered his spectacles to the end of his nose,
and said,

"Well, Frank, we are thrilled for you, but we read in God's word Jesus said, 'If you are
ashamed of me before men, I will be ashamed of you before my Father in Heaven,' so we
believe you should make this new commitment to Christ public before all these witnesses.
Why don't you come on up here with me for a moment?"

Quickly, John and Kaz both motioned for Frank to step forward and almost in one voice
said,

"I'll go with you."

Frank amazed himself how quickly he stood and moved to the center aisle. As the three
stood there, Rev. Rice came down to Frank, grasped his hand with both of his, and simply
said,

"Frank, have you asked Christ to be your Savior, and come into your heart?"

"Yes I have sir, in my bedroom, like my sister said." was Frank's reply.

"Then you are truly a child of God," said Pastor James, "And God will be everything in your life from this day forward."

When Frank returned to his seat, his head was spinning from the week's events. He did try to listen to the sermon, but from time to time found that his eyes kept wandering from the preacher to that front row where the young woman sat taking notes, occasionally nodding her pretty brown hair in approval of the pastor's oration. She would even lift her hand toward him at times saying her own approving "Amen." Unfortunately, it was always her right hand, and Frank never could see if her left hand was free of jewelry, particularly a ring. After the sermon was concluded, people gathered at the front for intense prayer, and a few people were anointed with oil, and prayed concerning their physical ailments. Kaz announced to the family,

"Let's go out the side door so we can walk to the park before we get home for dinner."

To exit the side door meant they had to walk again toward the front of the chapel, and exit near the corner of the platform. As they crossed in front of the little, elevated stage, Frank reached the little stairs at the same time the pretty, young woman was carrying her guitar down. As they met, the woman turned to Frank, extended her hand and said,

"Welcome, Frank. I am so happy for you, and it is nice to meet the rest of the Pawlak family." Frank who was never short for a response, did not quite know what to say, but he did manage a shy,

"Thank you. Nice to meet you too."

"Oh! I am so sorry, I have not even introduced myself." she replied. "My name is Opal, and I am the Pastor's daughter. Opal Rice."

"Oh, that's swell." said Frank. "I really liked your singing today."

"Thank you, but all the glory goes to God, you know."

Frank was not sure what she was saying, but it sounded right, anyway. They both agreed to look forward to seeing each other again, while Kaz and family started up the street.

"Opal." mused Frank vocally. "That's some kind of jewel or gemstone, isn't it?" Frank voiced toward his Pa.

"Yeah, it is. Pretty valuable one too, I think."

"Opal. Hmm, Opal." Frank spoke into the air.

"Oh boy, oh boy!" Johnny moaned.

"What?" quizzed Kaz.

"I think Franky may have found more than Jesus in that service today." Johnny teased like a mischievous boy again.

Frank quickly responded, "Awe, shut up, John, or I'll slug ya one right here in the street."

Then the whole family began to laugh as Frank simply walked ahead of them, waving his hand as if to say, "Forget about it." But, biting his tongue out of the corner of his teeth, he sheepishly dropped his head and smiled an interesting smile.

Life in the Pawlak household became quite different in the months to follow. Church, and this new way of life became a priority that affected everything from speech, thinking, to behavior. These changes were evident and dramatic. The family's new church devotion promoted a powerful lifestyle often referred to as "separation from the WORLD!"

Much of the daily routine continued for the family such as Kaz's and Johnny's daily toil at the box car factory, as well as Lilly's and Sophie's work at home and outside jobs. Both girls had reached that inevitable place where income was just more important than continuing their education. Eddie was reaching his teen years, and he was palling around more with his buddies, Sammy and Mike. Mary was becoming less sociable, and spending more time at home with her stomach and feet problems. There was still time found for fishing and hunting in the appropriate seasons, but the newfound religious standards were eliminating more and more of their pastime and recreational habits. The use of tobacco and alcohol were the first evils to be evicted from the house. Cursing and vile language, which had never really been too acceptable to Kaz and Mary, would now be considered hell-bound blasphemy. A great deal more careful attention was paid to pursuits, and only the most modest attire would insure their new message to an evil world. This applied more to the women and girls than the men. The word the church would promote at every opportunity was the term, "Holiness." This meant that many of the entertainment venues they had enjoyed in the past were no longer a place a true, born-again, spirit-filled, holiness person of God would be seen. The list was pretty long and clear. Taverns, bars, restaurants that served those demonic potables, liquor stores, pool halls, dance halls, motion picture houses, bowling alleys, roller-skating rinks, and yes, even sporting events or ball parks. Nowhere could the latter den of iniquity have hit any new convert harder than when Frank was kindly, but assuredly informed that in as much as he had become a real Christian, and had even had a supernatural experience with God, he could no longer involve himself with his former evil practice of playing organized baseball. The reasoning was that baseball games were played on "The Lord's Day," and to do so would be breaking one of the Ten Commandments, "Remember the Sabbath, and keep it Holy." Another reason this baseball behavior must be sacrificed at the altar of God was because they sold and drank beer, "the devil's brew," and they smoked and chewed, "the devil's weed," tobacco, both players and fans alike.

The ultimate proof that Frank had truly believed his encounter with God was genuine and life-changing was when he simply explained to his friends, family, and coach,

"When I gave my life to Christ, I experienced something I never felt in my life before. Not even from baseball, as much as I love it."

Years later, Frank would say, "What I found in God was so powerful that if those people at that church would have told me to lie my head on a railroad track, I would have done it." In the following decades, when the church lightened its code of behavior to allow many of those previously forbidden practices, Frank's children would secretly resent the church from preventing their father from pursuing a professional baseball career. They not only loved to play the game but, selfishly, thought, "If Dad would have made it to the pros, we might have gotten World Series tickets every year." The only person who seemed to never regret the decision was Frank. His sincere, and unwavering devotion would become his trademark for life.

"Why did you pick the coldest day of the year to get married?" Johnny grumbled toward Frank, while struggling to pull his winter galoshes over his freshly polished dress shoes.

"Opal said that a year and half was long enough for any courtship, and she did not want to wait for a traditional June wedding."

Frank and Opal had become a vital team to the Church. Frank loved to sing and play the guitar. He and Opal would often perform duets and trios with her pastor-father. They loved the new music that was circulating through the churches of these growing movements. Frank was still working on the railroad for Rev. Young, and Opal had acquired employment for the Reverend's wife. She cleaned their house in Porter, helped with the laundry, and did some cooking, often thinking about the day she would be able to do these things in her own home, with her own husband, and hopefully her own children.

Opal really enjoyed the dusting of the furniture most, especially Elmer Young's personal study. She loved to read, and Elmer had a very extensive library for that day. When the lady of the house, Virginia, noticed Opal's interest in each book that she dusted, Virginia assured her that her husband would not mind at all if she would like to read any of the literature she found. With that permission Opal worked as fast as possible to gain an hour each day before she had to return to the train station for her trip home. She would use that hour to consume page after page of the amazing books she would find. Classics, novels, biographies of famous people, religious commentaries, and travelogues of places around the world she could only dream of seeing someday. As she performed the house work, helped her father prepare for the busy Christmas season at the church, and designed the kind of wedding she wanted soon after the New Year, she found on Elmer's roll-top desk an interesting little book. It was small, thin, and black. The book had three gold stars on the front cover. Under the stars were the words, "Minister's Service Book."

"Virginia, what kind of book is this?" Opal asked, while she held it in one hand, showing the cover to Virginia who was sorting some papers across the room.

"Oh, that is Elmer's Star book," she replied as if Opal would know all about it.

"What is a star book?" quickly came the response.

"It is a preacher's book. It has all kinds of services that a preacher performs. You know, like how to baptize someone, what to say at a funeral, blessing of children, and... Oh! One you would be interested in, a wedding. There are all kinds of wedding services in there."

Opal's mind began to spin into creative thought. She wondered, "Since my Dad has already said he did not want to perform my wedding ceremony because he wanted to walk his daughter down the aisle just sit and watch his daughter get married, and he had already suggested Elmer Young perform the ceremony, and Frank and Elmer had become real brothers in the faith, maybe, just maybe I could have a greater hand in the ceremony."

When Elmer arrived home that evening, Opal was still sitting and intently reading the various wedding ceremonies in the little book.

"Good evening, Opal," Elmer greeted as he stepped into his study.

"What has your attention so much tonight?"

A bit startled, she rose from his chair at the desk and said, "I did not know there were so many different ways to marry people."

Elmer responded, "Well, everyone's a little different so why should every wedding ceremony be the same?" While he was still laughing at his question, Opal softly asked,

"Elmer, since you are going to do the wedding for Frank and me, would you mind if I found some things here that you could say? I mean, I just like the way a few things are said here."

"Opal, your father already warned me that you can be a 'take charge girl,' and you would probably come up with a few of your own ways for this wedding." Then reaching for the little book, he closed it, handed it back to Opal's waiting hands, and said, "Look, I have an idea. Why don't you just take the book home, and write your own ceremony? I will just read it the way you put it together."

"Really?" Opal shouted, "Oh, that would be wonderful, Elmer. I have some really great ideas."

"Whoa, whoa now, girl." Elmer firmly replied, "You can write your ceremony, but leave a place for me to preach a little and at least say the things I have to say to make this wedding legal."

"Oh certainly, thank you, thank you so much."

Opal stayed up late nights, drafting portions of the different ceremonies she loved into one, final piece of work. It was no little surprise to Frank, or her father that she would make one very, non-traditional adjustment to her wedding vows. Where the Bride would always vow to "Love, honor, and obey" her new husband, Opal had neatly edited her part of the vow for life. She would vow to, "Love, honor, and CHERISH" this man. The year was 1936. Opal would have been totally unaware of anything resembling a woman's rights movement, or something called "Women's Liberation Organization," but she may have been one of the first women of her time, and certainly the first in her family to stand by her position. She would remind others in years to come,

"I vowed to love that man, to honor that man, and to cherish that man to my dying day, but I never vowed before God to obey him."

This rather individual spirit and strength of character would come to serve her, her husband and her family in ways no one in that little church could have imagined, when those in attendance looked at each other, and asked with their eyes, "Did she just refuse to obey her husband?"

That vow arrangement was just the concluding surprise of several on Frank's wedding day. After arriving at the church before the ceremony, Frank was told to wait in the room that had been prepared for the groom and his best man. In a few minutes, Opal's brother, James Junior would join him as another tradition had been slightly redesigned, in that her brother would serve as his best man, and his sister, Sophie, would serve as her maid of honor. Frank was not really nervous until The Rev. Elmer Young entered the room of waiting. Elmer was not dressed like the railroad foreman Frank was accustomed to, but adorned in the long tailcoat, stiff collar, and formal tie of a clergyman. To Frank's further surprise, two other men followed. It was none other than Opal's pastor-father, James, and his own dad, Kaz. Pastor James quickly moved across the room to extend his hand toward his, soon to be, son-in-law.

"I want to be the first to congratulate you, Frank." said Opal's father in his familiar, kind, yet professional manner. He continued, "You are a fine man, Frank. I just wanted to tell you before this ceremony gets started how honored we are to have you in our family, and thankful our daughter is marrying a fine man of God."

A bit uncomfortable and awkward, Frank could at best only nod his head in response, and then simply squeeze out a scratchy throated, "Thank you so much. That's swell."

Then he felt the presence of his father moving up to his right side. Suddenly and firmly Frank, now taller than his dad, felt his father's huge hand grasp his shoulder.

"Franky, you're getting a wonderful girl. I really like Opal, and it is pretty amazing how this is all coming together today."

Kaz dropped his arm to his side, locking his hands behind him, and taking a step away from Frank, he began to speak in a rare, serious, but reflective manner.

"There is something I never got around to telling you, Franky, about how I met your Father-in-law. I never even told you that I met Opal long before you did."
Frank reached for a nearby folding chair, and gently sat down, never taking his eyes off his dad. Kaz Continued,

"You see, Frank. All you know is I found Christ, and turned my life over to him while you were in California. But you don't know how. You see, I actually went with a friend one night to attack a preacher at a tent meeting, and run him out of town for bringing some crazy, new religion to our city. A wonderful thing happened that night. Instead of attacking the preacher, I listened to him, and found out he really had what I was looking for all my life. That is the night I gave my life to Christ."

Frank wondered why his dad would pick this day and this time, just a few minutes before the wedding was to begin to tell him these details. Kaz turned, and with one statement brought the entire scenario together,

"The preacher I went to drive out of town, who led me to God is the man now standing in front of you, and the man who will be your father-in-law before this day is over."

James, having never known of the plot that night, turned toward Kaz and inquired,

"You came to run me out of town that night? What were you going to do?"

"Ah! We had a basket of rotten tomatoes, and we were going to smash you good!"

For a moment the two men stood in stark silence, staring at each other while Frank, Elmer, and James Junior awaited the next sound. It took only seconds before Pastor James broke into hilarious laughter, and Kaz began to shake and wheeze out heaves of asthmatic laughs. After a time of uproarious chortle, things settled again. Both fathers had removed their spectacles, and were wiping away the joyous tears of laughter from the corner of their eyes. Kaz turned again toward the quiet, head-shaking groom, and said to his son,

"For love of Mike, Frank, it looks like God was already thinking about you and Opal on the night he was saving me."

****

Within a short time, Frank and Opal were blessed with a family of their own. One little boy, then two, so close in age like Johnny and Franky had been, and just as lively. Opal's boys would bear the names of the original dynamic duo. Her firstborn was Frank Jr, and her second, John, whom they called Buddy.

The custom of many American families of that time was for new parents to use last names of family friends to give their children as middle names. Little Frank would be called by the family, Manson, the last name of an ancient acquaintance of Opal's side of the family. Frank Jr. would actually be the third generation to carry Manson as a middle name. Although their second child was named John, during the time that Opal was pregnant with this child, they would often tell Frank Jr. he would soon have a little buddy to play with. After John arrived, Buddy became the name he would carry. Later, it was shortened to just Bud.

By the time Frank and Opal were fully engaged in raising these boys, the Great Depression was declared a thing of the past, and America was again on the move toward economic recovery. The evidence of this may have reached this young family to some degree. There was work again in more places, and Frank had even followed his grandfathers and father to the box car factory. The reality though, was that this growing family was still barely scratching out an existence. There was simply not enough money to properly house, clothe, feed, and care for a family of this size in a manner that would insure a hopeful future for any of them. Housing consisted of inferior rentals with, at best some form of shelter. But they made the best of it with an attempt at cleanliness, moderate food supply, and loving support. The two mainstays were that Frank and Opal would do all to secure their love for their children, and were ever committed in their personal trust in their God.

While Opal dreamed of better conditions for her family, she prayed that something would come along that would make her children's future better than their present. The greatest challenge with having small boys was protecting them, and maintaining their health. There would be no extra money to keep them healthy by means of regular doctor visits or medicines. Opal knew that if a disease, injury, or malady of any kind were to touch her husband, herself, or her boys, it would take a supernatural miracle to produce a recovery.

What she could not know at the time was the word "miracle" would often come to be the only means available in times of need. Neither could she have envisioned that the word "miracle" would become the one word that would best describe and define their lives. As a longtime family friend would one day reflect on her relationship with this humble family,

"Anyone who has never witnessed a true miracle has just never known the Pawlaks."

****

"He's not breathing, Frank! He's not breathing! Can't you do something?"

Opal's frantic cry pierced the fuel-oil aroma of the small upstairs apartment, while the wind and snow outside produced that howling sound that only a Lake Michigan January can orchestrate.

"For God's sake, he is not moving, and he's turning blue!"

Frank's panic laden voice shouted as he thrust his huge hands around both sides of their eighteen month old little Buddy. It had been over a solid week of sleepless nights for the entire household. No one remembered such an epidemic of infant croup for many years. The home remedies were of no avail. Vaporizers ran day and night. Every known menthol rub was regularly applied. Frank and Opal had even been persuaded by the "Old Country" immigrants to use the "Grippe cure" practiced back in Poland.

This procedure involved a lighted candle and a small juice-sized glass. The glass would be held over the candle flame until filled with heat. The heated glass would be quickly pressed to the patient's, or you could say, victim's chest and held until the vacuum would suck the skin upward toward the uncomfortable source of heat. This action would then be repeated several times in different areas of the chest and back. Each application would produce an inflammation mark under the surface of the skin in the shape of the glass's mouth. A better description of the purple discoloration would simply be to say the body received several hickeys. It was believed that this actually pulled sickness out of the lungs and bronchial areas. Part of the cure was to keep the patient indoors until the hickeys all disappeared. Usually about two weeks. The old-timers swore that it was the cure of the grippe, which was the old country word for any form of influenza.

Buddy had been so infected with this respiratory malady that he would go into uncontrol-lable, croupy, coughing fits. Night after night he would literally hold the rails of his baby bed and jump up and down in breathless coughing fits until he would nearly pass out. The most painful part for Frank and Opal was that these home remedies were the only course of action possible for their second child. The fact was, there were other medicines, doctors available, and even hospital care available but not for young couples like Frank and Opal. Painfully, the truth was there was no money left after bare existence for any such luxury. There was an additional challenge; an ever-present philosophy and practice within their realm of religious belief. Because these new Pentecostal believers had witnessed many amazing, and what they called, super-natural phenomenon, a fervent part of their teaching was that if you had enough faith in God, you would not need to trust modern medicine.

In Frank's and Opal's case, however, it was most likely their desire to adhere to the teachings of the church, and please their parents that would espouse this anti-medicine faith practice. It was much easier to proclaim the faith stand than admit to the financial incapacity. Either way, the result was the same. It was not uncommon to hear young parents in these circumstances express phrases like,

"Our Buddy was so sick, and ran such a high fever for the past two weeks that we were afraid we might have to take him to a doctor."

As Frank held his non-breathing, blue faced, large for his age, baby in both hands, Opal exclaimed,

"I will boil some water! Bring him to the kitchen so we can put him over the steam."

Frank desperately shouted back, "He will be dead before the water boils." With a panicked sense of rising hopelessness, Frank barked out an order like an Army General taking the highest, and most fortified mountain of the battle,

"All we can do is pray!"

Those capable hands and arms that had often stretched above the outfield walls to steal a sure home run from an opponent's bat, and those same huge hands that had rolled out the dough that would feed hundreds of men in the CCC Camp in California, would now raise a suffocating child above his head, almost touching the low, apartment ceiling. Frank's voice bellowed upward as if to force it through the very roof. Opal sank to her knees at his side, and began to sob as any mother would, watching her child die before her eyes.

"Oh, Lord!" Frank desperately shouted upward, "This is your child, not just ours. You gave him life, please do not take him from us. There is nothing too hard for you, Lord. Please touch our child. Please, Lord, heal him now. We can't do anything else!"

Almost in perfect unison with Frank's final words, the sound of a deep suction was heard. Frank stopped praying, holding the child at arm's length in front of himself. Opal silenced her wailing cry and looked upward. Then they heard it. A cough, followed by a gasp for air, and then the most precious sound they had ever heard in their lives, the screaming cry of an angry and frustrated eighteen month old. Within a few minutes the screaming baby tired, silenced his crying, as Frank gently laid the sleeping child back into the bed. Buddy slept the rest of the night, which had not happened for two weeks. That night, there was never another cough, and the child awoke the next day with no evidence of the croup. Their Buddy was totally well, and robustly running the apartment floors as if he'd never known a sick day in his life. Frank and Opal had no idea that frightening night, that this was just the first of an almost innumerable amount of events, over many years, that would have no other explanation than the, often misunderstood, and misused term, MIRACLE.

****

Frank Manson was three and a half, and Buddy was two years old when Frank and Opal found themselves expecting their third child. Opal told her sisters,

"Maybe we will get a little girl to go along with this matched set of more than energetic boys."

However, when their new arrival came into this world during a ferocious, February blizzard, the word spread quickly through the family,

"Frank and Opal have had their third boy."

The pregnancy and the delivery seemed to be without any exceptional abnormalities. Although the new boy, named for Opal's younger brother, was a normal-sized child at birth, the next few years would hear him often referred to as "Little Freddy." A name tag he would come to resent, and enough motivation to prove himself just as big, capable, and athletic has his two oversized, older brothers. In spite of the fact that all was well with this new, little addition to the family, within a couple days of Fred's birth, Opal began to run an unusually high fever. Over the next twenty-four hours her condition went from serious to critical.

A serious urinary tract infection, kidney blockage, and a septic condition found Opal in the intensive care unit of the hospital. The alarmed doctors explained to Frank that if her condition did not make a quick and remarkable turnaround, her organs would soon begin to fail, and she would be too weak in her post-delivery state to live. Opal appeared to be in a comatose state, but what others did not learn until later was that Opal was conscious, and she could hear every word, including the grim predictions of the doctors.

"God," Opal silently cried from somewhere deep in her motionless body. "I trust you with my life. Now God, please trust me with the three boys you have given Frank and me." She continued her breathless, voiceless, and motionless plea, "I make you a promise today. If you will let me live and raise these three boys, they will be raised for you, and they will hear of your love and power everyday of their lives."

Frank left the side of his suffering wife, returned home to relieve his sister's care of his two older boys. After reading some scripture, he finally slept a few hours.

****

The morning was still dark, bitter, and cold, stinging Frank's large nose. The only thing his ears heard in the quietness was the frozen crunch of each step he made in the snow-covered sidewalk leading to the front door of the hospital.

"Pardon me, nurse," Frank softly spoke, not wanting to wake any nearby patients. "Would it be possible to get into the intensive care unit to see my wife? I have to be at the factory early and I wanted to check on her."

"I think we can do that, Sir," the nurse on duty whispered in his direction. "What is your wife's name again?"

"Pawlak, Opal Pawlak." Frank whispered back even a little more quietly.

"Frank, are you looking for me?" A strong voice came from a couple doors away. "I'm down here, Frank," the recognizable voice came again.

The kind nurse simply smiled at Frank's startled and confused eyes, motioned her palm upward and extended her arm in the general direction of the voice from the hall as if to say,

"You may proceed, Sir. She's all yours now."

As Frank slowly shuffled his galoshes-covered boots along the wooden floor of the hallway, the words were already forming, and pushing their way toward his gaping mouth,

"What happened to you? Opal, what's going on?"

Before she could utter another word he felt it. He had not felt this sensation in his body since that night he was shaken awake in his bedroom with Johnny. There was no light, no aura, no music, no angels, but there was something in that room. It was only he and his wife standing beside that hospital bed. There was only a dim light from a small lamp in the corner. But there was a presence, a power or an unseen force. It was almost like an invisible person was there with them. Opal reached for both of his huge hands. She held them to one side of her face and said,

"Oh, Frank, sometime in the night a man came to my bed in that other unit. I thought it was a doctor or worker, but he took my hand from my side, and said,

"Opal, you can get up now." Tears streamed as she continued, "After I stood up he simply walked out of the room. Then, the nurses came in, laid me back down and began to work on me. Ten minutes ago, they moved me to this room, and I heard you say my name."

Frank returned to the nurse's station and asked,

"What is going on with my wife?"

"Well Mr. Pawlak, we're not sure, but she has no fever. She just woke up and she seems very well." she responded. "We called the doctor, and he said he wants to run more tests, first thing in the morning. That is really all I can tell you now."

Frank and Opal held each other tightly, and assured each other that something amazing was truly happening. Frank went off to work, and Opal went off to the Lab for testing. After a few more days of observing, both Opal and the new baby, Frank arrived at her room. Her bag was packed, Freddy was securely wrapped for the cold trip home to meet his brothers, and release papers were in her hand. She simply had one thing to say.

"Frank, let's go home and raise these three boys."

Frank agreed, "Let's go home and raise them for God."

On their way home, Frank posed one more question,

"Hey, what did the doctor ever say he believed happened to you?"

Opal smiled, cuddled her beautiful new boy, gazed out the window of the car, turned her eyes up toward the clear, cold, winter sky, and replied,

"Oh, he said he had no explanation. His exact words were, 'It could have been nothing other than a MIRACLE.'"

****

The Pawlak home was a little noisier, and considerably more crowded with three boys at play. And though, formally named Frank Jr., John, and Fred, among the siblings, aunts, uncles, cousins, and close friends, they would be referred to for life as Manson, Bud, and Freddy.

Grandpa Kaz, however, quickly adopted an identification for his trio of grandsons that served as terms of endearment, and perhaps a little prophetic glimpse into the future. He would often approach this threesome of super-active, and undeniably Polish looking lads with his own selected names. Briskly rubbing their extremely, blond, tow heads, and declare, in his somewhat broken English,

"Manson the meanest, Buddy the Bum, and Freddy the best of a Joe."

Opal's father, James, would come to realize that pastoring both the Michigan City, and nearby Chesterton congregations had become an overwhelming responsibility. This was especially true in light of the fact that neither congregation was capable of financially supporting a pastor. Different from the older, and more traditional denominational churches, with large, national organizations that could support pastors, these new, upstart church groups depended fully on bi-vocational leadership. James was not only pressed for time in his pastoral duties, while working secular jobs, everything from wallpaper jobs to mobile sales routes, he also held a strong conviction that his call was to be a pioneer in religious enterprise. He held the personal conviction that he was to go to communities that did not have a Pentecostal believing church, and create one. He followed this pattern the rest of his pastoral career. As a matter of fact, when a church grew strong enough to financially support him, he took this as a signal it was time to move on and start a new church in a new place.

The next couple pastors at the Michigan City church were able to grow the membership to the point they were able to move from the 10th Street, wood-structured building, into a large auditorium on the main street of the city. The same Franklin Street that Kaz and his mother Anna had traversed the night Uncle Marek carried them toward Otis in his horse-drawn wagon, would be the site for the family's chosen place of worship.

Kaz would stand outside the front of the church, known previously as the "old Uptown Theater," and study the beautiful electric streetlights. He would wonder at the changes in this same block of the city where he had seen those first street lighters as an eight-year-old immigrant.

The Sunday service had long ended, and still there was a large percentage of the congregants in the auditorium that morning. One attraction of this type of church was the relationship building, and genuine friendliness that was enjoyed before and after each service. Adding to the unhurried behavior of the congregation was the fact that this early December morning was already snowy and cold, and no one was in a rush to get to their cars, or walk the cold streets home. Especially, since the city bus system did not run on Sundays.

Manson and Buddy had already been in and out of the building several times that morning to play a few minutes in the new snow. Upon one of their returns inside for warmth, Frank heard the strong voice of the Pastor call the attention of the remaining members.

"Quiet, Manson. Pastor is saying something. Listen, listen." was the admonition from his father, Frank Sr.

Opal gathered Buddy next to her side, and held Freddy, partially wrapped in baby blankets for their trek home.

"Folks, I have some very serious and disturbing news to share with you before you leave today." The room quickly quieted as every ear was fixed on the pastor's every word. After a short pause, and deep breath he continued. "We have just received word over the radio that the Japanese have attacked our Naval base at Pearl Harbor, Hawaii. The attack is happening at this very time as it is early morning there in Pearl Harbor." He continued to explain as much as possible that reports were early, and still unverified, but it appeared our forces were suffering terrible losses. At which he projected, "If this is actually happening, it means America will have been attacked and newscasts are predicting that President Roosevelt will have no alternative but to declare war on Japan, and probably Germany too. As much as we have tried, we will not be able to stay out of this War. It looks like the world will be at war for the second time."

The pastor asked the quieted and awed audience to stop for a moment, and pray for the victims of the tragedy unfolding in Hawaii. After the Prayer, Frank and Opal gathered their boys, and began the long, cold, walk down Franklin Street. No one said a word, not even those passing by on the street until Manson looked up to his father who was holding his gloved hand and said, in a sweet five-year-old voice,

"Pearl Harbor sure sounds like a pretty place."

Frank and Opal, like almost every family in America, placed the Stewart Warner tube radio in the middle of the round wooden kitchen table that afternoon. The radio would only be turned off a few hours at night through most of the rest of that week. Even after the boys were fast asleep, the glow of the tall glass tubes shining through the slots on the hard cardboard cover over the back of the radio would leave an eerie glow in the darkened kitchen. The accompaniment of the winter winds, howling through the poorly insulated apartment, spoke an ominous warning of dreadful days ahead for an entire nation. The wood framed radio would declare some of the most memorable proclamations in the history of this advanced, young empire called America.

"On this day, December 7, 1941, a date which will live in infamy..." would be words, so embedded in the memory of this generation of Americans that it would take future generations and future disasters to replace its power. President Roosevelt would ask the joint Houses of Congress to ratify his privilege as Commander in Chief, to declare war on the Empire of Japan and the nation of Germany, and all their Axis cooperatives under the command of Adolph Hitler, and the advancing Nazi powers. This first generation of American Immigrants would hear the clarion call for all young, able-bodied Americans to prepare for the reprioritization of their lives, professions, and even their families, as necessary.

Over the next several months these families of industrial manufacturing workers would see their places of employment fall into the Government's hands. They would suddenly see work centers like Pullman Box Car Factory, and many others, redesigned to produce whatever the nation was going to deem necessary to supply and equip the formation of the most powerful military history ever witnessed. This meant box cars would now be produced solely as equipment and weapon transport for the war. The steel mills, automobile assembly lines, rubber plants, petroleum centers, ship builders, airplane manufacturers, and every supporting, off-shoot enterprise would be reconfigured into what would be commonly known as "The War Effort."

Suddenly across America new plants would be erected and thousands of new workers were employed for an entirely new, manufacturing enterprise; Ordinance. It was a rather benign word that sounded less threatening, and certainly less realistic to words like bombs, grenades, cannons, shells, bullets, guns, and torpedoes.

Perhaps the greatest domestic change to the American cultural structure would be that women, moms, grandmothers, and wives would soon be called upon to remove themselves from the traditional role of stay-at-home caregivers. They would be encouraged that they, too, had a major role in defeating the evil powers of dictatorship, and protecting the freedoms that only a free democracy could provide. By the hundreds of thousands, American women entered the workforce, and not just in the typical clerical or service industries. Homemakers would now be replacing the many vacancies left in the heavy industry by the absence of their husbands, brothers, and male friends. Men from every walk of life were snatched away by draft or volunteerism. They were assigned to previously unheard of locations in North Africa, Sicily, Italy, France, Belgium, Germany, Bataan, Iwo Jima, Marshall Islands, Okinawa, and hundreds of barely pronounceable locales, which could not be located on a Geography classroom map.

This Second World War in less than twenty-five years would also require personal sacrifices and adjustment to everyday life. Soon, rubber tires were unavailable, gasoline was rationed, as well as food items. New clothes would have to wait. Household goods and building supplies would disappear. Electronics and appliances would be luxuries, even the wealthy could not acquire. Children's clubs and parties would be replaced with gathering drives. Parents would enlist their children to participate in paper drives, rubber drives, tin can drives. They would encourage their children to cooperate with conscientious events, gathering all the disposable products throughout town. This would be a very patriotic endeavor as this tonnage of refuse could be reproduced into every need our fighting forces would require in their battle for freedom and liberty.

Frank soon left the box car factory to work for a time at a huge ordinance plant in a small village called Kingsbury. Opal would even work there from time to time when she could get help with the boys from other members of the family. But eventually, the demand for more box cars to the war effort would build the employee force to astounding numbers at Pullman Standard Company, and Frank would return there the duration of the war.

****

"Someone is at the door." Kaz called from the back porch of the little house on Kentucky street.

"I hear it, I hear it, Ed." Mary hollered back as she dropped the bedspread she was arranging on Johnny's bed that morning. She thought to herself, "That man is going to drive me crazy being around the house all day, barking out orders to me."

It had been almost a year since the box car factory had told Kaz he could not work there anymore. The factory doctors made it very clear that those fainting spells and breathing problems, as well as those outbreaks of sweating and weakness were associated with an obvious malady in his heart. It was just too dangerous for him to work in those conditions. It did not help that the management was getting less sympathetic to his lack of production caused by the longer and longer periods of recovery required before returning to his duties. They simply retired him out of the factory, arranged some small stipend of monthly support, and assured him nearly forty years of those conditions had taken its toll on his body, aged far above his fifty-four years.

Mary was nagging Kaz each day to find something he could do to fill his time, away from the house preferably. He did his best to oblige. Often he would take Manson and Buddy on their bikes to fish at the pier. The boys were always a little beset when Kaz had to stop and rest frequently on their expedition. He would sit for a few minutes on a business stoop along Franklin Street, reach in his shirt pocket, and slip a little white pill into his mouth.

"Hey, give me a piece of that candy." Buddy insisted.

"No. You can't have this candy, Bud. This is old man's candy. It is not for little boys."

The explanation was neither understandable nor satisfactory to such a little guy, but he would soon forget the fuss when Kaz would take a deep breath, feel the effects of the little nitro tablet under his tongue, grab the long cane fishing pole, and resume the journey toward what would be an exciting fish kill.

"Mamie!" Mary squealed like a young girl upon opening the front door. "What are you doing here this time of the day?" Seeing Emil at the bottom step behind her beloved friend, she quickly enquired, "Emil, how is it that you are not working today?" Before either could answer, Mary noticed the rather solemn look on their faces. "Here, here. Come in quickly, both of you."

She was closing the door behind them as she called in the direction of the back porch,

"Ed, come in here. Emil and Mamie have come!" She called in such a high pitched tone, Kaz not fully understanding what she said due to the hearing loss that only a factory can produce, assumed she must have injured herself in some manner. He came bursting through the door, seeing his old friend standing with hat in hand squarely in the middle of the front room. Kaz proclaimed his usual,

"Well, for love of Mike! Look who found his way to his old pal's house." Then pumping his hand as vigorously as the night they dedicated the new bandstand all those years ago, he quickly asked the same question as Mary.

"What the heck are you doing out of work at this time of the day?"

Emil and Mamie sat down slowly on the sofa, as per Mary's and Kaz's hand gestures. Emil softly explained the purpose of their unexpected visit.

"Well you see, Mamie felt like we should come talk to you about something that has her pretty upset." Emil continued, "To tell you the truth, I'm not really happy about this whole thing myself."

"What? What is it?" Kaz inquired.

Mamie moved her small, lace handkerchief, which had been neatly folded in her gloved hand and began to weep, the silent kind of crying that tears out your heart. Emil finally said it all in one phrase,

"Our Kenneth enlisted in the Navy today."

Mary reached out for Mamie's other hand.

"Oh, my dear!" except this time Mary said it in her native, Polish tongue, and her own Americanized version of, "Oh my goodness!" which the family knew, only too well.

"Whoa, je oh cochani!"

Mamie burst out in anguish, "Why would he do this? It is too dangerous. He could get killed!"

Emil reached his arm about the shoulders of his pitiful wife, and pulled her closer to his huge chest. He began the impossible task of consoling her, while moving his eyes from Mary to Kaz as if to appeal for help.

"I told her as a young, single, healthy man he would most likely be drafted into the Army anyway, and he wanted to beat them to the draw, and go in the Navy." He continued, "Besides, on a ship he will be much safer than on the ground, should there be any fighting stuff that goes on."

Kaz interrupted, "Hey, Kenny is so smart, he won't see no fighting. They will make some kind of big shot out of him, and he probably will spend his time in some big office somewhere, making plans."

"You know, Ed may be right." Mary quickly inserted, "I saw that article in the paper about him graduating from High school and that picture with all those smart kids."

Emil, Kaz, and Mary continued to trade alternative possibilities to Mamie's fear-filled distress for several minutes. Then, Kaz said,

"Let me make us some tea. Maybe with it being so warm outside, I will make some of that new iced tea that those hillbillies at Pullman's were always drinking from their jugs. It's real good and sweet."

Mary confessed to Emil and Mamie that they were also very worried about Johnny and Eddie being drafted into this War thing.

"I know a lot of the boys and some of the girls ran right down and signed up for the service after Pearl Harbor, but we explained to the boys that if they wait this whole thing might be over quick. Then, maybe the draft will take the guys not working first.

Kaz explained, "I told them that the Army might go by the alphabet. You know, A first. And with their name starting with a P they might not get that far. Anyway, we hope not."

After they finished the cool tea, Mamie's emotions seemed much more under control. Kaz and Mary walked them down the front, and somewhat rickety porch stairs. Neither couple had any idea that Johnny's friend, the Pohl's son would not find himself in the safety and comforts of a front office, but rather the cramped and volatile confines that cradled the firm body, strong hands and accurate eyes of a brave young tail-gunner. He would fly amongst the fiercest onslaught of the Japanese Kamikaze attacks over the blue waters of the South Pacific.

Even though the military draft would not be conducted according to Kaz's possible reason, Johnny and Eddie continued working their jobs, while warily watching more and more of their friends and workmates receive the letter with the greeting,

"Your Nation is in need of your service."

Frank was pretty safe being thirty years old when the War Began for America. And having those three boys also placed him even further down the list of considerations for active service. The practice of seeing more and more of their community youngsters pressed into the obvious expansion of the War, was made more sobering by the newspaper's daily list of those wounded, missing, or killed in action. Funerals and long trips to the cemetery happened with increasing frequency. Immigrant parents were being seen more often at the side of their first-generation, American sons, as flags were folded, and Taps played its mournful sound. For many others the relief for those parents whose soldiers returned home was short lived. It was but small consolation to the horrible, life-changing physical and emotional wounds that brought them home, totally different men than they had sent away.

Johnny's mouth became noticeably dry as his fingernail pulled open the end of the envelope seal, and his massive thumb slid the length of the flap. The three fold letter, one sheet, pink in color, was slowly opened. The upper left corner of the page had a small, square , printed box. Inside the box at a severe angle was a date that had been rapidly and haphazardly stamped in red, as well as a somewhat smeared court stamp. On the right corner was a printed line with a handwritten date above, and the words, "Date of Entry." Fixed squarely in the center of the page's heading was the colorful circle with the words, "SEAL OF THE PRESIDENT." Centered below, and in extra dark ink were printed the dreaded words, "ORDER TO REPORT FOR INDUCTION." The thirty-two year old strong man, with no wife or child found no need to read past the first line. He knew what the rest of it said, and he knew well what it would mean for his immediate future. Johnny quickly scanned the next dozen lines.

To John Pawlak
Order # 38749

Greetings,

Having submitted yourself to a local board composed of your neighbors for the purpose of determining your availability for training and service in the armed forces of the United States, you are hereby notified that you have been selected for training and service in the Army.

A few more words detailed the time and place to report, followed by a simple signature of the Director of the local draft board.

John had remained a civilian for the better part of fifteen months following the Pearl Harbor attack. Eddie's notice would come only a few months after Johnny's, but what they knew so well was that voluntary entrance into any branch of the service would not just be joining the Army, Navy, Army Air Corp,(later to be renamed the Air force), Marines, Coast Guard, or Merchant Marines. It would mean you were heading to the true battle fields erupting throughout the World.

Johnny was quickly placed with the infantry. His childhood training as a hunter and excellent marksman made him a prime candidate to be placed on the front lines. Eddie pursued a different track. His love for heights, planes, and adventure placed him right in the middle of one of the largest paratrooper outfits the Army would ever develop.

Within days of receiving his draft notice, Johnny was thrown in the rigors of Basic Training. This training had no theme, but prepare to kill, or die. After a fast six weeks of what John thought was physical Hell, even for someone as well conditioned as he was, he found himself on the lower decks of a huge Naval vessel. This massive ship was built solely for transport of American Military Personnel, heading to places across the ocean where awaited a world at war.

"Johnny, Johnny!" several new friends from the boot camp yelled down the hatch over John's head, "It's the Statue of Liberty, John! You gotta come up and see her."

John had seen pictures in school books of the famous Lady in New York Harbor, but could not imagine actually looking upon this symbol of welcome to whatever freedoms and opportunities lay beyond her extended torch. As he bailed out of the attached cot, where he had been reclined for a long time getting the vessel underway, he moved with excitement toward the steps. As his foot neared the top of the step he could only imagine again the stories his father had told of running up the stairs on that cattle boat fifty years ago, as an eight-year-old boy, to see America for the first time. Just as quickly, John halted every muscle in his body. He could only see a little of the deck on this massive ship, but he could still hear the enthusiastic encouragement,

"Get up here, Pawlak! You gotta get a look at this."

To their surprise, and perhaps to his own, sullen feelings poured down upon John as if someone was pouring a barrel of cold oil from the deck. In a moment it changed his body temperature, and a chill ran up his arms where a moment ago his hands had been pulling him up the ship's stairway.   He shuddered as he thought he heard a deep, dark voice.

"You're never coming home from this." were the words that pressed hard on his breast-bone.

John knew deep in his heart he could not allow that voice to take any control on his thoughts. His mind flashed as fast and bright as the thousands of tracers he would watch stream across the battlefield skies over the next two years.

"No...this is not true!" burst out from that same pressured chest impaled by the dreaded declaration of eminent doom. To his amazement, John felt a smile break across his lips. His eyes connected with that of his requester at the top of the steps, and he confidently said,

"Naw boys, I ain't coming up there now. I want to see that old gal when she's waving me home."

With that, John stepped backward, step by step until his feet were again on the floor. He crawled back up into the bunk, and with a mixture of sounds above, engine vibrations below, and the upward and downward motions of the slow-moving, steel giant, a peace came over his mind. He whispered in the quietness to himself, "No matter how tough it gets, God is with me. I'll make it, I'll be ok."

Johnny's voyage across the Atlantic would be anything but the sea cruise he had watched on newsreels, where the wealthy booked passage on the Queen Mary. The massive waves of the Atlantic produced day upon day of violent movement and growing misery. Sea sickness was so rampant among the 1800 soldiers that most could not get out of their swinging bunks. The use of toilet facilities were basically impossible. The floors of the ship between the rows of bunks became cesspools. The feces and urine accumulated produced such horrid stench only to partner with the nausea and vomiting created by the vertical lurching of the vessel.

Not until the sea finally repealed its unkind welcome, the last day of the journey, that these, mostly unwilling passengers found out where they were going. They only knew they were not tourists, but pursuers. Nonetheless, Johnny felt some sense of relief when his staggering feet finally touched land.

It was Hot. The hottest day Johnny had ever felt in the month of May. He carried his heavy duffle bag across his back, and newly issued rifle over his massive, right shoulder. His steel helmet was as hot as a frying pan and it kept falling over his sweat-filled eyes. The heavy boots sinking deep into the hot sand dune before him, made the trudge up the hill nearly unbearable. To top it off, there were several shouting voices of command screaming angrily.

"Don't even think of stopping, Soldier until you get over that sand dune."

Johnny thought to himself, "Never have my legs hurt like this. This blasted sweat is in my eyes until I can't see."

Johnny thought, if only he could stop long enough to get a drink from that canteen on his belt...but, then he would hear among those nearly two thousand men around him,

"Move it, Soldier. Don't stop now."

At one point, Johnny did look back toward the voice behind him. Then he saw it; the shimmering ocean, its blue-green hue with that huge, grey, Navy Cruiser that had carried them to who knows where. When the last of the troops made it over the crest of the dune they were ordered to "Fall out." That is exactly what they did. Each, to a man collapsed, mostly on their backs, and without instruction thrust their hands to the water canteens at their sides.

"Hey, Soldier." came a voice to Johnny's right, "Are we in Hell?" the voice inquired. As Johnny pulled the canteen from his mouth and spurted some of the priceless liquid from his lips, he actually burst into laughter, like he had not known in several weeks.

"It can't be Hell, buddy," Johnny hollered back "because I will never go there."

"Oh, really? How is that so?" the exhausted soldier asked. Johnny quickly responded,

"Because I belong to Jesus, and He won't ever let me spend one minute in Hell."

"Well, pal," the voice shot back in Johnny's direction, "In case you didn't notice, I didn't see Jesus on the boat with us, and I got a feeling you won't find him over here in Africa, either."
He continued, "But you may see the Devil. His name is Erwin Rommel."

As Johnny drew one more swig from the canteen he realized he had never been this confused before as he whispered the words,

"Africa?, Rommel?

"On your feet, people!" the booming voice commanded from the back of a truck that had just pulled up in front of the sprawling, green-clad beings. "I bring you a welcome from your new Daddy, General George S. Patton, and he has a job for us to do. We are going on a fox hunt boys. But this ain't no fluffy, red-tailed puppy from the Shenandoah Valley, this is a 'Desert Fox!' Now, move forward."

From July through August there is hardly a hotter place on earth than the deserts of North Africa. The daytime temperatures of 115 degrees to 120 degrees Fahrenheit were the norm. A unique reality that each soldier would confront was that the night time temperatures in the desert could drop so low that one would feel the chill to the bone. Within a day or two of arriving in the desert the full force of warfare would meet these young Americans with shocking reality.

Huddled in a hastily dug foxhole in the sand, Johnny trembled with each explosion of mortar, followed by concussion, after concussion from tank fire between enemy combatants. Screaming commands came from before and behind. Rapid gunfire played a constant tune as faithful and unnerving as the drone of a Scottish bagpipe. After the first, long night of sleepless mayhem, the very hot Sun began to rise.

"Hey, Cummings." Johnny called to the nearest soldier he recognized, "It is finally quiet. Man, my ears are ringing like mad." Then a strange but calm feeling came across Johnny's thoughts, "Unless all that gunfire knocked this world around last night, that direction must be east, because the Sun is over there."

Suddenly, his ringing ears were filled with a loud and rough voice,

"Better get you a C-Ration out, boys, and eat up that great breakfast Uncle Sam gave you. Drink water, lots of water."

With face wrinkles beyond his years, the Lieutenant passed over each fox hole and repeated the encouragement, while slowly inspecting for the effect of an initial battle on each wide-eyed, and somewhat dumbfounded young man at his feet.

Johnny leaned back against the wall of the foxhole, peeled open the ration tin with the little attached key on the bottom, and delved his, considerably, dirty finger into the dog food-like mixture of mysterious meats. He consumed the contents in his usual rapid eating pace, and drank the entire canteen of water without stopping, preparing to climb out and go to the awaiting water truck to refill his canteen. As he ascended the hole and stood for a moment, stretching his legs, he took a quick visual scan of the area. He could not believe his eyes. There were vehicles burning in every direction he looked, and then something he'd never anticipated. From some of those trucks and tanks a few hundred yards away, he saw what looked like huge strips of cloth, hanging out some windows, and loosely falling down the side of some of the burning tanks. His focus cleared, and he squinted his eyes against the warming Sun. Those were not strips of cloth, they were bodies. Everything in him wanted to look away, but everything in him was moving his legs closer and faster toward the horrid scene. As he approached the carnage, the unthinkable unfolded before his eyes. Some of those limp, hanging strips of cloth began to move. Then he heard it. Moaning, crying, and screams that would embed themselves in his ears, heart, and memory for years to come.

"Hey! Hey, somebody has got to help those guys." Johnny called to all those around the area. "They are our guys!" he cried out frantically. "Come on, Come on! Somebody, we gotta get to them."

His reaction had all the emotions that panic could release when two silhouetted men came running toward him.

"Stop there, Soldier! No further, stop right there! You hear?"

Recognizing the three stripes on each of the men's upper sleeves, Johnny continued,

"But Sergeant, they need help! We have to help them!"

"Attention, Soldier!" barked back the soldier with no uncertain tone of command.

At that, Johnny stopped moving, and pulled himself together enough to stand at attention.

"Medics are on their way now, son. The best thing you can do is about face, and return to your post, immediately. Do you understand, Private?" The sergeant questioned in a strong voice that demanded an answer.

"Yes, Sergeant." Johnny's shaky voice spoke back softly.

"And where is your rifle, Mister?" snapped the Sergeant.

Johnny began to move his eyes, for the first time, off the terrible scene before him, and slowly scanned his body as if to search for his weapon.

"I must have left it at my post, Sergeant." Johnny quietly replied. He remembered from his training that there was nearly no sin so unforgivable as to be separated from your weapon in combat.

"Then, I highly recommend you return to that post and acquire your weapon immediately, before you end up like one of those poor souls you are so concerned for."

With his proper "Yes, Sergeant!" and salute, Johnny began his trek back to the security of his foxhole. After laying his rifle across his lap, he stared at the weapon for some time and wondered to himself, how long would it be until he killed his first enemy. Then a troubling thought began to walk across his spinning mind. What will it feel like to fire the weapon. He knew with such accuracy, this would not be a squirrel on a cool fall day, back home in Shocks Woods. Nor would it bring the thrill of downing a rapid, and darting, direction-changing rabbit crossing a local farmers field of harvested corn on a snowy, cold, Indiana, winter day. The somberness began to sweep over him as he reasoned with himself. Johnny had come to make most of his decisions in life based on his, ever increasing knowledge, and personal convictions found in his frequently read Bible. Deep in his heart of understanding he knew that the Bible Commandment, "Thou shall not Kill" referred to "Murder," or taking a life unjustly, or motivated by evil. But his thoughts seemed to amplify in his head, "Can I really take another life? Could I pull the trigger?"

Johnny rubbed his thick hand along the wood stock of his Army-Issue, Springfield M1 903 Bolt-action Rifle. As he lifted it from his thighs, and felt the 8.7 pounds, it actually felt more like a toy to those arms that had helped lift those 700 pound box car wheels at Pullman's. He thought of the power in his hands as he ran his fingers under the 24 inch barrel on the 43.2 inch weapon. Johnny was fully aware that the 30.03 or 30.06 Springfield shells could be delivered from that barrel at the rate of ten to fifteen rounds per minute. Each shell could travel at 2,800 feet per second. What made these facts even more sobering was that they were effective in striking their target up to three thousand feet away, and held the capability of traveling a full range of 5,500 yards, the distance of 55 football fields.
Each rifle held five rounds in its clip, and could be attached to a 25 round box magazine.

Johnny held the gun stock to his right shoulder, flipped up the rear sight, and focused with both eyes opened as his dad had taught him when he was a boy on their hunting ventures. As he peered down the top of the barrel to line up the front site with the rear, his eyes moved a few inches past the end of the gun, and there, sparkling in the morning African sunlight was the long, shining bayonet. This was a reminder to Johnny that the firing distance and power of the rifle may still not be sufficient.

The questions came again, "Can I pull that trigger and hurl that bullet through the body of a man my age, or most likely younger? Could I take the last breath of life from another mother's pride and worry? Which sound will haunt me most, the screams of my wounded and dying friends, or the screams and tears of a father and mother who receive the news that their hope and dreams just died on a battlefield, riddled with the bullets from a young American's gun? Had Pa not traveled to America a generation ago, I might have found myself on the other side of this battle."

Johnny stood to his feet, placed his helmet firmly on his head, placed his rifle over his shoulder, adjusted his dusty and wrinkled fighting uniform, and ascended again out of that foxhole in the full heat of the desert Sun.

The shade of the command tent was a welcomed relief as Johnny bent his head under the attached canopy at the front of the command post.

"Who goes there?" was the firm greeting from the MP security guard at his post.

"Private First Class, John Pawlak"

"State your business, Private." recoiled the over-officiate young MP.

"Request a meeting with the OIC, Sir."

Johnny couldn't quite decipher the strange look on the MP's face. Was it the fact that the young military policeman was only a corporal himself, might have considered responding in the usual way to being addressed so, "Don't call me sir mister, I work for a living," This common retort was meant to show the fraternal loyalty to the enlisted and drafted foot soldiers, and the mild chagrin of those college-boy officers within the tent. Holding decorum, however, he questioned Johnny further,

"And what shall I tell the officer in charge of the purpose of this visit?"

"Just tell him he has a loyal and devoted soldier that is facing a major crisis, and would appreciate just one minute of his valuable time."

To Johnny's surprise, the MP turned quickly and entered the tent behind him. Johnny quickly lowered his head and said an internal prayer, "O Lord, I need your wisdom. Please let me not get into trouble. And Lord, if possible, please let this man see me. I ask above all that you give me favor this day."

Just as quickly the MP returned and simply says three words,

"One minute only." Then he pulled the tent flap aside and Johnny stepped into a world he knew nothing about.

"Step forward, Son, and state your crisis that seems to be more important than this damn battle we find ourselves in."

Not exactly the favor he had been praying for a few seconds earlier, but he knew from this stern tone in the Major's voice he better talk fast.

"Sir, I have a crisis of conscience, and I need to make an urgent request."

"State your request private and quickly!" fired back the Major.

Johnny was a little surprised at his clarity of thought and speed of words when he said, "Sir, I would like to request to not have to carry a gun any longer in my time of service to this cause."

The Major looked up for the first time in the direction of Johnny's eyes. He slipped his dark-framed, reading glasses to the top of his head, and pushed back slightly from the layout of maps he had been studying.

"Are you a conscientious objector, Son? Because if you are, this is a Hell of a time to let us know."

Still at attention, Johnny responds, "No Sir, I do not consider myself a C.O., but I am a Christian with strong feelings, and I would never want to endanger one of my fellow soldiers, and honestly sir, I am just not sure I could kill another man, even the enemy, Sir."

"Do you understand, Private, that if I gave you permission to not carry a weapon in this battle, I would not be able to give you some safe, cushy assignment? I would have to place you somewhere even more dangerous than you are now, or my bosses would believe I was making an exception for some gutless coward that slipped in among us."

"Permission to speak Sir?" John softly fired back,

"Speak, man! Speak! This is already taking too much of my time."

"Sir, today I saw dying and wounded men that need immediate help and I was not allowed to go to their aid because it was not my job. Perhaps I would be best fitted to help our troops in some way rather than to be the aggressor you need in a soldier."

For a moment Johnny could not believe those words had come from him. He neither thought or talked with that kind of vocabulary or power of reason. He felt for a moment like one of those smart debate team kids in school was speaking, not him. For a moment he wondered if it was the Lord doing the talking for him. His thoughts were abruptly interrupted by the firm voice of the very obviously, aggravated Major.

"Hand me that rifle, Private." The Major held up one hand as if to say, "Just a moment." He wrote something on a note of paper, stamped it with an ink stamp and then while finishing his signature with one hand, he reached for John's M1 with the other hand.

For a split second, John wondered, "Is this how a dishonorable discharge and Court-Martial begins?"

The Major took the weapon, and rather disgustedly threw it against the inside wall of the tent.

"What is your name again, Private?"

"Pawlak, Sir." Johnny's shaking voice squeaked out,

"That's Polish, is it not?"

"It is sir, both my parents came from Poland." Johnny continued. At which the Major replied,

"Well, for God's sake, Mister, please don't tell that to anyone else. Just in case you are a yellow bellied, gutless wonder, my Polish grandmother would be turning over in her grave in Poland to think of a strong, scrapping, young horse like yourself, not being a brave fighting Pole like she always said her people were."

"If you don't mind sir, where in Poland does she rest?" Johnny tried to show interest, thinking he probably just stepped over the line.

"Some place called Poznan, but what is that to you?"

"Nothing sir, nothing at all." Johnny knew that if he said his family came from the same place, this warrior might issue a Court-Martial on the spot.

"Take this note, Soldier. About two hundred yards behind this compound you will see a battery of Medical vehicles. Report to the Doctor in charge and he will give you your new assignment."

As Johnny prepared to say, "Thank you, Sir." the words were cut off my one last declaration from the Major,

"Listen, Pawlak. Where I am sending you, you will wish everyday you had that gun in your hand. I would not worry too much about it, because a coward like you won't last that many days out there anyway. Now get out of my sight."

As Johnny made his way toward the trucks with the obvious red crosses on the sides, his emotions were conflicted. On one hand, he wanted to thank the Lord for receiving what appeared to him as favor. He would not have to carry a gun. On the other hand, words like gutless and coward were laying heavy across his shoulders. Was he really those things the Major had called him to his face.

The lead Doctor in charge of the Medical Unit read the little note Johnny had given him, and simply said,

"Welcome, Private. I don't know why you would want to join this group with no medical experience and all, but it looks like we are sure going to need some people like you. We are not too formal around here. There will be way too much blood and guts for that stuff. I am Captain O'Leary, but everyone just calls me Cap."

Johnny did not quite know where the strange accent came from, but he soon learned when he was told to pack the truckload of wounded soldiers, that Cap could not have hailed from anywhere but good old Boston. That evening at dinner, in an actual mess tent, Cap came by Johnny's table and started a little small talk.

"Pawlak, noticed the Polish name. You're not a New Yorker by any chance?"

"No, No," Johnny responded quickly, "I'm closer to Chicago, Indiana actually."

"Oh!" Cap shot back, "Well, I'm O'Leary. Maybe you heard of my Grandmother, her cow kicked over that lantern that burned down Chicago."

With that, the Captain threw back his head and roared out in laughter, then he slapped Johnny on the back. It was hard enough to sting, but somehow it felt like the first act of acceptance Johnny had received since his first day in the Army. What Johnny did not know was that Cap's slap on the back was a well-understood signal to anyone in the immediate area that he needed to speak privately to the subject of his inclusion. One by one, the other military medical workers began to take their trays and move toward the other end of the mess. Soon Johnny found himself and Cap alone at the table. The dialog of the meeting began with some education on Cap himself.

"Pawlak, let me tell you a little about myself. Everyone here knows I don't want to be here anymore than the rest of you poor slugs. I had a great position at Boston General, and it is still waiting for me to get back to it. I golf, and I have a paid membership at the country club. I have a wife that would knock out your eyes, and if I caught you looking at her I would knock out your other eyes, if ya know what I mean. But I was personally invited to this party by none other than the Commander in Chief, himself. Yep, FDR showed up at my office and explained that the war effort was going to need the best qualified surgeons in the field. He even told me I was the best of the best. Then I found out that lying politician told that to every surgeon he visited."

Johnny wondered to himself where this story was going, and why the Captain was even talking to a peon like him. The Captain continued,

"Little did I know that from the looks of things here, I will save very few lives. That's where you come in, my big, strong, Polak friend. We will be attacked again tonight by Rommel and his tank driving crazies. We lost big last night, and it will probably continue that way every night til we turn this tide around and run his furry little tail back to Egypt and then Germany." He continued, "Well son, you will find out tomorrow that you will serve one purpose, and one purpose only to this group. Patton wants us to account for every casualty we suffer. That means we have to find, gather, and retrieve every wounded soldier out there. We even have to account for and carry back to this compound every boy killed out there tonight, and every night til we wake up from this nightmare."

Then Johnny heard the reality of his newly appointed situation.

"Private," Cap took Johnny by the shoulders and turned him face to face, and slowly said, "The Old man thinks you are a coward. I don't know if you are or not, I don't even care if you are, but I care about those we can save, and getting the bodies of those we can't save back to their Mama and Papa so they can cry their eyes out, and start their own road to death one day at a time. "

The Surgeon Captain turned red in the face, his grip on Johnny's shoulders tightened to a squeeze, and his angry, hopeless eyes bore down on Johnny's with his final proclamation.

"You will lie in these foxholes at night and watch with amazement the greatest fireworks show you have ever seen. If it were not for the devastation it could be a great night of entertainment. Then, when the sun comes up and the shells stop falling, and the guns go silent, you come in Johnny boy."

Johnny had not heard that term since his dad used to compliment his latest stringer of perch on the pier with a,

"Hey, Johnny boy, now that's what I call fishing."

Johnny refocused on the voice before him, and the strong breath forcefully exploding against his entrapped face.

"You will hit that field each day, and you will gather those bodies. You will dodge the sniper bullets that try to prevent you from retrieving each fallen soldier. You will pay no attention to their screams, their cries for their mothers, their pleading for their wives, or their calls to their children. You will ignore their prayers for God to let them die, or their curses of any God that would allow this. You will pick up bodies that split in half in your hands. Arms and legs will fall off while you are carrying them over your big, tough shoulder. You will wash your clothes each night just to ring out your brother's blood, then you will do this all over again the next day, and the next day, until we win this battle. Then you will be sent to the next, hell on earth, place we've prepared for you."

With that, the first rounds of artillery began to announce from a distance it was evening. It would soon be dark, and the devastation would begin another long, ugly night for the future history books.

The plane door opened, and the noise of the wind was deafening as the cold chill of the night rushed right down Eddie's neck and back. He could not really see the doorway because of the twelve jumpers connected to the jump wire standing in front of him. He quickly rechecked his connection and patted down the front of his body for one last assurance that all was in place.

His mind flashed back to those days that he clung to the top of a tree limb, waving up and back, and devouring every moment of thrill that a ten year old, tree-climber could consume. For just a moment, he recalled himself lying in the pile of leaves on that cold, autumn day, with his severely broken arm throbbing beyond any pain he had ever experienced. Then it happened. He heard it just as clearly as if the paratrooper behind him had shouted it in his, helmet-covered ear, but it was his Pa's familiar voice,

"For love of Mike, Eddie!" came Kaz's familiar tone, "If you keep climbing these trees we're going to have to get you a parachute!"

Being drafted into the war didn't seem nearly as distressing to the adventurous, if not a bit cocky, party boy. This became especially true when he graduated from jump school. The idea of heights, and floating like a bird through the air, watching the ground rapidly ascend toward him, fulfilled every dangerous dream encamped in his vivid imagination. However, this felt very different. It was night. It was cold. This was not the old Snake Town neighborhood, where welcoming arms would be waiting. Here would be enemies with real weapons hoping to gain the praise of their comrades, and the reaffirmation of their own self-worth. Eddie knew one blast of a Nazi Army rifle exploding through his torso would accomplish all the above. As first jumpers began to holler, "Geronimo," and disappear at the doorway of the plane, Eddie's mind shifted to his brother, Johnny.

Like his parents, Kaz and Mary, Eddie had read the few letters John sent home. Many of them were greatly censored, with whole sentences neatly removed by a sharp pair of scissors. He knew John had been in North Africa, and then had moved to Sicily. News reels at the local theater kept the family aware that, in spite of the rugged and mountainous terrain, the U.S. forces had captured Sicily by the fall of 1943, and they assumed that Johnny was a part of the march into Italy.

Neither Eddie or his parents would have known what horrors Johnny had already experienced. The prophecy of the angry Medic Captain had been more than fulfilled in Johnny's first six months at war. The dangerous recovery of dead and wounded men, the daily bloodbath, and the heinous sights and sounds had already become the norm for Johnny. The effects of this inhumane theater had not only taken its toll on Johnny's body, displayed in a thirty pound weight loss, but his mind was beginning to suffer. Involuntary motor tics and breathing gasps would become his companions for decades to follow.

Eddie was suddenly snapped back from his mental journey as the jumper directly in front of him exited the transport vehicle. The full power of the wind blew against his face and body. Being the one standing in the door, Eddie stared out into a starless night. Dropping his sightline, he looked toward earth he could not see, in a country he could not imagine. He heard his fine tenor voice sing out a note his mother would have longed to hear him bellow from the stage of the Metropolitan Opera.

"Geronimo!" rang out through the dark Italian Sky, then silence. "It is so quiet." Eddie said to himself. Only the occasional rustle of the huge parachute far above his head could be heard. After the initial relief that the jump wire did its job in releasing the chute, he began to feel the ominous questions, "Is there anyone on that dark ground below that can see me? Am I framed within the enemy's gun site?" He began to look around to see where his fellow jumpers were. First, he scanned left, then right, and of course downward, looking for those who preceded him out. Just off to his right, he did see a short glimpse of a parachute, but then it disappeared as quickly as he spotted it. Eddie felt an unusual blast of air from his right. "What is that?" he said to himself. Another strong push of air, and he felt his body a little less vertical. Now with a strange angle for his legs, he realized he was not descending as much as he was being pushed sideways. Eddie called upon all his training, and began to pull at the control and directional cords in hopes of regaining a steady fall. The fear crept its way into his thinking. The drop zone would be somewhat assured of a clear landing with this size of intrusion behind enemy lines, but if this was some unexpected weather condition, they could all be pushed far off their intended landing target. Eddie had never experienced winds like this before, and he faced the facts this could end up very badly.
He heard his own voice, "Very bad, very bad, very bad." He was frightfully repeating over and over again.

He could not yet see land when he began a mental replay of his recent life. All the beer had tasted so good. All the songs were so much fun to sing. All the late nights and noisy parties made him feel so alive, and the girls. Oh! The girls. He loved the way they would run their fingers through his thick, blonde, wavy hair. And all he had to do was lay a few notes across those vocal cords, and every girl believed they were in the arms of Frank Sinatra, Dean Martin, and Perry Como all in one. He mused to himself, "Oh yeah, those guys were all Italian weren't they? And here I am falling into Italy."

"There it is!" He screamed, "Land below." For now, the playboy crooner felt a little less scared, but he still had a bit of consternation within.

He could see the images of some open fields intermingled with what looked like thick, wooded forests. These huge parachute contraptions were made to get you from a plane to the ground. They were certainly not the directionally controllable, lightweight apparatuses that future military sky walkers would be able to land with pin-point accuracy.

The thud was pretty hard, and the shot of burning pain made its way up each leg, and seemed to release just above Eddie's shoulders. He rolled to his side, laid there a moment as if to see if all parts of him were intact, then jumped to his feet to pursue his lines and gather his parachute. While wrapping his gatherings as fast as possible he began to spin his head from one side to the next, half looking for his fellow troupes and wearily espying for any sign of the approaching enemy.

"This is strange." Eddie whispered to himself as he realized there was in his sight, neither friend nor foe.

Once he gathered the military gear and his emotions, he quickly moved from the conspicuously open field to the nearby thick Italian forest. It was after a good hour of hiding within the woods, checking his ammo and gun, and eating a quick food ration that he finally began a long slow draw on his water canteen. As he leaned his head far back for the drink he saw from the bottom of his slightly opened eye lids the lightened eastern horizon. After another hour of stillness and intense listening for any sound of familiarity, he finally uttered the words,

"Oh my God in heaven, I am alone." Then he leaned back against a huge, white-skinned, birch tree, and with a little emotion in his voice whispered, "Dear Jesus, I am lost in an enemy's land."

A moment later, he heard the sound of branches cracking, the low hum of voices and the movement of what had to be a sizable group, advancing toward his direction. Eddie ran a few feet when he heard it, the gruff voice to his right,

"HALT!" Then another voice, "Stoppen Sie!"

****

After taking the mail out of the box and starting toward the porch, Kaz leafed through the several items in that day's delivery. When he came to the long, business sized envelope, he was surprised to see the U.S. Army seal in the return address corner of the envelope. At the top step, Kaz noticed how perfectly balanced Mary had hung the decorative star flags in the window. It was with pride that any passerby would know from those little banners that this household had two sons fighting for the cause of freedom with our forces somewhere in the world. Kaz turned at the top step, and sat down on the worn, uneven platform of the porch, he drew from his upper shirt pocket his eye glasses, and placed them on the bridge of his large nose. The words seemed so formal as it began with the salutation,

"To the parents of Private Edward Pawlak" and then it had Eddie's Military I.D. number, and a darkened photocopy of his dog tag. The letter read,

It is with sincere regret that we inform you that your son, Private Edward Pawlak is presently MISSING IN ACTION.

The letter went on to explain that the Army was making every effort to locate their son and would keep them notified of any progress in that endeavor. Then the letter thanked them for their son's dedication and assured them of the President's hopes and prayers for a positive outcome in this situation.

As Kaz slowly rose to his feet, he felt the familiar rise in his heartbeat. His mouth was too dry to even think of slipping a nitro under his tongue. He removed his glasses, dropping the rest of the mail on the porch, and with glasses in one hand and the letter in the other he proceeded into the house. "How will I tell her this now?" he thought.

She had been so depressed lately. Seeing both her boys go to the war, and having buried both her parents, this was almost more than any woman could bear.

"Mary." Kaz called out in an unusually quiet tone for him.

Coming from the kitchen with the dish towel still in her hands as she had been finishing the last dishes from breakfast. She responded seriously,

"What is it Ed? What's wrong?"

Kaz held up the letter and tapped it with his glasses several times and said, "It's about Eddie, Ma."

With pure terrified panic, Mary cried out, "Oh, Beloved God, No! Please No!"

"Wait, Wait, Mary," Kaz reached for her folded hands at her mouth, "He may be alright, we don't know, we don't know yet."
Kaz pushed the letter toward Mary's face, "It says here he is missing, just missing."

"What does that mean, Ed? Just missing?"

"I really don't know Mary," Kaz continued, "They just don't know where he is right now, but I will go talk to the Army people and see what they think it means."

Mary began a rapid fire of questions with each one raising in volume, intonation, and hysterics.

"What do they mean missing? Is he lost? Why don't they know where he is? Is he wounded? Are they just not telling us the truth?" and finally screaming at the top of her voice, "Oh! Jesus, Jesus, Jesus, has he been captured?"

Mary hurled her body on the sofa, pulled the dish towel over her head, buried her face into the crocheted cushion, and repeatedly wailed two words: "My Eddie, My Eddie, My Eddie!"

CHAPTER 6 - 1943-1953

Several Months passed, and no word came as to Eddie's status. The only thing Kaz and Mary did hear was that Eddie may have been a part of a group that parachuted into Italy, but the officials could not speculate. They would only tell them that, for security reasons, they could not share details or locations. Then they would always encourage them that Eddie was still on the list of MIA.

Kaz felt at times that he was living in a strange dream. He still enjoyed his times with his several small grandchildren, and tried to put out a little garden when he could. He would see some of his old buddies from the box car factory and found his greatest solace in the occasional letter he would get from Johnny, fully engaged in the overthrow of Mussolini, and victory over the Nazi powers In Italy.

Kaz received most of his comfort through his faithful attendance at church. He loved the church and church family, and they in turn loved him dearly. As the difficult Christmas of 1943 was approaching, Kaz had another challenge added to his deeply troubled life. His dear mother Anna had begun to fail in health, and that, rather rapidly. Her weak heart, limited mobility, and solemn withdrawal from the family reached its deepest level when she suffered a serious stroke.

Kaz spent as much time as he could at his mother's bedside. Although she was paralyzed on one side of her body, and appeared almost comatose to those who would visit, they still would bring the great-grandchildren to see her.

Frank and Opal's eight year old, Manson, would visit and stand at the end of Anna's bed thinking how short she looked. They would tell the children to talk to her. The doctor said she could still hear them, and it might make her want to wake up. Often Anna's granddaughters Lilly, Sophie, and Helen would stand by this courageous lady's side, and they would recount the stories of her famous apple peeling days, and her wonderful dishes of bigos and pierogies. Sometimes they would look at each other, smile a little and look away as if to say, "We still will never tell the stories of our little trips to the drug store for our Babcia's special delivery."

The Sophie lamented to the others,

"If only Johnny could be here, if he could come from the war, I know Babcia would wake up for Johnny. He could speak Polish to her and I bet she would wake up."

The fact that Johnny had spent more time with Jan and Anna as a boy than he even spent with his own parents, Kaz and Mary, made Johnny's absence for Anna's last days even sadder. Sophie sat holding her Grandmother Anna's motionless and paralyzed little hand between her own hands. Anna struggled some for each breath and they did not need the doctor's report that she would not be lasting much longer. In the quietness of the room Sophie thought to herself, "What an amazing woman. What courage, to leave her husband behind, and journey with Sophie's father, an eight year old little boy, to board that ship and head to a new land to seek out a good life for her family yet to come."

Her thoughts changed as Sophie vividly reflected on the darker parts of her grandmother's life. There was the reclusive side of Anna that they never fully understood. The aloneness she seemed to prefer as she aged, the secret drinking that was not so easily hidden as time moved forward, or the distance in her eyes even when trying to converse with her. So often it was like she was in another place or another time. This granddaughter was feeling so alone herself. Brothers gone to war, sister married with children, hard working job to make ends meet, and the constant care of a more and more difficult and demanding mother. These feelings seemed to help her relate empathetically with the sad, little lady that lay before her. She too knew it was of no use to bemoan her place in life, her disappointments or her absence of a romantic interest. Even so, she knew Anna was dying with an inner pain she had carried from her beloved Poland, and she would carry it to her grave. Yes, Sophie had heard the horrible story one time, and one time only. She was warned like the rest who ever heard it,

"Do not ever repeat this story! Forget about it. There is nothing that can ever be done, so it is not worth telling. Let it die with your grandparents."

So it would be, the story, behind the story, of why the Pawlaks came to America would disappear with the last painful and sorrowful breath that Anna Pawlak would draw that day. It would remain untold for almost seventy years, when Sophie felt in the closing days of her life it would be safe to share at last.

****

Jan and Anna did not come to America just because they heard of a wonderful land of opportunity. The facts were that before they had a son named Kaz, they had another son whom the family chose to never disclose his name. This son was bright and beautiful and filled with joy and zeal. He was a rather rambunctious lad at times with wit, charm, and a touch of impishness. While fully engaged in a local Catholic school, taught by a team of priests, near Poznan, his behavior, on one particular day, became an unacceptable challenge to his instructor. The teaching priest became so irritated with the boy's actions that he pulled the boy from his desk, and began to slap the boy's face.

Witnesses said the anger grew even more visible in the instructor until he began to hit the young, Pawlak lad with his fists. Finally, in total uncontrolled fury the priest removed his own shoe from his foot, and began to strike the boy in the head with the heel portion which had been equipped with the familiar steel, heel plate to insure wear resistance. After several blows blood began to pour from the young boy's head and then from his nostrils until he finally collapsed on the floor and lay silent and unconscious. He never awoke from this beating.

Jan and Anna were crushed beyond words. After burying their eldest son, Jan began to pursue answers so that those responsible would be brought to justice. He ran squarely into the power of the alliance between the government and the church of his day. Most public officials were either priests themselves, or deeply devoted to the church, and they believed that to accost or accuse the church would have personal ramifications, if not eternally damning results.

For many months he met only stone walls in every effort to bring these atrocities to light. He surprisingly found himself and his family becoming targets of ridicule and even threat. It was after all efforts had been exhausted that Jan came home one day to announce to Anna his total disdain for the church and religion. He promised he would never find the door of a religious establishment again. He also broke the news to Anna that he had contacted his old friend Marek near Chicago, and he would do whatever it took to move them, and the only son they had left, as soon as possible, to America.

****

Kaz sat at his mother Anna's funeral service. He could not help but think of the irony in his family. After his father, Jan's venomous detest of the church, he, his children, and even his grandchildren held their faith and love for God as the most important value of their lives. If ever there was an amazing paradox of faith it was from the disappointment of Jan Pawlak to the deeply embedded consecration of his eldest grandson, Johnny.

Johnny was still pulling the bodies off the frontline battle fields of Italy. Each night, during whatever quiet might afford a little sleep, Johnny would always say his prayers, on his knees, before trying to lay down in the foxhole and sleep. His sleep was always delayed by his tormentors. These now hardened, angry, and somewhat hopeless soldiers would taunt Johnny at his prayers. They would scream at him and often throw shoes or handfuls of dirt his way, cursing whatever God might be listening.

"Hey Johnny!" they bellowed. "Who ya praying to, buddy?" continuing their diatribe, "You talking to God? You really think he hears you?" With a few more expletives, and even louder voices and cynical laughter, they would insert obvious blasphemies, in hopes of making Johnny's faith a source of true ignorance and aggravating display.

"Well, your God ain't listenin' Johnny, or we wouldn't be in this Hellhole. Now, would we?"

Ironically, after Johnny would fall asleep under such a verbal onslaught, the next day's battle would seem even more intense. Stranger still, was how many of those same challengers, when struck down in battle, would make their first cry for help,

"Johnny! Johnny, help me! Johnny, pray for me! Johnny, please! Johnny, I don't want to die like this! Please, Johnny, don't let me die! Help me, Johnny! Pray, Johnny pray!"

The winter in the Italian Alps proved to be a slow and painful trudge in driving back the Nazi forces with the strange bed partners of Adolph Hitler and Benito Mussolini. As winter broke and spring began to show the first visages of green these troops had seen in many months, the fighting slowed. Mussolini had become more of a liability to Hitler than an asset. It was obvious that the Third Reich had problems arising from the east, as Russia was making the turn, which Stalin believed would happen with the engagement of America in the West.

Johnny was even getting a few letters from home, yet for some reason his letter had not gotten through to his folks in some time. It was extremely painful for Johnny to hear from his parents that Eddie was listed as MIA. What was move distressing was the months that had passed with no answer. This circumstance would most often end with confirmation of capture or death.

On June 4, 1944 the allies had totally captured Rome. Mussolini's body was hanged and viewed for days by an elated public. The best news Johnny had heard in months was that the soldiers would be given a free day to visit the historic and meaningful sights of the Roman Empire, which had once ruled the greater part of the world.

Johnny stood nearly at the top steps of the ancient ruins, as his mind tried to imagine the gladiator battles of the past on that Coliseum floor. He also thought of the horror of those who had stood for their convictions to the point of being human play toys for the ferocious lions. He questioned his own resolve as it applied to what he considered mild persecution for his faith. After leaving the ruins of the old Roman Coliseum he spied another soldier from his outfit.

"Hey, Soldier," called out the young medic, "Where are you going next?" and quickly added, "Want someone to tag along with?"

Johnny replied, "Sure, that would be swell."

With that, they extended their hands toward each other and gave the traditional, one motion, shake. Johnny queried,

"What were you going to see next?" the battle buddy, turned tourist, responded,

"I was headed toward St. Peter's. You know the Basilica." He stopped mid-phrase, pulled from his shoulder bag a small Brownie camera and continued, "If my blessed mother knew that her little Boston Irish boy, Blair Murphy stood at the altar of St. Peter's and did not get a picture, she would forget about lighting candles for ten years after I die, just so I'd spend more time in purgatory."

Johnny thought for a moment about how long it had been since he and Pa had discussed the many doctrines of the Catholic Church. Johnny soon learned that this excited Irish Medic could spout off these teachings of the church as if each were unquestionable fact. Johnny had to admit, as he ascended the steps to the church, that he was thankful that this beautiful building had not been destroyed like so many other historical structures of significance. He knew that Catholic believers held this holy site sacred. They believed it had been the Church of St. Peter. It mattered not at the time that his church affiliation was different. He was simply amazed that he would ever see something so important on the other side of the world. Both soldiers stood in awe while allowing their eyes to scan first forward and backward, then from side to side. They stared at edifice, one hundred and thirty six feet above them, almost twice the height of the Spaulding Hotel back in Johnny's Michigan City home. He wanted desperately to capture the reality of the God he believed in, being a God that saw the horrors he had witnessed. Unfortunately, the little guy with him was not the type to hold any emotions inside as he delivered to Johnny the fastest, and most complete tour guide recollection on every intricate detail of the historic structure.

"Yup, Soldier, it took one hundred twenty years and seven months to build this baby. It was amazing that it was built in a Renaissance and Baroque style of Architecture. It is two and a half football fields long and a football field and a half wide. Yeah, brother, this is what I call a church."

"Wow, that's really something." Johnny replied, not really knowing much about the words that Murphy was throwing around, like Renaissance and Baroque.

With that, the little medic started in again. This time he was throwing around names Johnny was sure he'd never heard before. If he had, he was probably daydreaming of fishing or hunting in school when his teacher was covering that stuff.

"You know, everyone knows Michelangelo but he was just a small part of this building. Bramante, Da Sangallo, Vignola, Della Porta , Maderno, Bernini, and Oh! Yeah, Carlo Fontana, all the greatest architects of the day really built this thing." Then with even more gusto he continued, "St. Peter himself, yeah the Disciple of Christ, and our first Pope is buried here."

Johnny finally forced in a question, "But where is that painting that Michelangelo did while lying on his back. I don't see it up there, or is it just too far away to see?"

Murphy turned his body directly toward Johnny, looked him straight in the face, and half laughing asked,

"How far did you go in school, mister?" Johnny sheepishly replied,

"I got almost half way through eighth grade."

"No, no, friend. That is a different place than this. Michelangelo did that in the Sistine Chapel, but it is close. Here in the Vatican, and we can go there next if you like."

After another hour of seeing the sights and listening to the medic drone on about everything he had ever learned about this pilgrimage site of his dreams, they started for the front door with all intentions of moving on to the Sistine Chapel.

"Hey, Pal, I never did get your name." Murphy vocally realized,

"Pawlak is my name. John Pawlak." Johnny quickly replied.

"Oh, great. You are Polish. So I am with a good Catholic brother today."

"Well, not really," Johnny responded.

"Well okay you're maybe not a good Catholic, but you are Catholic anyway, right?"

"No, not really." Johnny said again as they approached the porch and top step of the entrance, "But that is a long story for another time." Johnny quickly changed the subject, not feeling it necessary to get into a heavy debate with such a devoted enthusiast. "Hey Murphy, you want to get that picture for your Ma? I'll take one of you climbing the steps then I can get one of you in front of the place."

"Sure, John. That would be great." Murphy said as he handed Johnny the camera, saying something about how he had protected that little camera he won in a poker game off some Australian bloke back in North Africa.

Murphy quickly moved to the bottom of the stairs as Johnny stood on the top step, placed the camera at his belt line, and focused one eye through the little view window on top of the camera. Once he lined up his subject at the bottom of the step, Murphy placed one foot on the first step as if beginning his ascent. Johnny's big thumb slowly pressed the little, square, grey, ribbed button at the corner of the camera opposite the viewfinder, pushed it down until he heard the inner click and announced,

"There you are, Sir. You just made history."

The little medic quickly ran up the stairs to pose in front of the massive doors while Johnny ran to the bottom and repeated the same function he had performed from the top. He took a second to wind the little silver handle on the side of the camera, making sure the film had fully advanced to its next available exposure space.

"Now!" shouted the photo subject of an adoring and waiting mother back in Boston, "You come back up here, Pawlak. Put your best smile on that homely mug of yours, and let me get a picture I can show my Ma. She won't believe I saw such a strange species of animal, a non-Catholic Polak."

For some reason Johnny took off his envelope shaped uniform cap, folded it in his belt, pushed his hair up and over to the side, exposing his face. He felt like the war had moved far away for just a moment.

"Hold still now, or this picture will not be clear." ordered Murphy from about half way down the stairs.

Just as Johnny was holding still and awaiting the sound of the click on the camera, something moved in the corner of his left eye. It was a movement starting up the stairs over to one side. He tried to hold his pose, but his head moved to the left to view the photo intruder.

"You gotta hold still now, man! You moved your head, I gotta take another one." Murphy whined a bit aggravated.

Johnny was totally disengaged with the process. That body walking up the stairs, a soldier for sure. Johnny began to feel the strangest emotion. His mind whispered, "That walk is familiar. Look, how he swings his arms."

The head above those square and thin shoulders was bowed down, watching each step being taken. A crazy thought flashed through Johnny's mind, "Gee-Wiz, that kid reminds me of Eddie."Why now?" Johnny thought, "Why would Eddie come to my mind?"

Before Murphy could holler again for Johnny's attention to the photo at hand, the young soldier lifted his head to set his vision on his goal of the doors behind and to Johnny right side.

"Oh! My God in Heaven!" Johnny whispered audibly.

He saw it, that flock of blond hair under each side of that hat, and that familiar, large nose, those thick lips. His mother's lips. Before the climber even noticed the hatless soldier at the top step, Johnny bellowed to the top of his voice,

"Eddie, Eddie!" Their eyes fixed. Stunned beyond words they quickly moved toward each other.

"Johnny? Is that really you?" Eddie squealed.

They instinctively, and without hesitation did something they had never done before; they threw their arms powerfully around each other. Not since Johnny held Eddie's feverish body to his massive chest, and ran him through the streets, that cold rainy night, to get him to the hospital for that broken and infected arm, had these two brothers been in each other's embrace.

Johnny pushed Eddie to arm's length and declared,

"For love of Mike, Eddie! What are you doing here? You can't be here. Don't you know? You are Missing in Action!"

"Missing in Action?" Eddie queried. "Do I look like I'm missing in action? What the heck are you talking about?"

Murphy, thinking that his new Polish friend must have met an old buddy from boot camp or maybe even from home, ascended the steps and joined the reunion celebration.

"Hey Murphy," Johnny shouted, "Meet a ghost. This is my kid brother, and he ain't here, he's MIA."

Eddie interrupted, "Johnny, what the heck is this MIA crap you say?"

"I've been getting letters from Pa for months saying they have your butt listed as missing. Ma is nearly out of her head over it." Then Johnny settled his voice a bit and raised the overriding question at hand, "What happened? Where have you been? Are you AWOL, or what?"

By this point, Murphy was as interested in this exchange as he had been in the surroundings of the Basilica just ten minutes earlier. Eddie began to partially explain,

"I jumped into this spaghetti bowl at night. Somehow, I got separated from my entire Company. I hid out in the woods until the next morning. Then, I thought I was being captured when these German talking guys found me. But they weren't no Germans. They were a bunch of guys from the Third Marines. I moved forward with them for a couple of days and they hooked me up with an Army Infantry Brigade. The Commander of this group said he would contact my Company and let them know they had me, but would also request me to stay with them. He said they need an extra man, or a thousand. So, this Major tells me with my luck as a paratrooper, I better become an infantry man. So, we have been fighting just a click or two ahead of you guys I guess."

All three soldiers burst out in laughter and looked up and back at each other as if to say, "This is all too crazy to even believe."

Johnny broke up the hilarity with a sudden shock of reality. "Listen Eddie, we better get to the Red Cross and have them get the word home to Pa and Ma that you are fine, and that we even met up in Rome."

Murphy agreed that is what they must do immediately, and after thanking them for the amazing day, he excused himself to catch a few more sites.

Before long, Johnny and Eddie found the Red Cross tent near Johnny's encampment and told their amazing story. The worker was totally enthralled with their discovery, and he wrote down all their vital information. He assured them they will reach the center back home and have their parents notified as soon as possible. The worker also assured the boys that this is not an uncommon occurrence. With the disorganization of information that comes with the battlefield and the chaotic forms of communication, accurate information was a premium luxury not afforded on a regular basis.

What Johnny and Eddie would not know for sometime is that whoever handled the notification of Eddie's discovery was more of a journalist than a communication expert. Instead of notifying the parents, the line of communication was taken to the local Newspaper back home. Someone at the Newspaper saw an amazing print story in the unusual factors that surrounded this event. Assuming that the parents had most likely been made privy to this wonderful news, no one even contacted Kaz or Mary at the time.

Two days after the brothers' reunion in Rome, the complexion of the War would take on the most ominous shade, as the conflict climaxed to determine between the continuation of free democracy or totalitarian control. The future of the whole world hung in the balance.

****

When Frank's and Opal's fourth boy arrived within the fourth year of the War, it meant their family structure would take another, more challenging turn. Not only was Frank's income far less than a family of six required these days, but the immediate alarm was that this child had arrived on the scene, over two months prematurely. Richard arrived in this world weighing slightly above two pounds, and actually fell beneath that weight a few days of his birth.

Although new medical advances were forthcoming with the approach of the flourishing fifties, during the lean, war years, a child born with this many strikes against it seldom survived more than a few hours or days. The best the hospital could do in 1944 was to place the child in a rather crude incubator, try to keep it warm, and with the help of some intravenous liquids, hope to sustain the little life. The only thing the family could do was prepare for their loss.

Frank and Opal Pawlak were people of faith. They had witnessed events that could never be explained or defined as anything short of a miracle. So, as others were amazed, they just kept praying for their little guy, whose head could fit into a tea cup, and his body would have been fully comfortable in a shoe box. It took six full weeks, but the day finally arrived that Opal would hold her fourth son in the front seat of the borrowed car, and journey home to introduce her other boys to the fella that would be known through childhood as "Dickey."

"Frank, you have to stop at the Polish Pharmacy and get this prescription filled for the baby before we go home." Opal instructed as Frank threw his arm over the seat back to pull out on the street, behind the hospital parking lot. After finding a good close parking slot in front of the pharmacy, Frank brought the car to its vertical placement, turned off the key, pulled up the emergency parking brake, and placed his large dress hat atop his head. As he exited the car, he slammed the driver side door. He was not angry at all, it was just his firm belief that a door would be assured closed when he bit his tongue to one side of his mouth, and swung the door with the same velocity he once swung a baseball bat. Within about five minutes, Frank pulled the car door open, quickly slumped himself behind the wheel, and obviously angry, thrust the written prescription toward Opal, and announced,

"You will have to go get the baby's medicine!"

"Why? What happened in there?" Opal asked. Frank snapped back,

"Well, I handed Marszalek the prescription, and he asked me, 'Frank, how old is the child?' I answered him right back, 'He is six weeks old today.'"

"Well, that's right, Frank." Opal interjected.

"That's not the whole story!" Frank snapped back at her. "Then he said, 'Well what is the child's name?' For the love of Mike, I stood there like a fool. Six-week-old kid, my kid, and I could not even, for the life of me, remember the kid's name." Now, on a roll, Frank continued, "See if you would have let me name one of these boys, Tex, or Rex, or Tiger, I could have remembered its name."

Opal threw her head back and began to literally wheeze with laughter, and she continued until Frank finally caught the craziness of the moment. Finally, he placed his fist in front of his grinning teeth, and he began to laugh uncontrollably. Opal eventually caught her breath, and she placed a sympathetic hand on Frank's arm.

"Frank, it is totally understandable. We have not had this baby at home with us, like the other three, for six weeks. Even though we visited and spent time with him, you were just not used to using his name."

"Oh! I remember now! It's Richard something, isn't it?"

"Yes, Frank." Opal snickered, but we have been calling him little Dicky, and that is where the confusion probably came."

"Well, you still have to go in there." Frank said as he reached across the car to take the baby gently in his big hands. "What kind of Father will that Pharmacist think I am, having a six week old kid, and not even knowing its name?"

As Opal stepped out of the car, Frank could hear her still laughing until the front door of the establishment closed behind her. Frank held the tiny little guy with both hands lifting him in an up and down motion, in front of his face. His previous concerns about how they were going to feed one more mouth soon dissipated. With an odd, but loving, little sing-song tone in his voice, Frank always said a silly phrase when picking up a baby,

"Oh! They're so mean to the baby, so mean to the baby." And then, he whispered, "Thank you Lord for sparing this child. Surely you must have a plan for this little one."

Not long after Dicky's arrival, Opal's brother, James Junior, stopped by the house to see the toy-sized child. He spent a few minutes playing with the baby, then said,

"Hey Sis, you know that place where Bertha and I live out on Coolspring Ave? It's just too small for a family our size, we're going to be moving soon."

James Junior's life had been an amazing string of events, for one just twenty-four years old. His rowdy, good time, fighting, truck driving, musical adventures included marrying a young girl from his Dad's church, just barely his own age of sixteen. By now, they had five, stair-step, children of their own, and one more on the way to their eventual total of seven babies in thirteen short years. James Junior had several dubious distinctions among his many excellent talents. The better Junior was a hard working, bundle of personality. The latter could work for both worthwhile causes and personal damage. Among his talents was the ability to use his large fingers to form some of the most complicated guitar chords any musician could accomplish. His driving skills at the wheel of anything, from a gasoline tanker to a box cargo-carrying, semi rig, made him a highly sought, over the road driver. This lifestyle served a certain element of men, as the modern day, cattle-driving cowboy. Deeply embedded in this multi-gifted character, was a fun-loving, heavy-drinking, independent-thinking, hunk-of-muscle that just did not like the rules too well. And he never took a step back from anyone, like himself, who wanted to compare their manliness and ego, with a good-old-fashioned fist fight, inside or outside of any bar in town. This particular feature of his personality contributed to his entering two different branches of the military, and being kicked out of both. No one was ever able to explain how this could happen, but it did.

As James Junior held Dicky in one large hand, he did not seem at all like his rowdy reputation. Even Opal observed a sensitive, maturing man, especially when he began to share his real purpose in coming to visit.

"I wanted to let you know, I understand the downstairs apartment would be too small for you and Frank as well, but the people have moved out of the upstairs place. It has no more room than ours, but there is a sizable attic above the apartment. Most of the floor has been finished, and Frank could set up several beds there for your boys." He carefully handed the baby back to Opal and added,

"I know the previous renters were only paying fifteen bucks a month. I could talk to Old Lady Bies and see about it for you."

For a moment Opal thought it would be nice to be at the outskirts of town, with some fields and woods for the boys to roam. She then remembered the little pond back in those woods. Brinkman's, they called it, and she could almost see the boys splashing around there in the summer.

"Well, what do you think, Sis?" James Junior pressed

"It really sounds like something that might work." Opal said, "I know that would be a lot of steps with a new baby and all, but I sure will tell Frank about it when he gets home. Maybe we can come by and check it out tonight."

Manson and Buddy ran up first to the front porch and as the little Franky began to shadow box around the porch he said,

"Look Ma! This could be a great boxing ring!" Then he began to mimic a fight announcer. "Joe Lewis moves to the right, dodges a jab, and throws a left hook." The whole time he pretended to be the "Brown Bomber," the only man who held the Title of Heavyweight Champion during the entire eight years of Frank Manson's life thus far.

The three boys, Manson, Buddy, and Freddy charged through the heavy glass and wooden door to the building's entrance. They paid little attention to the straight hallway leading to the lower apartment, since they had already been there several times with their cousins. Quickly they turned to the right and overtook the initial three-step landing. Then they darted out to scramble up the long stairs, hoping to beat each other to the top.

"Hey! Slow down, boys! Don't destroy the place before we get a chance to look at it." was Frank's half-sincere admonition.

Before Opal could navigate the first few steps upward, with baby in arms, here came the boys, one after another, straddling the stairway handrail, and hollering,

"Woo hoo! Look out below!"

The next words from Opal's mouth would be barked hundreds of times over the next dozen years.

"You boys, get outside, and don't come back in here 'til I call you!"

As she stepped first into the apartment, she was not particularly excited that the entrance opened directly into the kitchen. It also did not help that the room was very drab. A worn linoleum cover spread across most of the floor space. Across the room and to the right of another doorway, sat an old sink with a tattered and dirty skirt, attempting to cover the pipework below it.

"Hey!" Frank hollered from a nearby space, "It has indoor water, and a working toilet up here. James said there is an old pump in the basement that works some of the time, but we would still have to heat the water for dishes or baths."

Holding the baby a little tighter, Opal moved to the left and noticed the nice wooden framework around the wide opening leading into the large room. She smelled the odor of kerosene fuel-oil as she entered the room, noticing the spot in the corner, where the heating stove had set during the previous winter. The thought rolled across her mind, "I bet this place gets pretty cold when the temperatures drop below freezing."

Frank was ahead of her, standing in the small bedroom off the middle room, designed to serve as a dining room, originally. Before encouraging her to come and look, Frank realized that one little, tiny closet would never hold both of their clothes, or even his alone. Opal turned the other direction to see, what would be, from that day forward, "the front room." The two windows on the North and East side of the room would offer some good breeze on the hot summer days. In the far corner of the room she spied a small doorway, covered with a, once white but now yellowing bed sheet, hung from a make-shift, wooden rod. As she pulled the sheet back she examined another little room. She thought, "Much too small for a bedroom but it may have some use." She tried her best to imagine furniture arrangements in each of the rooms, her nesting instincts inspecting this potential abode.

"I can carry the baby for you. Let's go find that upstairs place your brother talked about." Frank suggested.

At the very back of the apartment was a door, and beyond that door rose a dark, wooden stairway, walled on both sides with tattered drywall, at least until it reached the wooden floor of the attic. Evening sunlight was streaming through the very small, permanently closed windows, just under the overhang of the building's tall roof.

Frank's and Opal's thoughts could not have moved in more diametrical opposition. His first words were,

"Hey, this is pretty good. I can stand in here. Plenty of room for some beds, and with those rafters on the side we can hang a bunch of clothes. That kind of makes up for the closets down stairs."

Opal's words filled the air before Frank could draw his next breath.

"Frank, this is awful. Look. The floors don't even cover all the beams. There are only rails and insulation on that side of the room, and it stinks to high heaven." She walked toward the little window at the front and touched its little, wooden cross design. "There is no way these windows open. If the place caught on fire the boys would be trapped. No heat could get up here in the winter, and can you feel how hot it is already. Just wait until August gets here."

Frank finally countered with what sounded, at least to him, like some real answers to her concerns.

"Listen, Opal. In time we can finish the floorboards. We can change out those windows to the kind that open. Besides, with a couple extension cords hung over the rafters for lights, I can get those fixtures from Kubic's Hardware that hold both a light bulb and a plug-in thing, so we could hook up a couple fans in the summer."

"That still won't answer the heat problem in the winter." Opal responded. To which, Frank kind of rubbed the side of his head and said,

"Hey, I can put in a little coal stove right at the bottom of the stairs, keep the door opened at night, and since heat goes up it will run right up that stairway. With some good blankets they will be warm as a bug in a rug."

With a bit of a mournful sigh, she slowly said,

"This is not what I want for my boys. There has to be something better, Frank."

"Opal, for Pete's sake," Frank, slowly rocking the fussing baby, expelled a frustrated plea,

"It's only a lousy fifteen bucks a month. Where else are we going to find this much room for that amount of money. I only bring home thirty-seven lousy bucks a week, and with food and medicine, and by the time we pay our tithes you know there is nothing left."

In an effort to prevent this from breaking into one of their famous budget arguments, Frank started back down the attic stairs with a last attempt to console his angry and frustrated wife.

"...Plus the boys will love that field between here and Mrs. Bies' house. They will make some friends around the neighborhood, and I can even take them fishing or swimming back there in Brinkman's pond."

By the end of his appeal, they had returned to the back room, toilet facility at the bottom of the steps. Opal heard the explosion of voices from the dirt driveway, on the East side of the building. As she hurried across the middle room to look down from the windows, she saw not only her three boys climbing the large tree at the far side of the drive, but also a couple other, unrecognizable lads in the tree with them. She slid the window upward and opened it, and bellowed through the torn window screen,

"You boys, get out of that tree, and get yourselves up here right now. Bring your new friends with you." Then, she raised her voice to another level of emergency, as she beckoned her tow-headed three-year-old,

"Freddy, you get down from there! You are too small to climb that big tree like your brothers."

The boys came crashing through the kitchen door, a cloud of elbows, knees, and noise. Manson and Buddy attempted to head off any trouble they might have created for themselves, by clamoring above each other's voice,

"Hey Mom, this is my new friend, Jack." To which Johnny interrupted,

"And this is my new friend, Louie." Then, almost in harmony they shouted,

"They live right up the road, over there." They both pointed in a Southwardly direction. By now, Freddy had joined the clatter and announced,

"I climbed the tree!"

"Yes, little man," Opal sternly replied, "We saw you."

After telling the neighbor boys how nice it was to meet them, and reaffirming their names, and exactly which houses they lived in, Opal calmed the boys by lowering her voice. She said,

"Well boys, I guess I need to tell you something. It looks like this is going to be your new home, and we are going to be moving here very soon."

The boys began to jump up and down with Christmas-morning glee.

"Well, you boys want to run up the stairs and see where you're going to be sleeping when we move here?" Manson quickly asked,

"Can we take our new buddies up there too?"

"Sure," Opal answered as Buddy asked,

"When we get down, can we get some of those plums from those trees on the other side of the house?"

As the boys' feet rapidly thundered up those attic stairs, the entire apartment rumbled like a mild, California earthquake Frank remembered from his CCC days in the San Bernardino Mountains. Opal could imagine how much louder those stairs would echo with the growth of her sons, and their many friends and cousins in the years to come. She also had no idea the nearby plum orchard would produce some of the most effective little switches for her prominent task of raising obedient and worthwhile citizens for their city.

It was a full-grown Manson, whom Opal said was blessed with the gift of exaggeration, who would declare as fact,

"Our mother cleared out that plum orchard next door to us, by sending Bud and Me to pick out our switches for whippings every summer."

Opal always slowly raised one eyebrow, and looking them both straight in the eyes concluded,

"Well, it appears the orchard was just not big enough to get the job done completely." Laughter always followed.

But on this hot day in 1944, Frank slowly turned to Opal and said,

"We probably won't even be here long. Maybe we will find a place in the country yet."

Shortly after James Junior and Bertha moved out, Sophie moved herself and her mother, Mary into the apartment below Frank and Opal.

****

June 6, 1944 one hundred sixty thousand troops, along with 30,000 vehicles were delivered by the most massive armada of maritime vessels ever sailed. This invasion force would come ashore along a 50 mile stretch of beach in a place called Normandy, France, with one purpose. That purpose was to gain a stand on the European Continent, and begin an assault that would drive the most powerful military force in the world to date, back to the Eastern fringes of the battlefield. Provided that the powerful Allies from the East would pursue in kind, hoping the enemies of liberty would be squeezed into a box, attacked without mercy or reservation, and annihilated from its top motivator, to its last willing supporter. The names on both sides would be amongst the greatest military giants in all of history. On the side of the entrenched protectors of the intended world-conquerors, Von Rundstedt, Rommel, Von Schweppenburg, Dollman, Saimuth, and Falley. On the side of the freedom-loving invaders, and intended liberators of the captive masses, Eisenhower, Montgomery, Patton, Bradley, Dempsey, Mallory, Ramsey, and Tedder. The U.S. and her Allies would be one 150,000 strong. The awaiting Nazi forces, only 50,300. However, the smaller force would prove to be the advantaged, dug in, defensive power predicted by the designers of the planned engagement. The "D-Day Invasion" of Europe would cost the Nazi forces as little as 4,000 to 9,000 causalities, and only about 1,000 deaths could be confirmed. The Allies documented over 10,000 causalities and 4,414 dead young men, strewn on the beaches of Normandy. The U.S. led contingent would actually lose ten men for every one man the Nazis would lose on D-Day. Yet no other battle would so change the direction of a war for these Americans, since the Nation's history would be redirected on Pennsylvania farmland known as Gettysburg, some eighty years earlier.

Eddie would soon move with his Company into the South of France, and Johnny would be moved from Italy under the new command of his old Sicily boss, General George S. Patton, to Belgium, in preparation for the largest and bloodiest battle of World War II.

****

It was a cool, fall morning when Kaz stepped from the porch and slowly bent his aching back, reaching to the dew-covered grass where the daily paper rested. Now that the Nation's boys were really over there, and all Hell was fighting the rest of the U.S. Forces in the South Pacific, with the more than formidable Japanese, Kaz read the daily paper for every little detail he could garner. The first couple pages were a bit damp, and he was again frustrated that the paper boy could not seem to hurl the rolled and tightly tucked spheroid all the way to the porch. He sat as usual on the top stoop of the porch, moved quickly past the soggy headlines, figuring they would dry eventually, he planned to read them last.

Somewhere about the third page in, he saw it. Black, bold print stared him in the face. Was this a dream, a nightmare, a vision, or had he just let this war and the absence of his sons finally do some serious damage to his brain? He looked away, blinked, and then refocused on the page. But there it was, clearly:

"PAWLAK BROTHERS MEET IN ROME."

He gasped, and began to read the article faster than he had ever read anything in his life. The writer with a magical touch of adventure told how the brothers met each other on the steps of St. Peter's Basilica, at the end of the Italian campaign.

"MARY..." He howled, and bounded through the front door. "Oh, MARY!!!"

The next few days put the entire family in an almost ethereal state of comfort and joy. Just to hear and know that their two warriors were alive, and apparently safe, was a feeling beyond words to explain. The new strength of this knowledge made Kaz's and Mary's Christmas of 1944 the best they had known for some time. The kindest element of hearing of the whereabouts of their sons was that they had no present knowledge that the greatest horrors Johnny and Eddie would encounter were still ahead of them.

****

Eddie was now pushing Northward through France as part of the Montgomery-Eisenhower line from Belgium to Luxembourg. His Company would continue beyond the line in an attempt to head off the Nazi troops retreating from Normandy, and coming as a back-side support to the German troops in their attempt to penetrate the Allied lines.

"Really a cold night, eh?" Eddie directed his question to the tall, lean soldier standing to his right.

"Are you asking or sayin?" drawled out through the slightly open thin lips of the boy they just knew as "Tall." He got the name when he told how his "Gram-paw," as he would say it, often reminded him that he was "taller than a Georgia pine," the kind that grew up near their Valdosta farm. This was a story Tall had often recounted.

Eddie did not respond to his question, but turned away to watch the tracers scream through the clear night sky. "If the effects of these lights were not so devastating," Eddie thought, "and the night were not so blasted cold, this array of night splendor would be as exciting as a Fourth of July back home at Washington Park."

Eddie first heard the sound, a wet thud. Then, he sensed what felt like little pieces of rice against his cheek. As he instinctively swept the side of his face with the nearly frozen, though gloved fingers of his hand, he felt something heavy hit his lower leg almost taking him off his feet.

"What the heck?" burst from Eddie's lips as he staggered for his balance, stepped backward, and looked down to see the long twisted frame of Tall slumped in the snow.

"Tall! Tall!" Eddie shouted as he fell to his knees, rolling the Georgia country boy on his side. "Oh, my God in Heaven." trembled from Eddie's shivering lips when he saw it. Tall's face was gone, and most of the head was not there.

"Medic! Medic!" Eddie screamed to the top of his high pitched, tenor voice. He continued to holler over his shoulder for any kind of help.

"Your holes! Get to your holes!" ordered the familiar voice of the young Lieutenant, "Before we're all killed. Get in those fox holes!"

The next three nights would be exactly the same routine. While Eddie and his Company would burrow as deeply in their bunker as the frozen ground would let them dig, they would cover their individual holes with branches and limbs, more for hiding purposes and warmth than mortar shell protection. As the three to four men per bunker would crouch and often tremble, the ground around them would shake from each nearby strike. Their only hope was that the landing shell would explode in front of them or behind them. Eddie even voiced a silent prayer from within a couple times.

"Lord, please don't let my name be on one of those incoming shells."

When the night of terror would end, the Sun would rise with the welcomed relief that the shelling would cease during the daylight hours. This would be the time to eat rations, drink all the water you could get, and try to secure your bunker for the inevitable, night-long onslaught.

"Pawlak! Pawlak! Hey, where is that Polish kid, the wavy haired one?" came the graveled old voice of Sgt. Baldy Bishop.

"Here. I'm over here, Sergeant." Eddie replied.

"Well kid, get your buddies and your butts over to that truck. You're getting moved up. Get moving, soldier. There is a war going on in case you haven't noticed the last couple nights."

In a matter of seconds Eddie and the other three in his bunker ran across the field, and jumped into the back of the troop transport. Speeding down a very rough road, the cold winter wind poured down Eddie's collar. The last thirty-six hours played again in Eddie's memory. Tall's head having been blown off right beside him, sleepless nights of earth-shaking terror, and now the cold fact he was probably being moved to the front where the fighting would be even worse.

The truck pulled up to a fairly clean and peaceful camp. Eddie was pleasantly surprised to hear that the reinforcements had flanked and destroyed the attack group, whose siege they had withstood the previous nights. He and the few companions enjoyed the unexpected break from the battle, and enjoyed the rare days of mundane camp duties.

Within a couple of days the rest of the Company arrived at the camp. While stepping out of the latrine, Eddie saw Old Sgt. Baldy Bishop.

"Sarge!" Eddie hollered,

"Hey, you're that Polish kid right?" Baldy identified him, and without letting Eddie answer, he quickly continued, "Well kid, you gotta be the luckiest SOB I ever saw in my life."

"Whatcha mean, Sarge?" Eddie asked softly. Without even taking a good breath the Sergeant continued,

"After you left us, we really got hit hard that night. No one was in your bunker and the first damn shell they fired that night hit your bunker right on. Bull's eye! It blew everything to smithereens. If you guys woulda still been in that bunker, kid, there would not have been one piece of your scrawny body to even send home to Mama."

Eddie walked slowly to the tent he had been assigned. He lay down on the army cot, and stared for a long time at the green canvas ceiling. To his surprise, something hot and wet came running from the outside corners of his eyes and rapidly down across his cheeks, falling on the collar of his GI issue shirt collar.
Quietly he spoke the words,

"O.K. God, you got my attention." He thought to himself, "Why me?"

He rehearsed the fact that three times he should have been dead. The ill-fated night jump behind enemy lines, the sniper bullet 4 inches high and a little to the right that ended the life of the kid named "Tall," and now moved out of a Bunker just a few hours before what would have been his total annihilation. Before he wandered off into a deep sleep, he remembered thinking that maybe his life was being spared for a bigger reason than fun, parties, girls, and drinking. Perhaps there is something more to this God stuff that Pa and the rest of the family are so enamored by.

While Eddie was trying to make sense of all that had transpired in his life, Johnny had little time to think about anything. He struggled and was even a little amazed that he could actually get four pairs of underwear, three pairs of pants, three army tee shirts, and four shirts on his much slimmer body. Along with three pairs of socks that made his combat boots finally fit better than ever, extra gloves and caps under his helmet made him warm if not almost immobile.

General Patton had sent the word down the lines for each soldier to put all their extra clothes on, in case they were captured. The idea was they might survive prison camp conditions a few days in what would be the coldest, and most horrid winter to sweep this area in fifty years.

An eighty-five mile line had been built with Allied forces to hold off the Nazi approach from the East. This was intended to allow more forces to flank the line to the North, and actually make its first insurgence into Germany. But there were a couple huge problems. The weather was the first. August flood rains had bogged down troop and equipment movement to a crawl, then the early winter blizzards only became more fierce with each late fall and winter storm. Hitler had moved a much larger force against the line than Allied commanders had estimated. Somehow Hitler knew if he did not prevent the Allied forces from placing a foothold on German soil, he would be caught in a trap of the American advance from the West, and the Russian advance from the East. His answer was to send two hundred and fifty-thousand German fighting troops against the dreaded Allied line. It was exactly what he had hoped for. Because of the horrid weather conditions and because he forced his enemy, Hitler actually pushed the Allied line back some fifty miles between Belgium and Luxembourg. This push and weakening of the Allied forces would become known as "The Battle of the Bulge." Little could the cold, freezing, fighting soldiers on either side know that they would be part of what history recorded as the single largest battle the world had ever known, or have yet known, perhaps until a biblical Armageddon would unfold.

The German offensive moved powerfully through the forest in the Ardennes Region. From December 16, 1944 to January 25, 1945 the combatants of the United States and United Kingdom would face Nazi Germany. 610,000 Americans alone would gather for this battle. 19,000 Americans would be killed. 47,500 were wounded. 23,000 Americans were captured or missing, and nearly 800 tanks would be lost on the American side. Although Adolph Hitler was a typical analytical Austrian/German, no accurate accounting could ever document the number of German losses in the Battle of the Bulge. Estimates had guessed as high as 125,000 casualties, and over 700 tanks lost. The battle moved from village to village, and town to town. Places formerly unknown would become the most famous names of the war; Bastogne, St. Vith, Viauden, Elsenborn Ridge and Wallaria.

If Johnny thought he had seen unforgettable sights of horror in the deserts of North Africa, or the mountains of Sicily, or the fields of Italy, nothing could have prepared him for these nightmarish sights. His gunless role remained the same: get to those fallen bodies, if wounded, shelter them and get them medical help. Should they be dead, do all he could to pull, lift, or carry that body to a safe place for accounting and proper handling.

Some days of the battle, Johnny could not tell if the moisture soaking through his layers of clothes was the melted snow or the flowing blood of the young bodies he carried in his arms, or over his shoulder. It was during one of the most terrible days of slaughter that

Johnny's Commanding Officer stopped him while carrying bodies to the Red Cross trucks.

"What is your name, Soldier?" the officer asked while scanning the putrid blood mixture smeared everywhere on Johnny's uniform.

"Private First Class John Pawlak, Sir," came the answer.

"Where is your rifle, Son?" a sympathetic and soft voice asked.

"I don't carry a weapon, Sir. I carry bodies." Johnny's winded voice responded.

"Come with me, Private." ordered the Commander.

Johnny soon found himself in a Field Officer's tent. As he stood at ease in front of the small table covered with papers, the officer made an astounding statement to Johnny.

"Son, take off those bloody clothes, and put these on." As he handed Johnny a clean stack of shirts, pants and socks, he continued, "I have watched you for days now, and I have asked for your file. I see where you were placed with the Field Medic team because you asked not to carry a gun. You know, Private, we consider non-gun carriers cowards." He paused for what seemed a full minute. "But...you are no coward. In fact, you are quite the opposite. I am putting papers in for some medals, I think you deserve, but I want you alive for those medals. Then the real shocker came to the stunned Johnny, "I am moving you, Soldier. I'm giving you a new assignment."

"Moving me where, Sir?" Johnny asked somewhat confused, at which the officer continued,

"Moving you back off this line. You've seen enough, Pawlak. You've done enough. I'm moving you with another Medic Company, but you're being transferred to the dental hospital detail back in France. You have pulled enough bodies off the field. The heaviest thing you will pull from now on is a rotten molar from a screaming soldier that we need back on the line. Now, go get your things while I call a jeep to get you to your nearest travel agent."

"Sir," Johnny replied, "I am wearing everything I own to my name. I am ready to go now, Sir."

As Johnny heard his own words, he also felt something he had not felt in a long time, a little smile came across his extremely gaunt face.

A motor pool jeep soon arrived, and a PFC mechanic at the wheel swept Johnny down a frozen, dirt road in the opposite direction of the continuing explosions and gunfire. As both soldiers fought to stay in their seats and the driver did his best to avoid the huge frozen ruts that the tanks and trucks had left behind, Johnny began to think of a warm cot with blankets, a warm medical tent with lights, and the only blood to see he would personally request, as he encouraged the numbed jawed soldier to spit into a basin. Blood, spit from the crater which had previously held a throbbing cavity-riddled tooth. Johnny would soon be extracting over one hundred teeth a day. Best of all, he would be able to assure the brave one before him with words he had never used on the battlefield,

"In a couple days you will feel like a new man."

****

The home front saw little comfort in the movie house news reels or the local headlines, even though more victories were being reported daily for the U.S. cause. It was short lived joy to hear Gabriel Heater assure the American families each night across the radio waves,

"All is looking good for our fighting forces in Europe and the Pacific tonight."

The newspaper pictures of sighting German U-boats, and Kamikaze planes being blown out of the sky from the decks of U.S. destroyers brought little relief to the hearts of the parents awaiting a child's safe return to their arms. The fact remained that most families in America were still attending funeral services, and standing around freshly dug grave sites for family or friends, who's fighting hero gave their all to the cause. A few days after Christmas this, too often repeated story would come closer to Kaz and Mary than they could imagine.

Mary's body froze at the window when she saw the familiar black 1938 Hudson Terra-plane pull up in front of the house. The fedora hat rose above the roof as the Pastor of the church moved slowly around the rear of the auto, beginning his trek toward the front porch.

"Ed, Preacher is here." were the only world out of her mouth.

For a moment she tried to make herself remember he was the pastor. An occasional visit was not uncommon, especially since Kaz's heart episodes were a bit more frequent. Kaz was even missing an occasional service at the church. This was always noticeable to the pastor in as much as Kaz had a vital function of the church. It was his self-appointed position to make sure the pastor always had a fresh glass of water at his pulpit before delivering the stirring message each week. Kaz considered this his ministry calling after reading in the Bible that if you were to give someone as much as a cup of water you would not lose your reward in heaven someday. This duty was treated by Kaz with such loyalty that even the congregation held him in highest esteem for his faithful gifting. It did not always go without a challenge. None would ever forget, and generations to come would hear the story of the one occasion where Kaz was delivering the cool clear water to the front of the chapel. While ascending the platform steps he caught his toe on the last step, stumbled forward, and emptied the entire contents of his responsibility directly in the face of the pastor. After the shocking gasps from the congregation, the ability to refrain was just impossible. The whole audience, including the pastor and Kaz spent the next several minutes in uncontrolled, hilarious laughter. While Kaz apologetically wiped the pastors face and suit lapels with his best clean handkerchief, the comic relief moment provided some joyful healing in the otherwise darkness of those days.

Kaz roused from his afternoon nap in the large chair, he had none of the fearful thoughts that were rushing through Mary's head. He understood if there were any bad news concerning either boy at war, it would not be the pastor's car to arrive, but the dreaded Army green sedan, feared by most families.

They gave the pastor a gracious welcome, but Kaz and Mary could not help but see the rather sober, if not grim, expression on the pastor's face.

"Folks I have received some bad news and felt I should come here first." His voice was kindly soft as he fingered the brim of his large hat, and he continued to stare somewhere between them and the rug-covered, wooden floor.

For a moment, Mary felt her breathing stop, feeling she dare not exhale until she heard the next phrase.

"Oh my." Kaz breathed out, "What has happened?"

"Well, I know how close you are to Emil and Mamie, and I felt you should be the first to know. Their son Kenneth was shot down over the Pacific yesterday. There were no survivors, and actually, neither the wreckage, nor the bodies have been discovered. The area is too full of Japanese warships to even perform a search.

Kaz could only express a winded, "Oh!" as if he had just received a strong punch to the solar plexus.

Mary made no sound, but quickly moved to the coat rack beside the front door. In a moment she had put on her winter coat, pulled on her boots, wrapped one scarf around her head and another about her neck, and burst through the front door. She gingerly negotiated an icy street named after the state of Kentucky, in the direction of her dearest friend's sorrow-filled home.

Because of Kaz's weak heart the Pastor offered to drive him to the Pohl's house, giving Kaz time to properly prepare for the weather. It also gave him time to rehearse his comforting words to Emil and Mamie.

When Mary's arrived at the front door, Emil opened and said,
"Mary, have you heard?" To which she swept by Emil, and simply said,

"Mamie, oh Mamie!" and wrapped her arms quickly around her weeping friend, swaying her from side to side, hoping that somehow the embrace would allow her heart to press into Mamie's broken heart.

"He is not dead, he has been captured!" were the first words to break through Mamie's crying voice. "No. I know. I gave birth to him, I know, He is not dead."

Mamie was unbending. Even at the memorial service allowed by the family, Mamie insisted for several weeks,

"He is still alive. He is being held in a Japanese POW camp."

After about two and half months Mamie showed up at Mary's front door. Mary invited her in for tea. As they sat beside each other on the sofa, and listened to the delicate, and intimate music of Chopin on Mary's record player, Mamie said softly to Mary,

"About 8:30 this morning my Kenneth passed away in that POW camp. I felt his heart stop, and I heard his last breath. He is with God now, Mary. I will see him again and I have complete peace."

The little Snake Town boy that played war games with Mary's little Johnny would never be found or returned. Though the Department of Military would declare him Lost At Sea and Killed In Action, one mother would say to her dying day she knew better.

****

The letters from Eddie and Johnny were getting home a little more often, but they offered little useful information as scissors had removed any hint of location, or action, or whereabouts. The firefights were no less ferocious, but they were noticeably shorter skirmishes, as the German forces were in a much more mobile condition than aggressively defensive. They were moving as quickly as possible in retreat from France, in order to reinforce the Nazi troops being squeezed from both West and East. By the end of August, Paris had been liberated, and now in the first cold days of January, the Allied troops were simply cleaning out pockets of German resistance.

Johnny and Eddie would not hear or know of each other's location or condition until the War's end, when they were safely home.

Johnny could not believe his good fortune to even get a few days to explore Paris, see the sights, and be lavished in the exceptional kindness and expressions of appreciation from the French citizens. He was a little embarrassed and awkwardly shy when the French parents would encourage their beautiful young daughters to simply hug and give a good kiss to that total stranger G.I. walking down the street. More than once the thought crossed his mind, "Maybe I'll find one of these beauties and just convince her to come make a life with me when we all get back to America." But a rather dark thought would come as he would look down at the trembling hands that were once so strong and still. He frequently jerked his head in a slight backward motion, which was really more a nervous tic by now, and made that quick, short snorting sound as if gasping for his next breath. His mind silently uttered a different thought, "By the time I get out of this hell I will probably not be fit to be anyone's husband or any child's father." He corralled his thoughts and redirected them to the next sight that lay before him.

****

Lilly heard the downstairs door slam hard and thought to herself, "Who in the world is coming here on such a snowy, blizzard day?"

It was one of those typical January days on the southernmost border of Lake Michigan. This was years before the advancement of meteorological education would offer a better explanation for these overnight and massive snow accumulations referred to as "Lake effect snow." Regardless of explanation, residents of this area understood what they saw; ten to thirty inches of snow could be dumped on them in a matter of a few hours.

Now the slow, plodding steps began their obvious labored trek up the steep stairway. As the sounds passed the halfway point of the upward journey, Lilly could hear the familiar sound of metal snaps clanging. She knew them as the sound produced by any unsnapped pair of winter, rubber boots; known to most simply as Galoshes. The thought did pass her mind how her Pa always wore his boots open like that for easy dress and removal. Any good Pole would know to leave their shoes just inside an exterior door to the house. Lilly quickly dismissed any thought that it would be Kaz, her Pa, on this miserable day.

"Pa, for love of Mike! What are you doing here?" Lilly questioned, in no quiet manner. She was a bit surprised that he stepped into the kitchen entrance with his boots still on his feet, seemingly unconcerned at the amount of snow and wet he was strewing across the linoleum-covered floor. Hearing Kaz's heavy breathing and wheezing exhaled from his gaping mouth, Lilly moved across the room, took his arm and said, "Here, Pa. Sit, Sit on this chair."

Kaz half-sat and half-flopped back on the old oak dinette chair, as he unsnapped the chin strap, and tugged off the heavy, plaid, hunting cap.

"I guess those steps are getting a little higher every time I get over here." He attempted to twist loose the top button of his heavy Mackinaw coat, and breathlessly continued, "I know Derby Street is a nice part of town, but I sure wish you could have found a place on the ground floor."

"Pa, what the heck are you doing out walking in this deep snow on a day like today." Lilly questioned while helping him pull his coat away from his shoulders, and securing it behind him.

Lilly's youngest little girl, Judy, came running to the room, and quickly launched herself onto Kaz's lap. After throwing her arms around his neck she said.

"Dza Dza!" She called out the shortened version of the Polish word Dziadosz, meaning grandfather, "I'm glad you came to see me."

Kaz adjusted his little treasure to sit comfortably across his shaky legs. Lilly began to scold her father,

"You know, Pa, maybe Ma is right. Maybe you are as silly a man as she is always saying! I mean, walking through this snow..."

Kaz raised one palm in her direction and interrupted with an even more shocking fact,

"Well she would have me sent to the looney bin if she knew the rest."

"What rest?" Lilly bent at the waist to get nose to nose with her father.

Having recovered his breath and feeling more like his old, mischievous self, he proclaimed,

"Well, for Pete's sake, don't tell her, but I just helped that Hamilton guy down the street push his car out of a big snow drift, then walked all the way here, and up those blasted stairs."

Kaz inwardly chuckled at the entire scenario, but Lilly completely lost it.

"Pa, are you really crazy? What were you thinking?" She turned and dramatically walked toward the sink, picked up the dry dish towel on the counter, and threw it into the empty side of the sink, still ranting over her shoulder.

"For goodness sake, Pa, with that heart of yours you should not be away from the fireplace today." She turned the knob on the front of the little, apartment-sized stove, slid the tea kettle atop the lighted burner, and settled her voice before she spoke.

"I will make you a cup of tea, but you'd better get one of those pills out of your pocket, soon."

Kaz looked down and realized he had created a sizable puddle of melted snow from his boots on the floor. He gently patted Judy's tiny shoulders in a dismissive manner, and he softly said,

"Judy, honey, maybe you better get down now, and play in the other room. Dza Dza doesn't feel real good right now."

Lilly heard the statement, and slowly turned from the stove to watch her little girl slide off her Pa's lap, and run toward the living room. The next motion froze every muscle in Lilly's body. She panicked as she saw her Pa thrust his head upward in pain. He pushed himself stiffly against the back of the chair, his hands racing each other to his rounded chest, as his body twisted to the left, and then descended, shoulder first, to the floor space between the puddle at his feet, and the door he had entered only minutes earlier. Lilly's scream drowned out the sound of his body hitting the floor. She fell on her knees in front of him, pushed his upper torso until his body rested on his back.

Lilly's children came running when they heard the scream, but they stopped at the doorway as commanded by their frantic mother.

Time slowed as Lilly assessed the horrid scene before her. "He is not moving, he is not breathing, his eyes are open and fixed on something not there." She decided to call her husband, Chuck, since he was a policeman. Then, she reminded herself there was only one son not away at war.

To her surprise, the party-line phone system of that day was open. She had never known it to be clear when she picked up. After reaching her husband, he assured her he would have police and ambulance service there as soon as possible. He also reminded her that most of the streets were impassable and it could be some time before they would arrive.

"Frank!" Lilly's voice cracked over the phone receiver. "Please come now! Frank, something has happened to Pa. He's unconscious on my floor. I think he has had a heart attack Frank." Then she burst into tears, "I think he's dead! Frank, Please come."

It seemed like hours to Lilly, but within moments, Frank was taking three steps at a time up to Lilly's apartment. As he burst through the door, the first thing in his view was Kaz's unsnapped rubber boots. He stopped quickly at the door. He thought he heard his Pa's voice say again as he had whenever his eminent demise was discussed,

"When I die, boys, I want to go with my boots on."

It was a saying popularized in the Western movies, and it bespoke the manliness of working or fighting to the end. Although Kaz had not worked in the old box car factory for the last six years, and Frank had no way of knowing the last steps of his father that day, Frank did find some comfort when he learned that his dad, wise or not, had worked hard to help push a car out of a snow drift in the last hour of his life.

It did take an unusual amount of time for the police, ambulance, and coroner to convene at the apartment. By that time, Sophie had joined her siblings at the scene. Others who heard came respectfully, but remained out front in the yard.

Kaz's trio of children discussed how they should break the news to Mary, their mother. The conversation moved to getting the word to Eddie and Johnny on the other side of the globe.

"Listen folks," the ambulance driver said apologetically, "I really hate to ask this, but with this weather I could not get any of our other workers to assist me today. I am going to ask if perhaps this good son could help me in taking your father's body down the stairs to the ambulance."

They were stunned for a moment, as the middle-aged gentleman stared directly at Frank. Both girls replied simultaneously,

"Oh, Frank!" and just a quickly Frank said,

"Yeah, sure I can help."

As the driver descended back down the stairs to retrieve the hand-held, canvas stretcher, and a heavy burgundy blanket. The blanket had gold embroidered letters on one corner, "OTT," the name of the funeral home. Lilly, Frank, and Sophie held each other's arms as they stood over the peaceful, motionless body of the man they loved more than any other. Memories whirled in all their heads. Lilly could see herself as a child lying in bed next to her Pa, telling outlandish stories of riding a bicycle to the moon, while she twisted, and giggled, and begged for more stories. Sophie held her hands over her nose and mouth and envisioned the excitement of seeing her Pa coming up that side walk, black from head to toe, slumped from an exhausting day in the box car factory, the conditions which no little girl could have imagined. Frank could almost hear the voice in his ears again, "Franky, ya wanna go fishing this morning" Well, come on, boy. You better get out of that bed before the fish are all gone."

Frank bent at the knees as deeply as he had ever done to scoop up a Shortstop's throw to First Base. He lifted his end of the stretcher, and felt the full weight of his father's lifeless body, pressing in the palms of his own huge, working hands. As he slowly, carefully reached back with each foot to secure the step below him, he gazed at the rounded form of his Pa's unmoving torso. He thought of the little eight-year-old, immigrant boy from Poland who rolled on the grass in Baltimore, and cried out to his mother, some fifty one short years ago,

"You were right Mama! Money does grow on the streets of America!"

After Kaz had been carried away, Frank and the girls agreed to meet later with their Mother and begin the painful task of the funeral service. Frank slowly plodded back home and climbed the stairs to his and Opal's upstairs apartment. She met him at the door, placed her arms around him, and assured him of her joint sorrow. Frank said nothing, but he moved on to the toilet at the back of the apartment. He stayed there a long time. A couple times Opal came by the door to say,

"Are you alright Frank?" She would hear his tongue slightly suck against his teeth making a distinct sound people often make before changing a subject, and she would hear the reply,

"Yeah, I'm OK."

Much later, Frank emerged from the toilet. His face was still quite red. He had washed it and wetted his thick, black hair, pushing it all back, using only his large fingers as a comb. He would not shed a visible tear again to anyone's memory. After grabbing his jacket he simply said,

"I'm going to go down to the Post Office and see if we have any mail they couldn't deliver today."

The walk through the snowy streets was a blur, and he barely noticed the cold. His words were few and short, but enough to get what he came for. Frank stepped out the front door of the Post Office, scanning the few pieces of mail that were held for his address. There was a little stop in his pace when he saw the Military Letterhead, and realized it was a letter from his brother, Johnny. From where the letter had come, he could not tell. Exactly when it had started its journey from the battlefield, he would not be able to decipher.

He skimmed through a few general greetings and statements between the missing, censored spaces. He was caught off guard by the closing paragraph, which put something as hard as a peach stone in Frank's throat, as he read the following words from Johnny,

"Hey, I wonder," Johnny wrote, "How heavy is Pa getting these days, since he is not working anymore?" Then he added the following in an attempt at humor, "Not that I want you to have to carry him or anything like that."

The morbid reality that Frank had just carried his father's dead body made him hurt for Johnny's and Eddie's lack of knowledge, more than his own loss and pain on the snowy sidewalk. Frank only related the story of his Pa's passing a few times through the years, but he was heard to say to his own children more than once,

"No one should carry their own father's dead body."

****

Between the Red Cross and the Military, word got to Eddie and Johnny quite fast concerning their Pa's death. Though separate from each other they appealed to the proper chain of command for any possibility of a leave home for their father's funeral. They had seen, more than once, sons of officers and high officials literally pulled off the battlefield for a parent's or grandparent's funeral back home. But these two lower-ranked sons of immigrants were told they were just too necessary to the challenge before them. A couple Officers even assured them that under this strategic segment of the battle there was nothing known as a Leave for Family Tragedy or Death.

As Eddie was leaving the office where he pleaded his case, he met a friend of a soldier who had just left for home to attend his decorated grandfather's funeral. It was both boys' introduction to a familiar military fact: "R.H.I.P." or rank has its privilege.

Kazimiersz Pawlak, like many other Polish immigrants of that era, would not obtain wealth or fame. He would not leave large portions of land or wealth, but he would leave generations to follow his example of honesty, hard work, family pride, and above all, a spiritual faith that would sustain and direct many of his, yet unborn progeny. Most of all, in the genetic bloodline of a man named Kaz would be strength to accomplish what Jan and Anna's good boy, and kind man could never have imagined.

Mary had, within months of each other, buried her father, mother, and husband. She also lived with the painful sleepless nights that only a mother with two sons entrenched on the front lines of a world at war, could ever understand. The family Pawlak that new world, and a new life without their Patriarch.

****

In less than five months of Kaz Pawlak's passing, the world would be enthralled and relieved with the news that the nation of Germany, and the Nazi army had unconditionally surrendered to the Allied forces. The six-year-long atrocity was finally over. Reports would say that on April 30, 1945, as the Battle of Berlin raged above him, realizing that all was lost and not wishing to suffer Mussolini's fate, German Dictator, Adolf Hitler committed suicide in the Fuhrerbunker along with Eva Braun, his long-time partner, whom he'd married less than forty hours before their joint suicide. The surrender followed within days.

Word of the surrender reached America on May 8, 1945, and what became known as VE DAY (Victory in Europe), set off days of celebration the likes of which The United States, and her Western allies had never previously known. Times Square in New York City danced day and night. Sounds of sirens, church bells, fireworks, and in some more remote neighborhoods, shotgun blasts could be heard.

In the typical Midwestern town of Michigan City, Indiana, two young sons of Frank and Opal Pawlak joined the celebration. They participated by unrolling their favorite cowboy cap-gun strips, and in the absence of their father's hammer, used good, round, baseball-sized stones to strike each powder spot on the strip, creating their own celebratory commotion. Franky and Johnny aka. Manson and Buddy raised their stone firing-pins high above their heads, coming down on the cap strip with every young, sinewy muscle fully engaged. The cap explosion would only be excelled in volume by the pair's rotating declarations of,

"The war is over!"

"Hitler is dead!"

"Uncle Johnny is coming home!"

"Uncle Eddie is coming home!"

"We won! we won!"

The War in the Pacific droned on for four more months, but Victory in Europe gave the American people the confidence that it would be just a matter of time until they could begin this celebration all over again. It would be many years before the magnitude of the bombs dropped at Hiroshima and Nagasaki would be understood. It was President Truman's resolve and intention to save an additional one million American lives, and bring this world at war to final conclusion at the cost of such Japanese devastation. On September 2, 1945, a formal surrender ceremony was held in Tokyo Bay aboard the USS Missouri. The date was declared to be "VJ Day" (Victory in Japan). From September 1, 1939, With Hitler's invasion of Poland, to September 2, 1945 in Tokyo, Japan, the second "War to end all Wars" would become the subject of more printed words than any event in history.

Even better news for Mary and the rest of the Pawlak family was that neither of her sons would be deployed like others from the European campaign to Japan. They were coming home, and hoped to be processed back to the normal, civilian life they had once known.

Eddie was processed out of active duty in a somewhat uneventful manner. Though he did come home with some thoughts about his survival and purpose in life, it was not long until reuniting with some old pals like Mike, Sammy, and Dave found Eddie again at the late-night parties, firmly gripping a cold beer in one hand, and a Michigan City beauty in the other arm. Leaning against the nearest jukebox or piano, he was back melting the ladies' hearts, or at least their inhibitions.

Then it happened, of all places, right in Eddie's mother's living room. The fact that his Brother Frank's wife, Opal, had a little cousin that used to hang around at certain times, was of no particular interest within Eddie's fun-time world. Before the War she was just a young-looking kid that he saw from time to time and place to place. This day, however, was quite different.

Opal had asked her pretty little cousin to go with her to Mary's house to meet up with Frank, who was always faithful to spend some time with his Ma since Kaz had passed. Eddie stayed with his drinking pals a little too long that day, and was by any description available, approaching the threshold of "Drunk." As he kicked his shoes off at the front door, even before his mother's order to do so. He knew it was the one consistent part of her welcome to family, friends, or strangers alike.

Eddie staggered toward the living room. It had become a habit, or his own personal tradition to reach up to the heavy wooden door facing between the front entrance and the living room, and with feet crossed at the ankles, he pumped several fast chin-ups, like he'd done ever since he first learned to do the exercise. He allowed his body to simply hang by his fingertips as he scanned the room to see if anyone noticed his amazing feat. His eyes suddenly connected with Opal's cousin as the thought sped through his somewhat dizzy head, "Hey, that kid grew up a lot while I was away." Still swinging in the doorway and staring at the beautiful, curly-haired blonde. That adorable smile and wholesome laugh, accompanied by a little turned-up nose that adorned a face that seemed to say, "Just try to look away if you think you can."

To her surprise, and maybe even Eddie's, the next sound that permeated the room was a piercing, brazen, and totally flirtatious "wolf whistle." It brought the entire house to a screeching halt.

Before long, Eddie was spending every free minute he could with the girl the family called Mary Evelyn. Mary was his preferred name when speaking to her personally, after all, it was his mother's name as well. He soon began to feel this was just the girl to settle him down, and help him start a future.
It would not be long until Mary Evelyn would make the, settle him down part, a necessary requirement for any hope of his future with her.

Mary Evelyn opened the door excitedly anticipating her evening walk with Eddie. The fact she had fallen so madly in love with him made what she saw and smelled even more painful.

"Hey, Kid." Eddie slurred across his slobbering lips. "Ready for some time with your Mister Wonderful again?"

His hair was half strewn across one eye. His shirttail was half out of his trousers, which seemed abnormally unkempt. A pungent wave of stale beer-breath triggered Mary Evelyn's sensitive gag reflex. Eddie was a bit taken back as Mary pulled away from him, but little had he expected the next sequence of events. A more sobering expression fell across his countenance when he saw her eyes suddenly fill with tears. Not just a slight tearing-up, but a gusher rapidly streamed down her beautiful cheeks. Eddie felt a rather hard sting to his breast bone, and he realized it was Mary Evelyn's index finger repeatedly thumping his chest with every syncopated word that flew from her mouth.

"Ed-die-Paw-lak," she slowly drug out the four syllables, "I watched as a little girl what booze did to my family. I saw the poverty and abuse inflicted upon my precious mother before my Dad was killed in the mines. I know how our life changed for the better when my mother married a kind, Godly man." Her prodding finger gave way to two clutched handfuls of shirt lapel. She made her final declaration with her little turned-up nose but a centimeter from his sizable, Polish, reddened nostrils. "I love you with all my heart, and I want to live the rest of my life with you, but I will not live one day with this drunkenness! I'm not waiting for you to decide where I fit in with your priorities when it comes to these, so called, friends of yours." Then she dropped her final bomb as hard as any mortar fire Eddie has experienced at war, "The man I marry will be a man that makes God the most important thing in his life. So don't come back until you decide if you're that man or not." She pushed him away, still weeping as she turned and ran into the house. The door slammed in such a way as to say, "Don't even consider knocking again."

For the next couple hours Eddie walked the streets, arguing with himself, defending himself a little, only to have his thoughts quickly turn to feelings of responsible shame. He walked all the way to the end of the pier, and back down through town on that same thoroughfare his father Kaz had traversed upon his arrival from Poland. Eddie began to realize the power of his earlier indulgences were losing their inebriating effects. Eddie reached 11th Street and waited for the South Shore Train, headed toward South Bend. He decided to follow its direction. Within a few blocks, walking on the south side of the busy street, a Westbound passenger train squealed its steel wheels along the rails, as it prepared to make the regular stop at the 11th and Franklin station. The noisy train suddenly thrust Eddie into a memory of the battlefields he had survived. For a moment, his introspection made him relive his foxhole thoughts about survival, and a God who may have a genuine plan for his life. As the sounds of the train faded away, another sound was heard. It was music and some muffled voices singing. Eddie lifted his head from the sidewalk. His eyes observed the large, cement porch across the front of the light-brown-painted, Christian church that bordered the railed street at the juncture where the street and rail line make a hard turn toward 2nd street, later renamed Michigan Blvd.

The front door at the top of the steps, leading into the church, had been left slightly ajar. As darkness was falling on the city, the light from within the church seemed almost inviting to Eddie's eyes. He quickly shoved his shirt tail into the waist of his pants, checked to see that his shirt buttons were all fastened, and brushed his palms against his chest and thighs in an attempt to rid himself of any dirt or food accumulations. Upon reaching for the door handle with one hand he used the other to push his hair out of his face and back on top of his head. The music softly played from the large organ at the front of the chapel, and the congregants sang so sincerely of their faith. His mind's eye kept moving from Mary Evelyn's tear-filled assault, to inner thoughts about his near death encounters in Italy and France. The kindly and softly-spoken preacher was not a strong focus of Eddie's comprehension that evening. But he couldn't help notice when at the end of his lecture, the pastor invited anyone who would like to make a serious change to their lifestyle to step forward and come to the front of the church.

"This is your opportunity to surrender your life to Christ, and truly become a child of God." The pastor encouraged his listeners.

Somehow Eddie pulled the pieces together in his mind, "This is what Pa and Johnny and all the rest were always talking about. And this is what Mary Evelyn meant when she said she wanted a man of God." Without hesitation, Eddie moved from the hard wooden pew to the front of the church where the Reverend Ford extended a hand to him and simply asked,

"Son, are you ready to give your life to Christ, and receive him as your Lord and master?" Eddie responded,

"Yes, Pastor. If I have ever been ready for anything, I am ready for this."

The pastor actually laughed a little at such an energetic response. After Eddie prayed a prayer with the pastor, he was then informed that if he was really serious about this step toward a new life, he would follow the same pattern Christ had followed when he was recognized as God's son, and he humbled himself to be baptized in water. Within minutes, Eddie was led behind the platform, given a white robe to change into, and he entered the baptismal tank, where the pastor dunked him under the water. Eddie came out of the water believing himself to be a truly new man.

Eddie and Mary Evelyn would soon be married, have two beautiful daughters, and spend their lives together. Mary would have her, "Man of God," and Eddie would use that velvety voice in church, stirring the hearts of many who called him their favorite singer.

****

Johnny's return proved a great deal more complicated than Eddie's. While suffering the rigors of daily battle in Belgium, his days were bathed in blood and bombs, and his nights were plagued with recurring, disappointing dreams of returning home. When his mind could find rest, he would find himself in the swinging bunks of the mammoth Naval vessel, as it sailed into New York Harbor. Friends would beckon for him to come above to see the Statue of Liberty. Excitedly, John climbed the steps to the deck for a glimpse of Liberty's light, only to be woken in the cold with a command to take cover. So frequently did this maniacal mirage haunt him that he decided to stay in his bunk when his homebound transport actually made it to America's Eastern shore.

"Come on, Johnny! You don't want to miss this, Pal."

"Yeah," came another voice, "Ain't this the girl you've been dreaming about?"

Johnny remained still, but his eyes darted around the floating barracks, his mind whirling and wondering if this was another fantasy. Had he waited much longer, he might have missed the object of his dreamful desire. Against his better judgment, and the loud voices of doubt in his head, he succumbed to the wooing of his mates, and climbed the narrow ladder from the hole to the sun-lit deck.

The slight haze in the air, and the grey-clouded, overcast sky could not have diminished the beauty John Pawlak beheld. A clear minded man in this same scenario would have surely shed tears at the sight that reminded him his war was really over. But this war-ravaged victim of Traumatic Stress Syndrome could only stare with rigid jaw, and disbelieving eyes. She was beautiful. Crowned with freedom, gowned in glory, her torch touching the heavens. Boys, turned men by war's atrocity found new, youthful elation, as they pointed, and patted one another. But Johnny stood with unwavering attention on the symbol his soul had so desperately needed to see. He whispered,

"Is it really you?" He refused to look away from her galant gaze. He heard her words, from unmoving lips,

"Welcome home, Son."

Upon his arrival back in the States the Medical staff recognized that Johnny was not a well man. Not only had the horrors of war taken an emotional toll on his mind, nerves, and body, but he was physically ill beyond words. The dreaded dysentery, not unusual among the troops, depending on location and conditions, had struck Johnny to a condition rarely seen. He was sent immediately from New York to a Military Medical Center at Ft. Campbell, Kentucky. His massive 212 pound frame of muscle and power was diminished to a scrawny 132 pounds.

"Are you John Pawlak, young man?" Came the firm and official sounding voice toward Johnny's skeletal back. Without turning over, which would have been an exceptional effort, Johnny gave a weak reply,

"Yes Sir, I am."

"Well let me come around to that side of the bed and introduce myself."

Johnny noticed first all the medals and awards on both sides of the tall man's uniform. He knew this must be pretty important. The second thing he saw was the red, velvet-covered case under the officer's left arm. The gentleman officer spoke,

"My name is Major Harlan McCoy, and I have a presentation to make today. Hopefully, it will be a little medicine to brighten your day." Then he began to read from a white sheet of paper. "It gives me great pleasure to present to you, on behalf of a grateful Nation, the following citations and medals for your dedicated service to your Country."

Johnny used all his strength to attempt to, at least raise himself to one elbow. Finding his body trembling in weakness, with fever raging through his system, he conceded to rest his head again on the pillow beneath him. Johnny could not completely comprehend all the Major was reading, but he understood something about North Africa, Sicily, Italy, and he fully heard the words,

"...The Battle of the Bulge." When Major McCoy finished reading, he removed the decorative box from under his arm, opened it, and turned it toward the bed. He held it near Johnny's face and said, "Son, you deserve all eight of these medals, and all of these ribbons. I am honored to know one of the bravest soldiers I have ever met."

As he closed the box and slid it under Johnny's pillow, he stood to a proper attention and saluted. He could have had no idea that the pitiful figure lying before him entered his Country's service as one of the strongest and healthiest figures in this man's Army. To Johnny's surprise, the Major then pulled a chair close to Johnny's bed, and softly asked,

"How did you get so sick, son?" to which Johnny began a story,
"I think it was in France. I remember the day. It was hot, and I looked across a large field. I saw a cloud of dust moving up the road. When it got closer I could see it was a wagon being pulled by two huge Belgian horses. The wagon was piled to the top with long loaves of French bread." Johnny was able to roll himself over to his back, while keeping his eyes fixed on the Major. He took a deep, cleansing breath and continued. "It was one of those French farmers. They were always bringing something to us in the field after the Germans were gone." To which the Major interrupted,

"Yeah, they really felt like we saved their butts. I guess we did." After the Major laughed and Johnny was able to force a smile, Johnny resumed his story.

"When the wagon stopped among our marching troops, the Sergeant let us drop out of formation and help ourselves to that beautiful bread. See, we had not had bread in weeks, so the guys went crazy after that stuff." Then Johnny explained, "I saw that the bread was covered with dirt and dust from that country road, so when I got mine, I broke it open, and just scooped out the fresh stuff from inside the loaf. A lot of those other guys just started eating that bread, dirt and all."

"Well you were pretty smart soldier doing it that way." responded the Major.

"I don't know about being smart, but all I could think of was if my Ma saw me eating that dirty bread she would have thrown a fit. You know she always said, 'Cleanliness is next to Godliness,' so I had no choice. At which McCoy laughed even harder. "I guess," Johnny mused, "I still must have gotten some of the dirt with the bread. I don't understand though, a lot of the guys sure got sick, but I was one of the few that got this dysentery stuff."

After assuring Johnny that the Medical staff would get him fully recovered, the Major saluted, and left. Johnny studied the display of medals and ribbons and thought to himself, "Frank and Opal's boys, Manson and Buddy will probably enjoy playing with these when I get home." As for himself, he felt like the medals would probably only bring back memories he so wished to wash from his tormented mind. As he lay back on his side, his head swam in its near delirious fever, he softly whispered the words,

"If I ever get back to Michigan City, I will never get out of town further than I can see the smokestacks at Pullman." It was a promise he kept for over thirty-seven years. Not until the vacant Pullman BoxCar factory would burn down, would he venture to visit Florida with his brother Frank.

Several months passed in the Ft. Campbell Medical ward before Johnny was fully recovered, beginning to regain his appetite, and adding a few pounds which his body so dearly needed. He packed his last few items in his duffle bag, and began his first steps out from among the twenty, war-torn, young men, still recovering in this Army Hospital. As he headed toward the hallway, he noticed one particular soldier with both legs gone. He stopped at the end of the bed and wondered if the wounded soldier might have been one he had carried during the heat of battle. John then realized the soldier's body was heaving up and down at the stomach as the result of the young man's uncontrolled, silent crying.

"What's happening, fella?" Johnny asked as he moved to the head of the bed.

The soldier removed his arm from over his face, and in a rather embarrassed manner, tried to gather his emotions.

"Oh, after everything else, I can't believe someone would do something like that."

"Something like what, Pal?" Johnny asked.

"After losing both my lousy legs, and then spending months in this hell-hole, they bring me some medals. A few days ago, while I was knocked out after my last surgery, some S.O.B. stole my medals!" Sobbing like a little boy whose baseball had just floated down the river and out of sight, he continued to wail, "If I can't get home with my own two legs, you would think, at least I would have something to show as thanks for what I left over there."

"Excuse us, Soldier. You will have to move for now." the stern voice of the white-capped nurse announced, as she pushed past Johnny at the bedside. Within a moment the nurse was inserting the hypodermic needle into the out-of-control, young, double amputee. As she turned again toward Johnny, she simply stated, "There, that will settle him down a little. Poor kid, he has been like that for days now."

Quickly, she moved off to the next urgency before her. In a matter of moments, the heavy dose of Morphine calmed both body and mind of the soldier in Johnny's stare. With one last, shaky whimper the boy, not yet 20 years old, took his drug-induced slide into an unconscious sleep.

Johnny placed his hand softly on the soldier's arm, and sent a quiet prayer upward,

"Dear Lord, please help this young, brave soldier. Help him recover, and get home to his loved-ones. Give him strength to adjust to his new life. Oh God, may he come to know you and know your peace."

Johnny patted the man's arm several times, then began to move toward the end of the bed. As he grasped the duffle bag to throw over his shoulder, he stopped, took one more, good, long look at the young soldier, and thought about how grateful he was to be standing on two good legs. His fingers slowly tussled with the drawstrings at the top of the green, faded, G.I. issued luggage. He opened the top and slipped his hand along the inner side of the bag. He pulled his hand from the duffle, having retrieved his velvet box of medals and ribbons.

"Here Soldier, I don't really ever care to see these again." Johnny whispered, "My medals will be the legs I dress every morning from now on." Johnny slipped the case under the pillow of the sleeping hero that lay before him.

Though his body had returned home, Johnny's return to social life would take more time. He started by secluding himself in an old shack, on an old friend's farm, out on Earl Road. He spent untold hours reading his Bible, praying, and trying to eliminate the night sweats, dreams, and screaming voices from the battlefield.

He returned to his overhead crane, hook-on work, at the box car factory, and later transferred to the newer, and more modern Joy Manufacturing Company. Johnny would venture an occasional bike ride toward his Otis roots, and he was in faithful attendance every time the church doors were opened. At night he would hide himself in the little shack, and lift his home-made weight set, rebuilding that barrel chest, strong shoulders, and massive arms he had laid aside somewhere in the European Campaign of World War II. It took over a year before he felt he could leave his sanctuary of solitude. Johnny was renamed, first by nephews, then the family caught on, and even church members called him "Uncle John." Life began to feel normal as he moved in with his mother, Mary, and sister, Sophie on the lower floor of a two-story, brick, apartment house.

No one could have imagined at the time that this structure, on the far side of the City limits, would become the center of the family's history. Fact, legend, and lore would know this humble residence for generations to follow, simply as "The Coolspring Place."

****

While it did bring comfort to Opal to know some adults would be within observation distance of her active, and often rascal boys, the mixture of aging grandmother, spinster aunt, and childless bachelor uncle made for obvious social, and mutual habitation disasters. The thunderous monotony of pounding feet, accompanied by boisterous hollering filling the stairway and hallway outside the peaceful trio's downstairs residence, was enough to give the Dalai Lama a complete nervous breakdown. Even though Frank tried to help his sons piece together bicycle sections to make one usable bike, it was just too tempting for the boys to see Uncle John's nice, Schwinn Springer Fork bicycle leaned against the side of the house. Certain that they would return before he came back in need of his bike, this reincarnation of the original Franky and Johnny, now called Manson and Buddy, would soon be dashing off to Stell's grocery, or Kienitz's store for some penny candy. Inevitably, they would tarry long enough to be noticed.

Opal held Uncle John in high esteem, especially as more knowledge came concerning his trials and exploits in the war. She was not, however above enjoying a lively argument with him on subjects from politics to the Bible. Often she would hear Uncle John, discovering his bike missing again, loudly proclaim the following accusation,

"Dem Dahg-Gahn Kids! Dem Daaahg-Gaahn boys. They got my bike again, and I need to go to the store for Ma."

Several times this scene had been reenacted, and even after Frank and Opal had warned the joy-riders,

"Leave your Uncle John's bike alone, and don't touch it again or you're both going to get a licking."

But on this particular day, while Opal listened to Uncle John rant and rave about "Dem Dahg-Gahn Kids," she could contain herself no longer. She stepped off the bottom step of the cement porch, and stomped across the grassless sand called the front yard. She thrust one hand into her apron pocket, and with the other hand, shot her pointed finger toward the face of this man, loved by all. Knowing how good he had always been to her boys, Opal still unloaded what she intended to be the closing argument in defense of her boys.

"John Pawlak, you listen to me. I am sorry the boys took your bike again. We have told them not to touch your bike, and their father will give them a good whipping when they get back, but I am sick of you calling my boys, 'Dem Dahg-Gahn Kids.' No! It really galls me. Not after I have heard all the stories of how you and my husband treated that little lady, called your mother, inside that very apartment!" Now, she was on a roll, like her Father James would say, "Only Opal can do."

"My boys have never run from me like you, two rotten kids ran from your Ma. Never would they have held their feet against a bedroom door to keep me out, or pull themselves up on the bedsprings so I could not even reach them with the broom handle. Yes, I know those stories. So I will tell you one more time." By now, she had garnered the attention of the Baylines, the Thompsons, and the Moldenhaurs, on the opposite side of Coolspring Avenue, as they watched through screened doors. Her voice reached super-sonic sound barriers when she screamed,

"Don't you ever call my children, 'Dem Dahg-Gahn kids' again! do you understand?"

After a lingering time of her outstretched neck toward his now slowly dropping head, Uncle John guiltily broke the silence and conceded,

"Ok, Opal. I am sorry for calling them that. I was just frustrated. You know I love those kids, and I'm good to them. I just need for them to not take my bike, Ok?

"Alright," Opal said, taking a slow breath. "Just come to me first before you start calling them names again."

As she moved to the porch, she redirected her passion toward her disobedient boys, and mumbled,

"Boy, they are going to get it when they get home."

As Uncle John began his foot trek to the store for his mother, he also mumbled to himself,

"Whew! Sure glad Frank got her, and not me. Poor guy! Maybe this single life is better for me after all."

Both boys were dealt with, as Opal guaranteed. She just stood at the window, hoping to feel a little breeze later that evening. She shook her head, and whispered,

"Well, I'll be shot!" She watched Manson mount the handle bars, and Buddy straddle the back fender, while Uncle John pushed his bike and jumped to the seat, peddling her boys in the direction of the candy store.

Over the next few years, not much would change at the Coolspring Place. The summers would hold torturous days and nights of such intense heat in the upstairs apartment. The winters would be just as miserable, when neither the kerosene heating stove, in the center room, the small Ben Franklin at the bottom of the attic stairs, or the opened door of the kitchen range each morning, could produce enough heat to provide adequate warmth. Yet, the place was never short on family love, laughter, tears, arguments, smells and atmosphere.

The beds in the attic were primarily chip-painted, steel frames, long weakened, metal-spring frames, and worn out, old, musty mattresses. In as much as there would never be extra money for luxury items, such as thick, warm blankets, Frank saw it as a very fortunate blessing when he discovered that the military surplus stores were well-stocked after the War. Among the best and most useful items were the big heavy wool army overcoats. Those coats served an even more vital purpose when Frank would, as he called it, "Pile dem on top of the boys." He tried convincing himself the boys would be plenty, warm despite the howling winds that slowly moved the hanging clothes on the rafters above. By morning, the small swirls of snow that had sifted in around the non-winterized windows, were not worthy to be compared with the light-frosted boards that awaited the morning bare feet of four little guys, now that Dicky had actually graduated to the upstairs, once he could crawl. Opal found a few old, rag rugs, and placed them beside the beds to warm the tiny toes.

The approaching summer would be little relief for Opal. She lay in her bed, directly below her boys, hiding from Frank the tears welling in the corners of her eyes, as she grieved over the impoverished conditions. Her thoughts were on her sons, and what they were enduring, knowing this was not how the whole world lived.

While Frank worked hard at the large factory machine shop, Opal ensured her three boys were fed, and on the school bus, headed to the township school which bore the same name as their street; Coolspring School.

Because they lived on the Southernmost side of the avenue, the boys were required to ride the old, yellow, school bus out to the country. Had they lived across the street, they would have been city residents, and could have attended Jefferson school, where their father, Frank had started school. It was only three blocks away and could have been walked every day. This was just one of the oddities they learned about "living on the wrong side of the street."

Opal listened to the grind of the school bus engine, changing gears on its move toward the Hartsburg house, and the highway leading out of town. She called Dicky to come eat some of the cornmeal mush his brothers had forced down earlier.

"Feed me mommy." the little guy begged, while Opal ran a comb through his brown hair, parting it right down the middle, the way Frank wore his.

"You're big enough to feed yourself now, boy." she said before placing the little spoon in his hand. As she turned to move some dishes to the sink, she thought it was either the odor of that morning's breakfast, or the heat still rolling from the open oven door, which she had opened to ward off the early fall chill in the air.

"Oh, wow!" she said out loud, as she moved her fingers to her lips, filling her mouth with air until her cheeks bulged on each side. The powerful wave of nausea almost brought up everything she had eaten, between serving her boys and getting their jackets on that morning. "I hope that milk was good." she said. Her cousin Lena had just brought it yesterday from their farm out in Springfield Township, and she said it was given from the cows that morning. Then a horrid thought swept across Opal's mind. Quickly she moved to the calendar behind the kitchen door, and counted days backwards. Not much in her life was consistent, save for hardship, but the one thing she could count on like clockwork was, what the ladies of that day, still with whispered voice called, "Their Monthly."

She said it slowly as even more nausea swept her now sweating face,

"Oh Jesus, no! Please, no." Then the truthful proclamation, "I...am...late."

She thought for a moment that maybe she was getting a little older, and things were just going to be a little more irregular now. She knew better, and like most facing this possibility, she began to rehearse in her mind the when and where this could have happened. In a moment she would never confess, the where came to her mind, before the when.

That night, as she lay staring at the ceiling, she heard Frank turn over and take that familiar, long, sighing yawn before dropping off to sleep. "If I don't tell him now, I don't know any time that will be any better."

"Frank, are you sleeping?"

"No, not yet." he quickly replied. "What do you need?"

"Well, I need to tell you something." she quietly spoke.

"Ok. What did those boys do now?"

For a moment she giggled, and then rather sheepishly said,

"It is not what your boys have done, Frank. It's what their Father has done."

"What the heck did I do?" he quickly snapped back.

Opal never said a word. She just lay there in silence, and listened to the wheels spinning in Frank's head. Then it happened,

"Oh Man, Oh Man. Man, oh Man." Frank repeated as he flopped on his back to say,

"You're pregnant. Oh Man, oh Man. You're pregnant again. Wow! Really? You sure?"

"Well I haven't been to the Doctor yet, but I'm late. I'm feeling sick to my stomach some and," she paused, and with a know-that-you-know expression on her face, replied,

"Yep, I am sure. There is another one on the way."

After they both lay there for some time staring at the ceiling, Frank reached for Opal's hand and said softly,

"Hey, another one won't eat us out of house and home any more than the rest of 'em are doing now." They both laughed, then Frank offered his form of consolation.

"Who knows? This one may finally be that girl we've wanted."

The pregnancy was officially confirmed, and the word spread to family, friends, and church folks.

"The Pawlaks are having another baby!"

As time neared for the baby's arrival, Opal was so often asked,

"What if it is another boy?"

She developed a standard answer, which most thought she was just kidding, until they realized there was no laugh after she declared,

"If it is another boy we are not even sending out announcements."

When the St. Anthony Hospital nurse and Dr. Bernoski lifted the screaming, little creature for Opal to see, she said it before they could,

"It is another boy, my fifth."

True to her word, she purchased no birth announcements, but thought it a more fun approach to purchase several penny-postcards, and simply wrote in her own hand,

"Unto us another child is born, unto us another son is given."
After Opal returned to the Coolspring place with the new baby, her second oldest boy, Buddy, just a few weeks shy of his own 10th birthday asked his mother,

"Mom, can I name this one, please?"

Opal, still keeping up the little front of disappointment in a fifth boy, quickly shot back,

"Sure, Bud. After five, I don't need to name anymore." She may not have been totally sincere about her release of parental duty but Buddy wasted no time responding,

"Great, I want to name him from the Bible." Buddy quickly grabbed the large Bible from the end table nearby.

Opal did not realize in the moment he had been thinking about this for some time, and he'd actually been looking at Bible names he liked. She thought he was going to just do one of those famous Bible dives, choosing the name from where his finger happened to land. He opened the Bible to the Old Testament, placed his finger on the page, and said,

"His first name will be Samuel." Then turning to the New Testament, he followed the same method, then announced,

"His middle name will be Paul. Samuel Paul."

Opal thought about it for a minute and said,

"Well, Samuel was a pretty important prophet in the Bible, and The Apostle Paul preached all over the world, so maybe he will grow up to be a great prophet, and travel to other places as a preacher someday." With that, she quickly moved away from the spiritual talk and biblical discourse. Her concern returned to her very practical world when she said, "I am alright with Samuel, or even Sammy, or Sam, but you know I really don't like nicknames too much. So, I better not hear anyone of you ever call him something like Sambo." They all laughed at the thought of a familiar comic strip character, having no idea in this 1948 Caucasian family that even this nickname of a character would be an offensive or hurtful characterization to the small minority group of residents, confined to a few blocks on the North side of their city.

Samuel Paul would later say of his name,

"I've never complained about my name, knowing how I received it. As I have read the Bible often, I realize my name could just as easily have been Mephibosheth Jehoshaphat or Lucifer Judas. So, I am pretty pleased with Samuel Paul."

This fifth boy would also learn early that his Grandfather Kaz, who passed away before his birth, also carried the middle name Paul. It would come to give him some sense of connection to the wonderful man he wished he could have known.

Frank, Opal and those five boys would know hardships for years, even after the War had changed the economic picture for many other families. They had known miracles, which were the only explanation, and means of survival for their share of challenges. In spite of meager existence, and a life below the national poverty line, they were building a family of hardworking, talented, and hope-filled dreams that would give reason to believe, perhaps, at least in the next generation, the Pawlaks would be just fine. Amid every economic shortage, some outlandish event would present itself as an opportunity for unforgettable humor.

On one such evening, Frank straddled the attic floor stringers, reaching for his wading boots, but he lost his balance and fell through the drywall at his feet. As he sunk, thigh-deep through the kitchen ceiling, the explosion dropped its mess on little Sammy, eating in his highchair. In perfect timely fashion, the radio began blasting one of the most popular recordings of the day, as the voice of Stuart Hamblen sang the words,

"This old house is a gettin cagey
This old house is a gettin old
This old house lets in the rain
This old house lets in the cold.

Oh my knees are gettin chilly
But I fear no fear of pain
Cause I see an Angel peekin'
Through a broken window pane." [1]

****

"It's a perfect summer day." Opal thought as she spread the blanket a few feet in front of the lowest step to the front porch. Soon she was sitting with legs crossed, in what was often called in that day, Indian style. This description probably came from what pictures were seen of Early American Natives like the Sioux Medicine Man, Sitting Bull. She lifted her growing four-month-old boy high over her head as she proceeded to bring him slowly downward to touch her nose to his. Sammy's squeals of laughter made the torturous heat of the apartment above her, seem far away, at least for the moment. She changed the name of a popular little song of the day as she began to sing,

"Sammy Boy, Sammy Boy. Won't you be my Sammy Boy?" Her strong alto voice was still ringing in the happy little boy's ears when she heard the deep rumbling sound, and felt the vibration beneath the blanket. It was obviously a powerful car, approaching from the West of Coolspring Ave. As soon as the shiny black sedan cleared the plum orchard, Opal heard the engine drop in sound, and watched the heavy front fender dart quickly off the street, coming to rest directly in front of the Coolspring place.

---

[1] "This Old House" by Stuart Hamblen (RCA Victor 1954)

"Hey there, Sweetheart!" bellowed from the passenger side of the car,

"How is my big sis, and her beautiful fifth boy today?"

"Junie, Junie!" hollered Opal, clutching Sammy, and with the help of her free hand negotiated her stance.

As the sisters ran to each other, and threw their arms around each other, they were both
conscious to control their reunion joy so as not to crush the bobble-headed, little creature
between them.

"Hey, Marsh! how are you?" Opal voiced over Junie's shoulder, as her handsome brother-
in-law made his way around the huge ornamented hood. "You're the last person I expected to see today." Opal expressed with a fantastic tone of glee, "You guys are so busy working all the time," Opal added, "And Elkhart is so far away." Knowing in Opal's world, fifty
miles might as well have been five thousand. "Please, let's go inside, and I will make some
Iced tea." Opal, gesturing with her free hand toward the front door.

"Wait, Wait!" June responded, "Give me that baby first." as she reached to take Sammy.
Speaking directly into the face of the little boy, being held safely in the crook of her arm,
she declared, "Hey, little Sambo! I'm your Aunt June, and this is Uncle Marsh. We are
probably the last ones in the family to meet you, but you are such a beautiful boy!"

Opal held back the little snicker at her sister calling the baby, Sambo, the name she had
warned the whole family against using. For Opal, the faux-pas was immediately excused
and forgiven, as the quick reminder of June's childless condition sent a sharp dart through
Opal's heart.

"Opal, it is such a beautiful day. Let's just sit out here with the baby for a while, before we
go into the apartment." When Marsh offered this suggestion, all quickly agreed that out-
doors would be better than the suffocation that waited atop those stairs.

June instructed her husband to get the Brownie camera out of the car, and in a few moments commenced the barrage of photo taking.

Opal loved her little sister, even though she had been as concerned as the rest of the family
when June's lifestyle moved farther away from the traditions, and highly religious practice

of the Reverend Rice's teachings. It was not just the lack of church involvement, but more-so, the appetite for modern fashion, which included the forbidden cosmetic make up, sleeveless dresses, hemlines higher than normal, an occasional glass of wine, and worst of all, the hellish act of dancing to music, that made June's time with the family either restricted or limited. If what the family and church of their time deemed "Worldly" would not have been enough to produce this strained relationship with June, the ultimate wedge would be driven in when June would marry a previously divorced man.

He was movie-star handsome, educated, and socially adept. Marsh provided a comfortable living, was a rather dapper dresser, drove a nice car, and to validate his other-world status with this family, he even played something called golf for his recreation.

"Opal, this child is perfect!" June observed as she ran one finger along his cheek, and played with the long, single curl of blond hair, which Opal had arranged on top of Sammy's round head.

Opal became uncomfortable as she saw tears begin to fill each corner of her sister's eyes. Her heart began to break for June. Junie was a beautiful, young woman, who had fair complexion like one of the matching-set, China dolls of the famous Dionne Quintuplets. Born May 28, 1934 these five Canadian-born infants were the first known quintuplets to survive. Their fame covered every magazine in the world, and June would even collect the little doll set with their likeness.

Another feature that June could use to her advantage when trying the newest outfit at the department store, was her beautiful figure. Endowed with an above-average upper body shape that certainly drew plenty of attention from the men of that day. What most would never know was this so-called advantage, was actually part of the painful story that haunted her most.

June had been stricken with the childhood disease of Parotitis, more commonly known as Mumps. In her case the condition spread to her breasts and ovaries, and though rarely the case, she was left unable to become pregnant. In a family where her five siblings would have twenty-seven children among them, she would be unable to produce one. Although never spoken, there were some in the family who would privately question if this was some judgment of God against Junie for her choices outside of their church world of that day. Those thoughts would not last long, as each would come to recall the many other family members who had certainly participated in uncomely and ungodly practices, yet somehow produced entire litters of offspring.

"Opal, it is not fair, just not fair! Junie began to sob openly.

"I know Junie, I know." Opal replied through her own tears.

"This is your fifth child, and I cannot have one. Why? Why is that, and how is that fair?" June questioned as she held the baby in her arms, even a little too possessive for Opal's comfort.

Her husband moved next to June on the blanket and offered a comforting arm about her shoulders. The conversation became unexpectedly serious.

"Opal, I don't mean to be offensive, but I have taken off work today, and I asked Marsh to bring me here. I need to present you with an idea." she laid the baby across her legs, pushed her long blonde hair away from her damp eyes, and passionately continued, "Sis, you already have four boys, and honestly you struggle to even provide everything they need, and truth is you can't afford this child." Then she lowered her voice, and steadied her emotions as she reached for Marsh's arm. "We are much more able to care for this baby than you and Frank. He will never want for anything. We can raise this child to accomplish so much more than you and Frank will ever be able to do." Then, she dropped the truthful intent of their visit. "Please let us adopt Sammy. Please, Opal. We want to adopt this child. Please, Opal. Please, I am begging you."

For a moment, Opal's mind was spinning in a whirlwind of confusion. Just a few minutes earlier she had been playing with her child on a blanket. Her day only became more fantastic when her wonderful sister had shocked her with her unexpected arrival. Pangs of guilt began to force their way into this swirl of emotions as she reflected to herself, "Was my joking about my disappointment of a fifth boy taken seriously by some who heard? Did the lack of formal announcements give anyone the idea I did not want this child? Had my outfitting this baby in a girl's gown been seen as a shame for my little son? How could anyone even ask me to do this?" Then another thought crossed her mind. "Do I not want the best for my child? Are my feelings pride and selfish insult? Maybe she is right. She could give a child anything. Will we even have enough food for these children?" She immediately thought about her brother James Jr. Just a couple years earlier, when he and his wife were sure they were going to divorce, and his wife being so weakened and sick that their youngest would have died, had it not been for a family couple intervening and caring for the child. They also pleaded with James to adopt this sick and starving child for the child's sake. James agreed, and truly, in more ways than Opal could ever imagine at the time this child's life was literally saved. Only June's voice could break the tornado wreaking havoc in Opal's mind,

"Don't be mad or hate me, Sis. I just had to try."

With that, Opal took Sammy gently from June's loving grip and handed him to Marsh. This cleared the way for Opal to pull her frantic sister over onto her side. She placed June's head gently upon her legs. As big sister brushed her hand over little sister's hair, Opal began a weeping voiced prayer,

"Dear God, You know how much I love my sister, and I know how much you love her. Would you please come to her now with your touch of love and grace. God you also know that I believe you gave me this fifth boy, just as you gave me the four others. I know I may not be able to care for this child like my sister, but could you please help me, and my Junie understand today, that I cannot release my responsibility as this child's mother." After a few more words of prayer, including a request for God to make a way for June to have her own child, she ended her conversation with God. No one spoke for some time, Opal continued to gently stroke her sister's hair.

In a few moments, June stood, reached down for Opal's hands, and helped her to her feet. After hugging her big sister again, June took the baby from her husband and placed him back in Opal's arms. With her emotions fully under control, she said,

"Thank you, Opal, for letting me try, and thanks for the prayer. Please keep them coming for me." Then, turning to her motionless husband, June said, "We better get back home. We will be back. I want to take the boys to Washington Park before the summer is over, so we'll come back soon."

Opal touched her sister's shoulder again and said,

"Hey, I love you, and I love when you write. Please write often."

June was faithful to her word. She did return before the park closed Labor Day, as was the custom for the winter on Lake Michigan. The boats would soon be lifted from the basin and properly stored to wait-out the severe winter ahead. The amusement park would remain silent of its wonderful carnival sounds and long summer evening smells.

Frank's and Opal's boys dearly loved when Aunt Junie came to town. She was fun, full of laughter, a little naughty, and most always had some gifts. Opal loved the times they could be together at a quickly arranged family gathering, even though they did not include Marsh and June as often as the other siblings. Opal's closeness to June continued through those wonderful letters she wrote weekly. Both girls had an above-average grasp of vocabulary and structural grammar, enhanced by their vociferous passion for reading. Junie's book club classics kept them both sharing their favorite author's latest publications.

One particular form of winter challenge would become defined by weather experts in the future as Black Ice. It was a phenomenon known well by Marsh and June. The condition would occur most often before a major winter blizzard. The overnight drop in temperatures from unseasonal warmth, called January Thaw, left just enough moisture on the highway to quickly freeze into an invisible thin layer of clear ice. To the natural eye, the black of the asphalt, or the white of the cement highway looked for everything as clean and dry, and free of danger.

"Oh my Gosh!" would be Marsh's startling comment as the tires on that heavy car he loved, broke traction with the road. Only his steady hand and winter driving experience quickly brought the rear end of the vehicle out of its fish-tale motion, and back to a forward direction.

Startled by the uneasy movement, June lifted her hand from the paper on which she had been writing, and reached for her husband's arm.

"It's ok, Baby!" Marsh assured, "Boy it is just such a sheet of ice out here today. I will bring it down to a crawl, and we will be fine."

As the clutch was pushed in, Marsh slowly moved the steering column gear shift upward, and just as slowly, let the clutch rise below his left foot. The engine groaned and the car pulled its speed down into second gear.

"There." He said, "We're good now, Babe."

June barely acknowledged His assessment of the situation and continued writing in her note book. Just as Marsh's muscles had released their tension from the little slippage of the car, his eyes widened, mouth gaped open, and June heard the fast and deep sucking sound being produced in her husband's lungs.

A steel-hauling, flatbed semi-tractor-trailer was fully jack-knifed in front of them, bounding the median strip of the four lane highway, and headed directly toward their vehicle. Marsh realized immediately that his only hope of avoiding unthinkable disaster was to turn the car in the direction of the huge ditch in the center of the highway. Serious fans of the Indianapolis 500 had heard the race car drivers explain that you should always take your car to the place where an oncoming vehicle first lost control.

Due to his recent adjustment to slower speeds, he was able, without sliding on the ice covered road, to turn quickly in the direction of the ditch. What he did not expect, or could not have predicted was just at the last second before leaving the road with his, now airborne auto, the semi-trailer unfolded out of its jack-knifed slide, and turned back in the same direction that Marsh and June's car was headed. In mid-air across the center of the median ditch the front of the powerful Mack Diesel tractor collided with the passenger side of the beautiful late model sedan.

Marsh knew he had sustained some painful injuries in the horrific explosion of metal and glass. He was aware of his still conscience state, and immediately turned toward his beautiful, young wife. Her broken, slumped, twisted, and already blood-covered body lay contorted, somewhere near what had been the front floor board and front right wheel. As Marsh tried to free himself from the steaming metal trap, others began to run to his car and assure him help was on the way. Within minutes, that felt like hours, emergency help arrived, and both were extracted from the vehicle. They were rushed to the largest hospital in nearby South Bend.

Pastor James and Martha were notified that their youngest daughter was involved in a terrible accident, and was in a coma in the intensive care unit.

June's husband would recover in a couple days, and be released from the Hospital. But he would only leave for an hour or two each day for the next fourteen days, as he would sit vigil over the broken and motionless body of the joy of his life.

June's father, James, and mother, Martha would do the same. They were joined by many family members and friends who had come to pray and lend their support.

"Junie, my baby." The words slipped from her father James' thin and trembling lips, "I don't know if you can hear me or not, but If you can, I want you to know that your mother and I love you with all our hearts." James placed his small hand in her thin hand.

"Junie, I must know if you hear me." Then he did the unthinkable, "Junie, If you hear me at all, please squeeze my hand, Baby."

Was it his imagination he thought or his emotional desire?

"I felt that, Junie. I know you heard me." He leaned even closer to her ear, and holding her hand, made one more appeal, "My darling daughter, my darling Junie. If you have been talking to God, and you know all is well between you and your Savior, would you please squeeze my hand twice." He softly urged, "If I am going to see you in Heaven, Baby, will you squeeze my hand twice?

James lay his body over that of his dying daughter, breaking into a full sob. Just as quickly, he stood upright, pulled his wire-rimmed spectacles from around his large, protruding ears. After wiping tears from both eyes, he replaced the glasses slowly, one ear at a time, turned to his beloved Martha, and announced,

"Mother, she squeezed my hand twice, very firm and slow. She has made her peace with God, and we can be at peace for her."

Within a matter of minutes, their vivacious, young beauty peaceably drew her last breath.

It was painful to see the coffin, strewn with flowers, sitting at the front of the Mishawaka church, which James and Martha had loved and left two decades prior to follow their call in life. Most difficult for them, was to stand in that cold, snowy cemetery, and place her remains in the frozen sod.

Not since James and Martha had lost their baby to the famous flu epidemic that swept the little coal-mining town so many years ago, had they known the pain, only a parent who loses a child can experience.

"Opal, wait a minute please." came the soft but clear voice as she moved toward the car, beginning their sorrow-filled journey home to the Coolspring place.

"What is it, Marsh?" Opal replied, wondering what more could possibly be said that had not already been said with every tear and hug.

"I have something for you Opal. I wanted to wait until now to give it to you."

Marsh reached deep into his heavy, cashmere topcoat, pulled out a folded piece of paper, and handed it to Opal with his leather-gloved hand.

"Don't read it until you are on your way home." was his instruction. "Someone brought it to me in the Hospital. It was a letter June was writing to you in the car when the accident happened."

Opal took it gently from Marsh's hand and slowly looked at it on both folded sides. For a moment she was relieved there appeared to be no blood on it anywhere. She hugged her sister's, widowed husband, and thanked him for his love and care for her baby sister.

As they drove off, she just held the note between her palms for some time. Not sure if this would be the best time to look at its contents. Finally, she unfolded the lined sheets of tablet paper and began to read,

"My Dear Sister,

I Just wanted to drop a quick line to you today. It was so great to see you at Lowell's house last week. Boy, those boys are getting so big. Hey, that Manson is a rascal, you know. Told me a couple pretty good jokes, but I won't get him in trouble by telling them to you. Ha. Ha.

   Buddy is sure a sweet guy, and that little Fred is a doll, and Dicky even came over and sat on my lap for the longest time. You know Opal, I still can't talk much about your Sammy, but I can't wait to see what all he becomes in life.

   Sorry about my handwriting today, but this road is so slick with ice this morning that we are barely able to crawl without sliding all over the place.

   I better quit trying to write in this mess, and I will write more later. Just know I love you with all my heart and one thing more I want you to know_____."

At the bottom of the paper, the blue ink line shot violently across, and up the sheet of paper, running off the edge. Opal gasped, threw her hand over her face, and began to cry all over again, as she learned the last words from her sister were expressing love toward her. Opal would always wonder what was the one thing more she wanted to say. She stared for a long time at that line, and she took some comfort that both sisters were so lovingly linked the moment their lives changed forever.

****

The shock and pain of June's untimely passing place a year-long atmosphere of sadness over the Pawlaks of the Coolspring Place. And the demands of five children, the stress of financial inadequacy, as well as the usual additional relative needing shelter during a, much too often, set back of unemployment, hardship, or marital insecurity, turned the small apartment into a scene of miserable chaos. It was not unusual to find the attic over-flowing with not only Frank's and Opal's boys, but numerous uncles, aunts, nephews, nieces, cousins, and on occasion Grandparents.

Opal was sure she was entrapped in a hopeless existence, where there was virtually no possible improvement, or relief in sight. It was only her strong faith in God, which kept her occasional thought of suicide from becoming an actual attempt. Her spiritual pursuits were her only true escape from hopelessness. She spent time praying or reading in the rare moments when her boys, and whoever else was staying in the home, were out of the house. The greatest relief came more often from the form of worship practiced in many of the Pentecostal churches of that time.

After each service, the church conducted an informal time for the congregation to gather at the front of the church, and kneel or stand at the long, wooden kneeling benches, re-ferred to as "the Altar" in their religious nomenclature. Usually, there would be anywhere from a few to several musicians, gathered on the platform, playing continuous, familiar hymns and tunes for worship. The normal method of this musical presentation was to have certain common elements. Volume was primary. In other words, it was loud. Enthu-siasm was an absolute necessity, and the theme was vital.

Sociologically, it's true that people, unhappy with their station in life, very often attempt to reassure themselves that a better circumstance awaits them. Hopefully, this relief was just around the corner. The theme of the energy and emotionally-charged music would build this hope to a fevered pitch. Outbreaks of response from the avid seekers of hope, gathered at the front of the auditorium, were the normal behavior. Loud, vocal outbursts of "Hallelujah," and "Praise the Lord" were accompanied by openly, expressive weeping. At times the level of response would elevate to actual physical response. Some would fall prostrate on the floor, completely powerless to withstand the presentation of, what they knew was, "the Power of the Holy Spirit." Jumping in place, running around the outer aisles of the pews, and on occasion, a convulsive shaking of the entire body would appear as an ultimate manifestation of God's entrance into one's personal life. Many different theological views would define, debate, or declare this activity as simple mass hysteria at its best, demonically inspired at its worst, or a return to biblical behavior, present in the ex-perience of the Apostles of early Christianity.

For Opal Pawlak, the debate held no interest. What was obvious to Opal, at the brink of a nervous breakdown, was this form of worship provided at least one place that she could literally openly weep from the depths of her broken heart. If necessary, she could scream at the top of her voice, and not be judged as one losing their mind. She would simply be viewed as one of God's beloved children, receiving a supernatural visitation of divine power.

Opal's feet moved slowly across the wooden floor of the busy Woolworth's store on a cold, January morning. She felt somewhat peaceful, and comfortable at the contrast in temperatures to the bitter-cold bleakness, just outside the large front windows. The smell of the hot dogs being cooked behind the lunch counter was an inviting call she considered splurging on herself, if she had enough change left from the bus ride to town that morning.

"Jolla!" Opal called across the large display table of scarves and gloves at her waist. The tall woman with red hair turned grey by Southern Indiana rural life was perusing ladies accessories, and hadn't noticed Opal's entrance. This dear lady was loved by all for her big heart, which matched her big face and big laugh, but seeing her dear friend brought no joyous greeting in this moment.

"Opal, Sweetheart." came the soft and sober reply.

Jolla Jones pulled her hand out of the leather glove she had been admiring, and quickly moved around the end of the large framed display, moving toward Opal with a sympathetic gesture, arms extended in Opal's direction.

"Oh, Opal, I am so sorry, so sorry!" she said as she drew Opal's shoulders toward her awaiting arms. "So sorry, Darling."

Opal stopped in a combination of confusion and immobility. She thought immediately, "What is going on? What in the world would this dear friend be talking about?

There was no one Opal cherished like her dear church friend, Jolla. This woman meant everything to her, and the family. They had shared any extra food they could find during the depression years. Jolla was the greatest woman of faith Opal had ever had as a friend. Her distinctive, deep-throated voice, and Southern Indiana drawl was all Opal needed to hear when Jolla would pray. It was like she had a personal connection with God.

Never was Jolla's friendship held in higher esteem than during a time when the first three boys were very young, and Frank injured himself while working at the large lumber yard.

Frank had nearly destroyed four of the vertebra in his spine. All medical courses offered no hope for any kind of recovery. In as much as the church believed in the power of prayer for miraculous healing, Frank was prayed over multiple times. He was even carried by some friends to visit a popular healing evangelist that had become famous in certain religious circles. But all of their faith and prayers combined had done nothing to improve Frank's condition. His crippling infirmity appeared more evident by the day.

On one particular night, Frank had been carried to a fellow church member's home. He and Opal could participate in what the church called, "Cottage prayer meeting." Frank was laid on the sofa, in the only comfortable position he could endure; his face to the sofa's back, and his back to the other attendees.

As time passed that evening, Jolla excused herself, and left by the front door. Upon her arrival at the front gate, she would later tell that she heard a voice from somewhere deep within her.

"Go back in there, and pray for Frank's back."

For a moment, she argued with the voice.

"Lord, we have prayed so many times for Frank. He has been carried to every person of faith we know. Who am I to think that one more prayer from a nobody like me will heal Frank?" Then she heard it again,

"Go pray again for Frank."

Then she reasoned from her recent knowledge. Opal had told her that evening before the meeting that the Doctor had given Frank and the family a letter that day. The Letter stated, in no uncertain terms, Frank had four torn vertebrae. The doctor went on to declare that Mrs. Pawlak would qualify for something called, "Mother's Aid," because Frank would never be able to work a job again in his life. In spite of her doubts, Jolla did return to the little living room, and as she entered, she looked across the room and saw Frank's back. She walked across the room, and placed her hand right in the middle of Frank's back. To her shock, Frank startled, and suddenly did the impossible. He swung his feet off the sofa, and stood up as straight as a tin soldier.

Frank would describe it with detailed enthusiasm in his voice for decades to follow.

"I had actually fallen asleep on that sofa, when suddenly I felt like I had backed up against a hot pot-bellied stove. My back felt like it was on fire, and I knew I had to jump to my feet."

Frank bent at the waist, touching his toes, and loudly announced,

"I am Healed, I am healed! Look, no pain! I have no pain!"

The entire room of people began to weep and celebrate the answer to what they had so often prayed. But now they were so shocked, no one in the room had the audacity to claim it was their faith that had done it. Even Jolla admitted that she had argued with God, so it was not her faith that did the miracle, even though her final obedience to the voice was pointed out by several that night.

To add validity to the miracle that Frank had just received, a fellow member of the church asked Frank if he would like a job. Frank went to work the next morning in the man's coal delivery company. Frank's job was shoveling coal off the ground and onto the delivery trucks. Frank never evidenced a back problem again, and he would work in heavy industrial factories the rest of his working life.

Opal's rapid temporary mental review of her friend, Jolla's, worth to her and Frank's family was just as quickly brought back to the reality of the present. She felt again the heavy grasp of Jolla's arms, and heard what seemed like an echo, repeating the words,

"I'm so Sorry, so Sorry."

Opal grasped Jolla's upper arms, pushed her away at arm's length and questioned,

"What, Jolla, What are you apologizing for? What are you talking about? What, Jolla, What's happened?"

"Oh my Lord, Oh my Jesus." began to flow from Jolla's stunned voice.

Opal interrupted her friend's panicked moans,

"Something has happened, something bad. Jolla,
what, what has happened?"

Now Jolla reached upward with her hands to place each one tenderly against both sides of
Opal's face. She forced her to the attention of her compassionate eyes,

"Opal, Sweetheart, you need to go home, now. Go home. I will help you get to the bus, or
we will get a cab but you need to go home, now."

Opal burst into tears, and her naturally-strong voice carried across the department store,
while stools at the nearby lunch counter pivoted to hear her shout to her friend,

"No, Jolla! No you must tell me what has happened. Please, Jolla, as my friend you can't
just not tell me."

"Opal, Baby," Jolla replied, trying to get control of the nightmarish predicament in which
she found herself.

"It is not my place. You have to listen to me, and just get home to your family."

"My family, my family?" Opal pressed, "What has happened to my family?" Opal unloaded all her emotions, "Jolla Jones, my dearest friend, woman of God, He has you here
with me right now for a reason! Please, please, I beg you, tell me what is going on."

With those words, Jolla grasped Opal's hands to her bosom, and looked upward to the art
deco plaster ceiling of the store, as if to plead for either divine intervention or exceptional
wisdom. Returning her eyes back to Opal's fixed, green fountains of relentlessly-flowing
liquid, she says,

"Opal, I just heard on the radio before entering the store that your brother James Junior,
and his wife, Bertha, and the three little girls were hit by the South Shore Railroad this
morning. Evidently, no one has been able to reach you."

The sounds of the store went away, and the high-pitched squeal that replaced it seemed to
plug Opal's ears like a cupped hand smiting her ears at the same time. Opal staggered and
Jolla grabbed her to steady her from falling. An incessant pounding began to strike each

of Opal's ear drums as her medically-treated high blood pressure soared to new and dangerous levels.

The next sound Opal distinguished amidst the fog enveloping her mind and body, was the closure of the taxi door. She could not make her arm lift her hand to gesture to Jolla, as she viewed her friend's wet face. The cab pulled from the curb.

"I'm numb." was Opal's first thought. "Maybe paralyzed. Why can't I feel my hands or feet?" She realized there was a voice breaking the roar of the taxi engine.

"Where do ya need to go, Lady? Hey, Lady, I got to have an address. Where do you live?"

"What?" Opal finally spoke.

"Come on Ma'am. Ya gotta know where you live."

Where do I live?" Opal thought for a minute, and then heard her own voice say the frightening words, "I have no Idea where I live."

Fortunately, the cab driver Jolla had placed Opal with was a native son of Michigan City, and he knew most of the generational families in town, at least by name.

"Ok, Sweetheart, let's try this. Can you tell me your name?"

"My name, my name," Opal felt pure panic. Could she remember her name?

"Opal, Opal Marie...uh. Wait, wait just a minute. I know, I think, uh, yeah I think, uh," Then as if reaching the end of the life saving rope at the edge of a cliff, she said,

"Pawlak. Yeah, my name is Pawlak. It was Rice, but now it is Pawlak."

Upon hearing the word Rice, her mind drew up a picture of her younger brother James Junior Rice. Jolla's words replayed in her head,

"Your brother James Junior, and his wife, Bertha, and the three little girls were hit by the South Shore Railroad this morning." She threw her head back on the taxi seat and began to cry a mournful groan from somewhere deeper than she or the driver could ever define.

"Hey, I know that name, Pawlak." declared the driver. "Is that the big, red, brick house out there on Coolspring Ave?"

Opal could only nod her head silently up and down with the relief that she was going to get home safely.

"Sure," the driver continued, "That is where Johnny Pawlak lives with his mother. I used to work with him at Pullman's and he would call me to take his mother to the bandshell for the Sunday concerts in the summer. Don't worry about a thing, Mrs. Pawlak I will get you right there."

When Opal entered the apartment, several family members were already assembled. They began to express how they had tried to find where she had gone that morning. No matter how many arms wrapped around her and how many more times tears would burst forth, Opal felt caught in this daze, and she kept asking one question:

"Where is Frank?"

She was assured again and again that he had been notified at the factory and was already en route home. Frank entered the kitchen door, and Opal ran to his awaiting arms. As they stood there, entwined for a long period of time, without one word being spoken, Opal's pounding ears began to ease, and the ringing subsided. She became aware that in spite of the meager surroundings she had come to despise, and the hopelessness of her children's station in life, she found solace with her face placed firmly on the chest of this good, godly man who loved her and the five sons, with which God had gifted them both.

The tragedy of a young couple, each twenty-nine years of age, was spread across the newspapers and radio stations throughout the entire area. Photos of the disintegrated auto, and tactful, but painful descriptions of the human mutilations of both parents, and the three, preschool-aged little girls were either kept for future scrapbooks, or destroyed immediately, depending on the mindset of friends and family. The tragedy was so deeply impactful in the minds of the Rice family, that from that time forward, most memories of the family would be remembered in one of two categories; before the accident, or after the accident. "James and Bertha" was the title given to the devastating event, and for decades the reference was understood by family and friends.

Adding to this tragedy, as much as any opera performed on the stages of European theaters, would be visions of the newspaper photo of Opal's youngest brother Fred, now a

Reverend himself kneeling before the three eldest of James' and Bertha's children. The caption under the photo read,

"The Rice Children hearing that they are now Orphans."

Grandparents James and Martha resented that term as they, without hesitation, took full responsibility of raising the older children as their own. For the rest of the family there was an awkward, yet thought-provoking reality in the photo. One living child was missing. This had been the baby that an elderly aunt and uncle saved in her early life. This sober fact remained as an ironic comfort; certainly, this child would have been in that vehicle, and would have joined the painful sight of six, rather than five caskets lining the front of the old Mishawaka church.

This remaining middle child battled natural feelings and questions as to why and how her parents could give her up, keep the other three, then reconcile their marriage, and have three more children. The fact remained, her life had been saved for a purpose known only to God. She would be cared for by adopted parents who loved her beyond measure, and made her the fulfillment of their every dream. She went on to live a life of strength and character, and know the true experience of a family she would have never known, except that her God knew how much she would be needed and loved.

In the midst of the tragic nightmare, decisions had to be made under the pressure of time that would prove not so well thought out at the time. One of those would affect Frank and Opal in a most vivid manner.

No Uncle could have ever been a greater hero to a young fifteen year old boy than was James Junior to Frank's eldest boy, Manson. Uncle James drove big semi trucks, played an awesome guitar, looked like a movie star when he flicked his cigarette ashes in the rolled up cuff of his blue jeans. James struck an impressive figure mounted on one of his horses, and he gave his tag along nephew a special place of manly inclusion in the pack, willing to share the latest nasty joke he had just heard on the over-the-road truck trail.

When word came that the funeral director needed a family member to identify the bodies in the morgue, the duty fell on youngest son Fred Gilbert. It was determined that this task would be just too difficult for parents James and Martha and perhaps Uncle Freddy, as all called him, would find additional strength in his clergy position. The unexpected happened when Manson made the request to join Uncle Freddy in the identification procedure. Manson argued that this was his favorite person in his life in many ways, and he would be able to honor his uncle this way. Even upon entering the morgue the director voiced concern at having someone this young take part. According to the experienced director, he had never in all his years of practice seen this kind of carnage. Both Uncle Freddy and Manson assured the director that he was mature enough, and he considered this his act of honor to the man he loved dearly.

As each victim, from smallest child, to eldest was uncovered, the sights seemed to intensify in horror. The two littlest ones were actually recovered, wrapped in each other's arms, and may have been wrestling in the back of the car when the accident occurred. This led to one of the many speculations as to how a driver like James Junior, decorated for safety, could be distracted to the oncoming commuter train, traveling at high speed. Other possibilities were that the crossing light was not working. Bud had shown Frank just days before the broken pieces of warning signal, which had been shot out at this crossing. Amazingly, the lights were repaired and in perfect working order within an hour of the accident. Another speculation was that the utility company in the area had been burning brush along the rail line that morning, and smoke may have been covering the tracks, obscuring the vision of a high speed train.

The engineer would even testify that he saw James Junior's car pull up to the crossing, come to a complete stop, and then just moments before the train arrived at the crossing, lurch onto the tracks. It was winter, there was snow on the ground, and some thought perhaps ice or snow on the bottom of James Junior's engineer boots could have slipped off the clutch causing the car to jump forward.

By the time Uncle Fred and Manson had viewed Aunt Bertha's body, they were clinging to each other for added strength. When they stepped to the table that held James Junior, the director again emphasized that this would be the worst, and perhaps the young man would be better to bypass this viewing. The fact that James Junior's body had been hurled hundreds of feet down the track after receiving most of the initial impact could have in no way prepared them for the sight. Upon pulling the cover back, Manson and his preacher Uncle literally dove for each other's arms. A combination of groans and wails permeated the room. Manson spent weeks of sleepless nights. He suffered shaking spells, and by all known symptoms, experienced a nervous breakdown that plagued the teenager for some years to follow. He was never able to put into words what he saw, and no one would desire that of him. The closest anyone could imagine was when, on the following Halloween night, one of the family entered the apartment with a rubber mask of unusual detailed gore. Long before the desensitization of modern movies would leave most of society shockproof, Manson screamed a horrible scream,

"Get that thing out of here! Take it away!"

It was removed quickly and disposed of with everyone's understanding. Manson did not have to explain his Post Traumatic Stress reaction.

One of the darkest aspects of mankind seemed to be displayed on the tragic day of this accident. James Junior had just stopped by his place of employment that morning, and he received his latest salary payment in cash. He tucked it in his large billfold, and attached it to the chain from his belt to his rear pocket, before beginning his trip from the Beverly Shores residence to the Pine's cutoff location he was moving his family to. Inasmuch as his body had been hurled hundreds of feet away from the place the train and car came to stop, someone arriving shortly after the collision found their way to James's body, saw the billfold, and quickly removed the contents and disappeared.

A childhood friend and former baseball team mate of Frank's who had become a noted columnist for the local newspaper wrote several articles about this inhumane atrocity, and pleaded with the dead body bandit to return the monies that would help the children, remaining under the care of the modestly financed grandparents. No response ever came, even when arrangements had been made to protect the perpetrator.

There was a long funeral procession of five hearses, and several family cars, which the funeral home provided at no cost in light of the highly publicized tragedy. A train of mourners and some interested observers, pulled from the front of the family church in Mishawaka just as it had done the previous year for the beautiful Junie. To make this entire morbidity literally chill all to the bone, the graveside interment was conducted on the coldest day of 1951's new year. Snow blew at near hurricane force, and stung any uncovered face or hand.

"Therefore, we commit these bodies to the ground, dust to dust and ashes to ashes, awaiting the great day of their resurrection." boomed the powerful voice of the family pastor, who had preached most of the family funerals.

He was perhaps the closest pastor friend that Rev. James and Martha had ever known. His closing prayer called upon the King of Kings and Lord of Lords to bring comfort to this pain-filled family in their dark hour of suffering. Upon the Amen of the Benediction, Frank and Opal turned from the tented side of the five burial sites to return to the cars, knowing these unbearable conditions were not the place to linger, even to express their heartfelt appreciation to the amassed throngs who weathered this day for them.

As Opal's turn from the scene, she became momentarily blinded by the painful flash of what appeared to be hundreds of light bulbs exploding all at the same time. The moment she realized where this unexpected onslaught of surprise and discomfort originated, she verbally exploded.

"What are you doing here? Who said you could be here? Get away! Get out of here! Do you not have any respect for people's feelings?" She shouted at an array of reporters.

Frank quickly put his arm around Opal's shoulder and attempted to pull her back from her onward assault of popping sounds, winding gears, noisy clicks, and the virtual multitude of flash bulbs.

"Come on, Opal. Never mind those vultures, just ignore them."

This was Frank's usual controlled approach to most inconveniences. As they moved through the tumult Opal questioned Frank,

"Why are they here? Who said they could be here? They have no business being here."

To which the always, peace-pursuing Frank would simply give as realistic an answer as his Father Kaz would have given in the same situation,

"This is news, Opal, you can't keep them away."

****

"Jimmy, before you leave, how's about singing one of them good old Gospel songs we love to sing?" came the request from the tiny, toothless Appalachian lady.

Without a word, James softly pulled Martha by the wrist toward him, and with his other arm beckoned his frail, little sister to snuggle to his side. As the trio of brother, sister and wife stood on the wooden porch of the Kentucky mountainside shack, James began to softly sing some familiar words of one of their favorite church selections.

"I'll meet you in the morning by the bright riverside

When all sorrow has drifted away
    I'll be standing at the portals when the gates open wide
At the close of life's long weary day."

Then Martha and her sister-in-law joined in the singing with the nasal, twang-filled sounds of what would be later defined as America's true musical creation, "Bluegrass music."

"I'll meet you in the morning
With a how do you do And we'll sit down by the river
And with rapture old acquaintance renew.
You'll know me in the morning By the smile that I wear
When I meet you in the morning
In the city that's built foursquare."

Upon finishing the eerily prophetic wail in the song, James and Martha said their farewells to the dear soul on her porch, and they slipped into the front seat of the 1952 Nash Ambassador. It was the first new car that the Reverend James had ever owned, and thus, the reason for the trip to the mountains to see his loving sister. Within days of their return, James sank into a downward spiral of physical decline.

"Mother." as James would so often call his beloved Martha, he called out from the bedroom.

Martha quickly placed the waffle Iron back on the shelf, wiped her batter-covered finger tips and hastened to his side. Upon entering the room, she softly seated herself on the side of the bed, taking James' outstretched hand.

"What is it, Daddy?" to which James just as softly, yet with clear and exacting voice replied,

"Martha, I need to tell you a few things, and you need to listen well." She moved even closer to his face.

"I'm listening, Daddy."

"I'm getting ready to go home now. I can't stay any longer, and I have some final instructions for you."

At the top of his list of final requests, he asked that she keep James Junior's three children together, and not let them be raised by anyone else but her. After sharing a few more things he felt she needed to tend to he simply laid his head back softly on his pillow, closed both eyes, took a deep peaceful breath, and departed his present existence.

Martha would find herself again, gathered with family and friends at the Mishawaka church, only this time she stood alone. It would not be June's coffin or even Junior's family's stretched across the front of that church. It would now be the body of the love of her life that took her from those Kentucky hills as a fifteen-year-old girl, spending a lifetime building churches and loving people. The long procession, again wound its way through the streets of the city James asked her to leave all those years ago. She would oversee his body being laid beneath the soil next to their daughter, son, daughter-in-law, and three granddaughters.

The familiar Funeral Director remarked to Frank and Opal, as they walked once more from this much too familiar scene,
"I know Rev. Rice battled Diabetes, but I'm sure it was the last two years of heartbreak that took his life."

****

If Frank's and Opal's five boys bore any particular matching attributes, it was certainly their active minds and active bodies. Sports was beginning to play a vital role with the oldest two. Although Frank's game of choice was baseball, Manson and Buddy began to gravitate toward basketball. This was influenced by the fact that they were growing up in the State of Indiana, where every driveway, garage, or country barn was adorned with a basketball backboard and hoop. Long after the cotton nets had disappeared at the hands of the insufferable winters, the bare basketball rims made the shooting skills of Indiana boys among the best hoopsters North of Adolph Rupp's Kentucky all-stars. A healthy, if not contentious argument would persist for years to come as to which State produced the best players.

Perhaps, a more influential reason Manson and Buddy loved Basketball was that even before their teenage years, it was obvious that they were going to both grow to above-average height. Their little Township school coach, as well as themselves, understood they would quickly develop into a "bookend" set of brothers that anyone would love to have on their team. Manson and Bud would try to stretch each muscle of their bodies on a regular basis, in anticipation that their new nightly measurement would show one a hair taller than the other. Both were regularly thrilled, and terribly disappointed to see that they had either grown over, or fallen short of the other. These growth spurts rotated on a regular basis as they aged.

Bud finally ended up a couple inches taller than Manson at six feet, two inches. This was fairly tall for a boy not yet in high school, and certainly served his game well, underneath the basket, scoring and fighting the much shorter boys for the rebounds. His patented hook shot mimicked that of the most famous tall man in basketball at the time, George Mikan, who would go on to be enshrined in both the College and Professional Basketball Hall of Fame.

Manson, never short of confidence, accepted his final six feet height as plenty. His natural gifts of foot speed, ball-handling expertise, and an above-average accuracy in shooting the classic, one-handed, set shot at extremely long distances. This skill made him the most regularly listed high-scorer of each game. His natural quickness, and long legs also produced several ribbons of accomplishment for high-hurdle events at the County-wide Track & Field tournaments.

Fred would not garner the abnormal physical size of his two older brothers, but would far surpass them both with lightning speed. He not only duplicated his big brothers' dribbling and passing skills, but actually exceeded them. To all observers alike, his body only appeared about half again as large as the basketball, which he maneuvered with the same efficacy as America's most popular traveling basketball show, "The Harlem Globetrotters."

Dicky was about to join the ranks of other first-grade attendees. Of all the boys it was Dicky who seemed to have the most pleasant sweetness. Frequently he'd flash a bashful little smile when spoken to, and he was quick to find a comfortable lap to place himself upon, if given the slightest opportunity. What made his pleasant personality a bit of a surprise was not just the difficult way in which he entered this life, but he had been left with a walking difficulty, requiring special braced shoes. Due to the combination of failed experimentation in early reading classes, in which the teaching of phonics would be replaced with attempted sight memorization, Dicky would quickly fall behind in grasping the initial concepts of sight reading. Also unknown for many years, was what many educators considered an early grade school anomaly for some children. It never alarmed anyone when Dicky would write most of his letters backwards. Teachers would simply take his hand with the #2 pencil, set between his fingers, and try to show him how to reverse his previous creation. Dyslexia was an unknown word to the educators, and was certainly not something the average family ever encountered in that day.

This disorder within the brain, affected the way its victims would see, and try to translate verbally or graphically, what the eyes were observing. The place it would display itself most often, was in spelling memorization. For Dicky, his mind could audibly comprehend, and even place in memory the spelling of a word, but the memory was short lived.

Opal worked with Dicky before placing him on the bus for school. Before leaving the apartment, he could recite all ten words on the spelling list correctly. Unfortunately, by the time he had the words recited to him in a classroom test, he could not recall their character and image to write them on the paper. The ultimate result; these words could also never be recognized by sight, thus complicating an inability to read. The only answer the school had available was to hold him back from first grade, believing that somehow another round of the same would have a different effect.

Finally, he was promoted to the second grade, and the third, while yet still being unable to read. At the end of the third grade, the school failed him again, making him repeat the grade.

Opal could not stand this humiliation for Dicky, and she began to search for a school that would, at least place him in the fourth grade, where he would only be one year behind. It would mean attending a private school. St. Paul Lutheran School in the middle of the city.

The sacrifices were huge. Opal took in extra Laundry to pay for the private school, as she, still peeved with the public school, enrolled Sammy, a second grader, in the school at St. Paul's, as well.

Dickey still struggled, but he was treated so kindly, and given special attention that he made good progress, as long as it did not involve reading or spelling. Greater than his learning challenges, were his personal feelings about his own appearance. He detested the new glasses he had to wear, due to his weakened eyes. His pigeon-toed walk made him feel different than the other kids, even though his passion for basketball placed him more and more on the ball court.

His school challenges would continue until the day he turned sixteen, and he could officially walk out of school. That day he would walk to the IGA Grocery Store, begin bagging groceries, and become, in time, a successful grocer, while still unable to read or write.

He became a master of "faking it" for many years, until he saw an offer on TV promoting a self-learning program that could teach phonics to anyone who had never learned to read. With the help of his wife and grown children, he did learn to read.

****

Opal was entertaining a friend in the Coolspring place living room on a warm Summer day in 1951. A discussion ensued between the two ladies about women having babies as they neared that forty year marker.

"We'll, I'll tell you one thing," Manson spouted off, as usual, without any invitation to enter the conversation. "If my mother has any more babies, I'm out of here."

Opal slowly moved her eyes from the attention she had been paying to her friend's previous statements, and she slowly rotated her head in the general direction of Manson's moving body, crossing the living room. He was intending to get a fresh shirt from the little room at the front of the apartment.

"Well," Opal slowly dragged out the word as if his had been written with at least ten "L"s on the end, then gazing directly at the back of Frank's head, as he passed, she firmly stated, "You better start packing your things while you are in that room."

Manson stopped in his tracks, suddenly spinning his body around to face his mother, and shot out an attacking question.

"Surely, you're not telling me you are pregnant again!"

At this point, both Opal and her friend could not maintain their composure any longer. They both burst into a full explosion of laughter.

"No, this can't be happening! wailed Manson. "I'm sixteen years old, driving a car, working a job, and my mother is still having babies. This is crazy!"

Opal placed a crossing-guard hand between she and Manson, and reminded her eldest son, in that voice that only Opal could produce,

"Young man, I don't remember coming to you for advice as to whether your father and I would expand the breadth of our family size."

On a cold January day in 1952, Manson and the other four boys would all be just as excited when Frank and Opal Pawlak would bring into this world their sixth child. But what promoted this event to astronomical proportions was that, after introducing to this world five rambunctious boys, Opal Pawlak would finally get her little girl.

Opal recovered in the hospital with her new, delightful, little girl, and Frank took the boys that Sunday to church.

"I would like to make a special announcement today." said the pastor before the congregation. "We want to congratulate Frank and Opal Pawlak on the birth of their new child. Furthermore, I have the special joy of announcing this sixth child is finally a girl."

The audience burst into uproarious applause. The Pastor seemed to feel it was an appropriate time to add a little levity to the scene. He continued,

"You know, Brother Frank," as was the custom of reference in the church at that time, "When the Lord said to multiply and replenish the earth, he did not mean for you to do this all by yourself."

At which Frank, never missing an opportunity to fire back a hilarious, ad-libbed response, cried out to the pastor,

"Now you tell me!"

The pastor almost never got the congregation or the service back under control that day. Frank would be overwhelmed with the onslaught of well-wishers, pumping his hand and saying,

"Wow, finally got that girl. Bet Opal is out of her mind with joy."
Frank repeatedly said,

"Well, she has been a good wife, and she gave me five boys for a basketball team. I thought I would go ahead and let her have a cheerleader!"

By the summer, even Manson found that having a six-month-old, beautiful, little baby girl in the front seat of his 1951 Ford would attract more girls to the side of his car than any fender skirts, blue dots in his tail lights, fuzzy dice hanging from his rear view mirror, or wolf-whistle horn. It was not a popular term at the time but his little sister, Valery Joy would become, for sure, the best "chick magnet" an overly flirtatious sixteen year old boy could ever hope for.

CHAPTER 7 - 1953-1963

Over the next couple years, the Coolspring place became even more a center for perpetual motion and commotion. The sound of the basketball pounding by the hour on the dirt court seemed to never cease. It banged off the backboard and rim, firmly attached to the long, straight, limbless, pine tree that had been brought from the nearby woods for this exact purpose.

The large, cement, front porch, the old unpainted, dirt-floored garage, the large field between the two-story building and Mrs. Bies' house, and the often automobile-filled, grassless, front yard made the Coolspring place an ideal loitering center for youngsters throughout the old Brinkman section of town. Car hoods were raised to tweak one more feature on the young men's polished cars. Trunks were opened to store a few more sandfilled gunny sacks, providing enough weight to lower the back bumper to "really keen" levels. The blast of someone's portable radio, screamed out the latest songs from a whole new music genre called "Rock and Roll." Sometimes, the atmosphere would fill with the strongly pervasive wail of the day's most powerful country music hero. The night sounds would familiarize the entire neighborhood with the latest releases by Elvis Presley, Jerry Lee Lewis, Little Richard, and the likes of Hank Williams, Lefty Frizzell, and Johnny Cash.

When Buddy was about fifteen, like many young boys at that time, he thought he would try his hand at smoking the "Devil's weed," tobacco. Opal realized that each time Bud returned home from his evening walk, he had the fragrance so unfamiliar in their house, cigarette smoke. Not only was the odor on his clothes and hands, there was also the strong anise-flavored smell of the popular breath mint of the day called Sen-Sen. These mixed odors now covered Bud's new fangled, wireless, portable transistor radio.

It was not nearly the church's, still firm stand against the use of tobacco in any form, as it was her memories of that night when he was a baby, which infuriated her. She still remembered how God gave him breath when there was literally no more to be found in his lungs.

"I know you are smoking, Bud, and I can't stop you or beat it out of you." Opal declared while pulling the front of his shirt so his tall, lanky body could descend to her, below average height. Eye to eye and nose to nose she made her position known, and she punctuated it with an adamant guarantee, like only Opal could do,

"If I ever see you in my presence with a cigarette in your hand, I will shove it down your throat."

No matter how many years Bud smoked, he never lit or held a cigarette in the presence of his mother for the rest of her life. If she happened to draw near while he had one in hand, he would simply slip it down his side to the ground and step back on it. When asked why he simply replied,

"That woman made me a promise one day, and I am sure she would keep her word."

It was not unusual for someone to add to the hot summer night, the excitement of a newly-found firecracker. The sleeveless, or rolled up tee shirts beckoned an occasional six-inch punch contest. Young men took turns smashing their fists into each other's, tightly-braced, upper arm from a measured six-inch distance. This measurement would be calculated by placing one's little finger against the opponent's muscled arm, stretching the aggressor's hand toward himself until his thumb was fully extended toward his own chest, then placing the other fist to the end of the thumb. Without drawing the fist back in any measure, the puncher would thrust his fist in a forward-only direction, traveling the estimated six inches until the punchee's ache-induced arm consumed the full blast of the assault. It was only one of many ways that true masculinity could be displayed among the highly-hormonal, young men assembled at the Coolspring place.

Youngest son, Sam was more than a casual observer, he was an avid fan of the testosterone testing. He found the life and activities of his older brothers and their bevy of friends, enemies, and associates to be the greatest form of entertainment. Even more than the new Wells Gardner TV that finally found its way into the Pawlak house, the activities, music, sports, cars and storied adventures of his big brothers held him spellbound. Life on Coolspring Avenue woke his young mind to a world of possibilities that he could someday apprehend for himself.

****

Before long, the usual scenes at the Pawlak compound began to change. Manson travelled on weekends with invitations to perform Gospel music, and even followed his grandfather and uncle's vocation as an itinerant preacher. Within the family's church circles he was called an "Evangelist." Manson's multi-instrumental talent, and exciting preaching style soon had him traveling to other states to fulfill the many invitations offered to him. It was, however, in one of the services to a nearby community known as Kingsford Heights, that he would be introduced to a pretty, young lady who had relocated from the state of Georgia. Their romance budded quickly, but within a short time, her family relocated to Detroit to work in the auto industry. This meant many long weekends that Manson would be making a run to the Royal Oak section of Detroit. Bald tires, speeding tickets, and barely enough gas money for the round trip, would be absolutely no deterrent to transforming this little lady from interested fan to fiancé in short order. They made it to the marriage altar on a beautiful June day in 1956.

Around the same time, Buddy left the, not so luxurious attic of the Coolspring place to take up residence with his Grandma Martha. Her place held several attractions for the young man. First, there were no little ones crowding up the place. Grandma's waffle breakfast, and her famous chocolate cake, which she called "Wacky Cake," were especially delightful temptations. These amenities, plus a room of his own made Bud feel as though he were moving into the Conrad Hilton Hotel.

By November of that same year, Bud was walking that marriage aisle himself. Finding a career as a full-time butcher, he quickly found himself madly in love with the most beautiful cashier from the large grocery store where he was now a meat cutter.

For Sam, the sadness of his two big brothers departing for regions unknown was quickly dispelled with the reality that he would be promoted from sleeping on the scratchy, nylon frieze sofa in the front room, to one of the real steel-framed beds in the upper attic. His elation was short-lived, when he experienced the environmental challenges of the elevated space.

"Mom! Mom, I can't breathe." Sam cried out in the darkened attic. "It is too hot, I can't breathe."

The scary images of large winter coats hanging in the corner of the attic during this record-setting, blistering heat spell conjured images of walking monsters in Sam's young mind. Adding to the suffocating scene was the fact that no window could open, and the fan at the bottom of the stairs kept blowing the fuses in their part of the apartment.

Frank placed copper pennies behind the fuses in the past to make them work, but the possibility of them catching fire was just too dangerous. Opal's fear that the apartment would catch fire, leaving her boys trapped in that attic made Frank promise he would no longer try to jury-rig the electrical box.

"Mom, I can't sleep. It's too hot up here." was Sam's reprise.

"Come on, Sam. Shut up and go to sleep." his Brother Dick unsympathetically pleaded.

"I'll give you a nickel in the morning if you go to sleep." came the bribe offer from middle brother, Fred.

Considering Fred's frugal disposition, which would benefit him the rest of his life, Sam knew how frustrated Fred was becoming with his tirade, to offer real money.

"Mom, really, I'm dying up here it is so hot."

Opal's room possessed the only window. It offered only little relief from the horrid heat and humidity that a summer night could afford in the Midwest. She found the strength to calmly and peacefully offer some sympathetic vocal relief when she called in the direction of her bedroom ceiling,

"Lay real still, Son. Lay real still, and it will get better."

It wasn't what he hoped for, but Sam gave it a try, settling his thrashing body. He tried to ignore the sweat flowing from the sides of his forehead, and irritatingly trickling into his ears. Somewhere in the next few minutes he fell into a heavy sleep.

Though this scene was repeated several times, Sam never imagined that night how many times in his later life he would find himself crying out in complaint to his God, "This is miserable! I can't stand it! I can't take this!" only to hear the tender words of his mother,

"Lay real still. Lay real still it will get better."

****

No nine-year-old boy in the summer of 1957 could have been living a more exciting and fun-filled life than Sam was experiencing. Every morning he'd race through his bowl of cereal as if a race track flagman was holding a green flag at the doorway of that upstairs apartment, ready to wildly make the flag pop in the wind and send the signal to this blonde headed package of energy. The signal would say "Go boy, today's race has begun, hit those streets."

"Hey, hey! Hold on there, wild man." Opal shouted as she grabbed for Sam's arm. She placed a brown paper sack in his hand and barked out her order. "Here is a lunch I made for you. Don't lose it, and I don't want to see you back here 'til supper time. Do you understand?"

Without a word, Sam straddled the wooden stair rail, descending to the bottom. He dismounted the rail like Hop-A-Long Cassidy would have jumped from his faithful steed on Sam's favorite Saturday morning TV Western. Running out the door like "a mild mannered reporter for The Daily Planet, he could clear all four cement steps of the front porch with "a single bound."

Quickly atop the J.C. Higgins bicycle and standing tall on the rotating pedals, he began his trek toward the house on the corner of Coolspring and Hoyt Street. His friend Ricky grabbed his Montgomery Ward Hawthorne bike, and together they moved just a few houses to Big Dave's place. David was named that because he was twice the size of any boy his age.

Once to Earl Road, they moved quickly to Wabash Street, made the short turn to the church parsonage to see the pastor's middle son, Randy, already waiting. After gathering a few more additions to this harmless gang of motor-less street marauders, the decision of the day had to be made. With more arguments than some Supreme Court sessions have experienced, the benefits of which direction they would venture first were heatedly discussed.

"The beach!"

"No, Mt. Baldy!"

"No, Ames Field!"

After multiple nominations filled the noisy ballot, all would agree to the democratic form of resolve. Then a vote, preceded by a few healthy threats (after all this was the Chicago area), and finally, a slim majority prevailed. The result of the first decision of the day was of little consequence. Before the final trip of the day toward home and supper, all of the desired locations would have been visited.

From swimming, to racing the bikes, to finding pickup ball games, to a couple fistfights between friends, or new friends to be garnered, each day ended with sweaty, dirt-filled faces, grimy neck lines, dusty clothes, and a promise to each fraternal pal,

"See ya in the morning. We'll do it again!"

****

"Hey, Randy. Let's go up there behind the VFW where they're going to build those new houses."

Sam suggested on a hot, summer morning to the pal he considered truly, his best friend. Perhaps, it was because they had so much in common.

Randy was the preacher's son, and although Sam's parents were not pastors as such, their church life was almost their total life. Maybe it was that Sam loved to spend the night in the church Parish house, called by the people in this type of church, a Parsonage. All Sam knew was they had multiple bedrooms, and a shower, where he first saw "Soap on a rope." He knew his best buddy must be really rich. His family even traveled one time "overseas" to a place called Jamaica.

What may have bonded Sam and Randy into such a camaraderie was their whole church experience. Very early in their lives they both felt a certain appeal, and sincere interest in the proclamations of the church. Both had made declarations of faith into Christendom at early ages. They loved the vigor that their church style afforded, and they were enamored with the regular assortment of entertaining guest speakers and musicians who graced the platform of the Wabash Street church. So sincere, and somewhat emotionally motivated were these to friends that they even made pacts between themselves. While some of their other friends were slightly cutting each other's finger tips, placing their oozing fingers together to declare themselves "Blood Brothers," Randy and Sam felt this was a bit too pagan for them. Instead, they took a Bible and placed their hands upon the top to swear, unaware that the contents of the book they were using had admonished true believers not to follow such a practice. They vowed that someday they would get a travel trailer, and go from church to church, all over America and preach the true Gospel as they had heard it delivered to them each Sunday morning, Sunday evening, Wednesday evening, and every night of those two and three week long, protracted Revival meetings.

After a typical afternoon of adventure with Randy, Sam peddled right on past the Cool-spring place, all the way to Franklin Street, heading across from Bronco's Liquor Store, and forced his way into Kenitz Store to reward his freedom with a Baby Ruth Candy Bar, and a handful of red-licorice, silver-dollar candies. Having obtained the newfound energy that only a sugar rush can provide a carefree boy, he started his journey home.

"Excuse me, young man." Said the gruff voice of the, overalls-clad man, exiting the front door of the Coolspring place just as Sam was attempting to enter.

Sam really did not appreciate the stranger's big hand ruffling his wildly straggling mop of hair. As Sam's eyes and furrowed brow followed the large man's steps off the porch, he realized he had not even noticed the large, wood-slatted sides of the red and white farm truck. Sam had seen this kind of truck in the country whenever they visited his mother's cousin to bail hay, chop corn, or simply pick up fresh milk from the cousin's milk cows.

"Hmm," Sam thought, "My mom must have had some special company." He rudely mused. "Looks like a dumb old farmer to me."

"Well, you look like you've had quite a day, I'd say, young man." Opal voiced as Sam made his first steps into the apartment.

Sam was about to receive the most horrid announcement ever dispersed to any young man in his station of life. His mother simply said,

"Well, I have some amazing news for you, Sammy. We are going to be moving away from this place, and not just moving, but moving out of this stinking city and into the country! We are going to be living on a farm from now on!"

You could not have punched Sam in the solar-plexus with a Rocky Marciano uppercut that would have sucked the breath from his lungs any more than this announcement.

"Wait, Mom. What are you talking about?" Sam continued, "Moving? Moving? We are moving from here? Not living here? Moving from Grandma, Uncle John, and Aunt So-phie?"

It began to sink in deeply. "Moving to the country? I hate the country. Moving away from my friends? Away from Ricky? From David?" Bursting into tears, Sam cried out, "From Randy?" The questions flew. "Where will I go to school? Not Coolspring? Where will we go to church if we are way out in the country?"

Opal attempted to bring consoling arguments with all the benefits of country living, including bedrooms, yards, fields, gardens, and the possibilities of new friends. All Sam's mind could repeat was,

"The beach, Ames Field, the Dairy Queen, Kenitz..." On and on the list marched across the boys world as he knew it.

Opal explained,

"That man you saw leave in that truck, he has a big farm out on Highway 39 in Springfield township, and he has a big house that we can rent. He will even move us with his farm trucks. We will be out of this hot apartment. You won't have to sleep in the attic anymore. You boys will have some bedrooms you can share."

Sam was crushed and inconsolable. His world might as well be ending. Within a couple weeks Sam sat on the ledge of the large cement porch, and watched the last few items being placed on the big farm truck meant for carrying animals to the slaughtering house. Several of the neighborhood kids Sam was used to running the streets with stood around or straddled their bicycles. They hung their heads a bit, but no head hung as low as Sam's that day. Nothing as terrible would ever happen to Sam again. Not understanding the true difference between life and death Sam mused, "I wish I were dead today."

He did adjust some to the sounds and smells of country life, and he even found some areas of interest like hunting and romping the nearby fields, but he missed his friends and the only city he had known. To make matters worse, within months of moving out to the country his parents found a nearby village close to the farm that did not have a Pentecostal church.

Opal, calling upon her past experience with her pioneer, church-planting father, James, soon contacted church officials in that region, informing them if they wanted to found a new church in that community, they could be assured of a large family to help.

Thus, Sam was not only removed from his home, his city, his friends, his relatives, but now his church, which he loved so much, and even his best friend, pastor's son, Randy. He would not be attending an established church in a finely built structure, but would be going to church in a little, converted, storefront building, wedged between two taverns, which were allowed to be open on Sundays due their location across the Michigan State line. This geographical placement led to numerous stories of attempted church services shared with loud, staggering drunks, finding the wrong door at the most inappropriate times.

Sam resigned himself to his fate, and actually made new friends, as his mother had predicted. He became so involved in the new church venture that his early thoughts of becoming a minister some day began to feel more like a calling than a possibility.

Just as he was growing accustomed to the new reality, matters got geographically worse when Frank and Opal announced to the family they were moving again, less than two years since the last transition. This time, they relocated to a more modern house and a larger plot of land, where Frank and the boys could hunt their own land, raise a garden, and even have a horse and some pigs. All these deeper country amenities, which delighted his mother, only served to sever Sam's ties with his beloved Michigan City.

The frustrated youngster found himself in another country school, where the morning bus rides were so repulsive to Sam. Most of the fellow students on the bus were farm kids, which meant farm chores before school each day, which meant the fresh odor of barnyards still on the clothing of his classmates.

The annual class trips would include such bizarre locations as a local slaughterhouse. Shocked students watched animals being forced into a stall, struck in the head with a sledge hammer, and not quite fully dead, be snatched by their hind legs with a metal leg apparatus, upside down on a moving, overhead conveyor machine. Children grimaced as workers took a huge knife to the still kicking livestock, and opened the animal from chin to crotch, pulling innards from its body to the trough below. Boys vomiting, girls screaming in tears, and a few fainting students would make a country school's annual outing the delight of the desensitized rural community. Sam could never understand the fulfillment of the laughing slaughterhouse workers and, the somewhat demented faculty members of the country school.

There was one place of solace on that farm land for Sam; a rather large hill to the side of the house. His brother Dick would take his first car, a 1953 Pontiac Chief, and drive it through the field, up to the top of that hill, and run it down again as fast as he could, trying to avoid rolling the big heavy car over at the same time. It mattered not if the high-weeded hill was absorbing the hottest sun of the summer, or sprouting the new green under growth of a wet spring rain, or resisting the cold ominous chill of a late-fall evening, or even the deep heavy snow of the latest winter onslaught, Sam would walk to the top of that hill almost every day.

Once atop the highest vantage point on this farm, he felt the pain of missed friends, sensed the wind blowing in his face like the days he would speed his bicycle along the lakefront. Amidst the singing wind in the nearby woods he could hear the laughing voices of his old buddies, who now may as well have been on the other side of the world. Even though he was adjusting well to his new school, playing on the basketball team, working the lunchroom, or devouring every subject he studied at the hands of more than capable teachers, he vowed to himself that day, I will get out of this country life, and back into the city someday.

The longing of the displaced pre-teen could not consider how much his mother loved being out of that horrible upstairs apartment, with its disadvantages and fears. His misery in that moment was unaware of her enjoyment of the beauty of nature, and its open spaces. How could he know that fourteen years in the Coolspring place was an incarceration for the Kentucky-born mother? But did she know that the parole from her prison served as a sentence for her city-born son?

Sam stood atop that pinnacle point with the same question every day, "What's over that hill? What am I missing out there today?"

The boy made himself a promise.

"Even if I become a minister someday, I must know what is over that hill, and beyond the woods. I will do all I can to find out."

A roving and roaming spirit grew somewhere deep within the heart of this restless young man.

"There has to be more. There has to be something else. There is so much for me to see in my life."

These thoughts were becoming more than a passion and theme for Sam. He would make it the preeminent question for his entire being and existence on Earth. "What's over that hill?"

****

"Ah, cool, cool, so cool."

Sam sighed as he lifted one more scoop of running cold water to his, obviously, fevered face. For a moment he thought about the funny story of how his Grandpa Kaz had washed his sunburned face, from the new toilet bowl on the ship that had brought his first ancestors to America.

"I have to play tonight. It is the championship game of the Jr. High County tournament." Sam whispered to himself with each fresh application of cold water, as his frantic thoughts continued, "I missed two days of school this week and two practices but Coach Harry will still start me. I know Glen and Nicky are the best players but the coach really needs me under that basket for those rebounds."

Sam knew that there would be no leaving that farmhouse that night if he didn't pass his mother's inspection of face and forehead for satisfactory coolness. He quickly applied the last cold washcloth against his face, patted it dry with the small hand towel, zipped the quilted team jacket, and with basketball uniform and equipment, post-shower towel and spray deodorant in tow, rapidly walked through the kitchen to the back porch exit.

"Hey, just a minute, young man." came the vocal command from Opal, "You come over here right now."

"Aw, Ma!" Sam barked back at his mother, knowing that moving any direction other than her location, at the end of the dining table, would compel her pursuit of him.

Her hand moved exactly as Sam had predicted, first to his forehead, then quickly aside each facial boundary.

"Oh! You really feel pretty cool. That fever must have really broken last night. Ok, you have a good game, but don't overdo it. You still have been sick this week."

With a deep sigh Sam quickly pulled away from her clutch and burst through the door into the cold, crisp, late winter night, very thankful that the cold water treatment had worked, at least long enough to fool his nearly, non-deceivable mother. It did not take but the first few minutes of the game until it was obvious that Sam was not only unprepared to play, but physically unable.

"You're coming out now, Pawlak." Coach Harry told Sam during the time out.

When the team returned to the floor the coach said,

"Pawlak, come sit here by me. What's wrong with you tonight? You act like you don't even know where you are."

Sam could feel the fever again raging through his body. He thought it strange that even though he had run the gymnasium floor for several minutes, he had broken no sweat, and his body was actually chilling. The nauseated churn of his stomach was keeping him from offering the coach any reply whatsoever.

"Are you sick, Sam?" the coach interrogated further.

Sam could only nod his dizzy head up and down.

"Then get to the locker room, and stay there 'til we come in at half time." The coach ordered with a totally frustrated roll of his eyes.

Sam hated the circumstances but also welcomed the relief as he narrowly made it to the locker room toilets in time to grasp each side of the porcelain commode, and began to violently vomit. It was that kind of regurgitation that originates at the bottom of the feet before expelling from the front of the fevered face.

Sam laid on the dressing room bench and repeated his familiarity with the toilet throughout the remainder of the game until he was finally taken home by the coach. He spent another entire week fighting off what everyone knew as the influenza, but what his Polish family would know much better by the much more descriptive title "The GRIPPA."

After a few weeks Sam started to complain that his knees felt strange. He complained that they felt tight. Some mornings they seemed unbendable. Opal took Sam to a doctor she had heard of near their country home, but he simply explained to Opal that her boy was entering his teen years soon, and what he was experiencing was not uncommon. He diagnosed the problem as simply, growing pains."

****

"That's pretty good, Dad." Fred yelled out the window at the top of the stairs. "No, No Pap, that's too far! Bring it back a little bit." Then loudly Fred proclaimed, "There. There. Perfect! Stop and leave it right there."

This performance ritual was not uncommon when trying to get the best television reception from that educational channel in Chicago, almost 80 miles from their rural location. But turning the antennae produced at best a snowy picture on the old, black and white screen. This particular channel was seldom of viewing interest of this family, but this was different. This was Indiana, and this was High School March Madness. This was the State Basketball tournament where basketball was king.

The Michigan City Red Devils were always a basketball power in this Northwest, heavy industry-laden corner of Indiana. The city nestled itself against the "The City of Broad Shoulders," Chicago. The second round of the tournament was called the Regionals. The tournament location was again at the death trap for Sam's and his family's beloved team. The East Chicago Washington High School Gym had crushed the hopeless hope, for the Michigan City fans, year after year. To no avail, the team never seemed to make it past one of those local powers like Gary Roosevelt, Gary Froeble, Hammond High or any one of several great and talented teams.

This night presented again the possibility. The High School of his brothers, the pride of his beloved City, from which he had been exiled to this God-forsaken farmland, might just pull it out this time. Sam lay across one of the three beds shared by his two older brothers, still at home, and he followed every play of the game through strained eyes, as the reception faded in and out. The breeze outside would move the antenna. There was one distraction that Sam was resisting until, in the last minute of the game, it became obvious that his beloved team would again fall in the night game of the Regional, and the city would repeat the famous refrain, "Wait until next year." The distraction was again this nagging discomfort with his knees. This time there was even more pain. His elbows and wrists also seemed a bit achy. His left leg really was hurting more than usual. Sam never mentioned it, but when he awoke on the Sunday morning, he was more than surprised that his knees were really hurting. As he sat on the side of his bed and began to lift to his feet, a sharp pain surged through each knee. He quickly sat back down with an inward alarm, "What the heck...?"

Somehow, as he began to bend his knees and circle his feet at the ankles, the discomfort eased a bit and he finally stood, took a few steps, and slowly limped his way down the stairs to the restroom at the bottom. In fifteen minutes or so he was washed and ready to return up the stairs to dress for church and the normal Sunday events. The others noticed his slower gate and limp.

Even after Frank offered a post church surprise and suggested they travel to Laporte for a fried chicken dinner at Emma's Café, Sam's Dad teased him about his noticeable limp. As Sam struggled to get in and out of the car and restaurant that day Frank heckled,

"Hey, you're walking like an old man today." He continued, "I'm supposed to be the one getting old here, not you."

Little sister, Valery could not avoid the temptation to join in with sibling chortle.

"Hey buddy, if you're going to play for that new High School next year you better quit hobbling around like an old grandpa."

The only pain that Sam now seemed to feel was somewhere in the pit of his stomach. The reality hit him full on. I don't want to go to that school. That is not my Michigan City School. That is just more of the country.

The fact that the school was in a small community of a few hundred people, that it had a beautiful new Gymnasium and even had a football team, it was still country. Those smelly school bus rides to and from home, and above all, it was not the school of his dreams.

After the usual return to church for the traditional Sunday Evening service, Sam slid into bed early, a bit depressed about his future high school years, and even more confused about these strange aches and pains in the limbs of his young body.   What Sam could never have understood, was the siege of winter flu he had suffered a few weeks earlier, had left a working infection in his body, caused by a severe streptococcal infection. Because this event went undiagnosed and untreated, Sam was left with no viable means to prevent any future, and more dangerous conditions.

****

"Mom! Mom! Oh, God! Oh Jesus, help me! Mom!" The screams were best described by the familiar term, blood-curdling. "Help, somebody, help me! I can't move!"

Sam's pitiful and tear-filled screams were alone. Frank, Fred and Dick had left for their jobs sometime ago, and only Opal and Valery were downstairs. Opal did not let her premature onset of Arthritis in her knees, back, and hips prevent her from negotiating the stairs at above-normal speed. She called to her youngest son, whose wailing was not unlike an animal caught in a leg trap.

"What is it? What is wrong?"

Opal was already shouting long before she could reach Sam's bedside.

"I can't move my legs, Mom!" was Sam's panicked cry. "I'm paralyzed. I am paralyzed, Mom."

After assessing the alarming circumstances before her, Opal tried to calm Sam by assuring him he would be alright. She tried to get him to attempt again to move his legs. Somewhat relieved that his hands and arms all moved with his upper body, the panic of his inability to move his lower extremities came like waves over her emotions. She was, however, able to calm herself, and tell him she would call their regular doctor in the nearby village.

After making her call and returning to Sam, whose legs still seemed motionless, she explained that the Doctor had already called for an ambulance to come transport him to a hospital in Laporte where he would meet them. Even Sam was surprised when his condition was replaced by a resentment he had not expected.

"Laporte?" he questioned, "Why not St. Anthony's in Michigan City"

Opal quickly explained, "This Doctor does not work with the Hospitals in Michigan City. From out here we have to go to Laporte."

Sam thought to himself, "What could be worse? I can't move and now they are going to take me to some hospital in the town of Michigan City's most hated rival."

Even the word Laporte tasted putrid in his mouth.

After Sam was assigned a room in the Community Hospital, the short, funny-looking little doctor entered the room.

"Hello, Dr. Cohen." Opal fearfully said, "He can't move his legs. He says he is paralyzed. His...his...legs have been bothering him for some time." She tearfully stuttered.

Dr. Arnold Cohen calmly placed a hand on Opal's shoulder and asked,

"Is his Father here?"

For a moment it was the distraction he knew this panicked mom needed.

"We are trying to reach him at the factory in Michigan City, and we have told him to come here if he can get a way. He rides with someone else to work so it could be a while." Opal took a deep breath.

Dr. Cohen firmly said to Opal, "Please step out in the hall for a moment."

The Doctor, having quickly nodded toward Sam, physically conveyed the message that he did not want to speak in front of the boy. He continued,

"Now, Mrs. Pawlak, I am ordering an entire battery of blood work and x-rays to be immediately performed on your son. I can tell you we must all stay calm, but this could be serious. I will tell you straight ahead that with such an onset like this, we must eliminate some things first."

"What kind of things?" came Opal's speedy response? The Doctor continued in a soft tone,

"Well, number one is childhood Leukemia."

In a little more volume than the Doctor would have preferred, Opal shot back,

"Leukemia?"

"Now, now, Mrs. Pawlak, you must stay calm. We will look for everything, and I am confident we will get the answers fast. You go back to your son now and keep him calm, and I will get back to you just as soon as I possibly can. I will assist and watch over all the testing. Ok?

As he kindly motioned her back into the room, both Opal and Sam could hear the Doctor's metal heel taps click on the tile hallway and the sound diminished as he moved farther from them.

"Can you seem to move your legs any yet, Sam?" Opal asked as she moved over to the bed and placed one hand on her son's thin but athletically muscular thigh.

"Not really, Mom. When I try I feel like someone is sticking an ice pick in each knee." He explained in a shaky-voice reply. Then he said what Opal least expected, "Leukemia?"

He had heard his mother's carrying voice in her low-toned conversation with Dr. Cohen. Sam certainly did not know what the word meant or any medical factors of its dreadful possibilities, but he had heard the word often. He remembered how each time they traveled to family members in nearby Mishawaka or South Bend, or when they visited Dr. Cohen's office in the small village that held the High School Sam dreaded attending, that they would pass a certain house. The house was a one-story, fairly-modern, limestone structure that sat atop a hill with a wonderfully groomed front yard. In the front of the house was the largest picture window that Sam had ever seen, and upon each passing the entire load of passengers in their car would notice and mention the hospital bed positioned in the picture window. The story would be repeated how the young boy in the bed, watching the world pass him by, suffered from a dreaded condition known as Leukemia. Sam remembered how that the family had a friend who visited this pretty home and told the parents of a Pastor they knew in South Bend who believed in something called "Divine Healing" and they would love to help take the family for this Pastor to pray over the child, and assured the parents that medical miracles had been declared after this Pastor prayed for terminally ill persons. It was said that the parents thanked them, but assured them that they had their full trust in their doctors and medical workers for the needs of their child.

As Sam lay in the Community Hospital, he clasped his hands behind his head and began to sob, unconsoled by his mother, who could do nothing but the same. Somehow they knew that each was remembering the same thing; the day they drove by the picture-windowed, limestone house and saw no bed, and no boy in the window of that home. Further research brought the news they had expected, leukemia had taken the young boy's life.

Minutes that felt like hours brought the sound of those metal heel taps down the dark and dimly lighted halls of the outdated little hospital. Soon Dr. Cohen stood beside the bed listening intently to Sam's heart.

"Well, Mrs. Pawlak," The doctor began while flipping pages of his clipboard that would soon be placed in the metal pocket at the end of the old, steel, hand-cranked bed. "I have some good news. There seems to be no evidence that Leukemia is in any way a factor in what we are looking for."

"Oh, Praise God!" burst out of Opal's mouth.

"Yes, Praise God indeed." Dr. Cohen echoed but with a noticeably less enthusiastic expression than Opal's. "But," interjected the little doctor, "We do have a serious matter here."

Opal slowly raised her head to make eye contact with the little, Jewish physician, and even more slowly asked,

"Yes? Something serious, you say? What is that?"

"Well your boy suffered a rather bad strep throat a while back, and that streptococcal infection stayed in his body, kind of hid for a little while, but in time did its dirty little deed. Your son has a very serious onset of Rheumatic Fever."

"You keep using the word serious." Opal reminded the Doctor.

"Yes Madam that is exactly what I am saying, but why don't we talk down the hall where we can sit, and I can explain a little better. These good nurses can get your son ready for his stay with us."

Sam thought to himself, "Here I am with the problem, and they are going to go talk about it without me. That's just not fair."

After a few steps down the hall, Opal was pointed into a small office. She sat in an office chair across from the doctor. In a relaxed manner Dr. Cohen began his explanation of the diagnosis.

"Well, it appears that what we have here is a serious, and fairly critical condition. First of all, your Son is not paralyzed in the clinical sense of the word. He has feeling in his legs, and he simply cannot move them because his joints, especially his knee joints seem to be locked up to him. In other words, when he tries to move them, the pain is so severe that his brain is telling him to not move, and he thinks he is unable to move them." He continued, "You see, I could go in there and bend his leg at the knee but the pain would be so awful he might faint." The Doctor leaned over the little desk as if to gather Opal's full attention, and also help relieve the terrified confusion on her face. "Listen, let me clear a few things up, and explain in common words what is happening here. When we use the word Rheumatic, everyone thinks first of the arthritic conditions like rheumatism, but that is not what this is, even though it is affecting the joints." He took a long deep breath and continued, "Rheumatic Fever is actually a heart problem. Its real name is Rheumatic Heart Disease. That strep infection I told you about has not only gotten into the bloodstream, but has actually attached itself to your son's heart, and just keeps building strength, pumping this infected blood throughout the body. It produces the first and most painful symptoms in the joints."

"I'm not sure I understand what you are really saying." Opal interrupted.

"Ok, listen." Dr. Cohen encouraged, as he now slipped his glasses up to the top of his head, "I will make it simple for you. Do you know what sedimentation is?"

"Kind of, but go on." Opal said. The doctor slowly began to illustrate. "Look, when you cook beans or greens, you call it cooking them down, don't you? Opal nodded in the affirmative. "Alright, what happens with Rheumatic Fever is the Streptococcal infection has been cooking itself in the bloodstream, and as it has traveled through Sam's heart and body, the fever's heat has cooked down the infection until it has left some residue. We call this sedimentation. Just like the sticky stuff in the pan left by the beans, greens, or your morning oatmeal."

"Oh! I am getting the picture." Opal declared.

"Yes, Mrs. Pawlak, this is exactly what has happened, except there is a bigger problem. This sedimentation is a bit like rust left in a pan. It does some terrible, and even permanent damage. The pain in the joints, the swelling is just that stuff sticking to the joints, but if that stuff sticks to the heart valves, arteries, or inner wall of the heart, your son could possibly become a serious heart invalid for however many years he has left. If it's not caught, stopped, and reversed now, that number could be much fewer than any of us want to think."

At this, Opal dropped her face into both hands and began to weep again at the shock, clarity, and candor with which Dr. Cohen had spoken.

As they both returned to Sam's hospital room, the doctor explained some of the testing that would be performed, but also explained the first order of treatment would be to start a series of powerful Penicillin injections.

The next thirteen weeks of their lives were filled with long hospital stays, and agonizing bouts of joint pain traversing Sam's nearly 13 year old body. Serious weight loss, colorless skin, and long tear-filled routines several times a day became the norm. The nurses' hands would literally tremble from the force they would have to apply to inject the thick, pasty concoction of Penicillin into Sam's skeletal buttocks.

His greatest relief would come when a new roommate was brought to that children's ward, and he could entertain his new roommate with his comedy routines, or dramatized Bible stories. Other relief came from watching the neon bear across the street from the hospital, blinking on and off from the furniture store outside his window. Perhaps, nothing was ever as sweet as when his big brother Bud would stop at the Dairy Queen drive-in up the street, and bring him that thick chocolate malted Milkshake almost nightly. Sometimes, as he would suck the icy delight through his straw, he would shudder a bit. Not from its cold but from the reminder that tomorrow those thick painful penicillin shots would begin another round.

****

As Opal held the phone to her ear and waited she wondered if her request was even sensible, or was it just the weakening of a mother, watching her youngest son travel such an unfair road for a vibrant young boy.

"Yes, Mrs. Pawlak, Dr. Cohen here. Sorry to make you wait, but I have a lot of patients today at my office. How can I help you?"

"Well, Doctor, I wanted to ask your opinion on something concerning our Sam."

"Sure, fire away madam. What is it?"

"Well, you know in our Christian faith, the Easter Holiday is very important, and our oldest son, Manson is a pastor of a church in the Southern part of the State. Since Sam is home now from the hospital, we were wondering if you thought it would be ok to take him that far to visit his brother over the Easter weekend?"

There was a long pause, and then the sound of a throat clearing, followed by a rather quiet voice,

"Mrs. Pawlak, I released Sam to go home for the holiday and I'm even foregoing his four shots per day for the weekend, but there is no way he is strong enough to make a two hundred mile automobile trip. This would mean even more days without the shots."

Opal began her sad-voiced argument, "But if we laid him in the back of our station wagon and kept him down a lot..."

The Doctor cleared his throat again and interrupted her.

"Listen, Mrs. Pawlak. I was just getting ready to call you, I have a little bad news. You see, the latest test just came back from the hospital, and I'm afraid what we feared has happened. It appears that the Rheumatic fever has done some pretty severe damage to Sam's heart. This could, with a lot more treatment, perhaps just leave him with some heart murmur, and treatable condition. Or he could be in for some of the more difficult challenges we talked about when this whole matter began."

"I understand, Doctor." Opal tearfully responded. "Ok, we will explain that for now this trip would just be too difficult."

"I'm sorry, Mrs. Pawlak, but this is the wiser approach. I will see you in my office Monday. Have a good holiday."

It was early that Wednesday evening that both Frank and Opal explained to Sam what the doctor had said about the trip, and they even shared the newest information about the potential damage to his heart. After dinner Frank said,

"I can stay with Sam tonight while you attend the midweek service, if you want to go." Opal answered,

"No, you go, Frank. Give the church the updates, and have them continue to pray. Besides, Mr. Lawton, the Principal is coming by today with a new batch of Sam's studies, and I want to be here for that. The good news is he said that with Sam keeping up his classes at home and in the hospital there is no doubt that he will graduate from Jr. High school with his class."

After the Principal had left, Sam began to feel the familiar symptoms he had learned to recognize too often. Shortly before Frank returned from church, Sam could hold his emotions and disappointment no longer. With overwhelming frustration he began to cry and vocally explode,

"It is not fair, just not fair! I gave my heart to Jesus as a little boy. I have loved God. I love his word. I have not gone out and done the horrible things like other kids have done. I don't cuss or blaspheme God, and here I am with all this mess, and those people seem to get by with everything, and live with great health only to live like the Devil for another day. Mom, this does not make sense. I just don't get it. Why me? I don't deserve this kind of life."

Opal had nothing to offer, but,

"Come on Sam. Getting yourself all upset is not going to help with the pain, it will only make it worse. Let me get you a big glass of lemon ice cream, and I will make a float out of it with some ginger ale I have in there."

As Opal opened the freezer door, she let the blast of cold air prevent the well of tears that had built during Sam's painful tirade. She could not allow her son to see that not only did she feel his pain, she had suppressed the same onslaught of questions he had just spewed from his sick sofa bed, in the small living room of their home.

Early the next morning Opal was hearing Dr. Cohen again tell her he had another ambulance in route to take Sam back to the Hospital. This high level of pain again meant the condition was raging through his one hundred pounds of skin and bone. He could not make it through this weekend without his painful treatments. Frank, Opal, and Sam waited for the hospital bound transport so familiar for the last thirteen weeks.

The TV was on against the adjacent wall from Sam's recline. The program playing was one of Sam's and his mother's favorite musical variety shows. It was The Tennessee Ernie Ford Show. As was the custom of many Country musical artists of that time, the show

always closed with an old hymn of the church. The connection between the Grand Ole
Opry and the First Baptist Church was extremely close. That morning, Ernie Ford's closing hymn came from a deep list of traditional southern Gospel favorites. Father, son, and
mother listened intently as the deep baritone voice of one of America's favorite singers
sincerely sang the words,

Tempted and tried we're oft made to wonder
Why it should be thus all the day long
While there are others living among us
Never molested, though in the wrong

Farther along we'll know all about it
Farther along we'll understand why
Cheer up my brother, live in the sunshine
We'll understand it all bye and bye.

Opal was weeping openly as she expressed to Sam,

"There, son. There it is. That is your answer from God to those questions you were asking
last night." She continued, as if encouraging her sickly child, but she knew she was gathering these words just as much, if not more, to her own troubles and weary heart. "God has
a plan for you, Son. This will all make sense someday."

At the ending of her last words of consolation the reflection of sunlight swept across the
living room, and again the ambulance backed up to the familiar location. Still unable to
place enough weight upon those pain-filled knees and ankles, the workers lifted Sam's
body onto the stretcher. After the familiar journey, they backed up to the emergency entrance of that old Community Hospital.

A gurney was pushed from the head and pulled from the feet down the hospital corridor
by Ambulance workers. Again, Sam began to count the hanging light globes in the ceiling
above. After counting five or six of the old light fixtures, he suddenly sensed something
different. He felt the strong hand of his Dad firmly placed on his chest. Looking back
toward the head of the stretcher to see his father's beautiful blue eyes, he was taken aback
when he realized his father was not there. No one was there. Sam's presumption was that
his Dad and Mom, who had followed the ambulance in that old station wagon had quickly gotten out of the car, and caught up with the attendees. He thought his dad was simply
placing his hand on his son's boney chest to assure him they were right there with him.

Sam felt extremely confused. He strained his head and neck to see both hands of the Ambulance driver firmly at each side of his head guiding that end of the stretcher. He then pulled his head up to make his eyes see the same scenario from the other attendant at his feet. But this was weird beyond words. There was still, right in the middle of his chest the absolute feeling of a man's strong hand pressed against his breast bone and upper chest.

When the stretcher was secured beside the hospital bed, the two workers gathered up Sam's skinny legs and skin-over-bone, shoulders. They lifted in unison their patient, placing him on his back, in that all too familiar bed. That's when it happened. The moment Sam's hind quarters touched the sterile sheet, it was like the reaction of an electrical shock. Sam's body sat up straight in the bed. This was something that had not happened in weeks. To Sam's startled attention came another totally unexpected response. There was no pain anywhere in his body. He examined his hands, twisted his wrists in every direction. He pumped his feet, turning them at the ankles in rotating motions, first to the right, then to the left. He pulled his toes and feet up and down like an exercise seen in one of Charles Atlas' body-building magazines. Then the final test would be his knees. Sam quickly pulled his pajama legs above his formerly swollen knees, but they looked more normal than he had seen them in months. He began to bend his knees up and back toward his abdomen. With that, Sam giggled, fell back on the bed, and began to rotate his legs in a bicycling motion.

"I'm well! I'm well! No pain anywhere!" Sam literally sprung to his feet in the bed, yelled at the top of his voice, "I'm healed! I am well! Look at me, I am well!"

At that moment, his father Frank entered the room, having heard the commotion down the hall and thinking something horrible must be happening to his son. But one step in the room and Frank made just one sound,

"Whoa."

It was the kind of sound Frank made when a large coho would strike his retrieving bait, and he knew it was an above-average fish fight ahead. It also was that same sound Frank made every time he saw a baseball batter strike the ball with an unmistakable sound that said, this park will never hold that ball.

To the startled ambulance attendees and nearby admittance nurse, Frank's sound could have been interpreted as the sound one makes when being struck with a fisted uppercut to the solar plexus. Frank knew that he had not felt or experienced any atmosphere like this since the night, almost thirty years prior when he awoke in the darkness of his bedroom, beside his brother Johnny, and felt his body shake uncontrollably, as his sister begged God to personally go to her godless brother, and lead Frank to an epiphany that would change his life forever.

The workers quickly exited the room with a confounded expression that said, "We're leaving this to the rest of you. We brought this crazy to you and now it is all yours."

By now, Opal simply leaned against the corner of the room and quietly allowed tears to flow down her face, saying under her breath,

"Is what is happening here what I think may be happening here?"

She had witnessed it with Buddy's strangulation croup, Frank's incurable back injury, Freddy's hemorrhaging Tuberculosis and horrible ring-wormed head, but could this be happening again? Another miracle in this family named Pawlak.

The family basked in this unusual set of circumstances, and the hospital staff tried to quiet Sam, while they continued the normal admission procedure. They all heard the sound of Dr. Cohen's heel taps.

As he entered the room, he agitatedly asked in a stern voice,

"What is going on here?"

Sam sat up straight, effortlessly swung his legs out of the bed, slid off the side, and stood erect before the doctor.

"Look at this, Doc! I have been healed! I am well! it is a miracle!" At the same moment, Sam, never lacking for dramatics, noticed the cold metal bedpan which his frail body had come to hate because of the combination of the device's coldness to his skin, and hardness to his pin-cushioned rear side. Grasping it with one hand, and thrusting it over his head, he announced to the doctor. "And I will not need this thing anymore! I am well! I feel like I could hit the basketball court right now, Doc!"

"Well, I suggest that you hit that bed again first. Whatever is happening, we've got some things that must be done here. Now, settle down here, and give me some blood." Came the harsh demand from the little man who did not even stand as tall as his almost thirteen-year-old patient.

Opal walked over and motioned for Sam to follow the Doctor's orders.

"But Mom, I don't want to give anymore blood. I am tired of getting poked. Look! I am well! Let's just go home."

Opal wrapped her arms around Sam, half-laughing and half crying, she whispered in his ear,

"We know what is happening, Sam. But this doctor has no idea what he is about to see. Lie down. Let God finish what he has started today."

When Opal talked in this tone of voice it was a little spooky, but all who knew her, especially her children, knew they'd better pay heed. This was no normal woman they were dealing with, and they were probably in the presence of something more powerful than they could see.

After the first blood draw, the doctor and technician moved quickly down the hall. Sam could almost imagine sparks flying off the doctor's heel taps, not unlike the taps of the priest who had hired his grandfather Kaz and friend Emil to terrorize the itinerant preacher who became his other grandfather.

In a relatively short time, they would all hear the banging taps, rapidly returning to the room with only one order to the young technician at his side,

"Take more blood."

Sam caught his mother's eye with a pleading glance, "Can this just stop?" His mother gave him that little nod that said, "Patience, son. One more time."

Off they flew to the lab, somewhere deep in the caverns of the morbid edifice. Sam was pretty sure the laboratory must have looked a great deal like that of Dr. Frankenstein. He was also sure that a Boris Karloff type was in charge of the details of all that blood.

After repeating the blood-letting procedure one more time, a markedly long hour passed. Sam lifted his hand to those in the room.

"Hush! Hush! Listen, I hear him coming."

This time, the metal heel taps were very faint. The steps seemed extremely slow, to the point the heel protectors could be heard to almost gently slide across the floor. As the shuffle arrived at the door, Dr. Cohen stopped, leaned against the door facing, and studied several documents in his hands. He moved partly into the door frame, pushed the paperwork cradled in his left hand downward to his side. As the doctor raised his dark horn-rimmed glasses to the top of his head, he silently stared at some imaginary point between Sam and the boy's parents. He took a deep breath, closed his lips, and filled both cheeks with the air that was pleading to escape his rather distorted features. Finally, he slowly released the air from his rounded lips while allowing an audible moan to escape, as would a large migrating whale in the ocean's current. He spoke.

"I don't really understand what is happening here." Clearing his throat, and removing his glasses from his head and returning them to his face, he looked down toward the lab reports in hand. "Yesterday, this young man had enough sedimentation in his blood to kill two grown men. But," he paused, "Today we cannot find any sedimentation." He took one small step inside the doorway, as if to keep from exposing himself to the strangeness of the room. "There is not even any evidence that he has Rheumatic Fever, or I might say, had even had any Rheumatic Fever. Even his EKG reads differently than any previous heart test we have conducted. The doctor's eyes slowly looked around the room with the kind of look a man has when he thinks someone is about to jump out from behind a door, and stick a revolver in his ribs, demanding all his money. He slowly retreated one step backward to the safety of the escapable doorway.

"So What now?" Frank asked with a little smile, knowing what the doctor's reply would be.

"Well," the doctor said with both his palms turned upward in front of him, "I guess, you might as well get him dressed and take him home for now. But I want to see him in my office very soon, and I think, for safety's sake, we should continue the shots, at least for a little while, and see what happens here."

Frank, Opal, and Sam all restrained the explosion of joy and relief that was stirring within them to allow the confused, if not troubled Dr. Cohen to get a safe distance out of their sight and sound.

The little man turned to take one step out the door, then he suddenly turned back to the family, stretched both arms widely, and uttered a sarcastic and ironic statement that even he knew was a ridiculous convergence of words, attempting to put some conclusion on this most unusual phenomenon.

"Well, maybe it was just growing pains after all."

Once out of sight, the trio exploded with a combination of laughter, tears, and repeated whispers of,

"Thank you Lord!" and "Thank you, Jesus."

Sam literally bounced up and down in the back seat of the car as it headed past the neon bear and, to his surprise, Sam even declined his Father's offer for a celebratory milkshake as they slowly moved beyond the Dairy Queen Drive in. That day, Sam thought how his Dad's indistinguishable humming, that his older brothers often called "the unknown melody," was a beautiful concert to his healthy ears. Sam declared the Easter trip to Southern Indiana "Back on."

As the big station wagon moved down the two lane highways that cut through the wide Indiana farmland, Sam sat close to his Dad's driving position. Frank let him sit on the edge of the front bench seat, and actually steer the car. Sam loved when they passed through the little towns because it was there they would be stopped by a traffic light or two. Sam was allowed to shift the gear shifter built into the steering column, while his dad managed the clutch and gas pedal on the floor. That Easter Sunday, Sam's new sport jacket, shirt, necktie, highly polished black shoes, and rather dapper fedora, the kind Sinatra wore, announced to all that entered that little white country church pastored by Manson, "A new man is here."

****

Sam could not help but notice how strong his legs felt as he pushed both arms skyward until his feet left the ground. He could swing one leg up to the top of the fifty-five gallon, oil drum, and allow his right thigh muscle to lift his one-hundred-fifty pound body high enough to place his left leg on top of the other barrel.

Late spring days were still cool, but he found himself walking the hill less often, and spending more time standing atop those old steel barrels. The barrels were set upright behind the small barn. The barn was covered on the top and sides with shiny, corrugated, metal sheets. The barrels had a purpose. They were intended to become trash barrels, with at least one of them used to burn refuse in a controlled environment.

Frank was working longer hours at the factory. Some impending crisis was calling for larger military contracts in the heavy industry segment. It would be the first introduction to some new places with odd names; places like Laos, Thailand, Cambodia and Vietnam. All it really meant to Sam was His Dad was working later, and even on some Saturdays. It also meant Frank had not gotten around to cutting the tops out of those barrels Sam loved standing on.

Since Sam's amazing healing and astounding recovery, he spent time thinking often of his attraction to this preaching thing. Preachers were becoming his heroes, even more than ball players. He was always drawn to public speaking. He never really felt much stage fright or apprehension when asked to read a passage of scripture in Sunday School class or when asked to share something at school for "Show and tell time." What really began to capture his attention, and to some degree his imagination, was when his Dad had the radio blasting on Sunday morning with the sounds of radio preachers. Sam loved the sound of their voices, but even more compelling was their dramatic oratory, and persuasive arguments. He had his favorites, just like his friends who collected baseball cards. He knew their names, and the times of their programs. Among his favorites was the growly-voiced, powerhouse of a speaker named C.M. Ward and the Revival Time Radio, broadcasting on a nationwide network, representing the denomination that the Pawlak family belonged to.

At the close of each broadcast, while the choir softly sang a hymn entitled "There's Room at the Cross for You," Dr. Ward would move closely to the microphone and appeal to unconverted listeners via the radio waves,

"Mister, Lady, you can come today to the long, long altar, and know Jesus will meet you there."

Sam also tuned into a broadcast which closed each program with the speaker's little daughter, singing the title theme of the show,

"Harvest time, it's Harvest time
The fields are calling, the grain is falling,
Oh! do not wait, its growing late

Behold the fields are white, it's Harvest time."

Sam never fully understood why he felt like tearing up when he heard that song.

Some of those preachers would become superstars in their own right. Oral Roberts was building a massive audience by inviting people to simply place their hand on their radio, allowing him to connect with them, and send healing power to the infirm condition in their bodies.

Sunday night finished the long day of preachers for Sam when the highly distinguished, North Carolina drawl would declare that this exact time was every man's "Hour of Decision." The well-respected evangelist would one day hold the all-time record of preaching before more people than anyone in history, even surpassing Pontiffs in Rome. But to Sam, the young voice was recognizable as Billy Graham.

To Sam's great amazement, it finally happened. A preacher was actually going to be delivering his message on the new, and greatest life-changing medium known to man; Television. Yes, that same screen that would show the likes of Bob Hope, Red Skelton, Marshal Matt Dillon, Dean Martin, and all the famed movie stars, would now have a preacher in front of the cameras.
Sam sat frozen watching the first preacher ever to be seen across America coast to coast, the one, the only Bishop Fulton Sheen.

Although Catholic, and attired quite differently than the Protestant and Pentecostal preachers familiar to Sam, the magnetism created in front of that camera held this young teenage boy with a capture that forbade his eyes to even move from the revolutionary picture before him.

Now, with each foot firmly on top of a steel barrel, Sam would transform himself into any or all of those exciting orators he so admired. With spring wind blowing his flopping locks of blond hair, Sam preached to the waving fields, long weeds, and wild flowers preparing for the summer ahead. Changing voices to mimic one of his radio preaching heroes, and adjusting tone and volume upward for declaration and downward for intensity, the boy spread both arms in that patented Bishop Sheen manner, bellowing at the top of his voice those absolute truths he believed all needed to hear.

Sam never visualized himself speaking to a comfortably small contingency of church folk. No! Not this boy. Those fields waving in the wind represented thousands upon thousands of excited listeners, shouting "amen," and beckoning the preacher on his podium to hold back nothing, but give them more.

To the chagrin of Dr. Arnold Cohen, Sam never returned to any of the scheduled appointments as advised. The young barrel-top preacher had even convinced his mother, Opal, to continue any of those horrid penicillin shots would not only show a lack of faith, but would actually be an insult to the one who had provided the miraculous change of events in his life.

"Mom," Sam called with some introspection in his voice,

"What is it, son?" came the question, while Opal studied the tone and body language of her son's approach.

"I need to ask you about something, and see what you think."

Opal pulled the chair away from the table and motioned for Sam to take the one at the end. She loved to talk, one on one with her children. Even though she could challenge them, and even frustrate them with her strong opinions about their choices and desires, they each considered her a valuable confidante.

Sam quickly cut to the chase.

"You know Ma, I really think I am supposed to be a preacher someday like Grandpa, and Uncle Freddy, and Manson. I haven't told anybody but I have even been practicing some."

Opal turned her eyes away from Sam, and looking down at the table she made little circles with her index finger on the table top.

"Oh, well you may not be able to do that much longer you know?" She said, while fighting back the big grin she was needing to release from her face.

"What does that mean, Ma? I don't understand."

"Well," Opal said rather slyly, "Your Dad is going to cut those barrel tops out this weekend and you might lose your platform."

"Wait, What? You know about that?" Sam asked while hoping the flush of embarrassment was not glowing on his cheeks. Opal replied,

"Sure. You see, one evening I was in the yard hanging clothes, and I heard Valery's cat, Kitso crying and crying. I found her in the corn crib next to the barn. When I came out with her I heard this powerful preacher telling people how Christ was the only answer for their lives."

Sam hung his head with a kind of, "Awe Shucks" look, and then quickly smiled a little mischievous smile and asked, "Well, was he any good?"

Opal's little tease turned serious. She reached across the table and took both of Sam's hands in hers. For a moment, Sam remembered again how he loved the feel of his mother's hands. Strong enough to arm wrestle with her big sons, firm enough to smack the bottom of a little girl in a temper tantrum, and fast enough to slap closed a teenaged, smart mouth, yet soft enough to make all the pain of a broken heart disappear with one squeeze of a hand.

"The young man I heard on those barrels was so good that I have no doubt, if he stays humble, he will preach someday all over this world.

"Really Mom?" Sam's voice sounded excited with this confirmation,

"I said, 'if he stays humble.' Remember?" Then she sat fully back in her seat, crossed her arms and changed the atmosphere completely when she offered a proposal Sam was not expecting. "But I think there is a new place you should try out your preaching."

Sam wondered to himself, "Does she mean the Sunday school class, the youth group at church, or God forbid, not on the street like she used to do with her Dad when she was a young girl? That would be scary and embarrassing beyond words."

The real twist was thrown into this intense conversation when Opal suggested,

"I think you should make an appointment to go back and see Dr. Cohen, soon."

Sam sat back in his seat and literally whined,

"What? Go back to the Doctor? Shoot, he will want to start sticking me again."

Opal calmed her voice in hopes Sam would calm his, and continued,

"No, I mean for a totally different reason. If you think you will preach to thousands of people someday, you might need to start small first." She continues to clarify her thinking, "Sam, you are a miracle, you have received a miracle, but Dr. Cohen also was a big part of this. He has to admit and recognize that what happened to you was supernatural. I don't know anyone who could get him to listen like someone who has experienced what you have."

"But how would I do that?" Sam asked.

"Look," Opal explained, "You're his patient, and when he gives you an appointment you just take the time he would normally spend with you, and kindly ask him if you can tell him, in your own words, what you believe has happened to you."

"Ok then, if you really think I should do that, I guess if you set up the appointment I will try" Sam, grinning from ear to ear continued, "Can I take the barrels with me?"

His mother, very seriously responded,

"Son, I have no doubt the pulpit will always come easy for you, but this kind of thing will produce your greatest results."

****

"Hello, Doctor Cohen." Sam greeted the doctor as he entered the room. After closing the door behind him the doctor pulled the rolling stool underneath him and said,

"Now, what can I do for you, young fella?"

"Do you remember me, Doctor Cohen?" Sam asked

The doctor quickly looked at his chart, and as recognition dawned said,

"Yes, yes, you're the Pawlak boy." Then almost startled he chided his young patient, "You were supposed to be back here weeks ago. You have not kept any of your appointments, none of your shots. What is it? Are you having problems again?"

With a smattering of sarcasm, not unfamiliar to the little Jewish doctor, Sam recoiled with,

"Do I look like I'm having any problems?"

"No, no you really don't." said the doctor, noting the chart again in his hand as he continued, "Wow, you have gained fifty pounds since I saw you last." and with some unexpected language, he simply asked, "Why the Hell are you here now?"

Very respectfully Sam answered his question with a question.

"Doctor, when someone makes an appointment and pays for it, how much time do you usually give to them?"

Thinking it an odd question, the doctor furrowed his brow and replied,

"Well, that depends on how much time is needed, and how serious the problem is. Why do you ask?"

"Because my Mom already paid for this appointment, and she said I should see you alone, and you should give me the same amount of time you would give any other paying patient."

"Your Mom is a pretty smart woman. Seems she knows what she is talking about. Ok, you're on the clock, young man."

Sam did not understand what that meant, but by the way the doctor positioned himself he was sure it was his time to begin what he came to do.

"Well, Doctor Cohen, I don't know if you remember but I was healed from my Rheumatic Fever right in front of your eyes, and I want you to know I am still healed. I run every day, I ride my bike, play full-court basketball, and I have never had one more problem since I left the hospital. I also have not taken one more shot or even an aspirin for a headache."

"Well, good for you, son. I am glad you came by to give me that update."

With that Sam thought for a minute, "Well, that was easier than I thought. Good, that ought to get me off the hook with Mom." Then a sudden, little, inner, nagging voice seemed to say, "That is not what you came here to do. You came here to preach to him."

Boldly, Sam blurted out,

"But there is more I have to tell you."

"Oh well, Ok, let's have it then." came the invitation from the white-coated man.

Sam began slowly.

"You see, Doctor, it was Jesus Christ who put his hand on my chest that day in the Hospital. Not my Dad, not the workers, Jesus Christ. He is the same Jesus Christ that died on the cross for my sins."

Now a little of the barrel-top attitude began to embolden Sam, and he figured he had gotten this far; he might as well go for the gold. He suddenly raised his arm and finger toward the doctor and said,

"He also died for you, doctor. He will forgive your sins and become your Savior too." Sam really went for the throat. "Remember Doctor Cohen, you have seen Jesus Christ heal one of your own patients, and you will have to do something with that!"

Had Sam been raised in a good Baptist church he would have been trained in the method of evangelism that knows how to close the deal. He would have quickly offered the doctor the opportunity to pray "the sinner's prayer," and know true salvation right there on the spot, but he had an overwhelming sense that he probably had taken this about as far as he should go for now.

For an uncomfortable few moments the room fell silent. The doctor slowly stood from his stool, and moved toward the door. Then laying the patient chart on the counter, he reached into his pocket and seemed to change the entire subject when he asked,

"Do you mind if I listen to your heart for a little bit, son?"

Sam went from feelings of discomfort to embarrassment, and some trepidation as to whether he'd made a fool of himself. He continued to stare at the ceiling while following the doctor's soft request to breathe, rest, and even hold his breath. After the doctor placed the stethoscope back into his jacket pocket, he leaned his back against the door and said to the young man before him with mouth gaped open,

"Sam, I have to acknowledge something amazing has happened in your life. Your heart is perfect. Not even the slightest sound of a murmur, which always follows Rheumatic Fever, but as to what I have to do with what has happened to you is a little more complicated than you might be able to understand." Rather reflectively, he continued. "I have been taught all my life that Jesus Christ was a wonderful person, even one to emulate or copy. Maybe even a prophet, and not to rule out that he may have been the kindest prophet ever known. He may have even affected some people in such a positive way that their lives improved. Some may have gotten psychologically better to the point that some of their physical maladies may have gone away."

Sam's young mind was really trying hard to follow this dialogue. Then the doctor explained to Sam,

"...But to say that Jesus was the Savior, we use the word Messiah in my religion, or to believe he was God's only Son, and especially to believe he is still alive to perform these miracles you ascribe to yourself, would mean that all that I am and believe, and have ever been, through the history of my family, would be a lie. I would have to walk away from the things I hold dear to my belief, and even my tradition."

Sam realized that he had no words that could take this conversation anywhere from here. He simply stood from the examination table, reached out his hand toward the kind man, and said,

"Doctor Cohen, I just thank you for allowing me to share with you what I felt I must say to you. In our church we call it our testimony. I will pray for you in my prayers."

As the doctor firmly shook Sam's hand, he responded by saying,

"I think you would make a good Doctor. No, probably a lawyer. Nah! Preacher."

****

Sunday was still predictable in the Pawlak house. After the noisy preparation and radio preachers of Sunday morning, it was off to Sunday school and church service. After an extended time of handshaking and friendly talk, the trek home to the country was awarded when the back door opened to the amazing smell of Opal's pot roast, potatoes, carrots and onions, permeating the entire house. Each flavor blended into the other and produced a three-hour delight that announced to all who entered the house, "It is truly Sunday."

Dinner was most often followed by one of Frank's fabulous pie creations, or at least a dish of Vanilla ice cream, heavily covered with that good old Hershey's chocolate syrup.

Frank had assumed his usual after-dinner position, slumped on the couch, belt and top pant's button opened for digestive assistance. His thick bifocal glasses fixed atop that huge hump on the bridge of his large Polish nose, and in his he held the church denomination's national weekly magazine. The magazine was a consortium of stories about exciting events in churches across the nation, and intriguing stories of missions efforts around the globe. Included in each issue were a few personal testimonies of those miracles these churches thrived on. Toward the end of the periodical would be two full pages of listings, announcing where you could catch the latest and most popular traveling evangelist. The phrase "Coming to a church in your area soon!" was an absolute knock-off from the forbidden movie theaters, used to entice customers. The advertisements of which was the closest Sam and his family would care to know of those dens of iniquity, or so they were called.

Usually Sam would be out climbing the hill, riding the bike, or getting a few extra shots on the basketball goal attached to the corn crib, beyond the backyard. However, this Sunday, for some reason, Sam decided to join his dad in the living room, reading the new novel he had picked up at the library.

It was a great story about a young boy who wanted to return from his Civil War duty as a hero with at least one wound to show for his effort. Sam was fascinated with the ironic twist that depicted the boy coming to the realization that he actually was a coward, going A.W.O.L. from his company. While running and hiding in shame the young soldier becomes accidentally wounded, and is able to return home, not as a coward, but displaying what the author Stephen Crane described in his title as his, "Red badge of Courage."

Sam was an avid reader, even challenging his mother to an annual competition, in which each would try to read more books than the other in one year's time. Sam was so engrossed in the field battles described in the story that it took his Dad's almost rude interruption to break his concentration. Little had he noticed that his Dad had flung the church magazine across the room until it noisily landed against Sam's chest and slid to his lap, blocking the readability of the book cradled in his hands.

"Maybe here is where you ought to go to high school, Sam. Take a look at that place."

Sam gathered the discombobulated magazine and he perused the cover page.

"No, the back side." Frank instructed. "Look at the backside."

"Sam asked out loud,

"What is Canyonville Bible Academy?" Sam's question was soon answered when his eyes fell on the line, "A quality High School Education in a Christian setting."

His eyes immediately went to the small photos along the bottom of the page. Boys and girls were pictured walking along a tree lined sidewalk with books under arms, looking happy, smiles on their faces. There was another picture of basketball players in the heat of action, one player even snatching the rebound from the edge of the rim in the same manner that he approached the game. A couple classroom settings were among the montage of photos, and finally a picture of several hundred high school students, in what appeared to be a chapel, their hands fully extended skyward, eyes closed with facial expressions, not uncommon to Sam. These behaviors were what Sam had known his whole life as "worship."

His fascinated gaze was broken only when he heard his Father say,

"Well, looks like quite a place. Huh, Sam?" but with the same breath continued, "But the problem is, it costs money."

The comment brought back to reality that money, or the lack of it always brought exciting possibilities quickly to a screeching halt. Just as Sam was beginning to toss the magazine aside and re-engage his mind to the action of the Civil War story he had been consuming, he saw something else on the back of the magazine; a picturesque scene of heavy snow, weighing down the largest pine tree limbs he had ever laid his eyes on. Underneath the beautiful photo was this simple inscription, "The beauty of the forested Oregon campus."

"Oregon." Sam thought, as his mind backed up a few years to when Mrs. Miller's third grade class had read together that wonderful story, "Along the Oregon Trail." The adventurous tale of a pioneer family, and their Conestoga covered wagon, crossing the Mississippi River at St. Louis, passing through the gateway to the West, and the yearlong battle for survival that would eventually land them in their promised land of Oregon.

Through the past sickness, hospital stays and recovery, Sam had nearly lost that daily yearning to know what was over that hill, but now like a Lake Michigan undertow, later to be renamed a riptide, Sam could almost feel the unseen hands grasp his ankles and gently pull as if to release his feet from their much too stationary position.

"Wow!" Sam said out loud. "That is sure a long way off, but boy, would I love to go somewhere like that."

"Somewhere like what?" Opal questioned as she wiped the remaining Sunday dish water off her hands. She entered the room and gave the small towel a fling back toward the dining table.

"Well," Frank quickly responded, "Sam doesn't want to go to that high school he is supposed to attend, so I showed him a Christian High school out in Oregon."

Opal did not even leave a full beat between Frank's last word and her first response when she questioned,

"Oregon? I don't think so." Then as rapid as an old western Gatling gun, she fired, "First of all, you just turned fourteen years old. Secondly, Oregon is completely on the other side of the country, and thirdly, I might just ask, where in the world do you think you will find that kind of money?"

If that trilogy of arguments were not enough, she began to make it very personal.

"If you think I am going to lay awake nights wondering where my youngest son is, and what is happening to him now, on the other side of the world, well you have another think coming, young man. You will go to school where the laws and your parents say you will go, and you will find a way to like it. Furthermore, you will not walk around this house for the next four years with that, hanged dog look on your face." Turning toward the kitchen and gathering the towel that had fallen to the floor, she bellowed her closing argument to such a ridiculous idea, "If anybody is going to be depressed in this house it is going to be me, I'm the only one who reserves that prerogative."

Frank and Sam just stared at each other when Frank broke the silence by musing,

"Well, I wonder what your Mom thinks of the whole idea?"

They both covered their mouths to muffle the tear-rendering laughter that neither could control for several minutes.

When Sam's eyes cleared again, he refocused on the page before him, saw the small print along the bottom of the page, reached over to the nearby lamp stand, and having retrieved the ballpoint pen, he marked a large circle around the words, "Contact this address for more information."

"You know," Sam half whispered in his father's direction, "It won't cost anything to see what all is involved in a place like that."

"What is involved, Sam is money. You'll see." Was Frank's only response. Then he added, "You do have a whole summer ahead of you, and since you feel good enough to play ball and ride bikes, you might see if some of these farmers around here need some help. You're going to need some new school clothes anyway. Last year's stuff sure won't fit you anymore. Look how short your pants are getting. Those hillbillies call that, 'high waters.'

Sam's mind began to fly. "Hmm," he thought, "If I am going to have to find a job anyway for school clothes I wonder how much more I would need to go to a place like that school in Oregon? Maybe, just maybe...just maybe."

****

There was always something that felt so grownup about going to the mailbox, with the rural route address on the side, pulling open the hinged door, and seeing Mr. Samuel P. Pawlak on the front of the envelope.

"Dear Mr. Pawlak," the salutation read, just below the date. "It gives us great pleasure to have you enquire about our wonderful school here in Canyonville. Please find enclosed all the information you should need, and the appropriate application forms should you be interested in joining this family of education and spiritual growth."

Sam spent the rest of the afternoon absorbing all the vital information, costs, and personal requirements needed to attend. He also began to prepare like a defense attorney, to rebut each argument that would be flown across the table in his direction, when he would explain that he really wanted to flee the confinements of this open spaced countryside, in exchange for the wide-open freedoms of a private school campus. Never could he have possibly imagined that the number one obstacle to his venture would be removed before he even brought up the subject of the application forms.

Frank had barely finished his ritualistic practice of washing his hands in the kitchen sink, rolling up the machine-oiled smelling sleeves on his factory uniform work shirt, and flopping on the kitchen chair, beginning his table-grace prayer with a huge and tired sigh. Then he announced,

"Hey Sam, I may have a job for you."

Sam quickly gulped down the first mouthful of mashed potatoes he had snuck into his mouth near the end of Frank's prayer.

"What kind of job? In the factory?"

The factory was a place that always seemed way too confining for his style. He did not mind hard work, but preferred outdoor activity. This is why he loved delivering newspapers, and even the few times he had struggled with the hay bales that his big brothers seemed to handle so easily.

"No, not the factory." Franks said, "But it does involve one of the guys I work with in the shop." He explained. "Les Landis has a fairly new house in Brinkman Addition, and it has no basement. Just built on a cement slab. So what he wants to do is dig some basement space under his house where he can move his furnace and some other equipment below and make him another bathroom in his house. What he needs is somebody everyday to dig the dirt out from under the house while he is at work in the factory, then he can do the other work when he gets home in the evening.

"How would I dig it out?" was Sam's first of many questions to come.

"Frank," Opal interjected, "That doesn't sound too safe to me."

"Well, wait a minute." Frank said before slurping his first drink of coffee, "He has a plan. He showed me the drawings and they have been approved, and all. Sam will dig a small area and then Les will put this adjustable steel support post between the new floor level and a floor joist above. Once that is secure, then Sam will dig out some more space until it is the size he wants his new basement to be."

"Did he say what he would pay me?" came Sam's anxious sounding question.

"Yeah! That is the best part. He would give you a buck an hour."

"Holy Cow!" Sam said, "A dollar an hour, and for how many hours and how many days?"

Now Sam, who could add and subtract in his head almost as fast as his Mom could, out loud, leaned onto the table's edge fully prepared for the abacus in his brain to start sliding the beads across the strings. His anticipation was that the totals would be somewhere in the neighborhood of the necessary tuition, housing, food, books, and transportation cost, to begin his own journey along the Oregon Trail.

"Well, it would be five days a week, at least eight or nine hours a day, and probably you would be working with him on Saturdays." Frank then concluded, "You could be looking at maybe fifty dollars or more a week. So what? You could be looking at about five hundred bucks over the next ten weeks before school starts."
"Wow." Sam responded slowly, "This might be another God thing here."

He knew what he was about to share would need whatever spiritual slant he could put with his verbiage. He pulled something out from under his leg revealing the completely filled out applications for the school, which his mother had identified as "the other side of the world."

"Look. I have all the stuff they need for me to go to that school in Oregon, and it only costs four hundred dollars for the first semester and I can get work there on campus and in town, after school hours, toward the second semester and I already found out the Greyhound bus from Chicago stops right in front of the school. It only costs forty-nine dollars for a student ticket."

He stood and walked around the table, placing the papers between Frank and Opal, and softly said,

"All I need is my parent's signature saying yes and with this job I will have the money. Please, Mom. I really want to do this. It could be the most exciting thing in my life. They will even teach me more about becoming a preacher. I think God healed me so I could do this."

"Slow down, Sam." Opal said while examining the papers fixed fully in both hands. "Son, this is so far away and you don't even know yet if you can do this work for your dad's friend, and I really would have to pray about this and get a lot more peace than I have right now. So, for now, just return to your place and finish your dinner, and your father and I can talk about this more while you wash the dishes tonight."

Wait, and pray, and talk too often translated into Sam's mind as, "Probably not going to happen."

Sam slept restlessly that night, his mind kept wondering what the Kansas wheat fields looked like from the window of a bus, or how beautiful the Rocky Mountains must be, rather than just seeing them in a U.S. Geography book. So it was with utter shock that Sam came to the breakfast table and found next to his bowl of grape nuts that morning, a sealed, stamped, clean, white envelope addressed to Canyonville Bible Academy. In the left corner, return address section, the clear handwriting of his mother with the names Mr. & Mrs. Frank Pawlak.

"Mom, really?" Sam questioned as he held the envelope in front of him. "You signed it? I can go?"

"Sam, I don't want to talk about it this morning." Opal fired back without turning from the stove, "I don't want to ever stand in the way of God's will for my children, but right now, this is not my will, and I don't want to talk about it. Besides, you have to get dressed and I have to take you to Mr. Landis' house to start that job, and you may not even be able to do what he needs. So, you may not have enough money for that school anyway, and as I said, I don't want to talk about it."

Sam smiled at how much his mother had to say for someone who didn't want to talk about it anyway, but he also knew now would be an excellent opportunity to fill his mouth with cereal, and slip quietly upstairs to get ready for the manly job that awaited him.

The work was every bit as hot and dangerous as Opal had feared. Some days she would even bring Sam lunch, and seeing the white ring around his lips, and dark circles under his eyes, she would suggest he stop for the day before he would collapse.

Sam was too young to understand the fact that a man's desire is proven by his pursuits, but he knew this summer sweat, dirt, and backache was truly his ticket away from the things he hated, and the entrance to a whole new world that was just awaiting his arrival.

****

As the 1960 green and white Chevy Station Wagon settled along Woodland Avenue, across from the gate of the big compressor and mining equipment plant, Sam could already see his dad's familiar lope toward the car. That striped engineer hat pushed back and tilted to the left was an image which would never escape Sam's memory. Frank slipped into the front passenger side of that bench seat, quickly handed Opal his weekly paycheck, signed on the back, as he had done so many Fridays. Frank looked over the seat at his youngest son and nodded toward the army surplus duffel bag behind the rear seat.

"Got it all there?" he asked, then he reminded Sam with fatherly instruction, "Now this will be a long trip. Four nights and three days on a bus, and you have several stops and layovers in some big cities. So, stay inside, and don't get out and roam around."

"Well, Dad," Opal resigned, "Let's pray for him before you have to get back in."

This was a very familiar scene to Sam. Never did their journey to Mishawaka or Hartford City, the site of the church camp each summer, or down state to one of Uncle Freddy's churches, pull from the drive without Frank saying a prayer for protection upon the roads. Frank could have never uttered the first word of prayer until his cap or hat was slowly removed from his head. That same kind of respect was shown each time the National Anthem was played at a sporting event, and Sam just thought it right.

After Frank's prayer, which included the word "Lord," about every three words, Frank said his amen, and returned his cap to its normal position on his head. Then Opal quickly added,

"Sam, you're not too big to still kiss your dad." To which Frank turned as far as he could in the seat, and Sam leaned forward for their lips to briefly meet.

"Ok, Swell then, have a good trip, and reverse the charges and call during your layovers so we know where you are." Frank's final words were offered, and after letting a few cars pass by, he jogged back to the factory entrance without looking back.

As the South Shore commuter train pulled from the Eleventh Street Station and started its westerly trek toward Chicago, Sam had no idea how his mother sat with his little sister in the car and wept somewhere between sorrowful and hysterical.

Up the stairs of the Randolph Street station and across State Street, Sam rapidly marched with that duffle bag across his back. In his imaginative mind he was not a fourteen year old boy heading to a boarding school, but an eighteen year old Marine shipping out to Iwo Jima to plant that American flag on Mount Suribachi.

He could see both the bright Trailways and Greyhound signs hanging from the side of the multi-storied buildings down Randolph Street. Once his bag was safely in the luggage compartment, under the double decked Greyhound bus, he slid into a window seat about half way back, and thought, "This must be what Alan Shepherd felt when he prepared to be the first American ever launched into space."

Sam was fascinated that the several different busses he rode westward continued to roll across this huge country day and night. His only stops were for three to five hour layovers in places he had only heard about; Dubuque, Omaha, Cheyenne, and finally Sacramento. He did not understand that the bus business was at the height of its popularity as a means of cross-country travel. Neither did he know there would actually be stewards and stewardesses, on these long stretches, to bring snacks, drinks, and even full, hot meals. Most interesting was the time of the night when the bus stopped at some small place along the side of the road, and drivers would replace each other, while company workers provided pillows and blankets for each rider to, somewhat, try to bed down for the long night ahead.

During a longer than usual, six-hour layover in Sacramento, Sam ignored his father's instructions and allowed his venturesome nature to take over. After safely locking his duffel bag in the new fangled storage locker on the wall of the station and securing the key in his front pocket, he stepped out into the midnight air.

"California." he thought. I don't see any mountains like my dad talked about or even any swimming pools like the movies showed. This just looked like any other city. He walked a couple blocks from the station, stopped suddenly when he realized there was a man laying up against that building.

"Hey kid. Come here a minute." growled the long figure laying on his side. "Come here kid, and give me a hand."

"What do you want?" Sam asked from what he considered a safe distance. The figure replied with a slur,

"I need some help, kid. I need to get up. I think I had a little too much to drink tonight."

Just as Sam began to shift his weight to begin a slow approach toward the man, he heard another voice,

"You better get out of here, kid." came a voice from a darkened doorway a few feet away, "What the heck are you doing out here this time of the night, anyway? You ain't got no business being in this neighborhood. You better get out of here before you get hurt, Blondie, if you know what's good for you."

Goose bumps were crawling all over Sam's body. His mouth was dry, and he felt his heart beating in the front of his neck. With one lightning motion, Sam pivoted his body to face the direction of the bus station he had abandoned most recently, and ran harder than he had ever run down any basketball court. Nearly out of wind, he burst through the heavy wood and glass doors into the safe confines of the Bus station.

The mostly sleeping passengers, sprawled on the wooden waiting benches were no welcoming committee, but they were a beautiful sight to the young, foolish boy. He slowed his pace, found a seat for himself, and took another deep, cleansing breath, and safely giggled to himself,

"Well you sure got yourself out of the countryside, boy. Didn't you?"

The school was everything Sam had imagined, and more. The beautiful campus made him feel like an adult and mature just for being there. The classes were very different from Junior High. Students moved from room to room and different locations all over the campus. There were different and exciting subjects than he'd experienced at home. No more agriculture, a required subject in the country school.

Mr. Sanders taught Spanish, something he had learned while a missionary in South America. Algebra, a serious math class, was made fun when Mrs. Miles would take time in the class to show her many slides of Yosemite National Park in California. Of course, there was Gym class which meant a lot of basketball. Sam loved this because as a freshman he would not be eligible to play on the School team yet. English Literature and History were always Sam's favorite classes, anyway. He managed to get the afternoon job of mopping the Dining Room floor, and three evenings a week he could bus tables at the Blue Plate Diner, downtown. He loved that someone kept that jukebox in the corner playing constantly. His favorites were when Johnny Horton would sing, North to Alaska, The Battle of New Orleans, or Wolverton Mountain.

Another way the school helped to overcome his occasional waves of homesickness was the fact it was co-ed. Girls, yes plenty of pretty and proclaimed Christian girls. Sam had scoped out several possibilities of interest in that area, but soon found his need of money, and business mind, became a challenge for his female companionship hopes.

Because of Opal's regular health challenges, each of her boys had been taught certain areas of household work assignments. Sam's area of expertise, even at his young age, ironing the clothes. His mother taught him how to sprinkle a shirt with that old RC Cola bottle that had the sprinkler head attachment on top. After rolling them up to stay damp, and placing them in the fridge or cool place, they could be perfectly ironed to look like they were newly purchased in the finest men's store in town.

Sam placed some notices on the bulletin board in the student lounge offering his ironing services at a very reasonable price. In a setting where clean, freshly-ironed clothes were part of the regular dress code. In no time, Sam had built a sizable clientele which filled his late nights and Sunday afternoons with ironing.

It was not long until a delegation of fine-looking young women approached him with a proposal and a sincere request in the student lounge, since the men's dorm would have been off limits.

"Sam, look." their spokeswoman said. "You boys can get jobs all over town, but all us girls can do is babysit or take in laundry. See," she hesitated, "Your ironing business is really restricting our possibilities, so we wanted to ask you to leave the ironing business to the girls, and give us a chance to make some money too."

As she and several others of the girls softly batted their eyes in a manner to say, "Please, handsome. Won't you do this for us?"

Sam responded understandingly with what seemed like a workable compromise.

"Look, ladies." offered Sam, "Why don't you just lower your prices ten cents a garment, and you will probably get all the work you can handle?"

They seemed to like this suggestion, and strolled away approvingly. Sure enough, the girls posted their new advertisements, having undercut Sam's regular price, only to discover that by the next day, Sam had replaced his old ads with new ones listing an even lower price than they were offering. For the rest of that semester, Sam had plenty of walking change, but he could not have gotten a girl to even sit with him in church if his life depended on it.

Sam was facing the approaching Christmas season, and the reality that there would not be enough money to go home for the holidays began to set in. He soon discovered that all the other students, who lived primarily on the West Coast, would be going home for the Christmas break, but he and his roommate, being the two farthest from home would probably have to stay on campus over the holiday season with the school's cook and his wife.

Sam loved everything about the school, and especially loved the chapel services most, and the nights that guest speakers would come through. His spiritual life was getting stronger and the sure calling to be a minister was becoming his passion, but now the homesickness and the distance was getting heavier every day. Phone calls home were ending with fighting back tears by both he and his Mom.

Some guilt crept in when his mother told him she was not sleeping well with his bed empty upstairs, and she often shared how the little storefront church where they had been the last six years was seeing fewer and fewer attendees. Even many of his young friends had seemed to drift away from church when they began to attend High School. She did not know if the church could keep functioning much longer.

What a relief Sam felt the day he saw that letter from home in his mailbox at the school post office. When he opened it and read, he could hear his mother's voice of disappointment.

"Son, I have to tell you some big changes have happened here at home. For one, Mr. Hammonds, our landlord from Chicago came by Sunday afternoon and told your father and me that he is going to retire from his job in Chicago, and plans to move to the farm we live on. He actually gave us a date that we have to be out. We have looked everywhere for another place in the country but there is just nothing available that we can afford. So the bad news is we are going to have to move back into Michigan City. We found a small apartment for now. The only bad thing is it means stairs again as it is upstairs above another apartment."

Sam moved the letter away from his face and stared directly at the wall in front of him, then said aloud,

"Bad news? How is that bad news?"

His mind began to fly all over the place. "Michigan City! Back to Michigan City! Superior Street? That is right across from Kenitz' store near Ames field, the old neighborhood, THE OLD NEIGHBORHOOD, home, that's home!"

Sam felt the shaking letter still in his hand and pulled it again to his focus, and read on.

"To make matters worse, it looks like the church is not doing well with fewer and fewer people coming. They're having a hard time paying the bills anymore, so we don't know how much longer they can keep going."

Then came the part he was really waiting to hear,

"With us moving back to the city you would be able to go to the school you really wanted to attend, should you consider coming on back home. You could even be home before Christmas. I would love that."

Since Sam could never recognize the self-centeredness in the healed heart of a fourteen year old, he was left with little room to hear the heart-brokenness in his mother's voice. Sam could little understand that after knowing the beauty of yards, fields, flowers, and farm life, Opal's return to the city, much less, to an upstairs apartment, felt to her like a recaptured escapee from the Michigan City Prison hearing the steel doors slam behind him once again.

Sam flew out the door of the Student Center and bolted up the outside stairway at the side of the two story building. Breathless, he leaned over the counter that separated him and the office receptionist.

"I need to see President Bob immediately!" then lowering his tone from demanding to requesting, he quickly modified his words. "..That is if he is available to see me at this time."

"Is this something urgent?" she asked, rising from her desk and approaching the back side of the counter.

"Well, it's not an emergency, but it is really, really important."

After gesturing with her hand for him to take a seat behind him, she moved to the inner office behind the desk. In a few moments she returned saying,

"He can see you for a couple minutes but he has some important phone calls to get to, so be quick."

"Have a seat, Sam, and what gives me the pleasure of your company today?" came the most kindly greeting. Not what Sam had expected from the secretary's statements.

"Well, Sir," Sam softly spoke as he felt the President's hand guide his shoulder to the big leather seat in front of the desk.

Sam began to explain the letter from home and the changing circumstances for his family. He also went into great detail to assure the President how much he loved the Academy, but clarified his desire to attend the school of his family and hometown, and how that would now be possible if he returned home. When he finished, the President clasped his hands in a prayerful position, leaving both index fingers to settle under his chin, and spoke.

"Well, son, you are a good student here, and many of us have certainly recognized that there is a special call on your life. I really believe that what we have to offer here is the kind of foundation that would serve you well in preparation for the ministry you will have someday." Then with a little more precautionary voice he continued, "You know, this is also a wonderfully spiritual atmosphere where you are quite safely protected from some of the dangers and snares that can side track a young person during those High School years.

I have seen even the most sincere and dedicated young people go astray when they returned from this setting to the volatile and worldly circumstances in many of our Public High Schools today."

With that, Sam spoke up with a new gust of confidence.

"Oh! President Bob, I sure know what you are talking about, and I do understand the danger, but I will be very involved in a really good church, and my family will be right there if I were to slip in the slightest."

"So it sounds like you really have made up your mind already." Came the reply, "Well, Sam this is not so uncommon to us here. Especially as the first semester is winding down and we're nearing the holidays. It usually happens most with those students, like yourself, who are so far away from home. For a moment Sam thought again about the holidays. He remembered that he and his roommate would be the only students left on campus for two weeks. They had already been promised steak and all the trimmings every night from the Cook and his wife, who would be their caretakers over the holiday.

Another plan concocted by the Indiana and Florida boys, was to write many letters to their family, friends, and church members, bemoaning the horrible fate of being alone, away from home with just a couple of old people during Christmas. The goal of the letters, of course, was to produce a plethora of wonderful gifts, and maybe even some of those long cards with cash in them. These would all be supplied by contributors who were heartbroken for the boys, having no idea what a blast the boys would have with the entire campus to themselves. Then the little side-tracked journey was brought back to the present when the President continued,

"So, Sam, you begin to make the arrangements you need, and we will start the process of transferring you out to your new school back home."

The President rose to his feet, in the normal body language that said the meeting was concluded. Sam quickly stood, shook the President's hand, and bolted from the door. He took maybe three steps across the reception area and down the stairs, consuming three steps at a time.

"Home! I'm going home!" Sam hollered over and over again as he ran from one end of the second floor dormitory to the other end. Some students stepped from their rooms during this normally quiet study time ignorer to see what the disturbance was all about.

"Hey! Shut up, Pawlak! I'm trying to study here, you idiot." Came the angry voice of a fellow freshman from a room about halfway down the hall.

With that, Sam slowed his run, turned and slowly walked back to the room of the protest. To his own surprise, he felt his joyous celebration suddenly turn to an offended challenge. Once firmly placed in the center of the doorway, he had both fists on his hips, posed like John Wayne, and glaring directly into the brown, round eyes of the floppy-haired, Southern California surfer kid, he snapped,

"If you think you're big enough to shut my mouth, why don't you just try it, Sunshine?"

What Sam had not expected was that, without a second of hesitation, the other boy bolted mid-air, and flew toward the door, taking himself and Sam into the middle of the hallway. What followed was about fifteen seconds of fists swinging, feet kicking, bodies thrashing, and even a few attempted head butts.

"Whoa! Whoa there, gentlemen." Sam heard as he felt his body being pulled backward and upwards by his jacket collar. As he saw the other boy retreating in the opposite way by the same means of transport, both boys were still taking their last few flailing swings and kicks at each other.

The familiar voice of their Dormitory leader, Josh, a college student serving an internship by watching over these young High School lads.

"You two, get to your rooms, and don't you come out till I come and get you. Do you understand me?" This is over, now get to your rooms."

For a moment Sam began to feel some real shame come over him, especially when it came to Josh. Sam really admired Josh and thought he was about the keenest (the word for cool in that day) guy he knew.

Josh reminded Sam of his brother Fred, back home, and what Sam admired most was the deep dedication to God that both his big brother and Josh had in common.

Sam remembered his first week at Canyonville how the school conducted its annual fall Revival services. That meant church meetings every night, and because of the late services, no homework for that entire week.

Every night of the meeting, Sam sat on the front row, captivated by that year's guest speaker. She was a tall, thin, very holy-looking, woman. Her name was Sister Parish, and she not only was an exciting orator, but Sam was learning things from the Bible he had never heard, or even thought of. He knew some of the many churchy words, but her preaching explained their meaning and purpose so clearly that Sam thought each night,

"I can't wait 'til I can preach about those things someday."

Even more unimaginable to Sam was what was taking place on the campus each night. Long after the services were concluded, and the boys and girls had returned to their respective dorms, it was a regular requirement of the daily schedule that the dormitory leader would gather his or her students in the lower hall, and perform a duty called Vespers before lights out. This involved the leader reading some scripture, sharing a closing thought for the day, and then leading all in a song and a prayer before bedtime. But during the week of Fall Revival, an unplanned phenomenon took place. One night, during Vespers, while saying their nightly prayer, the boys heard an amazing sound. It was coming from the girls dormitory. It was a mixture of sounds. Yes, there was recognizable singing, but in the middle of all of it, voices cried out. Sometimes, over the singing would be an ominous wailing of girls' voices that might have bespoke some horrible event afoot, had it not been soon drowned out by hilarious laughter and a convergence of enthusiastic praise, not unfamiliar at all to these students. This passionate spiritual pursuit would continue until the wee hours of the morning. Some of those so involved never even went to sleep before dressing and heading to the next day's classes, and onto the next night's services in the chapel.

The next night the girl's dorm would be draped in total silence as the obviously exhausted ladies dropped into their beds and quickly fell asleep. Then it would begin to break out in the boy's dorm. Soon the same exuberance and voluminous behavior was being experienced by the boys, as if some supernatural visitation was being poured from heavenly urns. This seemed to rotate location from dorm to dorm each night throughout the Fall Revival.

Now, as Sam sat on the side of his bed, breathing heavily from the recent scuffle in the hallway, he felt true shame that Josh had to pull him from the other boy, and order him to his room to await the consequences of his challenged ego. He thought about how Josh seemed so close to God, and now how far from God Josh must have thought him to be.

Then another feeling replaced this serious moment, when a small smile found its way across Sam's lips, and he whispered the words,

"Whew, that felt pretty good. I have not done that in over a year."

Recalling a memory, he recreated the fistfight he had with Donnie in the last year at the country school back home. That morning, Donnie had spit on the back of Sam's head on the bus ride to school. In the darkness of his unlighted dorm room he mused, "Yeah, My brother, Dick said I should bloody Donnie's nose, and he was even there to watch me do it."

Even before leaving the spiritual atmosphere of the Oregon school, Sam was feeling an inner conflict between the things of God, which he found so compelling, and the inner gratification of calling out a rival in a violent hallway fracas. The upcoming march toward ominous challenges for his dreams and future could not truly be imagined for the transitioning teen, and the wisdom of the President's words were all but forgotten. He was heading home.

CHAPTER 8 - 1963-1973

The noise was thunderous. Not one person in the gymnasium was seated. The score was dead even, tied at 72 points each, and nothing was going to make the Holiday break sweeter than to pull out an overtime win against the hated Laporte Slicers. Their ugly black and orange uniforms looked absolutely ghoulish beside those shiny, satin-finished crimson and white of the Michigan City Red Devils.

The ball was being brought up the court by the little, flat-top haircut, J.B., but all eyes were in the corner. Vern, the sleek forward gave every appearance that he was not even involved in the play which the Coach had just diagramed on the small chalkboard, now laying discarded under the bench.

Suddenly, the crowd began to chant the descending numbers on the big lighted scoreboard at the side of the stage.

"Ten...Nine...Eight...Seven..."

At that very instant, Vern exploded from the corner of the court toward the top of the key. Midway to his destination, J.B. bounce passed the basketball in Vern's direction. Just as fast as he'd started Vern stopped, pivoted his body in mid-air, placing the ball high above his head, propelled his entire frame upward some three feet off the floor. He let the ball rotate in a backward spin off his finger tips, while thrusting his arms forward until the ball soared above the basket. With the sounds of, "Three...Two...One..." screaming from every voice present, the ball plummeted downward through the rim so perfectly the net did not even move from its hanging position. The noise from the jubilant crowd was deafening.

Sam, Dennis, and Phil pulled their collars about their necks, and headed out the front doors of the Gym, toward the warm Pizza restaurant on Franklin Street, as was this trio's after-game tradition, they stopped only for the several busloads of disappointed Laporte fans headed home along Pine Street.

The gathering of joyful Michigan City victors began to chant toward the closed windows of the line of busses,

"We are the Devils, Mighty, Mighty Devils."

To which the bus windows opened rapidly, and the angry Slicer fans began to retort,

"There ain't no City but the City dump!" speaking in degradation, using the one word term that had been emblazoned across the uniform jerseys of the victorious Michigan City Red Devil basketball squad that very evening.

After a few verbal slams back and forth, and a few snow balls precisely hurled within the opened bus windows, it was the emphatic vulgarities and gloveless hand gestures that surprised Sam the most. Not that they were happening, but that in the midst of his dream life at the High School he was so thrilled to be a part of, both the language and the gestures which came so easily from his mouth and his hands.

As he contemplated his new comfort with the foul language and behavior, Sam flashed back to the year before. He recalled with icy detail the week he had made that long return voyage on the Greyhound buses from Oregon. He returned by a different route. This time he took the Northern route through Portland, Idaho, Montana, The BadLands of the Dakotas, the wintry blizzards of Minnesota, Wisconsin, and Illinois, until he found himself once again in the same large Bus terminal in Chicago where he had begun his journey to freedom. Only this time, Sam had not calculated his money well, and was now penniless, and very hungry, having not eaten the last day and night of his trip. Just as he ascended the stairs, he saw one of the glass doors swing open, and there stood the most beautiful and comforting sight he had ever beheld, his Mom.

"Oh, Sam. There you are! We were wondering how we would ever find you here!" Opal wrapped her arms around him, and with tremendous relief, started out the door.

After getting settled into his little room at the back of the even smaller apartment, he soon gathered around him several new friends. Across the side street lived the Swanson boys and in the next block east were brothers, Bill and Phil, whose father worked In the office of the same plant Sam's dad worked. Over on Wilshire Ave. was Dennis whose dad was a block mason, and further down Gardena street lived Ricky. His Dad was the owner of a paint store way up on the North end of Franklin Street. When Sam returned home, it was to his delight that he could spend time again with his friend, the son of the preacher. Though Randy was soon entering his Senior year of school, a full year ahead of Sam, they still found some time to hit the beach. Mostly, if they had any time together it was quickly seized by Pastor Stewart Robinson.

Randy's father had led this small congregation on Wabash Street to become a thriving church within the city, and he was overseeing the final touches of the big, new church being built against the woods that bordered Woodland Ave, South of Coolspring. This particular day, Sam and Randy hung at their waists, over the edge of the highest pinnacle of the roof, some fifty feet above the ground. They strained every muscle to hold the fascia board in place while the Reverend drove the large nails back toward his own body.

"Ok, boys you can let her go. She will not be going anywhere now."

Sam thought how great it was that his old church would now have a structure that would rival the likes of the big Catholic churches in town, and even the Jewish Synagogue just a street over from the little building on Wabash Street. As Sam gazed at the huge platform in the front, he would think about the pact he and Randy had made on the Bible, those vows that they would someday cover the country as traveling preachers. He also wondered if he would himself ever stand on the big platform and preach In this, his original home church. But a sober thought passed over him: "I will sure have to get my act together, at least with God, if I ever have any hopes of preaching anywhere someday."

****

"You sit right there on the porch, and I will go across the street and get her." Sandy instructed Sam.

Not sure about this blind date, and going to a party with somebody you have never seen before, Sam thought, "I don't need any help getting girlfriends." After all, even Sandy had been his girlfriend when they were a little younger."

Growing more nervous, he began to pop his knuckles, never moving his eyes off the front door across the street. His study produced a litany of thoughts. His eyes scanned the white door, tall cement stairway, green house, black shudders, two stories, and an obvious basement below, with a driveway that passed by the side of the house to meet a white, one car, garage.

At that moment, the door opened and Sam leaned forward in his seat, hoping to get his first glimpse of his arranged date, and truly hoping she was not some poor, homely girl that Sandy felt sorry for, fixing her up with her life-long friend. To his surprise and relief, it was not the girl or Sandy. It was the girl's mom, quickly running to the car out front to hasten off for her evening shift at the family restaurant. Sam remembered his older brother saying when he told him who he had a date with,

"Hey, that is Vito's girl. And I don't know what she looks like, but if she is anything like her Mama, she will be a knockout. Vito's old lady is drop-dead gorgeous."

Just as the car sped away from the house, the door again opened. Sandy exited first, and then she held the door open as if to present the Queen of England at her coronation.

What Sam saw next brought a very confused emotion. First, he whispered,

"Oh heck, she looks just like Annette Funicello from the Beach Blanket movies with Franky Avalon." Then the inferiority that Sam hid so firmly behind a confident, and if necessary, boisterous façade pressed to the forefront of his mind. "Oh no, Sandy. What are you thinking, girl? That is so far out of my class, she won't even give me the time of day."

Then he began to take deeper inventory, as she pulled the beautiful, yellow sweater around her shoulders, keeping pace with Sandy's rapid, long steps across the street in his direction.

"Shoot, that sweater must have cost twenty bucks, and those shorts had to have come from one of the good stores downtown. Man, look at those fancy white shoes. Those babies didn't come from no rack at the Bergen center by the Drive-in theater."

As the pair of young ladies slowed their pace to climb the short stairs onto Sandy's family porch, Sam's quick-study scan moved beyond the clothes to the girl herself.

"Wow!" he thought, "Her skin is such a golden brown compared to my pale face, and her complexion is flawless."

He did not know enough about shape to give it much thought, but he did shift his eyes quickly upward so as not to be caught noticing those bronzed, muscular legs protruding from the glistening, white, dress shorts.

Sandy allowed her family's native Louisiana accent to slip into a pure mode of Southern Hospitality and propriety.

"Sammy," which only a few of his church friends still used, "May I introduce you to my friend and good neighbor, Maria." She pulled at Sam's forearm, bringing him closer to stand directly within inches of the girl's pretty face. "Maria, this is my lifelong friend, Sammy."

The sweaty palmed, teenaged boy quickly interjected,

"I really prefer Sam at my age." But he was quickly silenced when the young Sicilian beauty shyly replied,

"I think Sammy is a fine name, if you don't mind me calling you that." At that point, he found that even the little, crooked place on the bridge of her turned up nose was very attractive.

The party was a perfect setting for fun without too much uncomfortable dialogue necessary. The bond fire at the beach that night left a burning memory for a sixteen-year-old kid, who could not believe his luck in actually feeling this beautiful young creature snuggle into his side, under the wrap of his arm. He warmed her from the chilled lake air, and both of them pretended the raging bonfire was not warm enough to suffice.

As Sam walked up the back stairs of the new rented apartment on Spring Street, he thought how fortunate he was that his Western Union Telegram delivery boy job had provided enough money for him to have his own phone extension in his bedroom upstairs. The privacy and solace fed his independent nature. He could listen to the music he knew was unacceptable to his parents, and he even kept a bottle of his new favorite potable, Southern Comfort, undetected within the plaster wall of his closet. But what made this secret tower hold even more delight was that from the first evening they met, he and Maria would spend untold hours whispering into the phone in each of their bedrooms, reliving every significant, or totally insignificant event of their daily life. In time, words like love would enter the conversations, and for Sam, an occasional curse word would precede words of anger, disgust, and even hate toward his parents. He was especially wroth toward his mother, whom in his mind had turned from a caring necessity in his life, to an interfering and disturbing controller, who would not stop her incessant harassment in regards to his growing church absence. She also referred to his "Dangerous entanglement with that very Catholic girl," and what Opal deemed, "Her highly questionable family."

Bringing even more trepidation into Frank's and Opal's thoughts was the fact that Sam had a driver's license, and had purchased his first car. It was a 1959 Chevy Station Wagon. It was in pretty bad shape and needed a piston ring job so badly it looked more like a mosquito spraying vehicle for the City. As the faded blue and white beast roared about the city at above the speed limit, it burned and blew oil smoke from the tailpipe, until drivers behind this mass of rust and noise could barely see the car in front of them

Further complicating the situation, Sam left his Western Union telegram delivery route to take a job delivering Pizza, every evening, and of all places to find this gainful employment, it would be at none-other than the restaurant owned and operated by Maria's family. Truth be told, Sam had actually bought the car from Maria's father for the distinct purpose of working for the restaurant. Vito had even personally financed the whole deal for Sam and allowed him to pay him back at five dollars per week till the entire purchase price of forty five dollars had been paid back.

Things were drastically changing for Sam, especially in his relationship with his parents. The evenings filled with ball games and snowball attacks were replaced with breakneck and reckless driving. He drove across back yards, through fields, the wrong way down back alleys, and that was the normal night of Pizza delivery. The evenings were only interrupted by the seven or eight stops at the Checker Gas Station for another two dollars of gas and four quarts of oil. The latter being hand cranked from the fifty-five gallon barrel of greenish-black goop called motor oil. The oil sold for a meager fifteen cents per quart and was measured out in a glass jar with a tin metal pouring spout attached to the lid. As Sam slowly cranked out the liquid that would soon burn itself out of the car, he attempted to suppress the memories of standing on a barrel just like this one and preaching to waving fields of grain. Sam raced through town like a mad man knowing that there would be another large stack of pizzas waiting on the oven when he returned, the loud, cursing voice of his girlfriend's father, hollering,

"What took you so long? Look at all these pizzas waiting for you! You got to pick it up, kid. Let's go, let's go."

But it was the slower nights Sam really loved. Sometimes Vito would even let Maria ride with Sam. Oh, he did not drive any slower, but maybe even faster, thus providing a few extra minutes between returns to the restaurant to stop along a side street and capture, at least, a few moments of passionate kissing with this beauty he still could not believe was his.

Tuesdays were the best. Since it was a slow night, Vito and several friends of like personality and size would head into Chicago for the night. Their announced destination was the horse racetrack. This left the entire restaurant to Vito's boys and Sam. Most often, by early evening, the oldest boy, Tony would declare the business just too slow to stay open. The restaurant blinds were quickly closed, lights turned low, kitchen and dining room cleaned for the next day, and then the boys, usually joined by a few more buddies from the neighborhood, moved to the alley outside the restaurant drawing straws for what would become the Tuesday Night's Slap-Boxing event. Most nights the final bout came down to Tony and Sam. Their exchange of rapid, open-palmed slaps across each other's face gave them the feeling they were Cassius Clay and Sonny Liston, fully engaged in their version of the greatest fight of the century. These fights held no anger and usually ended when they both grasped each other in a laughing bear hug, gasping for air and conceding,

"That's enough for tonight."

The cold night air and stinging cheeks produced a sense of accomplishment as they headed for Sam's car, drawing warmth from a swig of the Southern Comfort bottle Sam kept safely under the front seat of his rattle trap wagon. Sam had added another new vice to his rapidly transforming style. He reached for the pack of Salem menthol cigarettes, flipped back the cover on the metal lighter and soon displayed with some pride how he could inhale deeply the cool-tasting smoke and blow it out both nostrils like every Hollywood tough guy from Humphrey Bogart to Marlon Brando.

****

"Good morning, Sweetie." Sam's gave his usual greeting as he reached the top of the back stairway entrance into Maria's kitchen. She greeted him with a little peck on his cheek, and ran for her textbooks.

As Sam gazed at the square metal-framed kitchen table he whispered to himself, "That's more lousy money than I have ever seen in my life." He moved even further from the table with a feeling, "I better not be even looking at that money if Maria's old man comes down here."

He could not help but stare at the piles of fifties, twenties, and tens loosely accumulated in piles like one would gather fall leaves in the yard. Then he did notice a very neatly arranged stack of bills on the other side of the table. "I bet those are two dollar bills." He mused, knowing those were often used at the racetrack where the Cadillac load of big men had gone the night before. Then, with both hands in his quilted winter jacket, he stretched his upper body a little closer to the table to verify his latest surmise. "Wait," he thought, "Those are not two dollar bills. Heck, those are one hundreds. That is a stack of one hundred dollar bills! Wow!"

As Maria rejoined him, taking his upper arm, he turned his stare away from the money-filled table. Sam, looking back over his shoulder spoke his present thought,

"Either your old man and his buddies are the luckiest suckers in the world, or they know horse racing better than anyone I can imagine."

Maria simply pushed him toward the back steps and said,

"That's probably not all track winnings. It is probably money from the restaurant."

Sam's argumentative nature thought, "If the restaurant is taking in that kind of money, looks like Vito could sure give me a little more than thirty cents for every pizza I deliver." But he knew better than to think that out loud. After all, this job did have its extra benefits, not the least of which included that pretty little girl sliding across the front seat of the car, and squeezing tightly against his body to make plenty of room for her brother Tony to catch his ride to school, as well. Wednesday mornings would always be, for some reason, a little unnerving for Sam as he never became comfortable with the huge amounts of cash money on the table each week.

It was not just money that impressed him in this newfound world, but because Vito was as much about fun and a social life as he was serious about work and business. When summer arrived and the lakefront basin was filled again with all those amazing yachts and sailboats, Sam knew he had hit the motherlode. Vito valued networking as a means of popularizing his business and increasing the clientele. This was how Sam found himself lying on the front deck of one of the most expensive and beautiful mahogany boats in the harbor, as it slowly motored, making no wake along the pier that led past the lighthouse, into the open waters of Lake Michigan. The vessel was owned by a major law firm in Chicago whose lead litigator had his summer residence within the sand dune area called Long Beach. The man at the helm loved to frequent Maria's family restaurant during those summer stays and had invited her entire family for this Sunday excursion. They were now enjoying a lifestyle that Sam knew his family had never known, nor would they ever likely participate.

Sam found himself a little startled when he realized that it was not Maria standing at his feet, but her father. Sam rolled to his back and sat up quickly to see Vito's large, harry chest and sizable, bare belly. But what caught his eye most was the can of beer in each of Vito's hands.

"Here Sam, you look like you could use one of these before the steaks are finished,"

As the large figure before him moved from his Sun-blocking location, and flopped his body on the highly finished front deck, Vito sat directly in front of the blond kid he was talking to.

"Hey, Sammy. I know you're too young to be drinking this stuff, and I could get into a of lot of trouble if you ever told anybody I gave you this stuff, but you're old enough to go get your head shot off in Vietnam, so you should be old enough to drink a beer with your boss once in a while. Don't you think?"

"I sure do, Boss." Sam said with a heavy emphasis on "Boss" as he reached for the open beer.

Sam got a bit uncomfortable as he realized that Maria's father did not just happen to come to him, but brought a drink with an obvious intention to enter into a purpose-driven conversation.

"You know, Kid. My grandpa came to this country just like yours did." Vito began,

Sam   quickly inserted, "Yeah, my Grandpa Kaz actually came to Michigan City right there through that harbor." as he pointed in the direction of the lighthouse, and the land behind.

Vito regained the conversation when he asked,

"What did your Grandpa do?"

"Ah, he worked his whole life over there at Pullman's." in a manner of speech that said, "He Really didn't do anything too important."

Vito quickly asked,

"Then your dad spent a lot of years at Joy's Plant. Didn't he?"

For a moment Sam took a sip of the warming beer, and wondered where this conversation might be headed. Other than negotiating his car purchase and moving to some quick work commands that this man had uttered he had never even had a normal conversation with the man. Sam suddenly recognized that Vito was about to reveal what this whole setting was about when his boss began to tell a story.

"See, my grandpa left the Old Country and landed in New York. Before long he was driving delivery trucks, and my dad did the same thing. Then my Dad's brothers got into some kind of trouble and my dad decided to get his wife and him out of there, and moved them to Chicago. That's where I was born and grew up. Sure enough, as soon as I was out of school I was driving big trucks. Then I started the restaurant just for some extra money, but the business took off enough for me to do it full time."

As Sam nodded his head, feigning interest in the little family history, he stretched his neck to locate Maria in hopes that she would rescue him from this uncomfortable isolation with this man he slightly feared anyway. Vito got to the point.

"See, I don't want my kids driving trucks or even running some back-breaking restaurant."

The man leaned even closer to Sam and started waving his finger up and back in front of Sam's startled but expressionless face.

"I want my kids to be teachers, or doctors, or even better." He stopped for a long slow breath, then raising his voice above the drone of the boat engine, he emphatically declared,

"A Lawyer. . . Yes, a lawyer."

Vito got up to one knee and looked toward the aft of the vessel, they were both enjoying, and with extended arm and pointed finger, he lowered his voice and said to the big-eyed young man at his side,

"You see that guy holding the steering wheel?" not being mariner enough to know the right word was helm. "Well, he may be the biggest lying so-and-so I know, but he is the smartest so-and-so I have ever met, and he has a nose for money like I have never seen. He is loaded, Kid. This toy you're sitting on doesn't even begin to touch the money, and stuff this sucker has. I watched him light a cigar the other night with a hundred dollar bill."

"Holy cow!" flew out of Sam's mouth. Suddenly, he had no more desire to be rescued from this story, but laughed and said to Vito, "Tell me more."

With this captured attention the big man shifted into an even more intense voice.

"Listen, Kid. You don't get this kind of money driving trucks, or running restaurants, or working in some boxcar factory, or machine shop. No disrespect to your family or mine, but you have to go where the money is if you think you will ever get enough of that stuff to really know what living is."

Almost every day that summer, Sam found some excuse to walk along that basin, on the pier side, and gaze at those toys owned by only very rich people, at least in Sam's mind. Then he would take the ride out to Long Beach and see those literal mansions hang precariously off the sand dunes. Many of those estates were only used during the summers, and boarded up for the harsh winters, awaiting the money players to return for their endless summer escapades.

Sam would replay his boat-top tutelage over and over, and reactivate Maria's father's words which had aroused something new in his psyche. He could almost hear this tough guy's voice saying,

"Sammy, Maria tells me you are really smart, and keep top grades in school. Now look you're going to be starting your Senior year this fall, and you need to be thinking about what you are going to do with the rest of your life. Before you get stuck in this town working for some lousy house payment and a few groceries."

Up to that time, the only thought that had really ever crossed Sam's mind when it came to his future life, was what had been there since childhood. He would be a preacher someday. But so much had changed. He was now finding out that there was another whole world. This world was exciting, fun, fancy, and luxurious, but what made this world even more magnetic was the fact that there was amazing amounts of money to be possessed. If only you positioned yourself in a way that could not prevent the flow of that money. Then he recalled Vito's conclusive suggestion that day,

"If you keep good grades you can get into any college you want. I'm talking about law school, boy." Then the man said it for him before he could even raise the challenge, "I know gotta think that there is no way you could ever find the money to go to a big law school, but that is where I might be able to find you a way."

"Whew, how could that happen?" Sam asked in the same hopeless tone he felt so comfortable in, when talking about money.

"Well," Vito stood up, and looking off to the west he said, "I know a lot of people, kid; with a lot of money, and some of them own many businesses. They might help someone smart, like you, if you were interested in really applying yourself to the Law trade."

Sam replied, "That would be a dream come true if something like that could ever happen."

"Well, kid," came the response, "These people have enough money to make any dream come true, and this would be the best part, When you get out of school and become a real lawyer these kinds of people could put you right to work being a lawyer for one of their own businesses."

The discussion was ended that day when Maria called,

"Papa, Sammy, come on. The steaks are ready for you."

As the, bewildered boy stepped from the deck of the boat to the floor of the yacht's lower level, he felt the firm had of Maria's father on his shoulder, and heard him whisper toward his ear,

"Yeah, Kid. You could end up a part of those rich suckers' big ole' family before it is over."

****

The hot August Sun burned down on Gill Field that afternoon. Maybe playing football his Senior year, with such a full load of classes and thoughts of which law school would be the best to pursue, was not the best idea anyway. But coach Osmand said he might be good enough to be a starting fullback, and carry the ball some. So he decided to stick with it a few more days. When he looked at the bulletin board affixed to the locker-room wall that Thursday, he saw that his name was still there, but not as a fullback, but second in line in the column that said middle linebacker. He felt a little more disappointment. Only an injury to the best player on the team would make a place for him to start. Only one more day of practice and the season would begin.

The other overriding factor facing him was that if college was not an option, he understood his draft number would certainly be high enough by graduation to get him drafted into the Army or Marines. With this thing in Vietnam already taking several of the non-college-bound boys from town to the rice patties of Nam, Sam knew he better make some serious decisions.

"Well, here is how it works young man. We have a special program in place," began the Air force recruiter, who lived near Sam's oldest brother, Manson. "We could sign you up now, before you start your Senior year, and place you on a waiting list. When you turn eighteen in April you would leave school, be immediately activated, sent to boot camp, and then you would be allowed to get your High School diploma through the GED program."

"This would guarantee to get me in the Air Force then, and keep me from getting drafted into the Army or Marines, right?" Sam grilled the recruiter across the desk.

Sam's thinking was that the dream of law school just would not happen for some poor kid like him, in spite of who his girlfriend's old man knew, and crawling on his belly through rice fields with the infantry, or dodging bullets with a bunch of crazy Marines in some sweaty jungle was not what he wanted for himself. Flying over all that chaos seemed a lot smarter to him at the time. The sales pitch was really on as the Air Force guy in that sharp, blue uniform, continued,

"Look, Mr. Pawlak, this would certainly be the smartest move for you. See, you would be able to finish your Senior year of football, watch the Red Devils have the best year in Basketball they may ever know, and probably not even see any of Vietnam. Of course, we can't guarantee that, but this thing probably won't even last another year. Could be over by the time you get in." Then, with the usual covering of his own backside, he said, "If you did end up over there, it would only be for thirteen months at the most, and you probably would end up somewhere like Tan Son Nhat, a very safe Air Base."

Neither Sam nor the young recruiter could never know that this war would last a total of ten years, would cost over fifty-four thousand American lives, and after an event known as the Tet offensive, places like that safe Air Base outside Saigon would have endless fields of dead bodies.

Back at practice, Sam was surprised and confused when he heard,

"Ok, Pawlak. For the first play of this last practice you get to be the fullback. Let's see how far you get against our starting line." came the simple instructions from the graveled voice of the old coach nearing retirement.

Coach V, as the boys called the tough old man, had been an honorable mention All-American punter for the hallowed Fighting Irish of Notre Dame, as a young man. The play was a simple dive to the right side of the center. John, the quarterback jammed the ball firmly into Sam's gut, and Sam, fully aware that speed was not one of his natural gifts, churned his legs as hard as they would move believing his strong thighs and determined attitude would show the coach that he needed this guy as a starter.

He heard it, that snap. Then he felt a strange sensation in his right leg. The linebacker who led the team in tackles, game after game, was draped around his lower leg, and that big ugly Brian kid had Sam's shoulders In a full bearhug. As the higher attacker twisted Sam's torso toward the west and St. Stanislaus church, the muscular arms and upper body of the assault on his lower leg turned, with all his might the single leg of the runner, in exactly the opposite easterly direction toward Lafayette Street, and the few kids watching from the fence. Sam felt no pain, but now some teammates began to order him to lie real still as they frantically began to notify the coaches and trainers,

"He's hurt! It's his leg, it doesn't look good."

Sam began to feel some throbbing pain that felt like an ice pick being pushed from the front of his knee to the bend in the back of his knee. He remembered being taught by a coach to ask a question: "Are you hurt, or are you injured?" If hurt, it meant to just get up and try to walk it off, but if injured, be still till someone can look at you. Then came Sam's answer at the same time that he released the scream he was not expecting,

"This is not good! This is bad! I've really injured something!"

Sam drifted off to sleep that night with the help of some medications that had never entered his body before. His leg was elevated on several pillows and the mass of wraps holding it in place nearly doubled the circumference of his normal leg size.

"Sam," Opal's voice would softly call from beside the hospital bed.

Sam's blurring eyes and fog-filled brain tried to focus in the direction of his mom's voice.

"I'm here, and so is your dad." Then she continued, "It is late but Dr. O'Leary is on his way, and they are going to have to operate on your leg, and they don't want to wait till tomorrow."

"Operate?" Sam questioned, "What the heck did I do to it?"

Opal placed her hand on Sam's forehead and began to gently sweep his hair up off of his forehead.

"Son, you really are hurt pretty bad. Your knee cap has been detached and twisted around to the side of your leg, and the Doctor is pretty sure you have torn one or more ligaments in your knee. It is hemorrhaging in there, and they can't wait till morning to get in there."

"O, God!" Sam responded while throwing his forearm across his eyes and tearfully began to moan, "What else could go wrong?" Why this, now? Not now." Then his attention suddenly diverted toward the door when he heard Maria's voice,

"O God, Sammy, no! What's happening?"

"How did you get here?" Sam quickly asked,

"Tony told me about it. He heard about it after his Sand Burrs practice." The term Sand Burrs identified the Junior Varsity team which her brother played for. "I ran all the way here. He said everybody was telling that you were badly injured."

Opal kindly moved away from her place at Sam's head and Maria moved in as Sam began to explain,

"I guess I tore up my leg pretty bad and they are coming to get me in a little bit for surgery."

"O Baby, I am so sorry. My Mom said let her know what she can do and she will check up on you later."

Opal fought back the feeling of resentment that another family, especially this family, was there to meet the needs of the child that she was responsible to see to. She also felt the pain of knowing that the climate between her and her son had become so strained and cold that he probably wanted the things another family had to offer, even more than any assistance from his own family.

After Sam assured Maria that she needed to get back home before too late, because he had no idea how long before they would come for him, she kissed his forehead and slipped out of the room.

Opal was worried about her boy, but his spiritual condition of his wayward heart would certainly surpass even her concerns of his physical challenge. So, with that in mind, she pulled from her purse a little newspaper clipping she had read just a few minutes before, while trying to ignore Sam and Maria's devotion to each other.

"Son, I know you don't want to hear this right now, but I think it is God's timing that I share something I just found in today's paper." She began to read a story from the sports page of a professional football player for the Kansas City Chiefs who had just gone into surgery the day before to have a very simple knee repair, and actually died on the operating table.

"Gee wiz, Ma! Really? I am about to go to surgery and you are going to read me some story about a guy who dies on the operating table during knee surgery. What the heck is wrong with your head, Woman? Are you crazy or just morbidly sick?"

At which Opal, bursting into tears shouted back,

"I am neither, but you are not right with God. I would not go under any anesthesia without knowing I had made everything right with God. You better listen to me, young man. There is a Heaven to gain, and a Hell to shun, and you better be right with God before you go into that operating room."

With that, she grabbed her purse and announced,

"I will be back in a few minutes." and stormed down the hall.

Frank lay aside the Field and Stream magazine he was perusing and said,

"She is just worried. I'll go settle her down a little." After patting the shoulder of his flushed-faced son, he added,

"She probably should not have shown you that story, but you know, she is right about the knowing-your-right-with-God part."

As Frank headed down the hospital hallway to search out the whereabouts of his anguished wife, Sam laid back on the bed, locked his fingers behind his head, slowed his breathing a bit and stared at the furthest corner of the room. After trying to balance his emotions between the audacities of his mother and his own inner turmoil in regards to the distance he felt from the spiritual joy and peace he once knew, he began to attempt some sort of communication with God. Sam was not sure if this amounted to prayer, or some form of extremely honest negotiation of a future barrister. He softly whispered in the direction of the ceiling,

"Ok, God. Here's the deal. If you know I am going to die on this operating table tonight then, right now I am confessing all my sins, and I am sorry for them. Please forgive me, and make sure I go to Heaven and not Hell, if I die." Then in an attempt to sound more honest than self-righteous, hoping that candor will earn more points than cannon, Sam continued, "But understand this, God. If I don't die in there, and I wake up from this whole crazy nightmare, I can't really promise right now that I am going to give up my lifestyle and jump right back into the whole church and religious thing." After his rather weak, "Amen" he mentally tried to convince himself, "There, I guess I have taken care of that stuff."

Sam was a bit startled from his somewhat questionable rededication when the soft voice of the white-uniformed nurse spoke,

"Pardon me, but I am going to give you a little injection that will relax you some, and we will prepare you for your procedure. The Doctor will probably be in to speak to you before we take you down, but if he doesn't make it he will see you and your parents afterward. You might feel a little drowsy and that is alright." After finishing the shot that Sam really did not even feel, she said, "Just rest now and this will all be over before you know it." Then she added, "Oh! Your parents are coming down the hall now. I am sure you will be glad they are here."

Sam quickly turned away from the door and thought it best to quickly pretend he had fallen asleep.

"Oh man! I wish they would come get this over with. My knee is killing me." Sam moaned as he, now lying on his back with his right leg elevated by several pillows, felt irritated with the time this was taking.

"It is all over, Son. You are back in your room. The operation is completed already."

Sam was confused.

"It is all over? When did they come get me? I'm back already? I don't remember a thing."

Opal stepped to the bed and said,

"Well that is a good thing. You sure would not have wanted to know what was going on."

About that time the Doctor stepped in the room. Upon seeing the pillows under Sam's leg, he quickly, and without warning snatched them from under Sam's throbbing leg, and with a simultaneous motion pushed Sam's leg, at the knee, until it was nearly flat to the bed.

Sam's scream was accompanied by an upward body thrust that began at the waist.

"What the heck are you doing?" Sam hollered,

"I am saving your leg, young man." The physician calmly replied, as he continued to explain to Sam and both startled parents, "I want this leg straight, not bent or propped up on some pillows. If this leg doesn't stay straight it will be bent the rest of your life, and you will limp as bad as I do."

Sam had not seen the doctor, in a conscious state, enough to have noticed his severe limp, but Opal had. She quickly asked,

"Is that what happened to you, Doctor?"

Doctor O'Leary, a bit taken back at her bold question said,

"Well, actually, in a way, Yes, Madam, it did. You see I broke my leg and it was not set properly, or given the right post-surgery therapy. I ended up having to have my leg amputated."

"Oh my!" Opal responded as she moved her hand to cover her mouth in an unconscious manner that said, "I probably should not have asked that question?"

"That is why I decided on orthopedic medicine. I felt like maybe I could prevent the misfortune of poor medical treatment, and do my best to make sure no other young man had to suffer these limitations."

The Doctor turned his attention to his patient and sternly lectured Sam.

"If you will do everything I tell you, young man, and not become some whiney little girl when it hurts, I can pretty well guarantee you will walk straight, have no limp, ride a bicycle, and run like you were meant to run. But it will take a lot of therapy, time in the weight room, and some stubbornness on your part to make that all happen."

"Huh, did you say stubbornness?" Opal retorted. "Well if that is what it takes, I can tell you, he will be your most successful operation."

Frank put his fist to his mouth and held back the explosive laugh convulsing in his chest, as Sam rolled his blurry eyes, and with a little grin said,

"Thanks for the vote of confidence, Mom."

****

The heavy cast started at the toes on Sam's right foot, and ran all the way to his mid thigh. The only physical therapy Sam could perform was to lift weights, strengthening his upper body as the cast and heavy bandaging would hold the leg and knee secure for the next four months. The restrictions, however, were only to his leg, and sometimes it was his stubbornness and powerful self-will that made the physical, mental, and spiritual war raging within him produce strange and even hilarious demonstrations. Sam had pretty well mastered the crutches till he could scale a stairway three steps at a time. He could use the heavy casted foot and leg to enhance his heavy-footed driving techniques. He maintained his pizza delivery job, and made quite a sight approaching each house or apartment with one crutch under his arm and balancing the pizza with the free hand. He also found that his pathetic looking condition produced some increase in his tips.

"Where have you been?" Opal asked as he pulled her station wagon in the opposite direction of Sam's.

"Well, if you aren't blind...?" Sam shouted back from the raised door at the back of his car, "I have had a flat tire today."

"Your boss called and said he has pizzas piled up on top of his oven waiting to be delivered, and he can't figure out where you are on a Friday evening, the busiest night of the week."

With that, Sam explained,

"This tire blew on my way to work, and when I got the spare out of the trunk it was flat too, so I rolled the stupid thing all the way to Sid's garage, got it fixed, rolled it back with this dumb cast and one crutch, while I might add, no one stopped to help me or give me a ride." A little frustrated shake came into his loud and angry voice. "All most of them did was point their fingers and get a good laugh out of this stupid kid with one crutch, pushing a tire down the street and back."

By now, Opal had passed and turned her car around to pull in behind Sam's. She watched him attempt to put the repaired tire and wheel on the old, rust-bucket car. This required Sam to struggle his way down to extend the casted leg on one side of the awaiting wheel hub, and the good leg on the other side. He had to use all that upper body strength he had developed to wrestle the newly patched and inflated tire in place. His goal was to align the five wheel holes to the threaded studs in front of him till he could push the wheel and tire assembly in one move, and once in place, grapple for the bolts, neatly cradled in the upside-down hubcap at his side. As Sam sweated, strained, and quietly whispered a few choice curse words, in a low enough tone so his mother would not hear him, he suddenly came to a dreadful realization,

"It is the wrong wheel! This stupid wheel does not even fit this car!" It was apparent that someone, probably the seller of the car had simply thrown in the tire storage place an old tire and wheel from another brand of vehicle just to make it look to the next buyer that the car came with a spare tire.

This was more than Sam could possibly take. He pushed the tire and wheel assembly in his hand as hard as he can to his right, grabbed the hub cap full of wheel nuts and flailed them like a boomerang into the street. While the thrown items were still noisily clanging on the pavement, he struggled his way to his, not so stable feet. He reached for the tire iron next to the fully-extended lift-jack and raised the iron high above his head, then threw the tool downward toward the ground with a virtual explosion of expletives that would make the proverbial sailor blush. The flying tire iron was intended for the asphalt street at Sam's feet, however due to its unbalanced design, it made first contact with the tire and wheel that the raging madman had cast aside. Upon contact, the ricochet effect spun the tire iron in a one hundred and eighty degree direction to make its final and painful blow directly on the knee area that was recovering from the previous surgery.

The cast cracked. Sam fell on his butt, and could no longer restrain the defeated and help-less position of slumped shoulders, and shaking torso, as he began to literally cry like a boy trying to ride a bicycle for the first time.

Amidst the pain, dirt, grease, tears, and anguish, Sam noticed some strange movement from the corner of his right eye. He turned in the direction of his Mother's front wind-shield only to see the most disturbing sight. Opal had both hands to her cheeks, and was uncontrollably roaring in laughter. As her eyes met those of her son's, she attempted to get a grip on what she had just witnessed, even trying to quickly dab the laugh-produced tears from the corners of her eyes. Sam struggled again to his feet, gathered the crutch under his arm, and moved as quickly as he had moved since his injury toward the side of his mother's door. He pressed his contorted face toward hers and began to scream to the top of his voice,

"WHAT IS SO FUNNY TO YOU?"

Opal exploded into unrestrained laughter, and responded emphatically,

"You are, Son. You are absolutely hilarious."

She seized the opportunity of the moment when, with an admonishing voice, she force-fully recoiled at her maddened boy.

"Just look at you! You are the most miserable person I know." She repeated the indict-ment as if to drive the point home, "You are so miserable without God!"

Sam, always feeling it necessary to get in the last word, and misguidedly thinking in his immaturity that the final word was the winning word, he screamed back at his mother, while trying to control own his tears,

"I am not miserable! I am happy! You hear me? I am happy!"

Opal looking deep into this visual and auditory contradiction could do nothing but once more burst into hilarious laughter.

What she could have never conceived that early fall day was that the war raging within her son was about to erupt in a full demonstration of war on the outside as well. This conflict would present itself in deeper and deeper displays of anger that was soon a convergence with Sam's growing tendency toward violence. Even before his injury, fighting had become a welcome enjoyment. He was not a bully, nor did he go searching for these encounters, but neither did he pass up the slightest opportunity to release his inner frustration with the, more than necessary, pummeling of a combatant's facial features.

Heated arguments between parents and son were becoming daily events. Especially with his mother, whom Sam always felt could never leave well enough alone. Before school most mornings, the inquisition would begin as to his plans for the evening, and before long the subject would return to his spiritual well-being, or lack thereof. The most sensitive to Sam would be his mother's reminders of his call to the ministry, and how far he had fallen from those desires. Somewhere in the angry and verbal onslaught of Sam's personal defense would come the subject of his constant attention to Maria, and growing infatuation with her family and their lifestyle, which stood in stark contradiction to that of his own heritage and family lifestyle.

One particular morning, the disgruntled commentary from both Opal and Sam had escalated to a full blown screaming contest.

"Now, that will be enough!" Opal shouted at Sam, "You are over the line with the things you are saying to me, and I will not tolerate one more minute of your smart-mouthed disrespect. I am still your mother and you are not going to speak to me like this anymore. I never took it from your brothers, and I will not take any more from you."

Sam, knowing that he was stepping into uncharted territory with the formidable woman, who never took a step back from anything or anybody in her life, made the decision within his own bound-to-win mind, and he figured there was nothing left to lose. With teeth firmly gritted, and neck muscles straining he launched one more verbal assault.

"Just leave me and my life alone! I am going to do what I want, and live how I want, and there is nothing you can do about it. I am not fighting with you anymore so just shut your mouth and get out of my life!"

Opal's reaction was as instant and anticipated as any of her children would have expected had they ever been bold enough or crazy enough to have told her to "Shut her mouth." With one rapid step across the kitchen floor, and both fists doubled, she began to swing at Sam's face and head. She managed only a few glancing blows and that probably because his now cast-less, but leg-braced knee was still not totally recovered. Sam covered both sides of his face and head in a Floyd Patterson style, boxer's defensive position. As he attempted to duck one of her mighty swings he saw it on the kitchen table. The silver steel blade reflecting the yellowed light of the room. He quickly grasped the wooden handle of the large Chicago Brand meat knife. Sam made a combination motion, pushing his mother away from his body, while taking another full step away from her.

"Get away from me, woman, or I will cut your guts out right here and right now. Do you understand?"

Opal stopped in her tracks, staring aghast at her son, and suddenly realized she was dealing with something so far beyond her expectations. She thought, "What is happening here? Has he gone totally out of his mind? Could he really do this? What have we raised here? None of my children have ever done anything like this."

She reached slowly for the chair at the table, and with eyes fearfully fixed on Sam; she lowered her body onto the chair. Sam held his threatening position for a little longer, and then throwing the knife toward the sink, he burst out of the room and headed for the front door repeating the same words over and over again,

"No more! No more! No More!"

Late that night when Sam returned home, he decided he would test the climate, and instead of slipping to his room upstairs he would come back to the kitchen under the pretense he needed a glass of water for the night. He was surprised to see his dad still up, and sitting at the end of the table, painting some homemade fishing lures he had designed from a few of Opal's unused table spoons. Frank had that serious tone in his voice that his children never tried to usurp.

"Your mother told me about your little mess this morning. You even threatened her with a knife."

Sam's mouth felt instantly dry as he tried to respond,

"Hey, listen..."

Frank raised his voice a bit and interrupted,

"No, you listen. This is not going to happen any longer." Then Frank leaned over the table, placed both elbows firmly in front of him and laid his big open hands upward from the table top and continued, "So you are really a big man now. Really a tough guy, huh? Well, why don't we find out just how tough you are? Why don't we just go outside now and find out how bad a guy you really are?"

Sam had never heard this tone in his father's voice, nor had he ever felt the kind of anger and power that was emanating from his dad's normally kind and jovial personality. A flood of thoughts rushed on Sam's mind. "This is scary. My Dad is inviting me to step outside with him. Holy Cow! Even if I could hit my dad, which I would never do, he would probably go crazy or something. I don't like what I am feeling here. I stood up to Ma but I have really brought out something in this kind man that I don't understand, and I don't like at all."

"Can I please say something, Dad?" Sam managed to squeak out from his saliva-less throat.

"Yes you can, in fact." Came Frank's still angered reply. "You can say you're sorry to your mother in that bedroom right now, and you can start living by the rules of this house, or you can find somewhere else to live, and we can still find out how tough you think you are."

Knowing that there would not be any safe and good result from one more sound coming out of his voice, and urgently wanting to retreat from this strange man he was first meeting at that table, Sam slowly turned from the room. Even more slowly he walked across the dining and living room floors, and timidly pulled open the sliding doors to his parents' bedroom.

"Are you awake, Ma?" Sam said hoping she would not respond so he could appeal to his dad to delay this restitution until tomorrow.

"Yes, Sam. I'm Awake." Came her weeping reply. She could not have avoided hearing Frank's elevated voice, with his challenges to Sam traveling from the kitchen.

"Ma, I am really sorry about what I did today. I didn't mean those things, and you know I would have never done that stuff. I just got too angry. I don't know what the heck is going on with me."

Opal never changed her position. She kept her face toward the front windows of the house, and her back to the doorway where Sam had placed himself.

"Thank you, Son. Now get up to bed."

Sam came back with a rather soft,

"Are you alright, Ma?" and Opal softly replied,

"It would all be all right son if you would get back in church and back to where you know you need to be."

Sam would have felt the anger again had it not been that somehow down deep inside of him, he knew she was so right. As he turned to make his way to the stairway that led to his room and the apartment upstairs, Frank was standing in the middle of the living room. Sam nodded toward his dad affirming that his dad had heard his apology, Frank moved toward the bedroom and repeated the same words Sam had voiced when leaving the house that morning,

"No more, No More, No more."

****

"Let's go. Get out of that bed, pal!" Were the first words that Sam heard on that early Christmas morning, as his brother Dick grabbed the front of his tee shirt and pulled him quickly in an attempted standing position.

"Oh God!" Sam called out. "What the heck are you doing?"

Sam grasped both sides of his pounding and spinning head, feeling the full effect of his previous night's indulgences.

"I don't care how drunk you got yourself last night. You're getting dressed, and I'm taking you home." Dick continued to bark. "It is Christmas morning and you are not leaving your parents to wonder what you are doing. So have yourself a merry little Christmas, little brother, and get your butt out there with the family."

The gift exchanges, Frank's traditional coffee cake, and Opal's attempt to avoid the subject of the previous night's disappointments at the hand of her youngest son, was simply a hangover fog to Sam that morning. No matter how much he loved his Dad's coffee cakes, the waves of nausea made even the thought of one bite sickening beyond words.

As the afternoon was coming on, Sam knew he had to get back to Maria's, or her Christmas would be very unhappy. Feeling somewhat better and wanting to approach the subject of his unfulfilled promise to his mother the night before he simply said,

"Hey Dad, can you run me back to Grandma's to get my car? I left it there last night." He hoped his dad wouldn't probe as the evening's details.

After hugging his mom and thanking her for the gifts, he started for the front door, then turned and said quickly,

"Sorry I didn't make it to the Christmas Eve service last night, Ma but I'll make it up to you. I will be in church Sunday morning, I promise."

****

"Hey Sammy, good to see you! I have not seen you in ages." voiced the words coming from the rather attractive blonde, standing one row in front of the pew where he had seated himself on this Sunday morning.

"Erin, is that you?" Sam questioned. "Wow, it has been a long time, girl."

With his mind thinking about the pretty little blonde girl that he was sweet on, what seemed like years ago, and a million miles ago. He quickly remembered hearing his mom say how she had married, even before finishing school, had a baby, and was already divorced.

"I would love to catch up and talk sometime." She said, taking Sam by surprise. "Maybe you could come by my apartment one day. I fix a wicked fried chicken. Remember I'm still a great Southern cook, and you could see my adorable little boy."

For a moment, Sam's male ego kicked into full gear, and he even felt a little unfaithful to Maria to think what was speeding through his mind. "*Wow.*" he thought, "*She is pretty good looking still, and she is a divorced woman who wants me to stop by her apartment. Hmm.*" "How about tomorrow around lunch time?" Were the words that flew out of Sam's surprised mouth.

"Yeah, I will have something ready. I'm really looking forward to seeing you again." came the smiling response from those thick beautiful lips that Sam had remembered kissing at a couple beach parties and hay rides in the past.

Toward the end of the service that morning Sam motioned to his mother that he had to get to work. He was going to slip out of the church while the pastor was entering that part of the message where he invited persons forward who needed some personal prayers. As he pulled from the church parking lot he thought to himself, "I sure am glad Maria is busy with her mom today, she probably would feel my guilt about the visit I have scheduled the next day, and especially if what happens is what I think could happen."

Sam had no idea what was taking place in the church after his exit. Sam's parents found their way to the front of the church, and when the new Canadian Pastor came to them, he took their hands and asked,

"Frank and Opal, what can I pray with you about today?"

Weeping, Opal simply said, "We can't take one more day. Either our son is going to kill us or we are going to kill him." Then she continued, "Pastor Yake, I know you can't put time demands on God in regard to when he answers your prayer, but I feel like I have to tell God I can't take twenty-four more hours of Sam's rebellion, his attitude, and his waywardness from God." Breaking into hopeless sobbing she again said, "We can't take twenty-four more hours."

As was often Frank's behavior when his wife was hurting, he simply placed his arm around Opal's shoulders, and without words simply bit his lower lip, nodding in agreement.

"Well, Opal," the young pastor replied, "I am not good at giving God timelines, but maybe in this case he is better at hearing them than we think." He bowed his head and prayed.

After an assuring pat on both their shoulders, and an encouragement to believe for the best, Frank and Opal slipped toward the kneeling bench and stayed there in a prayerful position long after most the congregants had left for their Sunday dinners.

As they drove from the parking lot on the last Sunday of 1965, they neither spoke another word to each other until they pulled up to the front of their house. Opal sighed a deep sigh and again repeated,

"Lord, we can't take another twenty-four hours."

****

"Get in here, mister." Erin excitedly welcomed with her Virginia accent.

Sam mused through his smile, as the lyric from a new California singing group danced through his head. "Those southern girls, with the way they talk, they knock me out when I'm down there."

While reaching for Sam's leather jacket sleeve, Erin quickly pulled him through the front door of her apartment, and throwing both arms around his neck, held him tightly against her body, like a grandmother would squeeze and rock a long lost grandson, returning home from the military.

"Jade East." She said as she released her grip, recognizing the popular men's cologne of the day.

Sam had taken some extra time that day to make sure he had nearly bathed in the stuff, and cleanly shaved. Every hair had been combed into place, with the help of his brother's WildRoot Cream Oil.

After taking his jacket and showing him the place where he could sit on the sofa Sam quietly asked,

"Is your baby sleeping?"

"Oh, no. My mother insisted on keeping him last night and letting me get a good night's sleep." As she sat down on the winged-back seat, directly opposite of Sam's position, she explained, "He is cutting teeth and I have been getting little sleep, and my mom watches him while I work at that rubber baby pants factory in Three Oaks."

"Why aren't you working today?" Sam questioned, to which Erin rather coyly said,

"Well, I called off today." Then quickly changing the subject she added, "I told my mom you were coming over today and she sends her love, and said you were always one of her favorites."

"Gee thanks. Tell her I said hi." Seemed like the proper conversational response at the time.

Sam's mind was bouncing all over the place, and suddenly settled somewhere with his eyes when he realized he was staring at that beautiful flowing hair, softly settling about Erin's shoulders. Part of the reason he was keeping his vision that high was an attempt to not stare at those shapely and attractive legs crossed at the knees and calling to a hormonal 17 year old. Attempting to verbally force his mind back to the reunion at hand, Sam asked, "So, anyway, how have you been? What's happening in your life these days?"

Sam became noticeably uncomfortable and startled when this beautiful, young divorcee stood elegantly from her chair, spread her open hands along her dress front, cleared her throat and moved across the room to take a seat next to him on the sofa. Erin never sat all the way back, but sitting on the edge of the sofa and turning her legs in Sam's direction in order to face him, she stared deeply into his eyes. For a moment, Sam recognized his true inexperience in a mature woman's world. He mused, "Ok, so this is how it works? Just like that?" He was kind of waiting for the next word, and really hoping she would do something to give him a clue what his next move should be, when he noticed something very strange. Erin had in her hand a folded tissue. He had not noticed while deeply studying her features how she had acquired it or where it came from. Her eyes fixed on his, having filled with tears that were just about to spill over those, long-lashed eyelids. As she moved the tissue toward the corner of one eye to capture the inevitable deluge to come, he thought, "Oh! I get it, the tears. This must be the part where she begins to tell me how miserable her life is, how lonely she is trying to raise a baby by herself, and how she really needs someone in her life whom she can depend on."

Sam shifted his body a little to the right, to see her better. He was pretty sure the next move would be to offer that comfort that only his muscular shoulders and chest could provide. "This could lead to the kind of experience that only a real man of the world understands." But she spoke first, and what came from her mouth could not have been more shocking than if she had begun to speak the most learned and perfectly pronounced Mandarin Chinese dialect, when she burst out, through tears,

"Your mom tells me you are not serving God."

Sam could not believe his ears. He jumped to his feet like he saw a rattlesnake between them on the sofa and recoiled as well, "I did not come here to hear some sermon!"

Just as startled, and just as quickly, Erin bolted to her feet placed both hands firmly on Sam's prized pectoral muscles and pushed him back on the sofa. Then in a voice a little bit like some wild, hillbilly woman in a Ma and Pa Kettle movie, she screamed, "You are going to hear one anyway, mister."

Sam somehow knew better than to jump again to his feet at that moment. "For love of Mike, this woman is like a young version of my mother. She is crazy. She is likely to punch me right between the eyes if I try to stand up again."

Erin simply stood over Sam, his groomed pompadour wave had fallen down his forehead and over his eyes, and he regained eye contact with the weeping girl, but his body language was anything but macho or confident. His head, still downward while his eyes rolled up to fearfully see what was coming next.

"Sammy, Sammy, Sammy, she repeated with the same sorrow that a sister would express while standing over a casket displaying her brother's remains. She gathered enough composure to start the sermon she had promised. "Sammy, you were always the preacher, our little preacher. We all knew it. There was never a question. You belonged to God. Not to any of us, and not even to yourself. You always knew the scripture memory verse every Sunday. You always beat all of us in those find-the-scripture-first Bible drills."

Sam's mind couldn't help retracing those years she was digging up so clearly. Years he had tried, and almost succeeded, to eradicate from his memory were flooding his thoughts. He saw himself again, like Ebenezer Scrooge, being swept back to Christmas past, particularly when she added,

"You always got the lead part and the most lines to memorize for the Christmas or Easter plays."

Unexpectedly, Sam began to feel something hot burning in the corner of his own eyes. His breath seemed to shorten and in a dizzying moment of elevated blood pressure, his body began to feel like he was slowly sinking into the cushion of the sofa beneath him.

Erin turned this attack on her old friend into a personal diatribe when she fell to her knees in front of the melting lump of self-centeredness.

"Sammy, this is killing me! I can't stand the thought that you are not even in church. You are not making God everything in your life. You are getting drunk and are always fighting, and I heard you even took a knife to your precious mother, and threatened to kill her." Her Virginian twang made that knife and kill part even worse than Sam really thought it to be. Then, without taking a breath, she unloaded. "I hear you even have yourself involved with someone who has no way of understanding the call that has been on your life, that you know has been there since the day you were born."

"Oh, Erin! Please stop!" Sam softly pleaded, "You have no idea what I've been through and where my life is, and anyway all that stuff you are throwing at me was a long time ago in another world, where there was never enough money for anything."

Erin pulled herself away from her advanced posture and sat back now on her legs beneath her. She reached to touch Sam's clenched fist, and in a somewhat conceding voice started again. "No, no, you are right. I have not been around. I do not know everything about your life but I know about mine, and you need to hear this, and then I will shut up and never bother you again." She slowly and in a much calmer voice began her story.

"Shortly after you went to Oregon, I started missing church and the youth meeting. Our friends were all in different High Schools then and I got caught up quickly in the new friends, parties, and especially the boys. One of my classmates had an older brother, already out of school. I met him at a party and was pretty excited that this twenty year old boy was really interested in me, a fifteen year old girl." She stopped long enough to cry silently for a moment, and gathered her emotions to speak again, "He had a cool car, was old enough to buy beer across the state line, and loved when I could soon out drink him. I got the results on my sixteenth birthday that I was pregnant. Then I started catching him with other girls. We fought a lot. No, I don't mean we argued. We fought."

Witnessing the force with which she pushed him to the sofa and the verbal onslaught that followed, left Sam little doubt that she was saying her battles with her husband became pretty physical. Then came the part he had not heard.

"You see, Sammy," she continued, "One night the baby was in his high chair at the table. My husband came in late for supper and I could smell the perfume all over him, and I saw the lipstick smear that he missed on his ear and neck and I told him we were over. I wanted a divorce and I would take my baby so far away he would never see him again. Before I could move he threw the glass beer mug across the table and it hit me right across the bridge of my nose. He stood, reached across the table, yanked my hair, and drug me across the table, slapped me several times, and then threw me to the floor. I knew immediately that my arm was broken, but before I could get to my feet, I watched in horror as I saw him try to smother my baby with a cushion from the sofa. He stopped for a moment, realizing what he had done. He cursed me and stormed out the door. I heard the tires squealing down the street as I hurried to the baby. Erin stood again to her feet in front of Sam, and with her voice somewhat elevated again cried out "He nearly killed our son. Erin returned to the chair, reached under the cushion to retrieve another tissue from the stash she kept beneath the chair cushion, and after blowing her nose she led toward the conclusion of her horrific story. "The baby's father will be in prison for a long time."

For some time neither Erin nor Sam spoke a word. Sam tried a couple of times, but no words came. Something else was happening to Sam that he could not understand or even describe. He felt like his skin and muscles were pulling away from his bones. His mind questioned, "*What is this? What the heck am I feeling? Something is very wrong with me. I feel like I am melting like the Wicked Witch of the West in the movie The Wizard of Oz.*" As he tried to understand his startling physical sensation, he was still giving his attention to Erin, expecting that perhaps she would break this atmosphere by speaking. Then she did.

"Sammy, I am sorry for my emotions today. I was determined to talk to you without all this, but listen. Oh, please," she began to cry again. "Please hear me. If I had stayed in church, if I had stayed close to God, if I would have avoided the first party when I saw the booze and drugs..." then she repeated the words, "If I would have stayed close to God, if I would have stayed close to God, none of this would have happened."

Sam could no longer control his own tears. He began to feel an emotion he did not expect, or had even long forgotten. He missed God. Just as powerfully as any of Sam's, once favorite, radio preachers, or visiting revivalist speakers, or dynamic orators at one of the many youth rally summer camps ever did, Erin began to connect her story to a place of application to Sam's life, with nothing left but to force him to a decision that demanded but one answer.

"Sammy, I beg you. Don't go one more day down this road I have travelled. God begs you to come back home to him. He has missed you, and you know you have missed Him." Erin stood, wiping the last few tears from her eyes. She pushed her hair back and said, "That finishes the sermon, I guess. Anyway, I did promise you some lunch if you would like."

Sam stood, amazed how much his legs were shaking. He still felt weird all over, but he cleared his throat enough to speak. "Hey, I hope you don't mind, but I just don't think I can eat right now. Whew." he said as he pushed the hair from his face, and with his fingers tried to put it like it was when he had entered this little apartment. "I better go, really. But thanks anyway. Hey, I really am sorry about all you've been through. You know, maybe if I had stuck around...well, anyway..." There was a long awkward pause between them, and Sam motioned requesting his jacket.

Erin said, "Oh sure, I'm sorry I will get it right away." She moved to the little closet down the hall, as Sam repositioned himself near the front door. As Sam wrapped the jacket around his body and began to zip the front all the way to his neck, Erin again put her arms around him, and half crying and half laughing said, "You were always our hero, Sammy."

Sam struggled with the keys again, almost as bad as the Christmas Eve night, but this time the blurred vision was from the tears gushing the reservoir he had built up trying to restrain his emotions with Erin. Soon, the old car was headed northward toward the 212 cut off. Needing to break the effect of this unexpected morning, he twisted the knob on his dashboard, and the AM radio began to blast sound into the warming front seat of the old wagon. It was a midday newscast just rattling off statistics about deaths in another province along the Mekong Delta. Sam quickly turned the other knob on the far side of the radio and it statically squawked the ear-piercing sounds until the first clear station came through. "*What is that song? That is sort of familiar.*" Then it hit him like a thunderbolt. "*That is that religious station out of Hammond, Dad is always listening to.*"

"I've wandered far away from God and now I'm coming home,
The paths of sin too long I've trod, Lord, I'm coming home.
Coming home, Coming home, Lord, I'm coming home.
Open wide those arms of love, Lord, I'm coming home.[2]

To his own surprise, Sam remembered every word of every following verse. To his greater surprise he heard his own strong voice begin to bellow each line. The driving was getting a bit hazardous, and Sam could barely see the lines of the four lane highway, because of the overflow of tears streaming down his face. In a rather surprising move, he reached for the pack of cigarettes in his shirt pocket, pulled them out and studied them in his hand. Knowing that in his upbringing, cigarettes represented a controlling factor in one's life that the preachers said, "Was evidence that you had not surrendered all control of your life to God." Sam squeezed the fairly new twenty-five cent pack of his favorite Salem's till they were no larger than a cigar's diameter. He hand cranked the window down and the twenty degree January air attacked his ears and nose immediately. In an attempt to gain the velocity of a baseball pitcher's fastball, Sam sailed the cigarette package out the window of the car, losing sight of them as the wind snapped them away. He was so consumed with these events that he gave no thought to the new no littering laws, until he noticed the sign that promised a ten dollar fine if caught doing just what he had done.

The location of the parsonage was a familiar one, but the current resident clergy was no longer Randy's dad. And Pastor Yake had only known Sam through the anguish of Frank and Opal for their wayward son. Nervously Sam pressed the doorbell and took a step back when the new Canadian pastor opened the door with a, not so welcoming question.

"Sam, what do you want?"

Sam could seem to only release the words, "You know what I want."

---

[2] "I've Wandered Far Away From God" by William James Kirkpatrick

The pastor produced a compassionate smile and replied, "Yes, as a matter of fact, I do know what you want, Sam, because I was just on my knees praying for you."

Without many words at all, Sam found himself kneeling in front of the large leather sofa in the living room of the church parsonage. The Pastor was kneeling right there with him and simply encouraged Sam,

"Sam, I am not the one who needs to pray today, so why don't you just go ahead and tell God what you came here to tell me."

Sam spoke to God as if he was somewhere in the back cushions of that sofa. He never stammered but started slowly.

"God, you know what a mess I have made of myself. I am really sorry." There was a long pause and Sam again burst out tearfully, "Oh God, I am sorry and I want to come back to you." He buried his face into the sofa, in a consolatory voice said, "If you can make anything out of this mess, I give it to you. I am yours from this day on. You have me, God. I will do whatever you want." He had no way of knowing at the time that the next phrase he uttered would become the thesis statement for his life and for his future, "I promise you God, anywhere, anyway, and anytime." His entire body was shaking while he could seem to do nothing but uncontrollably sob. He also felt like something was washing out of him like an infection being flushed from a horrible wound.

After a time, he returned to a peaceful state of breathing and finally got up from his knees, turning to sit next to the pastor on the sofa. The pastor was about to say something when that beautiful Grandfather Clock by the fireplace began to chime. After the little melody concluded, the deep strong rhythm of the hours began to ring.

Pastor Yake suddenly threw his head back and began to laugh a deep hearty laugh that came from somewhere down in the deep of his stomach.

"What?" Sam questioned with a strange smile on his own face.

"Oh my." retorted the pastor. "Sam, all I can say now is you need to go straight home and tell your mother what has happened today, and the decision you have made, and what you now plan to do with your life, and..." The pastor burst out again in laughter like he has just heard the best joke he has ever heard in his life, then continued to instruct Sam. "Just tell your mother that the pastor wants her to tell you what twenty-four hours means."

Pastor Yake's attention returned again to the clock as it rang out the twelve chimes which also coincided with the normal closing time of the Sunday morning service from the day before.

****

"There is another problem, Mom, and this one could really be tough." Sam tried to explain to his mother, who was still wiping tears and trying to control how enthralled she was with everything Sam had carefully explained to her about this unusual day.

"What problem?" Opal quickly asked,

"Well, Ma." Sam slowly said with a deep breath that followed, "It's Maria, her family, my job, and all that." Sam continued to speak seriously, "I really am crazy about Maria, maybe even think I am in love with her, but I know, and here is the hard part, I really have always known, if I am supposed to be a preacher and all, it would never work for us to end up together."

If ever Opal found a perfect time to show no response and offer no words of wisdom, it was now. Everything in her wanted to yell, "I have always known that, I have even told you that, don't you remember our wars over that?" but to her credit, or some supernatural hand on her shoulder, she spoke not a word.

"But the problem is bigger than that." Sam explained, "Her brothers and sister are not going to like this at all, and her brothers can get pretty hot. They are tough guys, and I am not sure what they would do to me if they thought I hurt their sister." He continued, "Her mom really likes me and even talks about when Maria and I get married someday, and what beautiful grandchildren she will have, and all that kind of craziness." Sam got really somber. "And her Dad, oh man! Her dad has been really good to me, and he kind of has some plans for me, like to help me get to college and law school, and hook me up with some of his rich Chicago friends. I mean he is also a really big guy, and who knows what he might do to me if I hurt his little girl? Really Ma, I could end up just disappearing or worse with the kind of people he knows."

"Look Sam," Opal spoke, "Sometimes we make decisions that make difficult situations for us, but you have told God you're His now, so you have to be totally honest with everybody. Who knows? This may be your opportunity to witness your faith to that entire family."

At that time, the only three words that stood out to Sam were "witness," "difficult," and "family," and none of them were being cataloged in his mind as positive. Like witnesses, would there be any at his murder? Or difficult, which now was interpreted in his mind as impossible. Worse yet was the word family. Yeah, that was the word Vito used when projecting the possibilities of Sam's Law future, "a whole new family" he said.

Maria hung her head and cried so much when Sam tried to explain.

"Maria, I don't expect you to understand, but believe me, the guy you have known the last year and a half was a fraud, a fake. That is not really who I am. I was living a lie, trying to make a new life for myself, away from all I really am, and all I really know."

It was of little consolation to Maria because she really loved the guy she knew as Sammy, regardless of who he really was. So the only comfort she could find was in running to her married sister. It was even more difficult for Sam to try to explain this life-changing twist when Maria's sister and brother-in-law had them both to their home and tried to tell stories of people they knew who practiced different religions, yet had great marriages. They even told of one couple where the man was a minister in a protestant church, and the wife remained a faithful practicing Catholic, and if that worked for them, then there was no reason the same scenario could not be successful for Sam and Maria.

Sam made sure he stayed out of sight of Maria's two brothers, awaiting the called meeting that had been arranged for the whole family. Vito, Tony, little brother, sister, brother-in-law, and Maria's beautiful mother would all be present to fairly hear this non-Sicilian, Polish kid explain how God wanted him to break the heart of their most prized jewel. Every member of the family kept their eyes riveted on Sam like they were peering into his very soul. He seldom made eye contact with any of them except Maria. She seemed hurt, but sympathetic to the tribunal he had to endure.

A little hand wringing, a very dry pallet, which was relieved when Vito motioned for one of the boys to give Sam a glass of water, and an inner shaking in the lining of his stomach. He hoped no one could see his tremor beneath the beautiful sweater Maria had given him for Christmas.

With language and terminology Sam was sure the family was unfamiliar with, especially in regards to his church background and personal beliefs, he did his best to explain that he never intended to hurt Maria. He thanked them for their acceptance and inclusion in their home, business, and family activities. He personally thanked Vito for trusting him with his daughter, and assured the big man how much he had learned about life just being around him. After Sam said all he thought he could possibly say without digging himself any deeper in their disdain, he sat silent. In a few uncomfortable moments all eyes finally broke their frozen focus on Sam and almost in perfect unison every head turned in the same direction.

For a moment, Sam felt like he knew what those early Christians must have felt on the floor of the Roman Coliseum, heavy boots pressed upon their neck, sword glaring down upon them, simply waiting for Caesar, with all eyes gazing at the throne, to turn the thumb up or down.

Vito shrugged his shoulders, opening both hands toward Sam, he asked,

"Is that all you got to tell us, kid?"

"I think so, Sir." Sam answered quietly.

Just then, the big man made a slight turn in the direction of his teary daughter, sheltered under her mother's arm. He spoke in a soft, but matter of fact tone.

"Well, little lady, all I can say is it looks like you lost this guy to a better man." Then he rolled his eyes toward the ceiling and nodded upward a couple times as if he were pointing her attention to some heavenly realm.

It took a moment for it all to sink in to Sam's understanding, and as the room filled with laughter, except for Maria burying her face in her mother's side, Sam breathed a big sigh of relief. He was not going to be taken out to the backyard and beaten unconscious. He would not feel the hands of Maria's father choking the last breath out of him, nor would he have to look over his shoulder every time he ventured into town. However, he did practice the latter option for a few weeks to follow.

Vito offered Sam a beer before leaving, but Sam knew well it was not really an invitation to stay and socialize, rather a suggestion that he leave, and the faster the better. Sam stopped to see if there were any last gestures he could extend toward Maria, but the glare from her mother coming over Maria's head let him know there would be no amicable farewells this night.

As Sam drove off to never enter that house again, nor ever see Maria or her family again, he drove by the restaurant, looked down the snowy alley, remembering the Tuesday night slap boxing contests. As he drove past the Pullman BoxCar Factory his mind thought of his Grandpa Kaz. Driving up Washington Street, he passed the old Barker Mansion, recalling the story of his Grandmother Mary's frantic appeal for help from the wealthy. He said an audible prayer.

"Ok, God. I will do all I can to not make you sorry that you chose me. God, I will be your preacher if you will let me."

****

"Sam, come over here a minute. Roger and I want to talk to you about something."

The big round-faced Canadian pastor called to Sam as if something both urgent, yet secretive needed to me discussed. Sam moved across the red carpet at the front of the church sanctuary, and slightly limped up the three stairs to the platform. At the south side of the stage was a single door that led into a combination reception/secretary office. Beyond the reception desk was a second, more ornate door. After motioning for both Sam and the Youth Director, Roger, to proceed to the inner office, the pastor followed and slowly closed the door behind the three of them.

"Have a seat, Sam." Pastor Yake insisted, pointing to one of the two leather chairs that sat facing the large wooden executive desk.

Roger chose not to sit beside Sam, but took a comfortable leaning position at the far front corner of the desk, and with crossed arms simply looked as if he were studying the young man whom the pastor, now seated in the executive chair, was preparing to address.

Sam was not sure Roger really liked him much. He remembered how Roger had come to visit Sam in the hospital during Sam's recovery from surgery. Sam also remembered how much he did not want to have any preacher visit him during that time. At the time, Sam did not want to hear the expected challenge to return to church so he acted like he'd fallen asleep during Roger's visit. What the young faker didn't know was even though Roger was a newly married college graduate, fulfilling one of his visitation responsibilities that came with his first ministry job, he picked up quickly on Sam's game of playing opossum. He even reported back to the pastor how that "Pawlak kid was such a phony, and a pretty bad actor as well."

The pastor began to speak.

"Listen Sam, the reason we called you in here was to discuss a little plan we are working on, and to see if you might be interested in helping us some." As the pastor continued, speaking rather rapidly, Sam moved a little forward on the chair to indicate his sincere interest. "Sam, with you having grown up in this church, you understand the structure of the youth department. You probably recall that the youth ministry encompasses those persons from thirteen to thirty-five years of age. Well, the problem we are finding is, however that may have worked in the past, it seems that there is a pretty big age span there."

He did recall how often the teens felt awkward sharing their weekly gathering, especially the social events where almost half of the group were married people, and some of those with infant and elementary aged children. It did feel nice though that these leaders would be interested in his opinion, or at least want to poll him about their new plan. He was pretty sure that he had been sought out because of the younger age group he represented, and maybe because he identified with some of the target group they desired to enlist. With both pastors aware that it had been quite recent that Sam himself was an avid part of this young segment of wayward society.

Sam was totally taken back by the next words out of the Pastor's mouth.

"Son, we would like you to be our Director and Youth leader of this new segment of our youth that would include the Jr. High, High School, and College age students."

Totally astounded and aghast, Sam was unable to control the sudden surge of his shoulders backward until his shoulder blades and elbows were penetrating the back of the seat he had occupied just a few minutes earlier. His neck stretched his head upward, and his lips parted as a natural physical reaction when one's jaw descended toward one's chest.

"No, no, wait. I mean...not no, but...No, well, but, wait." This string of singular syllabic grunts and sounds seemed for a moment unstoppable in Sam's mouth. Finally, he forced his hands together and began to rub one hand over the other, as if trying to rid himself of some highly caustic material, affixed to his fingers like glue. His eyes swayed from Roger to the pastor and back again several times until he silently screamed to himself, "Sam, stop.

Take a breath, get a hold of yourself. You are acting like a pure goofball." Finally forcing himself to speak some legible words, he responded.

"Oh, Pastor Yake! I love your idea, that thing about splitting the group to, you know, uh younger and older people, you know? And all of that kind of stuff, you know?

Hating that he could not seem to say anything without the inquisitive, "You know?" Sam filled both cheeks with air and slowly blew out till a faint whistle sounded.

The Pastor and Roger looked up and back from this totally discomfited young man to each other several times, and then, in unison, began to shake their heads and laugh at the sight before them. Sam lifted both hands out in front of him as if to say, "Give me a second and I will explain myself."

"Well, this is a little different response than I expected, Sam. Go ahead tell us what you think."

"Oh, Pastor. I, I mean, well, what I am trying to say is, I don't think I would be the choice to lead a group like this. Well, at least not yet." He actually stood in front of the desk, slowly shaking his head. "Pastor, I have only been back in church two weeks." Sam turned toward Roger and extended a palm-raised, open hand toward the department leader, and said in a regrettable tone, "I mean, Roger, just a couple weeks ago I was so far from God. I was getting drunk, and smoking, and cussing, and acting like some fool. I kind of feel like this is way too soon. You need to watch me a while, and see how I do. No, this is...no, I am not sure I'm ready for something like this yet, you know? I'm just getting my feet wet again. No, Pastor Yake. I don't think I'm your man for this kind of thing yet."

The pastor rose from his chair and walked around the desk, passing behind the chairs where Sam stood. He tapped Roger on the shoulder, reached with thumb and index finger to the finely pressed seam in the front of his suit pants. After lifting both cuffs from the top of his highly-shined dress shoes, he sat into the empty chair which Roger had left vacant upon their arrival to the office.

"Sam, come on and sit back down beside me for a second." Said the Pastor as he patted the seat beside him.

Once Sam had reseated himself, he kept his eyes staring forward in the direction of all those framed certificates attached to the wall behind the pastor's chair.

"Listen Son, let me explain why I have come to you. True, if you were a brand new convert, and you had just come into the church world for the first time a couple of weeks ago, I would never have considered this idea. You have had a call your whole life, and you have an obvious gift. The way I, or should I say, Roger and I see it, most of your life has been dedicated to the Lord. You have followed him and planned since a young kid to be in ministry. You just stumbled for a little bit, but you also have simply stepped right back to where you really always wanted to be. Besides, it will probably only be eight or nine months because I am sure you will want to get started with your Bible College training next fall."

This was still happening very fast in Sam's way of thinking. As the pastor's voice seemed to settle his panic, Roger finally chimed in.

"Look, Sam. If it'll help you feel a little more comfortable, I have several really good leaders in the older group, and I can spend the first few weeks there with you. You will lead it all, but I will just be there for some moral support, and to reign in the clown and goof-offs, if necessary."

"Whew, that would be a lot better then." Sam replied.

Quickly, the pastor stood again to return to his place behind the desk, and once safely fixed to his place of authority, he stated some conditions to this proposal. These he stated in no uncertain terms.

"The older group will continue to meet before the Sunday Evening service downstairs in the fellowship hall. You will take the younger group to the large classroom just off the downstairs lobby. We will put a piano in there and a small pulpit. Yeah, that's right, a pulpit." The serious man with the dark bags under his eyes that he earned from his driven work schedule gave Sam the appearance of someone much older than his mid thirties when he added, "You will preach to those young people. You hear me? No game playing down there. I expect you to save the games for your parties, but in that hour you have them somewhat captive, I want you to preach to them. If you need any help, Roger or I can help you make out a good outline. You will take time to pray, and study, and prepare a great sermon every week. When you preach to them, Son, I want you to set them on fire, and when you are finished, you need to get them on their knees, crying out to God."

Sam was already thinking about some of those great sermons he preached from the oil barrels behind the corn crib, and he was getting a little excited thinking that this could be the beginning of what he really longed for. Then the firm and emotional voice added,

"Look, Sam. If the Spirit really falls in those services, and God shows up for you, heck, you won't even have to worry about coming up to our evening service. We might just come on down and join yours. Now, go on home, and start getting that first sermon ready, because we are going to announce this change starting next Sunday."

As Roger and Sam left the pastor, walking back across the large stage, Roger slapped Sam on the back and said,

"You will do great, Sam. And hey, that part about bringing the folks down to join you on Sunday night. Shoot, he never said that to me before. Don't hold your breath on that ever happening, kid. You just better have everybody up there when he starts on Sunday night."

So, on the very next Sunday Evening, only three weeks after Sam had said to God, "I will be a preacher if you will have me," he stood before twenty-five young people, opened his Bible, and read a story from the Old Testament about Moses, a shepherd's staff, and a serpent. He said the words,

"Tonight, I would like to preach on the subject, "What is that in your hand?"

****

It was in early February of the new year that Sam read the note left in his mailbox by the youth office.

"Sam, this Sunday evening we are having a local Gospel Quartet perform in our service upstairs. I would like for you to have them sing a song or two in your youth service, so the youth might stay for our upstairs service once they have heard them. Thanks, Pastor."

So, it was a bit of a treat for the youth service when these three, young good-looking guys accompanied by a shorter than normal piano player. Their bright red matching sports jackets were almost as bright as the hair on the lead singer. He was flanked on either side by two obvious brothers with thick-oiled, jet-black hair. In another setting, and with a different musical genre, they could have just as well been Franki Valli and the Four Seasons. Their tight harmonies and popular gospel repertoire were entertaining to the youth, and their very sincere dedication to their faith values impressed the older audience later that evening.

After the later service, Sam was visiting with the brother' parents, who had come along from their home, some nine miles away.

"I really wish our daughter could have been here." Explained the mother of the two singing sons, as Sam shook the parents' hands, and assured them that the group who traveled as "the Royer Quartet," was an inspiration, to his youth group especially.

"Thank you." Responded Mom Royer, "but I really wish my son, Mike would have waited on this booking till their sister could have been home from Bible College." She went on to explain that the group most always included their sister, and in her, unbiased opinion, they were even more outstanding with her daughter's fabulous voice.

"Excuse me, Mrs. Royer but I need to speak to Sam just a moment if I can." came the voice from the smiling, little wavy-haired piano player from the group.

"Hello, and thank you for having us sing for your youth before the service tonight. I just wanted to ask you a personal question if you would not mind." Sam quickly could not pass up the opportunity to crack a joke when he responded,

"I don't care what they told you, I did not do it." And only when the little pianist stared at Sam with a confused look that Sam quickly reestablished a serious demeanor. "Sure, fire away."

"Well, my name is Jerry, and I also am the youth leader of my church in Chesterton. We have our meetings on Wednesday evenings in the basement of our Pastor's home next to the church, while the adults have a Bible study In the church itself. So, what I was thinking is, perhaps you would be able to come over on one of our Wednesday evenings, and preach to our young people like you did tonight."

"Wow!" Sam thought for the moment, "Am I really being invited to travel to another church group and preach for someone besides my own church family?" Then a little question popped up, "Is this how it all starts? I wonder if this is how Billy Graham got started?" but before his mind could wander too far, he quickly came back with a simple,

"Sure, I would be honored. Just tell me when you could use me."

The little fellow, somewhat older than Sam, already had a small calendar in his hand.

"Since this is the beginning of February how about..." and with a long pause that Sam was hoping would be broken with the words, "Maybe this Wednesday, day after tomorrow?" But instead came the proposal, "How about preaching for us the last Wednesday in March? That is Spring Break, and with no school we should really have a good crowd in attendance."

Sam tried to hide his disappointment and not let anyone hear his mind wheels grinding out the painful thoughts, "Oh! That is seven weeks away." He graciously responded,

"Yes, that would be perfect. I believe I will be free by then." As if to imply he had other such speaking engagements.

Sam did keep himself very busy in the weeks that followed. Almost every night he and a new friend who began to attend the church would peruse the local newspapers, or the church magazine that had been his father's Sunday afternoon read, for those advertised Revival Meetings within Sam's driving area.

Both Sam and this new friend felt that they needed desperately, a heavy diet of church services. Sam also felt there were many preaching skills to be studied if he could fill his nightly schedule, sitting and listening to those experienced in the trade, or "call," as they referred to it.

Finally, the late March engagement appeared, and Sam could hardly believe he was actually going to be the featured guest speaker for the nearby youth group.

"Hey, pal." said the young man who had been Sam's passenger and navigator for several weeks on those jaunts to South Bend, Gary, East Chicago, Goshen, Medaryville, Three Oaks, and so many other locations. "Before you go in and preach tonight, I want to give you a little gift I bought you today."

The plain beige paper was professionally wrapped in such a manner that one could have easily guessed what was in the flat, rectangular-shaped box. As Sam felt humbled by his friend's kind expression, he carefully separated the paper at the points the tape had closed it. The box appeared plain, slightly expensive-looking, and with a textured finish not normally seen on cardboard. When Sam separated the overlapping top of the box from the bottom, he smelled the fresh new leather as soon as he espied the beautiful, black, grainy-cover of the quality Bible.

"Oh Tim, you shouldn't have..." was by far more sincere than appropriate dialog coming from this appreciative friend. Then Sam read it out loud. "Holy Bible, Thompson Chain Edition. Oh Man, Tim!" Sam half shouted, "This is the one Bible I have wanted so badly. The way it is laid out, the sermon outlines nearly jump off the pages as you read it. Thanks Tim. Thanks so much. I will use it tonight. This will be my preaching Bible. Maybe it will be in a museum someday like Charles Spurgeon's or D.L. Moody's." Sam laughed, and followed up by asking, "Is this the one that was in the Bible Book Store up town?"

"Yup! That is the one." His friend gleefully replied.

"Oh, Man!" Sam said, "That Bible cost you almost thirty dollars. I could never repay you for what this means to me, Tim."

Tim simply urged,

"Sam, just preach it hard to these kids tonight. Help them get it straight before they mess up their confused lives." Sam couldn't help noticing how serious Tim seemed as he spoke.

After singing the Star Spangled Banner, the national anthem which opened every youth meeting in this particular denomination, the little pianist for the Royer Quartet stayed at the piano and led the enthusiastic young people through several more memorized choruses. The group engaged in some fervent prayer, and took up the weekly collection, then Jerry moved to stand in front of the nearly full parsonage basement.

Sam was reminded that his Uncle Freddy, Opal's brother, had built this basement when he had pastored this church, while Sam was just a small toddler. This was around the same time that the horrible train accident took the lives of Uncle Fred's brother James, his wife, and their three girls.

"We want to welcome everyone tonight, but there is one person we especially want to welcome home." The local youth leader continued, "We are so glad to have Patty Royer home from college for her Spring Break. Welcome home, Patty. We've missed you."

The exuberant young people burst into applause for the young woman who was best known as the faithful greeter for their youth services, before leaving for Bible College in Minnesota. All her friends believed she was destined to be a missionary in some remote part of India or China. They had all heard her tell how she believed this already about herself.

"Patty," Jerry spoke amid the welcome-home applause. "Would you stand a minute, and bring us a greeting? Tell how college life is treating you."

As the sister of the two dark-haired singers Sam had met seven weeks earlier stood to her feet, Sam pivoted on the front row folding chair next to his friend. From that moment, Sam never heard a word, nor could he tell anyone what the girl had said. He was smitten.

When she finished her greeting, Sam slowly turned himself to face the front again. He tried to shake off his distraction, and focus on the reason he had been invited. After preaching, using his new Thompson Chain Bible for the first time, he closed his message with a challenge for those young people to decide just what they had in their own hands, which in God's hands could determine the greatness of their entire destiny. The sermon which proved to be effective at home on his first venture into preaching was to be found even better-tasting on its second serving.

The car was very quiet on that ride home. Tim still seemed in deep self-introspection, and Sam had plenty to reflect on from the night of ministry, and the remarkable college girl he'd noticed. Just before Sam pulled up to the curb in front of the house where Tim lived with his single Mother, Sam broke the silence. Instead of his usual, "Hey, see you tomorrow" he blurted out a statement that shocked both Tim and himself.

"Hey, man. Did you see that girl tonight, that one that stood up from college and greeted everybody?"

Tim broke his moody spell and said,

"Yeah, what about her?" Sam quickly declared,

"Well, I'm going to marry that girl." Tim rather confusedly asked,

"Oh yeah? Well, do you even know her name?"

"Ah! Don't sweat the small stuff, pal." Sam grinned from ear to ear, and reaching over Tim and pushing his door open confidently concluded this amazing evening by saying, "God told me that was my wife. Besides, there will be plenty of time to find out her name, and who she really is."

****

Sam's quick immersion back into church activities helped him feel assured that he'd made the perfect decision for his life's direction. And being surrounded by all the many friends and relatives which had left such an indelible mark on his young life gave him the sense of connectedness and comfort that comes from the familiar. Seeing his Mom and Dad so peaceful and happy that their prodigal had returned home helped Sam release the feelings of remorse and guilt associated with his past couple years.

What a thrill it was to listen to Uncle Eddie, now a beloved middle-aged man, still moving the audience with his soft, crooning style, delivering the most popular versions of that day's great gospel music. Uncle Eddie sang songs with titles like "The Ninety and Nine," a tune adopted from the parable of Jesus about a shepherd who would leave ninety-nine sheep, safely in the fold, to search for the one lost sheep who had gone astray. Or another called, Ship Ahoy, a song depicting a drifting and damaged boat nearing disaster amidst the harrowing sea billows.

It was not unusual for the congregation to vocalize an exciting concurrence when Eddie would sing of the rescuing Captain, calling across the stormy sea to the one in peril. It was as if each listener could identify with the day they felt rescued from the sure disaster of their previously chosen path of life.

Uncle Eddie and Aunt Mary had two beautiful girls. Sam always considered the eldest, Susan, his favorite cousin, even from their early childhood. Perhaps it was that he identified with her light and fair features, not unlike his own. Only her curly hair surpassed his own blondness into a platinum white which older women had to buy from a bottle.

Since Suzie's parents were as involved with the church as Frank and Opal were, and Frank and Eddie were brothers, it assured Sam and Suzie plenty of time together at one of their houses. It also meant while other kids were playing cowboys and Indians, or cops and robbers or soldiers, Sam and Suzie often gathered the other cousins and neighborhood urchins to join them in playing church. During one of those childhood church sessions preceded by a tremendous summer storm, little Sammy noticed the large mud puddle had again gathered between the grassless front yard and asphalt street in front of the old Cool-spring place. To the future would-be preacher, the temptation was just too appealing.

Sam laid Suzie gently back into the several inches deep, mud puddle. All the enlisted childish church-goers, or players of the day, began to applaud and shout "hallelujah," just as they observed their parents doing, the Sunday before, at the old Michael's gravel pit, way off the County Line road.

When the parents heard the sound of rejoicing drifting through the open windows in the hot upstairs apartment, they quickly moved downstairs to see if it was the sound of a rousing revival or rambunctious rioting. Uncle Eddie saw it first. There stood his beauti-ful, fair-skinned, curly white-haired preschool aged victim of his fanatical evangelist, little nephew. The white hair was mud-caked brown. Her skin, covered from head to toe in some kind of gunk resembling road tar, more than a health-giving, Dead Sea mud bath. The gasp from the remaining adults on the scene quickly alerted the mini congregation, this may not be an acceptable form of worship to all present. Uncle Eddie nailed the high-est b-flat note he had ever accomplished, screaming and singing at the same time.

"Susan Pawlak! Just what the heck do you think you are doing?"

Both little skinny blond bundles of mud began to cry loudly, knowing that a good spank-ing was probably going to be the end result of their fervor and dedication, to what the church called, "the things of God."

Now, on this Sunday morning, the two favorite cousins sat side by side, passing a few notes among the other youth in the church, attempting to whisper out the sides of their mouths so their parents, who saw to it they always sat within a sight line, would not have to snap their fingers to bring them back to attention. Paying attention was no problem when Sam's favorite singer began his solo. He hung on to every word of the chorus. "Wow! My Uncle Eddie is an amazing singer." Then Sam's outlining, preacher mind be-gan to structure another sermon based on this emotional song.

Sam thought about how the simple words laid out the whole purpose of Jesus' life, and particularly as it related to Sam's own growing level of faith.

"Living he loved me.
Dying he saved me.
Buried, he carried my sins far away.

Rising, he justified, freely forgiven.
One day he's coming.
Oh! Glorious day!"[3]

The congregation shouted "Amen," Hallelujah," or "Praise the Lord," because applause was something that would have never been done in the church, as it would identify with, "The World," and sinful places of amusement. It was also taboo since it would have drawn the attention to the performer, instead of the God the singer was promoting.

Sam's eyes were drawn to the lone figure of another man sitting near the outside wall across the auditorium. This man was looking much older to Sam. His hair had thinned some and his massive shoulders were becoming a little more rounded than they'd appeared in the past. Sam noticed that while the song had already ended, and Uncle Eddie was returning to his seat, the other man was still looking skyward. The man's eyes were tightly squeezed with almost a painful look on his face. Both arms were stretched high above his head, and both huge hands were clenched in fists the size of small hams. The man's head kept rotating from side to side in the same motion a person might emphasize an emphatic "no," if being questioned. But across the quiet sanctuary, all could hear the single voice of the praying man. It was a clear voice, yet bearing a tearful sound. The heavy, broken, Eastern-European accent was uttering a series of short phrases.

"I tank you, Jesus. I tank you, Lord. Tank you for all da tings you always done."

In a matter of seconds a reverent hush fell across the congregation, only to be interrupted by the sound of some sniffing from persons, obviously tearing up at the sight and sounds. The Pastor stood at the podium, but did not speak. It was as if he was afraid to interrupt or interfere with some sort of spiritual phenomena taking place.

Sam, along with the other young people sitting together, could not take their eyes off the lone man. He was no stranger. This was none other than everyone's hero, Uncle John Pawlak. Most did not know all the details of the battle-ravaged veteran. They knew he had been to war, and they all heard he saw some terrible things that led to a few of his unique idiosyncrasies, but what they recognized most was his outstanding dedication to his God.

Twenty years after John had walked off the blood-bathed fields of WWII, and had conquered what a later generation would diagnose as Post Traumatic Stress Disorder, Uncle

---

[3] "One Day When Heaven Was Filled with Praises" Hymn by Chapman and Marsh

John would be considered, perhaps, the most loyal and loved church member this church had known since his own father, Kaz, faithfully provided the glass of water to the pastor before each sermon.

It was the boys however, that most identified with and admired Uncle John. The Junior Boys, they were called. The raucous Sunday school class of nine to twelve year olds were Uncle John's boys. Uncle John had committed himself to the life of a bachelor, falsely believing that his postwar emotions would disqualify him from being a good husband or father. But his love of nature and passion for spiritual things made a perfect fit for attracting active and sometimes rambunctious boys to himself and his Sunday School class.

Perhaps it was Johnny and Franky's wild and wooly ways that gave him the patience and the desire to affect these boys in a positive way. Among his recruiting and discipleship techniques was his regular visit to each boy's home, familiarizing himself with the home life and challenges of each boy, and winning the comfort and confidence of each parent to release their child into the preplanned adventures for these lads.

Almost every Saturday John would load that 1953 light-green Ford with boys from the church's neighborhood. He would transport them to the beach, a local park, or nearby woods where they could tromp the trails, climb the trees, hunt and gather seasonal mushrooms, or best of all, shoot Uncle John's 22 rifle.

Yes, it was quite a paradox of life to see the man who asked not to carry a gun at war now teach each boy how to shoot a tin can off a fencepost. Some became so adept that when August arrived they could fell a fat, bushy-tailed squirrel in the tallest hickory tree which housed the outing for Uncle John's Junior Boy's class.

It was no wonder that every boy in church could not wait till he turned nine, and hated when he turned thirteen. The thing that these boys would later relate as their greatest memories was not even the hot dogs and marshmallows Uncle John would prepare for each outing, but how he would gather the boys around the bond fire, read some scripture to them, and then urge them to always make Jesus the most important thing in their lives.

There were, of course, some boys who passed through that class that did not heed the words of Uncle John, and some went on to some self-destructive consequences. But there were also a sizable number of preachers, missionaries, and good church leaders who attributed their devotion and success to having spent many Saturdays and Sundays with Uncle John Pawlak.

What many of the younger set, and most of the adults never knew about Uncle John was that his greatest accomplishment was how his life had developed into a discipline of prayer, seldom matched by any man. As faithfully as the boys got the undivided attention of Uncle John each Saturday and Sunday morning, God received the undivided attention of John Pawlak most evenings, early mornings, and even many late-night hours, while others slept in peace. John actually spent so many hours kneeling next to his bed, praying for anything and everything that crossed his mind, that there were literally two worn-down trenches, at least a half inch deep on the wooden bedroom floor. These were the product of thousands of hours, where what some defined as a "Soldier of Christ," knelt to pray. He engaged in this practice as he had done nightly in the foxholes of North Africa, Sicily, Italy, Belgium, and France. This man had exchanged the war against the Axis of Evil to his own personal war for the eternal souls of his fellow man.

Sam sat, overwhelmed with this meaningful moment in church that morning, admiring the aging warrior as he communed with his God. He could not help but think how amazing it was that Kaz's and Mary's three boys, Johnny, Franky and Eddie, were not only there for him to see, but were vital fixtures in this sacred congregation founded by his maternal Grandfather James in that cold automotive repair garage almost thirty-five years before. Sam could not help but wonder where this journey would soon take him.

****

"Hello. Is this Sam?" asked the deep, low, growling voice on the other end of the phone.

Sam greatly enjoyed hanging at his oldest brother's apartment. He was especially fond of spending time with his two nephews, now about nine and six years of age. He also loved the fact that his brother Manson was a pure music fanatic.

At times Sam was called upon to watch the boys, while Manson and his wife were out for the evening. He could dig through the vast collection of long play albums. These gems were kept behind the cabinet doors of the new Zenith, color television. Sam would spend hours devouring the sounds of the latest and best musical artist.

There were some contemporary artists like the new kids from England, like the Beatles, Herman's Hermits, and the Rolling Stones, but Sam found he was particularly drawn to the more traditional pop artists like Frank Sinatra, Tony Bennett, and even crooning jazz aficionados like Mel Torme. The eclectic variety of Manson's musical taste also included great orchestras like Montovani, and pianists from Peter Duchin to Liberace.

So, with one of these musical greats, blasting in the background, Sam responded to the deep voice on the phone by saying,

"Can you hang on a second? I need to turn down the hi-fi a little." He lifted the record player arm so as to not scratch the 33 1/3 speed vinyl, then he returned to the caller. "Yes, sorry about that. This is Sam Pawlak. How can I help you?"

"Well," the voice on the other end began, "I don't know if you remember me or not, but this is Mike Royer from the Royer Quartet."

Sam motioned to the boys lying on the living room floor, giggling at the latest doings of Popeye and Olive Oil on the television before them, to hold down the hilarity a bit as he was trying to talk to someone on the phone.

"Sure, Mike. I remember you, and your brother too. From Chesterton, right?" then Sam continued, "Yeah, your group sang for us a while back, and I saw you when I spoke at the youth meeting over there in March."

Mike got quickly to the reason for the call.

"Your pastor gave me your number, but your mom said you were not home, so I should call you at this number."

"Yes." Sam shot back, "No problem. What do you need?"

"Well, I need a preacher, that's what I need." Mike laughed a bit and continued, "Here is what I mean. Our quartet is getting a lot of opportunities to sing at different churches on the weekends, and sometimes the pastors ask if we could do the whole service, and one of us preaches too. In the past, my sister has done most of the speaking for us."

Sam pulled the phone even tighter to his ear when he heard the words "my sister." His mind ran rapidly to the night in that basement youth service back in March, and the pieces fell together quickly in Sam's memory. "Yes, his sister. Yes, I remember well. That is the girl, the girl from Bible school." He recalled feeling so awkward when shaking her hand that night he could not even make himself look her in the eyes. "Yes," he thought. "I even told Tim I was going to marry her someday."

Sam's attention snapped back to the phone call at hand when he heard Mike's proposition.

"I just wondered if you would be interested in traveling with us some weekends, and doing the preaching for us." Then he quickly added, "All we can pay you would be some White Castle hamburgers, or a Pizza from time to time, but it is some great ministry, and I think everyone would enjoy your preaching."

"Well," Sam thought out loud, "My dad got me a job for the summer doing inventory at the factory where he works, but that never involves the weekends, so...yeah, I might be really interested in that."

Mike answered, "We are all kind of in the same boat. My dad helped get me a job in the steel mill in Gary, and I am working on my welding, so I work all week too."

"How soon would you need me?"

"Now, that's the thing," Mike announced, "We are doing a service this Sunday Morning in Rensselaer, and they really want a speaker too, would you be available?"

"Sure, I could do that." Sam blurted excitedly.

"We will also be doing their evening service, so we could use you for the whole day if you could prepare a second sermon."

Sam's mind began to drift a bit as he thought how he would have to get Roger to cover his Sunday Evening youth group responsibilities, and this on pretty short notice. His mind slipped off into a totally unexpected direction when he heard himself think, "Wow! This means I will be spending the entire day with that girl, Mike's sister, the one I have not been able to forget since that night I first saw her."

"Oh, absolutely! Sure, no problem." Sam fired back into the mouthpiece of the olive green, wall phone. "But I don't have a car right now, my old Chevy Station Wagon finally threw a rod and I just junked her."

"That is no problem." Mike assured Sam. "I am going to a meeting up in Hartford, Michigan Saturday evening to talk to a pastor about having us sometime, so I can pick you up that night. It will be pretty late but just tell me where to come get you, and you can stay at our house out in Burdick Road. We will go from there the next day."

After giving Mike the location where to pick him up, at Manson's house on Saturday, Sam began to prepare all he thought he would need for his first preaching road trip. Two good sermons, of course, his Thompson Chain Bible, both of his good dress suits, white shirts, ties, cufflinks, and both black and brown dress shoes. Finally, he'd better get a good haircut before Sunday so those church people won't think he is like one of those long-haired rebels that were beginning to infiltrate the youth groups at church. Besides, he would sure want to look as good as he did that night when Mike's sister, "What was her name? Maybe Pat" first shook his hand and said,

"That was a very good sermon. You are a fine speaker." Sam moved his eyes everywhere but in her direction, and he did not know why he had not thrown on the charm as he had perfectly displayed on so many occasions of the past.

As Mike pulled the two-tone, four door, 1964 Chevrolet Biscayne up the dark driveway of what was known to his family as "The old Burdick place," Sam could only make out the form of a two story house with a long porch across the front.

Because of the close proximity of Mike's parents' bedroom to the front door on the porch, they entered into a miniature lobby affixed to the end of the century old house. The little enclosure held a white door with several small window panes which opened directly into the kitchen. Across the kitchen was the doorless entrance to the living room.

As Sam held his suit carrying luggage bag over his shoulder with one finger, he felt his leg slide against the front of the sofa. He could barely see. The duo tip-toed across the dark and silent room. Mike silently pointed to a door at the east side of the room, and motioned for Sam to follow him. When the door opened, Sam could see a long stairway slightly illuminated by a low wattage light bulb, inserted into a ceiling receptacle somewhere in the small hallway at the top of the stairs. Once to the top of the creaking wooden stairs, Mike pointed to the first room on the right and whispered,

"You can go ahead and sleep in there tonight. I'll wake you pretty early in the morning." Sam whispered back,

"You probably won't have to wake me up. I am a pretty early riser, myself." Although that fact was true, Sam's real motive may have been more to impress Mike of his work ethic and ambition.

Sam had it driven into his psyche from early childhood, any worthwhile persons were early risers, and anyone who awoke after the sun had risen was certainly suspect of slothful behavior, if not a totally aimless character.

Sam quickly hung the clothes carrier on the back of the door, and after slipping into the welcoming bed stared out the window across the room. A thought drifted through his mind. "I wonder which of these rooms she is in." The last thing he remembered thinking in the dead quiet of this country home, so far from the noisy city he loved, "I can't wait to see her in the morning."

The smell of bacon frying and the sound of footsteps descending the stairs alarmed Sam from his heavy sleep.

"Oh, Shoot!" he uttered, a little disturbed that he had not been the first to awake that morning. He had planned to wake in his usual pre-dawn habit, and go walking in the fields behind the house. It was always his favorite time of the day, but he again thought he would impress the parents, or even better yet, the sister, should she be sitting at that kitchen table when this young, handsome, ambitious fellow, came in from his vigorous, sunrise exercise.

Sam quickly put on enough clothes to descend the stairs, hoping the lavatory would be empty, and he could quickly shave all twelve whiskers from his upper lip, brush his beauti-fully aligned teeth, wet and comb his hair, and splash on some of that English Leather he still had left over from his last birthday accumulation. He checked his posture, making sure all was in order before leaving the bathroom, just in case she had come down herself. It was obvious she hadn't, but he stepped to the kitchen door to greet Mom Royer, who was standing at the stove with spatula in hand. He heard Mike first, who had affixed him-self at the end of the table.

"Good morning." Sam's first words that were met with the anticipated,

"How did you sleep?"

"Like a baby. In fact, I really overslept a little." He said a little apologetically.

Sam noticed Mike examining an unfamiliar electrical piece of equipment in front of him, when Mike asked,

"Do you know anything about sound systems?"

"I can plug in a plug, but if it doesn't work, then I haven't a clue." Sam chuckled.

The small, thin, flat piece of equipment was about twelve inches deep and about twenty inches wide. It had several rounded knobs on the front, and a black power cord coming from the back. Mike explained,

"It's a Bogan Amp. Pretty new, but it has some kind of short in it. I think I got it fixed, but we will find out today for sure."

About that time, younger brother Dave stumbled into the room. Through his disheveled hair and sleepy yawns it was still evident this was the handsome young guy in the bright red jacket Sam remembered from February. He also remembered how impressive was the fine tenor voice this guy possessed.

"You guys better get with it this morning." were the instructions from their mother. "Your Dad has to work today and has already left, so he won't be here to help you load the car."

David groaned as he headed for the bathroom, Mike quickly stood and wrapped the cord around the small amplifier. Sam excused himself to return upstairs and get dressed in his preaching attire, thinking again, "Maybe she will be coming down the stairs when I start up." It was not the case. After Sam had affixed the shiny tie tack to his pressed white dress shirt, he heard the call from downstairs,

"Breakfast is ready, and you better get it and get out of here. It is getting late."

Sam had been looking forward to this great smelling breakfast since the aroma of fried bacon first woke him that morning. He also was pretty sure that if it was getting this late, the sister would have to be appearing at any time. As Sam was devouring the eggs, bacon, and fried potatoes, his mind still pondered the biggest unanswered question of that morning, until he sheepishly lowered his focus to the table and found enough courage to slowly inquire,

"Uh, where is your sister, Mike?"

Mike repeated the question like almost every Chicago area resident would do.

"Where is my sister?" Then dropped the bomb, "Oh! She is somewhere in Colorado singing with her college choir for a couple weeks. They are on tour out west right now."

Sam's mind shouted to his body, "No, Sam. Don't make a move. Don't drop those shoulders. Don't let your face show the shock you just felt in your chest. Keep your mouth shut. Do not scream that big 'What?' that has already formed on your lips. They will know you came here more to meet their sister than to travel and preach for them today." After feeling sure that he had held his emotions in some form of proper composure, he spoke,

"Oh, wow! That must be a wonderful experience for her. I bet she is having a great time. I travelled out west myself a few years ago, and boy that is beautiful country. Everybody should see it."

Sam realized that he was going to just keep spewing some ongoing list of short sentences until none of them made sense, and his uncomfortable disappointment would become obvious. He did notice Mom Royer had a little, what he interpreted as smug, smile as she turned away from the table. He wondered, "Did it show? Did she pick up on my interest? Did she see my disappointment? But his paranoid quandary was interrupted when Mike announced,

"Come on guys. Let's get the stuff loaded and head out."

As Sam sat on the front seat of the little church that morning, his emotions vacillated from enjoying the trio with the new pianist, and excitedly wishing they would finish their segment of the program, so he could get to that pulpit and preach the brand new message he had prepared.

Sam often questioned through the years why it was that when he would ascend to the pulpit to preach, he never felt the slightest twinge of nervousness. He heard others say how nervous they were before speaking in front of a congregation. He hoped it was not some self-centered arrogance. He even chastised himself for not being nervous, thinking perhaps it was a lack of humility he needed to overcome. But he knew he'd be a lying hypocrite if he tried to feign any display that said anything other than how much he loved to do this, and how excited he was for the next opportunity.

That morning, Sam shared a small portion of his journey from a family of preachers to his wayward trek, and his divine fortune at being allowed to follow in the family's call to ministry.

To Sam's surprise, several elderly people approached him that morning and began to explain that they had been former members of his grandfather James' church in a nearby town. In fact, they were members of the church when his grandfather had passed away, and his grandmother Martha had assumed the responsibilities of the church. It gave Sam a renewed pride and appreciation for the impact his ministerial relatives had on people, and it gave him the feeling that this preaching pursuit may be a more worthwhile endeavor than he had previously allowed himself to believe.

Following that first service, the lead singer announced his intention to follow his own urgent call to ministry in Mexico, and the quartet was in need of a suitable replacement.

"Hey Sam," Mike began, "would you be interested in becoming our regular lead singer for the group? I can't make this decision on my own. The whole group would have to approve, but Dave and Big Mike think it would be good. I would have to get my sister to hear you when she gets home, and see if she is in agreement too."

"Well, yeah. I guess I would like to do that if you think I can." Sam responded. "You know, I'm not much on harmony. When someone starts to sing another harmony, I just fall right into what they are singing, but I can stay on the lead part or the melody pretty well."

Mike said, "When my sister gets home I will call you and have you come out to the house so she can hear you sing, and we will see what she thinks."

As Sam walked up to his parent's dark house near midnight he thought, "Wow! What a crazy day. Here I thought I would get to meet Mike's sister, and be with her for the full day, and that did not even happen. But I might be with her every weekend for the entire summer. This may just be too good to be true."

****

It was the bedroom that housed Danny and Becky, the little brother and sister of the Royer siblings, which also doubled as the music and rehearsal room for the quartet. The room held two twin beds for the six and seven year olds. On the east wall of the second downstairs bedroom sat the big, white, upright piano. The northerly window had been raised upward to its fully open position, and on these hot summer nights the teenaged gospel quartet would spend long hours learning the latest songs from the long play records they had purchased at the latest gospel concert, known to those music followers simply as "The all night Sings."

These regular events in the nearby Morris Civic Auditorium of South Bend, or the Medina Temple Auditorium in Chicago were where the youngsters would sit enthralled with the talent, performances, and messages from the most noted groups of that day. Names like The Blackwood Brothers, The Statesmen Quartet, The Speer Family, The Oak Ridge Boys, The Happy Goodman Family, and a flood of rising newcomers would cross those stages to the delight of their enthusiastic followers.

The lobbies were transformed into virtual department stores of record sales, and the fans would pass by the beautiful, customized, shining, live-on tour buses, parked at the front curb. Many young singers like the Royers could only imagine that their weekend singing concerts, in relatively small churches, might someday lead to a nation-crossing profession of their own.

Sam studied her every feature as Mike instructed, "Pat, you just sit there on the side of one of the kids' beds, and listen to Sam sing."

Mike said it in a way that he was sure she would be impressed, as much with his find for a lead singer, as the singer's own talent. He also knew it would be a rather quick solution of replacing the vacancy he had to deal with. What neither Mike nor Sam knew at the time was, Pat remembered this fellow who was about to audition for her approval, only too well. She was unimpressed with him even before she heard him.

"Yes," she thought to herself, "I remember this character well from the night he spoke at our youth group In Chesterton. I tried to strike up a conversation with him. I told him how good I thought he spoke that night, but he never gave me the time of day. He would not even look at me. He moved his eyes all around the room like I was taking up his time, and he was way too important to get caught up in a conversation with some nobody like me."

She had no way of knowing how wrongly she had analyzed his behavior, nor how impressed he had been with her that night. She also could have never known how desperate he was to meet her again. Not to mention how she would have run from him as quickly as possible had she known that he told a friend he was going to marry her someday, without even knowing her name.

Pat's mind was flooded with thoughts of why her brother would bring one more character into this group that did just fine with only family members.

Just then, Mike nodded to Big Mike to go ahead and play the introduction to the song Sam had prepared. It was one the group was learning at the time, and it was quite comfortable for Sam, having sung it a couple times in his home church. The words began to flow softly from Sam's throat,

"In the harvest field now ripened, there's a work for all to do
Hear the Master softly calling, to the harvest calling you."

The frustrated thoughts that had been stirring in Pat's brain
softened as the clear, strong, voice seemed to rise from deep within his powerful-looking, barreled chest just a few feet from her. Her mind began to caution her, "Easy, girl. Don't let yourself get too caught up in what is before you. Don't make a move, don't show an interest, and of all things, for God's sake, girl, don't show what you feel right now."

The delightful shock to her ears seemed to explode to, of all places, her heart when even the cows and sheep outside the raised window lifted their heads to hear the next burst of vocal power. Added to the volume and strength of the auditioning voice was a stylish cry that spoke the emotions of a lyric operatic tenor.

"Little is much, when God is in it.
Labor not for wealth and fame.
There's a crown and you can win it,
If you go in Jesus name."

After the second verse and a reprise of the final chorus, Sam held the final high note as long as his breath would allow. By now, all eyes were on Pat. What would be her response? What would be the first thing she would say? Would she even be as impressed as the cows or sheep? Would it be a yes or no to make this guy the lead singer and preacher for this group that meant so much to them all?

Finally, she looked Sam directly in the eye. He withstood the temptation to let his eyes wander about the room in the intimidation of those beautiful hazel eyes, accented with those beautiful, thick, dark eyebrows. In a soft and controlled manner, some would call very professional, she spoke,

"You have a very nice voice, and I think you would be a good addition to our group. I am looking forward to working together."

Pat excused herself, and assured the others she would be soon ready to get on with the rehearsal at hand. As she slipped into the restroom next to the rehearsal room, and Big Mike began to play a few bars to the first tune they would practice, Pat pulled the door behind her, leaned back against the door, and let all her rigid and controlled demeanor slowly melt into a jellied sensation that left her unsure whether her legs would hold her up, as she experienced the deepest swoon she had ever known in her life, softly whispering the words,

"Oh...my...goodness! He is gorgeous!" Her mind quickly thought of a swooning Scarlet O'Hara, and she laughed at herself in a feigned southern accent. "Whatever shall I do?"

****

Well over a month of weekend travel concerts passed before the group found a Friday night free. Sam sought the opportunity to ask Pat for a formal date. The four weekends of late-night drives home for the work schedules that followed each week had already produced some quiet nights with Sam and Pat, not so secretly, holding each other's hand in the back seat of her brother-chaperoned Chevy. When David and Big Mike would fall fast asleep, and Mike's undivided attention would be given to keeping his sleepy eyes focused on the dark road ahead, Sam would even boldly adventure a quick kiss from the beautiful and gifted alto singer.

This Friday night, however, was different. It was a real date, away from her brothers and all those other eyes. So Sam, believing any girl would be as interested in a sporting event as he had always been, could think of nowhere more ideal to go for a first official date than the good old stock car races at the South Bend Motor Speedway. With any luck at all they might even get to see noted race drivers like Dick Good, Art Cross, or a future Indianapolis 500 winner, Gordon Johncock. The races were so loud Sam and Pat could not even hear each other if they tried to communicate. Sam suggested they go on a little further on Western Avenue to the Big Boy Restaurant.

Once home, they sat together on the porch of her safe, old farm house. She and the confident preacher were not yet ready to finish this first, eventful date. Instead, she retrieved a Mason Ball Jar from the kitchen. The exuberant pair, so filled with energy, life, love, and a world of adventure ahead of them, chased the Indiana summer lightning bugs across the large front yard until 3:00 in the morning. They placed them in the jar, and each secretly wondered, with every pulsating illumination of the magical creatures, what lights would shine on their lives unfolding before them?

With an uninhibited declaration, Sam announced. "God told me you're going to be my wife."

Stunned by the unexpected statement, she thought quickly about how a marriage to a good looking preacher did fit her own checklist, but she was scared out of her wits at a first date proposal.

"I'm not sure He has said that to me, yet." Pat calmly replied as she closed the lid on the jar she was holding.

Sam stood and touched her hand. "Oh, He will." He smiled and said. "Maybe I better get home tonight."

****

Decisions were made that summer that Pat would not return to Minnesota in the fall for her Sophomore year of college. Instead, she worked that semester at the book bindery in Laporte, to accumulate enough money to join Sam and her brother Mike for the second semester of school in a little Canadian Bible school recommended by Sam's pastor. It was the only school priced within a budget Sam could afford.

One of the side effects of the group's travel that summer was that Sam was often being invited to return to the churches to conduct extended services, called "Revival Meetings." So for the latter part of the summer, Sam left the factory, and traveled by train or bus to preach each night of the week. On occasion, the quartet joined him for the Sunday services.

****

It was Christmas Eve of 1966. Sam made up an excuse to summon Pat to go with him into town to acquire something needed for the festivities at the Burdick house. Instead of continuing west at the first intersection atop the hill, he turned the vehicle south, driving about a mile or so down the road toward Pat's old school. He turned again south onto Greening Road, and continued till the huge trees lining both sides of the narrow blacktop touched at the tops, forming a beautiful natural tunnel, even without summer leaves. He stopped the car, keeping the engine running because of the cold night. He reached into his pocket, and started the most important invitation he would ever make.

"Pat, I told you on our first date that you were meant to be my wife, and I know that now even more than I did then. I just hope you are coming to the same conclusion."

He opened a small, velvet-covered box, and turned it toward her. Her eyes were beginning to fill with tears and his voice was getting even shakier.

"Patricia Lee Royer, will you be my wife, and will you be my partner in our mission to win lost souls to our loving Savior, Jesus Christ?"

"Yes, I will." Came the simple answer, before both threw their arms around each other, parting long enough for a long kiss, and embraced again for several minutes.

"Well, you have to do one more thing to make this official. Before we tell the masses back at the house." She told him.

"Oh. What is that?" asked Sam.

"You have to properly ask for my father's blessing on this union." She said with a little grimace that bespoke, "I am not sure what he will say."

Sam was relieved when he saw the workshop light on, the door standing open, and the figure of Pat's dad in the back corner with his welding hood over his face. He could hear the big Lincoln Welder roaring out its noise. Pat sat in the car for a few more minutes, and watched Sam as he entered the workshop. As he approached, he made some obvious noise so as not to startle her father. The stocky, powerfully built pipe fitter lifted his helmet, lowered his working tools, and turned to see who was approaching his sanctuary of steel.

Sam knew that Pat's dad was not a man of flowery speech, but a rather gruff, get-to-the-point kind of guy. So he wasted no time when he announced,

"Well, Lloyd," knowing he dare not call him Dad yet, and trying to sound man-to-man in a rather boy-to-man moment, "Pat says I need to talk to you about something." Without hesitation the red-cheeked hulk of a man quickly said,

"Hey, she is your problem now." His belly began to shake in laughter which broke the awkwardness for both of them.

Sam said a soft "Thanks" and reached out to shake the heavy welding glove that held the powerful hand inside. Lloyd unexpectedly put an addendum to his humorous approval.

"All I ask is that you let Patty finish her college before you guys get married. She would be the first one in our family to do that." Sam quickly responded,

"Oh yeah, sure. Absolutely, I'll see to that."

When Pat entered the door, the collar was turned up on her beautiful leopard pattern winter coat, and she thrust her hand toward all within. Her hair was a bit mussed from the several times Sam had run his hand through it while making his proposal. Her eye makeup, unapproved by her mother anyway, was quite smeared from the tears that had been shed during the proposal, but she was smiling from ear to ear like any young woman, awaiting all the congratulations and hugs that would follow. Then came the clamor of individual requests to see the new diamond Sam had saved up sixty-five dollars to purchase from the kind jeweler who knocked off twenty percent for the obviously money-stressed young man madly in love.

****

Though Pat continued with her schooling as promised, it didn't take long for the young and impatient Sam to opt for the excitement of inspiring exuberant audiences and filling the altars, to the dry theological lectures of a classroom. But he couldn't shake the conflict he felt over this decision. Had he made the right choice? Was this God's will or his own? Upon returning home from the cold Canadian campus, he got the assurance he'd been seeking.

"Sam, I can tell you this much, boy: God is up to something with you." Opal said as they drove from the old New York Central Station in Michigan City.

He dare not do it outwardly, but inwardly he rolled his eyes and thought to himself, "Oh brother. Here it comes, that diatribe about how when God really calls you to be His preacher you don't need all that seminary stuff." He had heard this so many times from that side of the family, the family of preachers with no formal advanced educations. He had heard the famous stories of young men who knew they were destined for ordained ministry work and went off to those big schools and came home confused in their beliefs, and so educated they lost their passion, only to become "one more boring and dead preacher." Sam was prepared to stop her quickly and scream to the top of his voice, "I love learning. I want a good education. I do not want to be proud of my ignorance. I want more than emotion. I want to be a person of substance, knowledge, and enough wisdom to use the knowledge I acquire."

To his surprise, Opal did not go down this path at all. She struggled to gather her purse, swung open the door to the car, stood to her arthritic feet and legs, and she simply informed Sam,

"The phone has rung off the hook ever since you left. I have a list of at least twenty pastors who have called you, hoping you were available to come to their churches to conduct some revival services."

"Yes, Pastor. I have those dates available if you like. Now, let me make sure I understand. You want to begin this Sunday morning and evening, and then each night of the week concluding on the next Sunday night. Ten services, is that right? Ok, Pastor. Thank you, I will be there." Before hanging up his mother's old black desk phone Sam continued, "Sure, I will be more than happy to come to you on the Greyhound Bus." He paused for more details. "Oh, staying in your parsonage guest room would be an honor, sir. No sir, I have no eating restrictions, but don't put your wife out for me. No, no sir, I have no expected honorarium. A freewill offering on the last night will be very kind. Thanks again, looking forward to being a blessing to your wonderful congregation."

Sam's voice was dry and raspy when he put down the phone receiver, having completed the twentieth return call from the list of numbers his mother had taken in his absence.

"Mom, those were almost all long distance calls. By the time you get that bill I should have some money, and I can pay for all of them."

"Oh, thanks son, that will be a great help."

Sam knew he had one more call to make. He left a message with the college desk, and within a couple hours he heard her lovely voice.

"Hey Baby." he excitedly said. "Got home fine, and listen you will not believe what has happened. In the last three hours I have just booked sixteen meetings. All at least one week, and a couple want to go two weeks. Some pastors have asked me to keep a week open on my schedule in case it goes good, and they want to extend the meeting another week."

"That is fantastic!" Pat almost squealed with excitement. "Why wouldn't they want you? You're the best preacher I know."

"Thanks so much. I needed to hear that from you, I thought by now you would have figured I have lost my mind completely." Sam continued, "That means this semester will go fast, and we will be back together soon, and maybe we can even think about getting married a little sooner than we thought."

Pat quickly brought Sam back to a little promise he had made about a month ago,

"Remember, you told my dad I would finish school first." Sam slowed a bit and said,

"Oh yeah, that. Well, I guess I am going to have to figure out how I will get my college finished too." Then he added, "You know, I have heard about this college that you can do by mail. It is a part of our church organization, and someone told me they will accept their certificate toward my ordination." He surmised, "If that is possible, maybe I could get my college education, and continue in full-time ministry at the same time." and then he quickly and kind of teasingly added, "And maybe we could get your college that way, and be married, and do these church meetings together."

"Slow down, boy." Pat responded. "I am glad for the meetings. Just worry about being ready for those. We have time to see where this goes."

Sam quickly changed the subject, thinking about how much he was going to owe his mom in phone bills, he began to wrap the conversation with a lot of,
     "I love you so much"
     "I miss you already"
     "I hope spring gets here soon"

Then he finalized with, "By the way, the State Convention is in Indianapolis, right after my first meetings. I kept the dates open and figured I will be able to go there for three days. Maybe I'll be able to book more meetings when the pastors know I am home." Then he added, "The Speaker is some national leader of the church, and I saw he had been the former president of the college you attended last year in Minnesota." Sam concluded the call by saying, "Remember, I love you. Stay warm and I will write every day that I can."

****

"Well, hello Uncle Fred." Sam said while softly placing his hand on the shoulder of his mother's youngest brother.

Sam's favorite preacher, and amazing musician turned slowly to see his young, blond, wavy-haired nephew grinning from ear to ear because of the surprise he had hoped to bring to his uncle. Uncle Fred responded with just as much excitement.

"Sammy! Wow! I didn't expect to see you here, but I am so glad you made it to the conference."

After hugs and several hard pounds on each other's back, the way men of that day greeted male family or friends, Sam explained,

"I just finished a week of meetings up in Kokomo, and figured since I was only about fifty miles away I would come on down and find out how you important preachers run things."

The wheezing laugh from his uncle, and the assurance that he would have to find someone else beside his uncle to see any "Big Preachers" was exactly the kind of response that Sam expected from this youngest son of Rev. James Rice. He also knew that his Uncle Freddy, as the family called him, was really only famous within the circle of the very tight Rice side of the family. Having been James' son and following in his father's footsteps, Sam's Uncle Fred was the pride of Martha Rice's life.
Sam also knew that his Uncle Fred held a work ethic that allowed him to serve as a bi-vocational minister, like his father James. This meant pastoring small to medium sized congregations, while helping to support his family with some form of secular work. He had a wife who was willing to hold a full-time job as well.

"Yes." Uncle Fred replied, "My sister Odessa told me you had been preaching in Kokomo, and that you were staying with her during the meetings. She said you were really doing a fantastic job. She also said I should watch out because you were quite the speaker."

"Oh, you don't have to worry about that at all." Sam replied. "Besides, I hope I am alright. After all, I have studied the best." Sam said flatteringly as he lightly punched Uncle Fred on the shoulder.

"Ok, Ok. I see how this is going to be." joked Uncle Fred. "It looks like you are learning pretty fast. So, when can I get you to come over to the west side of Indianapolis and do some preaching for my church?"

"You name the time, and I will be there with bells on."

As his Uncle reached inside the pocket of one of those famous plaid sports coats and took out a little pocket-sized date book he mused,

"You know, Sam? We could start a Revival Meeting." His Uncle continued, "Easter morning, go every night that week, and end the following Sunday night."

"Oh, that would be great!" Sam responded, reaching for his own date book. He had learned one thing about his new profession: never be without your datebook.

"Well that settles it. You can stay with me and your Aunt Evelyn. Levi, and Freddy Jr. will love having some time with you too."

Sam became excited at the mention of his two cousins, whom he did not get to see often. He knew one thing for sure, there would never be a dull moment when they were together.

For now, the future planning would have to wait. As the music from the large organ and grand piano began to play the prelude to the opening church service of the conference, Uncle Fred interjected one more facet of the Easter week agenda.

"We will do some good advertising in the newspaper and distribute some promotional flyers in anticipation of your coming. I can see it now. HEAR THIS TEEN AGED EVANGELIST NIGHTLY."

As they entered the chapel, Fred made one more comment. "Your mom and your Aunt Odessa say you really are a good preacher." Then he returned Sam's shoulder punch from earlier. "But that is your mom and your aunt."

Both men laughed and slid across the pew to focus their attention on the event about to begin. Sam did not really even hear the moderator's opening remarks. He was still engrossed in the fact he would be preaching in his uncles' church on Easter. Seldom was a pastor willing to relinquish his pulpit on the Sunday that would produce the largest attendance of the year.

A word began to float across Sam's psyche; "Evangelist. Did he say Evangelist?" then he mused, "Me, an Evangelist?"

Sam sure knew the word. He was greatly fascinated and entertained when those itinerant preachers would visit his boyhood church every few months for extended nights of service. Then his thoughts took an unexpected turn. "Billy Graham is one of the most famous evangelists in the world. There was that Billy Sunday fella back in my Dad's day, the former White Sox baseball player that became a famous evangelist for helping to shut down many taverns and bars during Prohibition." As his thoughts wandered, he recalled Frank Sinatra's lyric from "Chicago, That Toddlin' Town."

"...the town that Billy Sunday, could not shut down."

He felt a bit ashamed of even associating his name with such giants, and the guilt really came heavy when he remembered that even St. John the Baptist, the cousin of Jesus, was considered an evangelist.

He had no way of knowing, nor did anyone else at the time, that just a couple decades later, due to the popularity of the television medium, the word Evangelist would suffer a major setback and become darkly associated with persons of questionable motive. Not since Bert Lancaster had exploded across the Movie screens as Elmer Gantry, the unscrupulous traveling preacher who used Bible thumping to reach the financially prosperous gains of a master charlatan, had the position of a traveling evangelist been more suspect. As Sam sat there pondering, he sincerely tried to resist any further thought of becoming something or someone of note someday.

When the later spring arrived and winter cleared, he was constantly traveling the highways of Indiana, Michigan, and Kentucky in what was called "the work of the Evangelist." The used 1964 Volkswagen Bus Sam had purchased from his cousin Bob was quite a contrast to the same models making their way up and down the California coast with passenger loads of social revolutionaries, known simply as "Flower children." Many of the same VW Busses would later cross the U.S. to gather on a Western Pennsylvania farm, and for a few days rewrite history through illegal hallucinogens, new expressions of nudity, and new-found sexual freedoms, all to the constant pulsating sound of the heavy sounds of Rock and Roll. But on this sunny spring day of yet somewhat tempered innocence, Sam came up with what he thought would be an excellent addition to his preaching paraphernalia. He stood rather proudly observing the words he had sprayed on the driver side door of his VW Bus, the stenciled proclamation for all to see.

SAMUEL P. PAWLAK, EVANGELIST

Whatever venture Sam enjoyed in self-promotion was quickly brought back to reality with the help of his two oldest brothers, the infamous "Franky and Johnny, Version 2" in the Pawlak history. John, whom the family still called Bud, took one look at Sam's vehicular artistry and sarcastically responded,

"Hey that is a good idea. Give me that stencil set. I think I will put on my new pickup truck door, 'BUD, THE BUTCHER.'"

Not to be outdone, Frank asserted with facetious sneer his opinion of his kid brother's ridiculous thirst for attention.

Manson chuckled, "Yeah, and maybe I can print on the side of my beautiful, white convertible Impala, 'FRANK, YOUR FRIENDLY UPHOLSTERER.'"

They were still laughing uncontrollably as they slammed their respective car doors and stirred up a huge cloud of dust from the snowless, dirt lane that led from their parent's house.

Within minutes, Sam found himself at the nearby VW dealership, matching cans of touchup spray paint with the faded red side of his vehicle. Before sunset the lettering was as buried under the paint as was his silly thoughts that he was going to be the next Billy Graham, Billy Sunday, or God forbid, John the Baptist.

****

"Can you believe this weather for January?" Gary hollered to Sam in the parking lot across the street from the dark brick church which housed the three day conference they had attended.

Gary and Sam had become pretty good friends in just the two weeks Sam had been in Kokomo, where Gary's dad was the pastor. He was a young married man who also had interest in becoming a minister, and Sam encouraged him to attend the conference with him.

"Sixty five degrees in Indianapolis the last week of January?" Sam bellowed back and added, "I didn't even bring the lining for my top coat." Sam turned out the collar in hopes that Gary could see from that distance his new London Fog, James Bond style trench coat. He had used some of his first pay, called by the churches of that time, Love offerings, to get that good coat. He continued, "Hope this weather continues till I get home. I didn't even bring any boots or gloves. Crazy Huh?"

Gary shouted back, "So we will expect you at our place by supper, right?

Sam put up a thumb skyward confirming his plan to stop back through Kokomo, eat some of Gary's wife's good fried chicken before starting back toward Michigan City the following morning.

"Only Indiana..." Sam's aggravated tone whined as he attempted to use Gary's window scraper on the many windows that surrounded the VW bus. "Sixty-five yesterday, and thirty-five degrees this morning. This is absolutely ridiculous, man."

Gary nodded in agreement and offered Sam a possible solution.

"Hey, why don't you just stay here and wait it out a little while. The TV says it is even worse as you go north. You don't want to get yourself in a mess."

"Aw thanks, buddy" Sam responded, "But these skinny tires really do pretty good on the road. Besides, I got to get home and see if I can get through to that gal in Canada. I haven't talked to her in a couple weeks. Anyway, as I get closer to the Lake this blasted Ice and sleet will turn into snow and that will be much easier to drive on."

Gary advised, "Just take it real easy on this ice, man. This stuff is dangerous."

Referring to Gary's southern upbringing, Sam laughed and put a little dig in by adding, "Hey, I'm a Chicago boy. I can drive this stuff. I'm not from Arkansas, you know." With that Sam jumped behind the wheel, placed a clean rag on the dash, knowing that the air driven heater would not do much of a job keeping the inside of the windshield clean, and he would have to keep wiping the steamed up windshield to navigate the icy roads before him.

He thought that staying off the four lane Highway 31 from Kokomo to South Bend would be a better choice, so he followed some of the not so familiar, two lane roads north and east. He knew less semi truck traffic would be a better route with the ice so heavy he could barely drive over 20 mph. He knew if he could finally make it north enough to reach Highway 30, that would take him west toward his familiar State Road 421. This two lane highway cut through some of the most fertile farmland in all the United States. Miles and miles of empty corn fields and soy bean farms made for wide open spaces, only to be slowed by a little village every ten miles or so. Town names he knew by heart, Brookston, Chalmers, Monon, Medaryville, Francesville, Lacrosse, Wanatah, Westville, and on to Michigan City. It was there that 421 would become Franklin Street. That meant home. The same Franklin Street that young Kaz had first ventured down almost three quarters of a century earlier.

The westward trek on Highway 30 was becoming more treacherous by the minute, and certainly by the mile, and every mile was taking a good fifteen minutes to traverse.

"Aha! There you are, girl!" Sam whispered out loud while making one more circular movement with the oil cloth against the frosty inside of the windshield. Old highway 421 now lay just a few hundred feet ahead of this struggling, flower power vehicle. Sam muttered to himself, "This old buggy may have been built in Germany, but it was never intended to plow through this kind of blizzard."

About a mile north of the Wanatah intersection, he could only see a few feet ahead of the noseless vehicle. The blinding snow, pounding against the windshield faster than the sporadic sweep of the windshield wipers could clearly remove, was only made more hectic by the fact the blades built up masses of restrictive ice. The sound of the little engine, not much larger than one found in most washing machines of that day, brought only more stress to the situation. The interior of the little bus was nearly as cold as the below freezing winds outside.

"For love of Mike!" Sam shouted in the exact same tone his father Frank or Grandfather Kaz would express. "Now the engine is missing. Trying to stall on me, are you?" Sam shouted toward the rear of the little rolling icebox. Then he thought, "I better keep the speed up a little more." He slowly pressed his thin dress loafer against the long gas pedal beneath him, but with the little acceleration the unexpected followed. The single rear-wheel pulling system performed excellently. Had it been dry pavement beneath that accelerated rotation of the working tire, the vehicle would have responded with increased thrust down the highway, and the engine speed would have adapted to the increase of power and stopped its previous sputtering to smoothly hurl northward to the desired location. One small factor suddenly changed the entire process and progress. Under the little tire, so anxiously desiring to respond to the physical command of the not so experienced winter driver was no pavement at all, but a pure layer of ice dangerously hidden under a cushion of the beautiful white, wind driven snow, which was accumulating at the rate of three to four inches per hour. As any source of traction was now totally eliminated, the rear of the vehicle was making every attempt to join the right passenger side of the VW Bus.

"Steady, girl. Steady." he firmly pleaded to the carriage. Then remembering his Dad's instructions about winter driving he could hear his father's voice, "Don't touch the brake. Stay off the brake, and turn the wheel back into the direction the tail is coming. No gas either, not until it gets straight again." Sam did just as he had been instructed, first pulling both feet away from the pedals and turning the wheel to the right. It worked, in that the old VW stopped its direction of spin, but the overcorrection took place and now it started around the other direction. Again, Sam was pretty adept at turning the wheel the other way. This redirection continued to proceed a few more times, "Left, left. No, now right." Sam cried out, "Whoa, girl! Come on, steady yourself!" Then frantically again, "Right, right. Now, stay off the brake!" Sam continued to call out the commands as if the vehicle not only understood but would actually respond. After about a football field of this frantic exercise in futility, the inevitable unfolded. This time there was no bringing her back. The tail end of the beast just ignored all commands, adjustments, pleadings, and even a couple of prayers.

Sam realized he no longer had control of his transport, but rather the transport had replaced him as captain at the bridge. She uncontrollably spun in a complete 360 degrees just as assuredly as a square dancer would respond to the caller's commands to "do-si-do." Due to the fact Sam had thought some acceleration would keep his engine from sputtering to a stall, the increased overall speed created enough G-force to catapult the entire VW Bus across the two lane road, over the deep ditch along both sides of the highway, and plant itself solidly out into the deep snow blanketing the harvested Indiana cornfield, some fifty plus feet from the asphalt. The red and white pride of the young itinerant preacher boy came to its final immovable setting, firmly wedged against a stretched wire fence, and deeply sunken in the early stages of what would be one of the most powerful and dangerous snow storms to ever invade this region of the country.

"You look like you have problems, friend." the half laughing voice descended on Sam's cold, wet head. The timing could not have been better. The big County snow plow truck driver had opened his passenger side door and shouted across the seat from his warm cab, "I can take you back to the corner for help if ya need."

The warmth of the cab was a welcome relief. Just getting from the ditched VW Bus to the road left Sam soaking wet. The unlined London fog was little resistance to the horrid conditions. The Florsheim dress shoes were no preventative to filling both feet with snowy, cold, melting discomfort. The cigar smoke was very strong, but as the driver clenched the burning Havana between his teeth he offered Sam some information and advice.

"Son, we are in for a real beauty, for sure. They say this baby could be the blizzard of all blizzards." He continued, "You ain't getting that bus out for a while. If I were you I would see if they have a room left up here at the motel, and worry about getting back here with a tow truck to get you out of that field sometime after this thing is over."

"Well, I sure appreciate the ride, and yeah, I think you are probably right. I will check with the Motel." Sam replied to the plow man, but the whole time he was thinking the last thing he wanted to do was sit around here for a couple days. "Maybe I can find somebody going through, and hitch a ride."

"Would you happen to have a room still available, by any chance?" Sam kindly asked the middle aged woman behind the counter.

"It's your lucky day, young man." She responded quickly. Just one left, and you'd be pretty smart to take it. We're really in for something here, you know?"

Sam slid his hand into his damp thin dress slacks. He felt the money clip and fingered the small collection of folded bills attached. Knowing he had a little over $200.00 at his fingertips, he was relieved to hear the room would only be $8.50 for the night.

"Good heater in that room, and your own little percolator for coffee." The desk clerk continued using her best selling techniques.

Just then, Sam heard a voice from across the rather small lobby.

"Where are you trying to get to, friend?"

Sam turned to respond to the athletic looking man in his mid twenties, and answered, "I'm trying to get to Michigan City. My car ended up in a field up the road, and I will have to come back when this storm is over and get it."

"I'm going that way. You can grab a ride with me if you like." The stranger continued, "I was going to stop for the night, but I think I can make it." Then came the irony as he explained, "I have a good little VW Bug, and that thing can get through anything. You know? They are really light, motor in the back, makes good weight on those rear tires, and with those tires so skinny they won't get bogged down in that snow."

Sam almost smirked when he thought to himself, "Yeah, that is exactly what I thought about my Bus." But he reasoned that it was a bug, smaller, just might work. After thanking the attendant at the motel Sam and the fellow adventurer headed to the little gray VW Beetle. As they pulled from the parking lot onto the highway they exchanged the normal introductions.

"I'm Sam."

"I'm Joe."

They briefly shook hands, Joe's gloved and Sam's still bare. Joe explained that when he got to Michigan City he had to pick up a work associate, and get on into Chicago where they both lived. The conversation remained usual small talk, local sports interests, a little Chicago politics, and of course, the miserable conditions before them.

"Oh, there on the left," Sam pointed and Joe observed, "That is my car, there in the snow." a little amazed that you could hardly make it out. It was already just a huge lump of snow covered with several new inches during his little venture to the motel and back.

It was probably about 11:00 am by the time Joe and Sam noticed what appeared as a line of cars stopped ahead of them. They had actually only driven about two or three miles past the stranded VW Bus.

"Well," said Joe, "Looks like we have a little hold up here."

Sam added, "Probably one of those train crossings. There are a lot of them between these little towns."

For the next three hours the little bug would not move a single foot northward. The only heat was from two little openings at the floor by each door. The heat was air driven and required the motor to be running, and even with the great gas mileage the VW's were known for, it was getting obvious this could not go on for several hours, or into the night.

It grew quickly dark, late afternoon in the shortest days of sunlight throughout the whole year. Both Joe and Sam were suddenly startled when a strong knocking was rapidly repeated as Joe's window. As Joe rolled the window down slowly, the howling blizzard began to pour snow into the car. A frantic voice barked to the duo within the quickly cooling vehicle.

"You guys better get out of that car and into my house for now. This storm is only getting worse, and no one is moving on these highways tonight." Then he urged, "Come on, fellas. Shut her down and get in here where it is warm. You will freeze to death out here."

"Ok. Ok, thanks." Joe replied.

The two young men found themselves in a very nice, modern tri-level house that set about a hundred feet off the traffic jammed, arctic arena they were officially stranded within. A sofa, a carpeted floor, a couple handmade quilts, a pillow each, and a great tasting hot chocolate and grilled cheese sandwiches did seem to make better sense than surviving the night in a VW, even to two young buffs who thought themselves eight foot tall and bulletproof.

Even though the snow was still falling, and the wind was now creating some sizable drifts, Sam and Joe expressed thanks to their wonderful hosts who had gotten them through the night, and surged through the thigh deep snow to Joe's car. After using a long handled snow scraper, carried by most travelers in this part of the Midwest, the little car did fire up, and in a few minutes the men were moving slowly behind some other vehicles that had forged ahead with daybreak.

"We have to be getting pretty close to Westville now." Sam announced to his driver. "I figure we are about two miles from the Highway 6 curve." Sam explained in a comforting tone and announced, "There is a large State Mental Hospital there, and right across from that is a truck stop and restaurant. I will fill up your tank with gas there, and with a break or two we should be on into Michigan City after that. Only about ten miles from Westville to Michigan City, and we will pass by a little community called Otis. That is where my Grandfather came as a young boy when he first emigrated from Poland."

Joe replied, "Well, I'm from Chicago, so as you might guess, I am a Polak too."

With that, they laughed and started a rotation of the latest Polak jokes they had heard. Just as suddenly, the laughter stopped, and so did the car. Joe swore out a frustrated line of curse words.

"What's going on?" Sam interrupted.

"We're stopping again." Joe whined, and explained, "Look at this traffic. Nothing is moving any further."

Sam tried to console them both with the idea that maybe the trucks are plowing ahead, and they would get started again soon. But after several hours of sitting, racing the engine in hopes it would force a little more heat out of those side vents, a certain ominous feeling was growing. They watched the snow continue to fall and the wind blow in almost hurricane force strength. The little German import they were stuck in was going nowhere fast. By 3:00 or 4:00 that afternoon the full darkness of winter had fallen on the stranded men, and with the car nearly out of fuel they both knew shelter was their only hope of survival that night. They both scanned the fields on either side of the car to see if their eyes could strain beyond the horrid blizzard in hopes of any kind of light which would bespeak a structure they might escape to. For a long time they said nothing. No knocking came at their window from a Good Samaritan, as had happened the night before. There were a few moments when the wind seemed to slacken its ferocity, and as the blowing snow weakened, Sam saw something on Joe's side of the car.

"There! Look Joe, out your window, that direction, about eleven o'clock. Look, look, as far as you can see." He explained, "I see a light. Do you see it? There Joe, I think it is one of those mercury vapor lights. You know, the kind the farmers put on their barns. I've played a lot of basketball under those kinds of lights."

Joe finally saw what Sam was trying to point out and said, "Boy, you're right Sam. I do see it, but that must be at least a half a mile away. Do you think we can make it? I mean, you don't even have boots or stuff."

Sam felt foolish when he thought how the rescuers from the night before had offered him some gloves, scarves, and stocking hat, and he kindly refused them, thinking he would be in a warm car and home in just an hour or so. He also felt a little ashamed that his youthful bravado had outweighed his common sense.

Joe projected, "If we can keep our eyes on that light, and walk fast I think we will get there. It may be now or never."
Sam only had one word. "Go!" He struggled with the car door. The snow had drifted against the side of the car till it was nearly half way up the door. As Sam firmly placed his foot on the inside of the door to force it open enough to squeeze his body out into the storm, he thought it odd that he heard Joe's door slam closed. Evidently the snow had not drifted on Joe's side as high as Sam's. Finally, standing fully erect outside of the little car Sam realized when falling thigh deep in the first few steps of snow, that this was going to be no easy or quick journey to shelter.

"OK, Joe. I'm out, buddy. Let's head that way." Sam paused for a moment to hear Joe's reply but all he heard was the howl of winter wind, and the sting of pelting snow flying rapidly by his ears and painfully needling his face. "There it is! There's the light, Joe. Let's head that way." Again, and eerily Sam silenced his call to listen for any response. He heard none.

Sam had never spent a day in the military but he had trampled many a wintry day with an old twelve gauge shotgun laid over his forearm, and worked a good rabbit field with his dad carrying the old familiar sixteen gauge, side by side, double barrel that his dad had bought through a Sears and Roebuck catalog some forty years earlier. In those hunting days Sam had always hoped they would jump a beautiful pheasant, and thus he had learned the military technique of keeping his head on a swivel, so as to not miss anything from any direction. Now his head was not only on a swivel to try to locate his traveling partner, but also trying to keep an eye fixed on that farm light in the distance, and shaking the gathering snow from his eyelashes and face. That awful night of wintry terror would only have been worsened had he even imagined in those first few minutes of attempted sojourn to survive what would transpire. When he stepped from one side of that VW Beetle car, on that deserted stretch of Indiana highway, amidst conditions known only to the Arctic Circle, that a young man named Sam and a young man named Joe would have a strange two days of friendship, only to never lay their eyes on each other again.

For what seemed like at least an hour, Sam followed the glow of that mercury vapor light in hopes that it would surely lead him to a barn, perhaps an active farm. Even better were the thoughts of a warm farmhouse, a welcoming and hospitable family, and visions of hot soup, homemade bread, and canned preserves to accompany the hot tea from the stove top tea kettle. Then it happened.

"The light, the light. Where did the light go?" Sam was not asking as much as screaming to the sky and the conditions about him. Even louder he called out, "Where are you? Oh, come on! Not now!"

His mind raced. "Did I get off the mark somewhere?" He questioned, "Am I turned around? Wait, wait, maybe it is back this way. Yeah, yeah, I must have turned around when I was trying to get that snow out of my shoe." He stood still and slowly pivoting in a complete circle, realizing why he could no longer find the light. "This must be what they call a white out." his lips tremble at the very words. "I am blinded by this snow. Which way is north, the lake, the town?" Full panic set in as he remembered how he'd stepped into the phone booth back at the motel the morning before to call his mother. He had told her he was not going to get a room, but was catching a ride with a guy. He told her he would be home later that day.

"She will be out of her head thinking I am in this storm maybe stranded on the road somewhere." He remembered the big storm in 1958. He was just a kid when his Dad and Mom took in about forty stranded people off the highway into their large farm house. He remembered that when they ran out of propane gas for the stove his dad built up the fire in the basement furnace, took the metal floor register from the living room above, and with ropes, let down one of Opal's large pots full of homemade tomato soup so it could set on the top of the furnace and provide hot soup for all the folks that were refugees in their house. Again, he allowed his body to think it was not freezing as he imagined he could taste the hot tomato soup so hospitably served to others stranded.

"Don't cry!" He commanded himself. "You're eighteen years old, and not some scared little boy. You're a fighter, Pawlak. Tuff guy, remember? Besides, no one will hear you now, and tears will only freeze on your Polak mug."

He started walking again, but each step was followed by a deep fall into waist deep snow. It took every effort to make his legs lift high enough to take another step. There was no light to follow. He took some comfort that his feet were not really cold anymore, then all his senses came to absolute conclusion, "I am walking in circles, my feet are getting frost bitten, I cannot survive this too long and I am lost." Direction, there was no such thing for Sam now. The snow has drifted over every fence row, even reaching the upper levels of the phone lines. The high-rise electric structures were either too far away or not visible in these white out conditions.

"What day is it?" He asked himself as he insisted on keeping his mind by continual conversation, and that audibly. "Let see, I left Gary's house Wednesday morning. I went into the ditch Wednesday, went to the Motel the same day, met Joe, that was still Wednesday, stayed in those people's nice house Wednesday night, then started with Joe today. Yeah, Thursday. This must still be Thursday night. I better just keep moving."

He mustered all his strength, thought to himself that these high steps in the snow and his aching legs reminded him of running the sand dunes along lake Michigan as part of his conditioning workouts, or even running thigh deep in the lake, and playing football in the water to strengthen those legs. He pretended he could feel the summer sun on his back and convinced himself the cold on his legs were just the crisp cold waters of Lake Michigan in the summer. This fantasy was brought to an abrupt stop. His last step was the worst. Sam fell into a very deep snowdrift, all the way to his armpits. But to his surprise something strange occurred.

"What is that?" Sam asked aloud, then again, "What the heck is at my feet?"

He wondered for a moment. Was it the ground? But he knew it was a surface harder than even the frozen tundra beneath him. He was able to lift one foot enough to make a stomping motion downward, and he heard it. Hard, maybe wood. He started to frantically dig around him as best he could. This would normally feel like an impossible task, digging yourself out of a snow tomb, but the panic and thrashing of his arms to remove snow from around his body, and seek the lower part of his anatomy as residual benefits, he was forgetting the cold, and even sweating a bit. After some time he had cleared enough snow from one side of his body till he could bend and reach below his right foot in an attempt to identify the hard surface that was preventing his form from descending to depths well over his head.

"I feel it." he muttered. "It is hard, but not wood; it is scratchy, kind of sandy, and gravelly all at the same time."

He continued working until he'd made an area large enough to move his legs and bend down and rub the surface with his frozen hand.

"Shingles, some kind of roofing shingles. It has to be a roof. A building with some rough old tar paper shingles." He became extremely excited. "That's it, a building, a shack, an out building, some animal pin, something is there."

With the first and smallest feeling of hope since emerging from the stranded car, Sam dug and dug in what he knew was one side of the roof till he uncovered and revealed a side of the structure.

It was his first good fortune when he saw a snow filled window opening. With a little more effort he could squeeze his body into the dry, and much warmer condition of, what he would learn later with daylight, an old abandoned chicken coop. Somewhere in that night Sam would actually become warm enough to remove his coat, hang his wet socks on an inside part of the facility, in hopes they both would dry a little. As he ate several hands full of clean, white snow, he began to apologize to God for the accusatory tones he had expressed when trudging through the drifts.

"Are you telling me, I walked away from my former life, made a dedication to you, and agreed to pursue this entire idea you had called me to some special cause for you, only to be stranded in a snowstorm, and freeze to death at the ripe old age of eighteen years old? Well, thanks God for everything. And by the way, what is that whole idea of giving me that girl, and telling me that we had some great future ahead together when now she is hundreds of miles away, and who knows if they will ever even find my pathetic body?"

"Thank you, Lord." Sam now whispered, thinking that maybe he might survive this storm another day or so, and when the storm let up he could yet get out to some help. "I might even live after all." he mused as he drifted off into a heavy exhausted sleep, and the icy world hurled its force around him, continuing to screech its howling voice into the deep winter night. The screaming wind would reach levels that sounded like some wild cat wailing in the distance. Throughout the night, Sam would awaken, move to the window space and raise his body up the snow's mine shaft he had dug, only to realize the white out conditions were not slowing. He could still not see even a few inches across the stark abandoned fields. He tried to half lay and lean against the wall of the previous aviary shelter. He could pull his top coat over him and recover enough warmth to help him ignore his growling stomach. Ignoring severe pangs of hunger, he warmed enough to doze off again. He repeated this action several times through that long night, so alone and apparently so unknown.

"Day light." The first audible sound he heard, and they are coming from his own mouth. He talked as if someone else were there, and stretching his stiff, shaking legs he wondered out loud, "Can I see anything yet?" He wrapped the thick London Fog about his shoulders and stumbled to the opening. "Oh, I better put this thing on." He mumbled, and inserted both arms,, fastened all the buttons to the top, turned the collar up. He used both hands to sweep away some of the drifted snow that had invaded the hole overnight. As the top of his bare head rose above the even higher snow levels, Sam mournfully expressed his new day's discovery. "O my God! No, please. No, this cannot be."

He beheld nothing; absolutely nothing but blinding, blowing, white. The unchanged conditions of another day and the horrid howl of the hurricane force gusts fell over Sam's body with such force that all his muscles declared, "We are through." The limp body of the overly confident young man slid backward into the coop and laid prostrate on the floor, as weeping was only interrupted by the heaving of Sam's chest.

"I will not survive another day without food and heat." He continued to emotionally sink as he considered his options. "If I stay in here and grow weak till I become unconscious, they will not find me till spring or maybe never. But if I try to go out there into that blizzard, I will surely die within minutes."

For a long time he could not motivate his body to do anything but lay there. To his amazement he must have actually fallen asleep again. Throughout a day that seemed like a week, Sam would sleep, exercise his limbs for circulation, crawl out the hole to see no improvement, and try to consume enough snow to provide liquid. His mind could not refrain from telling his snow filled stomach he was well into his third day without food.

"Ok." the survivor said to himself, "It is now dark again, must be somewhere between early evening and nighttime." Then he tried to recount, "Left Gary's house Wednesday morning, met Joe at the Motel, spent all day in the VW. We stayed in that man's house Wednesday night, left again with Joe the next morning, sat again all day in the VW, got out with Joe that had to be Friday night, walked and walked and walked, then found this place, yea that was still Friday night." He then came to the accurate conclusion, "This whole day must have been Saturday." He further concluded, "That means this is Saturday evening. For love of Mike, I have been in this mess for four days now."

That was the last Sam talked to himself for a while. Weakness was becoming exhaustion, evidenced by how quickly he fell asleep again. His eyes popped open as he was literally startled by the deafening silence in his ears. For a moment he wondered,
"Was this the beginning freezing to death, starvation or just a symptom that accompanied delirium?" He sat up, turned his head in each direction, thrust his index fingers into each ear as he had seen some noted healing Evangelists do in assisting the deaf in their faith while the subject was hoping for miraculous sound when the fingers would exit the ears. The utter silence after twenty-four hours of viscous assault made the quiet terrifying. When senses allowed his brain to reason, he knew what had happened. The wind had stopped. Moving as quickly as his body would allow, Sam thrust his head above the snow like a prairie dog in kind.

"Yes! Yes! Oh, Yes!" he screamed to the top of his voice. All he could see was everything! No snow, no wind, few clouds and even a few images began to twinkle in the sky. He was not ready to proclaim this a beautiful winter night, but it was everything the last four days were not. Dressed again in the top coat and even wearing dry socks under those $45.00 Florsheims he gazed as far as his eyes would allow and saw it. "There, over there, just like before. There it is." A Mercury Vapor barn light shined powerfully across the mile or better distance that cold night. Sam was more than thrilled to see light, and so encouraged that the historic storm had moved away to the east with all its magnitude.

One thing Sam had not considered in his jubilance, was that the pattern for this kind of winter storm was pretty predictable. The torrential downfall of snow was often followed by the high winds and drifting that Sam could now espy. Those drifts eliminated every road and every fence, and in this case even covered the low hanging telephone lines along the highways and country roads. But the most assured performance for the finale of this arctic intrusion would be the falling temperatures and sub Zero freeze.

"I must have been walking a couple hours by now." Sam muttered to himself, while still seeing the light clearly in the distance, and even better the distant form of some type of building. The conversation with self continued.

"I am really cold."

"Don't keep your hands in your pockets man; if you fall you will bust your face."

"But my fingers are killing me."

"But my feet quit hurting a little while ago. I am surprised how warm they are." Then would come the self admonishment.

"Just keep moving, boy. You will be there soon, you will get warm."

"You're tougher than this, man."

"Don't stop. You can whip this thing like a grown man. Yes you can, keep going."

Sam's mind moved mysteriously to his Mother Opal. He and she loved to share poetry, and amidst his personal motivation that night, came back the words of one of their favorite poems.

> IF YOU STRIKE A THORN OR ROSE,
> KEEP A-GOING
> IF IT HAILS, OR IF IT SNOWS,
> KEEP A-GOING!
> The last line of that great old Frank L. Stanton poem said to Sam's memory,
>
> WHEN YOU FEEL LIKE SINGING SING.
> KEEP A-GOING!

With that, Sam began to sing, mostly within himself, song after song, genre after genre, arrangement after arrangement until he was too weak to sing, and could only let his mind do the singing. He willed his weakening and numb body to keep a-going.

"Just three steps now, Sam." His cracked, dried bloodied, and almost unmovable lips tried to say.

Having accomplished that task, his blurred vision strained against the lighted wood and glass front door of the big farmhouse. It took an effort to form a fist from those stiff and frostbitten fingers, but there was no pain when his knuckles rapped three strong beats upon the little glass portion of the sturdy door.

"Where am I?" Sam gasped, staring at the ceiling light that seemed so far above his head.

He realized the warmth he felt, the pillow under his head, and the weight of a blanket and quilt across his body. Then pain, real pain surged through him. His feet throbbed as he forced himself to set up, pulled the bedding away from his legs and to his amazement found his aching feet wrapped in gauze bandages. It was then he noticed the same gauze was covering his entire left hand, and two fingers on his right hand.

"Hey, hey! Easy there, fella." a lady's voice said as she pushed opened the door at the foot of this large bed. "Just go slow now. You're alright." she instructed.

Her voice was a cross between that of a concerned nurse like the ones he had remembered from the long hospital stints with Rheumatic Fever, and a gruff, old prospector's wife you might see on a Saturday morning TV western with Roy Rogers or Gene Autrey. She carried a tray to the bedside, and inside, the beautiful sight of a large ceramic bowl, steaming with some concoction of vegetables and broth. Again the Midwestern Florence Nightingale began,

"Now, what is your name, young man?" he shakily replied,

"Sam. I am from Michigan City." She helped her patient sit up a bit against the antique headboard.

"Well, Michigan City Sam, why don't you try to eat a little of this soup while I take a look at those toes, and put some more of this goop on them."

She began to help Sam understand the lost period of time between his arrival at her door and his waking up in this typical country, farmhouse bedroom.

Never had anything tasted so wonderful. Even the heat of the soup was little problem for Sam's extremely chapped lips. The soup felt like it stayed hot all the way through his chest and deep into his empty stomach. After encouraging him to go slow the hostess explained that upon Sam's arrival he made quite an entrance.

"Yes sir, fella." she explained, "When my husband opened that door, you took one step inside and hit the floor like a ton of bricks. I guess it was that heat hitting your frozen body, right in the face." She continued. "Whew, then it got real harry. You started bleeding from your nose like a real gusher. My old man and a couple of the other guys carried you up here. When my husband came down he told me to get some warm towels on your hands and feet. Said you even had a bit of frostbite. Well, you were kind of awake, and kind of out of it. Just kept groaning and mumbling."

"What day is it, ma'am?" Sam softly asked, the lady of the house quickly answered,

"It is Saturday night about 9:00 pm." And then she began her own inquiry, "Are you a college student?"

"Well, yes. I guess you could say I am." Then Sam explained, "I went to college for a little while, but didn't stay and now I am doing some courses by mail."

"What ya studying?" She continued to smear Sam's toes with the familiar tin Watkins petro-carbo salve, the same black stuff that his dad would put on a dog that was bothered by a wood tick.

"I am studying for the ministry through a Bible college."

"Whoa," She responded, "You mean you are going to be a priest, then?

"Kind of like that, but in our church we just call them Pastors, or Evangelists, of preachers." Quickly turning up the bowl and consuming the very last drop, he kept his eyes down as to not see her reaction. After finishing her kind care for his toes, she moved away the tray and soup bowl, and promised some warm tea would follow. Then turning to his fingers for care she softly said,

"Well, ain't that something. We finally got something good out of all this trouble."

Sam thought she was saying something about the improvement in his frostbitten fingers, but he soon learned that was not what she was talking about when she continued,

"Having a priest, or minister, or whatever you are is like a special blessing after all that has happened here." Before he could ask what she meant, she continued, "You see, in just the last couple days, over forty people have found refuge in my humble, old farmhouse. And though we are most grateful for the lives that we've saved, there have certainly been a few nightmare moments too. Why, one young lady stranded here suffered a...a... pendix attack..."

"Appendicitis?" Sam inserted.

"Yeah, that's what they called it. We had to use one of the traveling truckers' CB Radios to get a helicopter to lift her out of here." She hardly took a breath before launching into her next tale of heartbreak. "My Lord," she moaned in a midwest country drawl. "There was a young couple who got stranded on the highway, just like you, and they had a little baby with 'em, only eighteen months old. Can you believe it? That poor daddy tucked the little one in his overcoat, and he and the mama ran, well, more like dug their way through the storm right up to my front door. My, they were exhausted when they got here. Then, oh my dear Lord, they were thrown into a shock when they found..." she paused and covered her mouth, fighting back tears, "...that little one was smothered in the daddy's coat. Oh, the way that sad mommy wailed. I never heard anything like it." The animated storyteller sat motionless, but her eyes darted around as her mind replayed the entire scene for a moment.

Sam began to feel perhaps his arrival here was not just happenstance, but he listened patiently as his hostess finished her story.

"We tried to call for a helicopter again, but because of the conditions getting worse they couldn't get out here right away. They had to stay here with their little deceased child another day, the poor dears. Why, they finally managed to get them lifted out just a couple hours before you..." Engrossed in her morbid tale, she caught herself and brightened just a bit. "Well, before you honored us with a visit."

She smiled a warm smile, then to Sam's amazement the lady's eyes filled with tears. "Tomorrow is Sunday. There are still a lot of people in this house, and they are pretty upset. Do you think if we help you down the stairs in the morning you could maybe give us one of them sermons you have been learning?"

Sam's pain and shock from his own experience turned into a strange emotion as he absorbed her suggestion. "Purpose" he said without voice. "Maybe God, you still have a purpose in all of this, and maybe I do too."

"I will be down there." He said resolutely. He lightened the heaviness in the room by adding, "Especially if there is still some of that bacon I smell cooking tonight."   With that, she stood, gathered the tray and her treatment items, and said while exiting the door, "I'll hide you a couple good pieces, might even have an egg."

For some time, the young survivor just stared at the far wall, recounting all that had happened, then he began a serious dialogue with God.

"Lord, what could I possibly say to this group? This is not a youth group in my church, or even a congregation of people who came of their own volition to hear the previously promoted guest speaker. They have been through a hellish experience. They are fearful and have seen tragedy, and it is not over for any of us yet. What could I possibly say?" He wished he had that Thompson Chain Reference Bible that his friend had gifted him before departing from the faith, and disappearing forever from Sam's life. At least he could do some word research like Hope, Faith, Peace, or Love, in which he would associate some biblical passages with each, and offer a positive encouragement in the midst of this negative event. Then he saw it. Right there on the little corner table behind the door sat one of those big white family bibles, the kind intended more for display than usage. He struggled to roll himself across the bed and lift his body to a sitting position. With just enough stretch he managed to grasp the corner cover of the book and move it over the edge of the table till he could place his pain filled, less bandaged hand around the width of the Bible, pulling it with one hard jerk onto his lap. He slid himself back toward the headboard with legs crossed.

"Whew, it's still a little cold." Sam said as he pulled the blankets up and around his shoulders and head, looking somewhat like Sitting Bull, and knowing that the old furnaces in these farmhouses seldom carried much heat all the way up from the basement to the second story of the house. "Ok, here goes..." Both thumbs met somewhere near the center of the golden edged pages, and pushing downward forced the opening of a Bible that had not been opened for some time. What happened then seemed ironic to Sam. "Well how about that?" came the question from his mind.

"The Book of Job." he began to reason, "Sure, that might work. Everybody, saint or sinner has heard of Job or at least of the trials of Job." but then he thought, "I don't know if these folks would be ready to hear that. Boy, if they think they have had it bad, well just look at what all this other bloke had to put up with." Sam had heard that misery loves company, but right now that only felt like multiplied misery. Then his eyes dropped below the bold letters at the top of the page where the title was printed. Right there, before his eyes were these timely words:

"For He saith the snow, 'Be thou on the Earth;' Likewise to the small rain, and to the great rain of his strength. He stealth up the hand of every man; that all may know His work. Then the beasts go into the dens, and remain in their places. Out of the South cometh the whirlwind; and cold out of the North. By the breath of God frost is given: and the breath of the waters is strained. Also, by watering He wearieth the thick cloud; He scattereth His bright cloud and it is turned roundabout by His counsels; that they may do whatsoever He commanders them upon the face of the world in the Earth. he causeth it to come, whether for correction, or for His land, or for His mercy."

The kind-hearted hostess offered Sam a comfortable seat in the big overstuffed chair that Sunday morning. His now tolerable feet were elevated on the ottoman before him, he looked kindly into each set of eyes in the crowded living room. To those in the adjoining dining room, and the mostly men who stood in the far kitchen as if it were the farthest pew of the church, Sam read the passages from the Bible. He took a few minutes to reflect on his own experience over the past five days, and asked those to consider a greater lesson from all this inconvenience.

"Perhaps, there is a God." He mused and stated further, "We all make our plans, live our lives, and yet there are events that overwhelm us, and we come to the stark reality, we are not in control."

After a few more suggestions of thought, Sam began some discourse on humanity's need of something more than is known in one's life. He later pulled all those thoughts into one question that demanded an answer from each: "What will you do with your life from here?" He felt an overwhelming sense of direction. It was as if God himself was lightly pushing on the back of his shoulder and saying,

"Go ahead Sam, you know you will never be here again. You will never see these people again. Do it, now!"

Using the familiar form of this engagement he had learned from some masterful communicators from childhood up, he said it,

"Maybe you would just like to bow your heads for our concluding prayer, and while you are in this position of humility and contemplation, you might answer a question. Would you like to surrender your entire life to God from this point on by accepting His son Jesus Christ, who died for you, as your own personal Savior?" Then he led them to the ultimate act that had become so familiar to the aspiring evangelist. "If that is you, and you know you should make this decision, would you make the first step by simply lifting your hand so I can see? I will pray with you."

To Sam's utter amazement, several hands began to rise across the two rooms, and even one young man leaning on the counter in the far kitchen, took one step forward to make sure he was in Sam's sightline, and lifted his hand. Seven in all, that Sunday Morning prayed with the frostbitten messenger.

After all had eaten some more good soup and grilled cheese sandwiches prepared by the "Good Samaritan" hosts, several other people found their way over to talk with Sam, and he even prayed with a few more.

Little by little, as the weather cleared, some of the winter refugees ventured toward the truck stop at Westville in hopes of things clearing enough to get their cars moving. More lanes had been plowed over night and in the early morning. Sam knew he wasn't ready to put on shoes, and head out yet, so he opted for one more night in the warmth of the upstairs bedroom.

Around midday on Monday, Sam thanked his host and hostess, forced his feet into his shoes, and welcomed the big boots given him by the farmer. With a stocking cap pulled fully over his head, some old work gloves on his healing hands, a heavy sweatshirt under his thin top coat, and a lady's knitted scarf wrapped about his neck and face, the young adventurer began the march down old highway 421 toward home. A very comforting thought came across his mind as he walked in the cold sunshine, "If I'd stayed in College, there might just be seven less people in heaven some day."

That thought certainly would have been dissected and debunked by wiser and more experienced heads, but for the young preacher boy, it seemed true in the moment.

He hitched one very cold ride on the back of a flatbed truck, hauling two large rolls of steel. He covered himself with the tarp that covered the load, because there were already five people in the cab of the truck. He felt the truck stop. He looked out under the tarp to see he was at the stoplight, of all places, Coolspring and Woodland Ave. He hopped from the truck, waved at the transport driver, and just stood for a long moment. He looked westward knowing his entire eighteen years of life had started just a couple blocks up that street, then he turned east and walked the mile and a half to where his brother Manson and family lived. Upon entering their apartment, his sister-in-law screamed and ran to him.

"Sammy, where have you been? Everyone has been so worried, and your mom is nearly out of her mind.

Sam had no idea that after he had last talked with Opal, they saw a story on the news how a young man's body had been found frozen somewhere in the area he had traversed. Feeling so safe in his mother's arms, he looked over her shoulder. He could see the making of the next winter storm, and he heard again the words, "He wearieth the thick cloud...that they may do whatever he commandeth them."

****

"Sam, I am sorry to call you so late but I would want you to know, Grandma Pawlak passed away tonight." Opal's report, though not a surprise still left him, for a moment, without words. When he finally gathered some words they were straight forward and controlled.

"I knew she was back in the Hospital, and when I saw her last she was even more frail than usual." He quickly inquired, "How is Aunt Sophie handling it?"

"She is doing alright. She knew it was coming, and I think she's been preparing for this." Then, as to the point as Opal could often be she added, "Truthfully, it will be a relief and finally take a lot off of your Aunt Sophie." Knowing her son's next question she quickly asserted, "Your Dad said it was time. For him this is so much easier than when his dad died. Anyway, I will let you know the arrangements tomorrow, hope you can make it home for the funeral."

After assuring his Mother that he would be there and sending love to his Dad, Sam returned to his quarters in the church parsonage in Ellettsville, Indiana. He lay back on the bed and studied the lamp's shadow on the ceiling, recalling the familiar features of the lady Mary whom his grandfather Kaz had first spotted so long ago at the park concert. He sorted through his own childhood memories of their long walks down Coolspring Avenue every spring and fall, and the smell of the fields burning so vivid in his recollection. He closed his eyes for a moment and could see her soaking her desperately painful feet while reading her Bible or listening with him to the old 78 records of everyone from opera legend Enrique Caruso, to gospel tenor Jack Holcomb. He could almost taste the rich Land O Lakes butter on the soft, wholewheat bread, and hear the fizz of the warm, iceless 7Up she would pour for him from the little seven ounce green bottle. He smiled in the dimness of the room when he remembered her old Polish belief that ice in the drink would give him a sore throat.

She had lived over two decades after Kaz's fatal heart attack. The absence of that man she so often called "Silly Man" had left her with little happiness. In fact it assured her loneliness and left her rather difficult attitude to be borne most heavily on the shoulders of her faithful and caring daughter, Sophie.

Sam felt a great sense of loss that this generation of Polish immigrants was now gone. So many times through the years he would wish he could have asked questions at the feet of his beloved grandparents, Kaz and Mary.

****

As dramatically painful as the NorthWest Indiana January can be to both the human body and the psyche, the summer weather can be a rapturous comfort that invigorates and heals all of one's senses. So was that June night on the front porch of the old Burdick place. Sam's feet pushed softly against the freshly mowed grass, providing a gentle resistance against the feeling of slipping off the edge of the aged and tilting wooden slats that comprised the porch of the hundred year old structure.

"Just listen to what I am saying and even more to what I am feeling." He spoke quietly, yet with a passionate intensity that commanded Pat's full attention. It had been perhaps the longest winter of their lives. But amidst this first truly humid summer night Sam was delivering the most desperate speech of his young life. The full moon seemed to grow even larger for that moment. The little lake that lay hidden behind the thick foliage across the road reflected the moon light till a soft glow seemed to rise just above the treeline. The multitude of lightning bugs wove their random patterns across the yard and out toward the corner of the property where the road took it's hard turn northward. The only real sounds were the occasional chirp of the night birds, and the deep basso profundo of the huge bullfrogs, sloshing about on the near shore of the body of water the locals referred to as Rice Lake.

"Pat, I do know we are young and sound reason would tell us we have plenty of time to plan for the future. Our parents would request much more preparation and security before we venture into a marriage, but I am asking you to hear me out."

Her bare feet, unable to reach the grass below, began to slowly kick one before the other as she leaned back and trusted the weight of her upper body to her two elbows firmly planted against the porch flooring. Her long black hair swayed from side to side in accordance with the nervous forward and backward rotation of her feet and legs. Her head lay far back and her stare seemed fixed far beyond the paint chipped roof where her eyes were directed.

He was midway through his discourse when, to his relief he felt her hand softly atop his on the floor deck beside her. He resisted the desire to gather her closer, and he fixed his own eyes toward a non-visible locale far into the darkness beyond the lake.

"Pat," he continued. "There are only a couple things I am really sure of at this point. One is, I love God, and know He has a purpose for my life. The other is, I love you, and I know we are to be together, make this life together, take this trip together for the rest of our lives." Less bombastically, but just as desperately, Sam went for it all with the declaration that defied all sound reason. "And we need to do it now, or soon. We, or at least I can't waste the next two or three years of my life, or our lives, abiding by what everyone else thinks or wants for us. I need you and I need you now." He leveraged one last verbal plea, pulling out the heavy artillery, as it were. "I am only half of what God needs me to be without you. I don't want to travel these miles, conduct these campaigns, and preach at these churches by myself. I knew the first night I laid eyes on you fifteen months ago that you were everything I needed. And forgive me if this sounds arrogant, but I also knew then and now know I am who God intends you to spend your life with, and further-more..."

Sam's voice fell abruptly silent at the sound of the front door of the house opening behind him. The twists of the door handle releasing the toggled apparatus, and the familiar squeak as the tubular spring stretched to give egress to the intruder of the moment. There appeared before the youth's twisted head and startled eyes none other than Mom Royer. His mouth was suddenly very dry as results of both his passionate vocalization and the unexpected intrusion on such an important scene. The first thought that shot across his mind was, "Did she hear what I was saying? And was she stepping in to put a stop to this nonsensical diatribe?" Before Sam could act, Pat broke the awkward atmosphere with the most unexpected and amazing statement that Sam had ever heard, in what seemed like a long life, in spite of his mere two decades of existence.

"Mom," Pat forcefully announced, "I think I am going to marry a Polak." The words had hardly traversed from his ear canal to his reasoning station when Mom Royer thrust upon both young lovers an emphatic, resolute, and somewhat conciliatory directive of her own.

"Well then, let's get this over with, once and for all!"

For two young people from blue-collar, middle class families it was determined early in the wedding plans that this should be just a small affair, with only family and a few dear friends. Pat's dad, Lloyd had made an interesting suggestion.

"Hey Sam, Lloyd suggested after raising the welding helmet over his face. "I'll give you a thousand dollars if you just elope."

Everyone took it as an attempt at humor, but Sam would say later, "If I thought for a minute Pat would have gone for it, I might have done it. Shoot! A thousand dollars then would have been a good down payment on a house, after all."

There was another complication to the small and intimate wedding idea. Both of these families knew everybody. Oh, not as prominent socialites or community leaders, but in both of their relative base, church affiliations, and neighborhood establishment, they were considered close family friends to hundreds of people. Complicating matters further was the large number of pastors and church leaders who both Sam and Pat had endeared themselves to through the years of gospel concerts and services. They would have very much expected to be invited to the event of this beloved couple. Many of the church adherents had known three generations of the Pawlak/Rice family.

The brand new Church facility was not only state of the art architecturally, but the pristine and eloquently designed sanctuary required nothing more than a couple baskets of flowers. This small family gathering had now blossomed to a waiting crowd of over four hundred persons.

As Sam stood along with his groomsmen at the front of the Chapel, next to Pat's lifetime pastor, his awe at the number of witnesses, and the grandeur of the moments was only exceeded by one sight. There at the back, atop the aisle to be walked, stood the most beautiful raven-haired goddess. Even the local newspapers grappled for every adjective at their disposal to sufficiently paint the picture of what Sam was beholding.

"Wow! She is so beautiful." the nervous groom softly whispered in the direction of the Pastor. Then he saw something that moved his eyes. "Hey, her dad looks pretty good in the suit too." He inwardly laughed at the fact they could not get Lloyd to agree to wear a tuxedo for any amount of money. "Wait." Sam thought, "Did he just wipe a tear from the corner of his eye?" He marveled, "That is the toughest old, steel working, pipe fitting, welding mass of humanity I know, and he is actually crying back there." To make matters even more uncomfortable, he noticed her dad slip a piece of tissue up under the wedding veil, as Pat too was wiping a tear." Sam quickly dropped his eyes from this scene at the back of the church, to the second row of beautiful wooden pews, and stared directly into the face of his Mother-in-Law to be. "Look, she is crying too?" She was wiping tears as singer Tom T Hall once described as "that silent type crying that tears out your heart." Looking to Mom Royer's side of the pew, there sat seven year old little sister Becky, holding her mother's hand and weeping openly over the loss of her big sister. It only got worse when eight year old, little brother Danny sat with both fists pressing into his eye sockets as his little body convulsed and shook, with what could only be described as pure tragedy.

Sam frantically questioned, "Why are they all crying? Do they think I am going to take her away, cut her throat, and hurl her body into a ditch somewhere? What kind of monster do they think she is marrying?"

A moment of relief did come when Sam allowed his eyes to float across the aisle to the more familiar gaze of his own parents. Then even more confusion attacked his psyche. "Now look at those faces. My Dad is smiling with a tremendous look of satisfaction. You would think he just hit a line drive home run off of Walter Johnson or Dizzy Dean, or even better he had just landed an eighteen pound Coho Salmon off the Michigan City Pier. What's that all about?"

The pinnacle of understanding was best plastered all over his mother Opal's enraptured face. Never had he witnessed his mother so joyful, so peaceful, and delighted. She was truly swept up in joyful celebration.

"Wow." He reasoned, "Mom looks like she is about to sing! Maybe even Dad, also." His mind suddenly slipped back to one of those lively, vigorous explosive Sunday night church services when participants would reach an emotional state of frenzy while singing and clapping their hands to an old song. One came to mind which bespoke of previous lives of grievous transgression having been reversed by a merciful God having taken all their former sins away. The reoccurring hook line of the song bore the words, "Goodbye, Glory, It's Gone! Goodbye, and Glory, it's gone." Somehow the entire scene at the opening of this September 9, 1967 marriage became very clear to Sam as he explained to his own mind. "Oh, I get it. Pat is the first child in this family to marry, a daughter to be taken from them, change her name, and become dependent on someone else beside them to care, protect and fulfill her every dream." Then he said to himself, "For my parents, I am the fifth boy to get married. There's only one fifteen year old girl left to raise for just a few more years, and yep, they are singing about this young dreaming wanderer, Goodbye, Glory, it's gone."

After the long and celebratory day the little brown Rambler American pulled from the parking lot of the church. The aura that settled within the little sedan was broken a bit when Sam alarmed Pat with the news,

"For love of Mike! I forgot to bring our wedding license."
Pat asked, "Is that important? Do we have to have it?"

Showing a glimpse of supreme innocence, naivety, or growing up in a world of protection or censorship, Sam reasoned, "I don't know if they will let us check into a hotel unless we can prove we are married.

"What in the world are you doing here?" Opal asked with an unusually confused look on her face.

"We forgot our marriage certificate, and we thought we would probably have to have it to prove we are really married if we try to get a room on the road."

The explosion of laughter that erupted from the brothers, sisters-in-law, and cousins gathered around Opal's kitchen table would have been the fulfilled dream of any great standup comedian from Bob Hope to Jay Leno.

With license in hand, and embarrassment on cheek, the young lovers resumed their trek to wedded bliss.

Many a paramour honeymoon in locations like Paris, Rome, Vienna, the Caribbean. But all the Samuel Pawlaks could afford was three days in Kentucky. With apologies to Kentucky he would always say, "Nothing wrong with Kentucky, after all, it is where my Mother's family hailed from."

After their short Honeymoon, Sam and Pat began right where they wanted to be, singing and preaching at a Youth meeting in Three Rivers, Michigan, and traveling through the night to open another "Revival Meeting."

They spent the next forty-two straight nights of their brand new marriage conducting services every night, housed in some Pastor's parsonage, or with some kind member who offered a room to the new young evangelist couple. It was probably not the best way to start a marriage, but they believed they were fulfilling a call on their lives, and they were as happy as if they had one lick of sense.

****

"Welcome to Clinton, folks." were the first words from the big smiling face of the man they all called Pastor Jack. The Dallas and actually, Oak Cliff, Texas drawl could not be denied. The big Texan found himself a cultural fascination of the local Southern Indiana residents, who themselves produced another distinctive accent of their own. "Let me explain what we've done as far as arrangements while yawl are a stayin' here." Pastor Jack's wife gestured for the heavy winter coats from Sam and Pat, and kindly motioned for them to be seated on the western design sofa. Pastor Jack explained to the slightly weary couple after their first four months on the road, "We have a dear lady in our church who has a lovely old home right near town and the church that yawl will be preaching at every night, for the next couple of weeks. Her husband, a railroad man, got some toes frost bit and is in the hospital. She will be spending the entire day with him, and just coming home for sleeping. She asked if we could perhaps house you in the fine upstairs bedroom of her place." Before they could agree, he continued to explain. "You will have the run of the whole place to yourself and she will have your meals prepared for you each day. She wants to do this to help you and the church a bit."

The experienced travelers were already pros at amenable appreciation. "Oh, that sounds wonderful." Sam quickly replied, and Pat chimed in,

"I am just sorry about her misfortune with her husband. We sure don't want to be a burden on her to cook meals for us."

"Well..." Jack said with a longer than usual drawl, "She wants to cook you a good dinner tonight, after your long trip today, and if you don't mind, join you for the meal. She does have one little request that could help her while you're here, if you don't mind."

Sam humorously replied, "Mind? Shoot, we are pretty used to singing for our supper, so to speak. Anything we can do for her would certainly be only a small act of appreciation for her generous hospitality."

Jack quickly stood and said, "Alright then, with that all settled, let's get you fine folk on down there and get you settled in. Y'all can have some of that good Hoosier cooking and get to the service at 7:45. Our folks are so excited to have you here, we ain't heard nothing about you, but that you two are the best."

The pot roast melted in their mouths. The dear lady was so kind and even a bit grand-motherly and Pat was so thrilled that even her little dachshund dog took a liking to them. That was, until half way through the meal, while the lady of the house excused herself from the table to take a phone call, Sam whispered to Pat,

"Look at my pant cuff."

While Pat had noticed the dog playing at both of their feet during the meal, she was shocked to see the friendly little fellow had chewed to shred the pant cuff on one of Sam's only two suits.

"Pat, I can't wear the same suit every night for two weeks. What am I going to do?"

Suddenly, before she could console Sam that she could alter the cuff, and if he walked a little crooked, no one would probably notice one pant leg being shorter than the other, the hostess returned to the table.

"Are you sure you have had enough to eat?" She sweetly asked and was assured by both they couldn't take another bite. "Well, I don't know if Pastor Jack told you but I did want to take the occasion of your staying with me to see if I could impose a bit on you to help me with a situation that I am really unable to perform myself."

"You name it dear, and we will do all we can do to help you." he responded.

The kind woman dropped her head, lowered her voice, and began the obviously difficult task of explaining. "I don't know if you noticed but at the top of the steps we passed by another room on the way to the room where you took your luggage."

"Yes, I did notice a room with the door closed. You mean the one that has that shade pulled on the inside?" Sam enquired as Pat nodded affirmatively.

To their slight awkwardness, her voice grew soft and even a bit shaky. "Well, you see we had a son, a wonderful son and a handsome boy. In 1943 he was drafted into the Army. He eventually lost his life In Bastogne. I think that's in Belgium. Anyway, it was during what they called the Battle of the Bulge, the battle there with General Patton."

Sam quickly interrupted, "I am so sorry. I know of that battle. My Uncle John served there also with General Patton."

She acknowledged with a little nod of her head and then continued, "When that Army car pulled up front here that day and that fella from the draft board stopped in, I knew. I just knew. After he left, my husband and I just sat here and cried for a long time. My husband went to his work shop out back and I went up to our boy's room. I just pulled the shade down on the door window and closed the door, and thought I would deal with that later." She looked up the stairway from the kitchen. "That was in the winter of 1945 and my husband and I have never been able to walk back in that room again. That door has not been opened in twenty two years."

By now, Pat's empathetic personality demanded she move herself around the table and place her arm around the shoulder of the pain-filled mother. As the elderly lady leaned her head toward Pat's shoulder, she cleared her throat and continued, firmly determined to get through this.

"When Pastor Jack announced you folks were coming to conduct these special services in our church, I felt like maybe this would be the time. I will be gone all day each day while you are here. I will be taking care of my husband at the little hospital near the end of town, and I wanted to ask a favor." Then she said it, "If you two would be so kind as to go into that room, remove everything you find, and dispose of it all at the city disposal just north of here, I would be more than willing to pay you for your work." Then she wanted to make her intentions even more clear. "You can keep for yourselves anything you find that you like or could use. Just put it in your trunk where I would not see it. I really can't remember what all he may have gathered in that room but neither of us feels like we could handle seeing it again. Apologetically she said, "I know it is probably unfair to ask this of a fine young couple like you, but I thought It might bring the closure we have needed."

Sam and Pat looked at each other as if to say, "Can we do this?" Simultaneously, both heads nodded an affirmative shake.

"Madam, we would be honored that you would entrust us with this important matter, and we assure you we will do it respectfully and as easily for you as we can." He assured their hostess.

"Thank you so much, and again I don't want to see anything or hear anything. Please use your discretion and... Oh, one thing more if you don't mind. Could you dispose of all the window coverings and clean the place real good so after you're gone, my husband and I can go in and redecorate? We might make it available to a local college student that needs a room."

The first evening service went really well, and the breakfast left the next morning was wonderful. Sam and Pat's hostess had already left for the day when they slowly turned the handle to the room, opening a virtual time capsule of over two decades passed. The only thing that could have made their entrance more mysterious would have been if it was at night time, and the door would have squeaked like the one on the old radio broadcast of Inner Sanctum. Both intruders quickly placed hands in front of their faces to create an impromptu fan and began to wave rapidly, using the second hand to attack massive cobwebs eerily attempting to attach themselves to the long awaited rescuers.

"Oh, this is awful." Sam half spoke and half coughed from his throat. Pat gasped for air and agreeably shook her head while holding both nostrils closed between her thumb and fingers.

"Let me see if I can get a window open quick." He suggested heading for the far side of the room that faced the street out front. Pat suddenly jumped and chirped out a little scream when Sam's attempt to pull back the curtain created an explosion of noise, dust and near strangling dryness.

"Look, Pat." He hoarsely directed, "That framework is so rotten that the curtain rods just fell out of the wood when I touched them."

He made several attempts to twist the window lock atop the lower pane, but he soon realized after twenty-two years of idleness it would not budge.

"The Mrs. said there are tools in the shed out back. I will run get a hammer and screw driver to get this window open." Then he cautioned, "Don't touch anything. You might hurt yourself. And step out in the hall every little bit so you can get a breath, I will be right back." Sam bolted from what he considered more a crypt than a room and hurried down the stairs and out to the owner's workshop.

As an act of good timing the morning sun broke through the barren window and helped illuminate the room. It was then Pat saw it, that framed picture atop the old Oakwood dresser. She whispered, "What a beautiful girl." As she stretched her sweater sleeve into the palm of her hand and gripped the cuff with her fingers, she could use her garment as a makeshift dust cloth. Holding the frame gently in her other hand, she began to make circling motions against the grimy glass surface within the wooden frame, until she could clearly see the beautiful brunette, and read the small inscription written in the corner of the photo before it's framing.

"To my future husband with all my love, Doreen."

As Sam stomped his way back up the stairs he found Pat sitting on the floor outside of the room. He thought at first she had followed his suggestion to get fresh air as needed, but then he saw her tears. She pushed both hands toward him to reveal the picture and softly said, "Sam, he was engaged. Look, this was his fiancé."

"Are you going to be alright? Are you sure you can do this?" He asked as he sat down on the floor beside her. She quickly responded,

"Oh, we have to. I know his mother could not face this after all these years.

"You just sit here for a bit and rest while I get us some fresh air in there."

As he moved away Pat thought to herself, "Yes, I could sure use some fresh air right now. This dust and my emotions are both pretty heavy. Maybe that is why I am so nauseous this morning."

Yet, she knew there was most likely a greater reason for her sick feelings. She had already told Sam that she had missed her last couple, what the girls of that time called their "Monthlies."

Most of the window frame paint had just about disappeared over the last quarter century, thus the windows opened easily and the room was soon aired enough to continue the journey into the past.

"Look at this, Pat!"

"Oh, Sam can you believe this?"

A series of "I can't believe this," prefaced almost every sentence for the remaining two days it took to clear the fallen soldier's room. The inventory of a young man's world included an old Rawlings baseball glove, an automobile wall calendar dated April 1943, several Sears and Roebuck catalogs with pages folded for future wish purchases. Under the bed were a box of rocks for an obvious collection, a big ball of aluminum foil made entirely from candybar and chewing gum wrappers. Baseball cleats, high top basketball sneakers, and a variety of college pennants that never made it to the walls. For Sam, the mother lode of a find was the "Hav-a-Tampa" cigar box with a sizable collection of baseball cards with players from the late thirties and early forties. But Sam had no idea what really lay before his feet when he opened the bedroom closet door; stacks and stacks of comic books. Not a few, but hundreds.

"Wow! This guy was really into comic books, Pat."

"Do you like Comic Books?" she inquired as she prepared more piles to take down the stairs.

"Nah, not really, but these are sure old. They're in pretty good shape. Look, 1935, 1937, 1940. Oh, here is Superman and all these crazy characters.

"You love to read." Pat said. "Why didn't you like comic books?"

"I do like to read, but real stuff. Never been very interested in that outer space junk or some alien goofy gook. Buck Rogers was a twit. I bet he couldn't even catch a football."

They both laughed as Pat said, "Well I will get some more boxes so you can pack them up for the dump."

The real truth was, in the days of his grandparents' church life, it was pretty well believed that comic books and even the "funny papers" were just too worldly and foolish a thing for a good Christian to waste time reading. Besides, the stories were not true, which meant they were really a lie, and reading them was promoting untruth and lies. If all that were not enough evil, they were taught that the only Super Heroes worthy of any boy's attention were God and Jesus, and as an old time preacher of that day would say, "If Jesus ever comes back, he better not find you reading no comic book."

So it was no problem for Sam to pack the trunk of his car and the back seats, and even the front passenger seat with this unrecognized treasure trove. He disposed of it deep into the refuse of the city dump. In as much as the front seat of the car was one solid bench seat, Pat was able to squeeze between the last loads in the passenger side and tightly against Sam's strong shoulders. She raised a rather sobering thought.

"Honey, if I am pregnant, and it is a boy, I hope he never has to go to any war."

He felt the rise of a scary thought amidst the backdrop of the most devastating year of something called the Vietnam Conflict and the dark, cold January sky of 1968. It came out in a new found expression of that era, "Ooh, that's heavy man."

Later that day, they deposited the young man's prized possessions in the city dump, and were karmically rewarded with the transmission in the little car failing. It meant the couple would be seeing the town at a much closer view because they would be walking for a few days, but considering all that had happened they felt like the most fortunate people in the world. Little did they know another series of events was about to unfold that would have a significant effect on their days to come.

"That is the first time I have heard that phone ring since we have been here." Sam announced while moving across the quiet and warm living room of the house they had been so wonderfully provided.

"Maybe you shouldn't answer her phone while she is not here." Pat cautioned.

"Well, I could at least take a message or see if she or Pastor Jack is trying to reach us." Sam already had the receiver from the black desktop phone, so they both shrugged their shoulders at the same time and he answered. "Hello."

Pat scooted forward on the sofa where she had been finishing up the alteration on Sam's ragged suit pant cuff. Her eyes got big when she heard him say,

"Pastor Van, how nice to hear your voice. Are you calling for me?"

The rather fast talking voice on the other end explained,

"Yes, Brother Pawlak."

Brother was a term that was still used by certain persons within the church organization of that day, but would soon be replaced by the more progressive, or as some thought, more revolutionary young clergy, to Reverend Pawlak, or Pastor Pawlak, or the almost blasphemous, Sam.

The State Director of the denomination, or as some churches would call their Bishop, the Superintendent quickly explained,

"We have a little congregation here on the west side of Indianapolis that is in need of a Pastor, and some of us here at the office believe you and your wonderful wife would be the perfect fit for that church."

Before Sam could even reply with a simple, "Oh really?" the full force of the sales pitch came sizzling through the earpiece of the phone till Sam thought the receiver was actually heating up.

"Yes, young man. With your preaching ability and the musical talent of both you and that lovely Royer girl, you will be just the spark plug that little church needs. You will have that place full in no time, and I have already told them they should have you in no later than this Sunday to hear you and then take a vote and make you their new Pastors."

Finally Sam got a word in, "Well, can you tell me a little something about the church itself?"

The Superintendent finally slowed his pace a bit and lowered his volume to make a few things very clear. "Well now brother, there are not too many, maybe twenty-five or so folks. They do rent a small store front building, maybe holds about fifty or sixty people, and it has a nice little parking lot in the back. Now, I talked with them about their finances, and they are not really able to support a Pastor yet, but if you would be willing to work an outside job, I am sure it would be no time at all till you would have that thing up to enough people that they could begin helping with a little salary."

There was a long pause from both ends of the conversation and Sam finally said, "Brother Van, I am honored that you would feel my wife and I could be good for that place, with us being so young and all. I will see if Pastor Jack can let us off here Sunday Morning. If so, yes. We could travel over and meet with those folks Sunday, but we would have to be back here for the meetings Sunday night."

Pat was not privy to the details on the other side of the conversation, so she listened as Sam explained. After some discussion they agreed that with a baby on the way, maybe this would present something a little more stable and consistent at this time.

When Sunday came, Sam and Pat were chauffeured by Pastor Jack's daughter and son-in-law to meet with the handful of people in the little store front building on the busy, little, residential street called Warman Avenue. It was located at the west side of the growing State Capital. Pat sang, and Sam preached to the little flock, and after some pleasantries they were headed back to the little town of Clinton. That afternoon they were voted in unanimously by the eighteen voting members as the new Pastors of the tiny Bethel Assembly of God in Indianapolis. As they rode in the back seat of that car, Pat slept against his moving chest. This husband of a few months felt like he had just conquered the world as he allowed a phrase to dreamily rotate within his mind, and with it the vision of his future, "Pastor and Mrs. Sam Pawlak."

****

"Here Pat, just slip in this booth at the back, warm up, and I will order us some lunch." He helped her get settled in the "mom and pop" restaurant on the main street of the little town, as they were glowing from the previous day's success in Indianapolis.

Clinton was most famous for its summer Italian festival. They studied the photos on the walls. Ladies dressed like old country villagers, bare foot and literally stomping grapes in large wooden tubs that would become wine and juice, later sold to the tourists.

"Are you Okay?" He asked as he sat down across from her and slowly stirred his hot coffee.

"I am really sick today. This must be morning sickness or something." Pat held her head in her hands and continued, "I don't think I can eat a bite. My back is hurting too; maybe that fall I took getting in the car last week, on that patch of ice, kind of twisted my back."

A moment later Pat excused herself. "I have to use the restroom. I'm going to be sick." She quickly slid across the vinyl bench seat and out of the restaurant booth.

"Can I do anything?" He asked.

She kept walking, but looked back at Sam and weakly winked one eye and said, "I think you have done quite enough, young man." They both laughed facially if not audibly. Then Pat added, "Maybe you better call Pastor Jack and have him come get us. I don't think I am up to trudging this snow all the way back to their house."

Sam slipped to the pay phone in the corner and read the Pastor's number from the little date book he always carried in his shirt pocket. He was assured the Pastor would have that big Chrysler New Yorker out front of the restaurant within minutes. Pat returned to the table and said in a rather apologetic way,

"Well, I'm sorry, but it doesn't look like I am pregnant after all. I have been cramping all morning and I just started my period, just must have gotten mixed up with my pills, I guess."

"Hey Baby, that's alright. We got a lifetime to make dozens of babies." Sam wondered why he was the only one laughing at that attempt to comfort. Pat just grunted and motioned to start for the door. Sam said, "Before we head back I better call your Mom and tell her you are not pregnant yet. She will be telling everyone since you told her you thought you were last night."

Sam was not prepared for the alarm in his mother-in-law's voice.

"Tell me again, what is happening?" She lightly asked.

"Well she started today, and it is a pretty bad one, so we guessed wrong. No grandbaby yet."

Mom Royer got Sam's undivided attention when she said, "Listen to me. She may be having a miscarriage. You get her to a doctor now!" She continued, "I have had two miscarriages and I know what I'm talking about. She may be in trouble."

For a moment, the word kept circling in Sam's head. Miscarriage? Miscarriage? And panic met confusion at the intersection of immaturity and knowledge. "I kind of know, that is like, not good. What does that mean, Mom? What does that really mean?"

Mom Royer slowed the emotion in her voice and said, "Sam, she probably is pregnant, and she could be losing the baby. Just get her help right away." With a tear filled voice she said, "Take care of my baby, and call me as soon as you know something."

Pat was motioning to him that Pastor Jack had arrived. They quickly got her to the Pastor's home where his wife helped her get to bed. Then they called for a Doctor just up the street who agreed to come as quickly as possible.

Sam was in the living room talking with the Pastor unaware that Pat had gotten herself to the small restroom off the bedroom when Sam heard a horrible scream, and Pat's call for help. As he ran into the restroom, Pat was standing beside the commode and crying hysterically, repeating the words,

"It's the baby, it's the baby! I've lost the baby."

The pastor's wife and Sam quickly helped Pat back to the bed and within a few minutes the Doctor arrived. Sam pointed him to the restroom and with some instruments he studied the small fetus, lifted it from the water and placed it into a small container.

"It appears to be about three months size. I'd better check on your wife." The Doctor consoled.

After examining her, he stepped out of the room and spoke to Sam. "Sir..." the doctor respectfully explained, "I have given your wife some medicine and taken some blood for testing. We will need to move her to the hospital for a day or two and she will need us to perform a Dilation and Curettage or a D & C.

Sam never felt so ignorant. The young boy, still three months and six days from his twentieth birthday could not really understand what had even happened, and the Doctor might as well have been speaking Swahili to him.

"Mom, everything is ok now. She did have a miscarriage, but she is alright. They are taking her to the hospital. They still have to do something to her. I don't know what it is but, you probably do."

Then she helped Sam settle a bit when she asked, "Are you alright, Sam?"

"Yeah, yeah. I guess so. This has just all been so crazy."

"Do you need me there?" she asked.

Sam tried to sound brave and said, "Oh, I know you don't like to travel, and it is winter and, and I know you have been kind of sick yourself and, and..."

"I will talk to your mom. Maybe if she could drive and come with me, we could both come down."

Sam expressed the relief he felt, "Oh, that would be great. I know Pat would feel better with you here. I just don't know what to do or really even what I am supposed to feel."

Mom Royer interrupted again and said, "Sam, I am so glad she is with you. It will all be fine."

These two would-be parents would learn that there was an element in their profession not so different than in the entertainment world. "The show must go on." Anyway, that was how they felt that same evening when Sam held Pat in his arms, then the young preacher walked out to meet the frigid air of the night, leaving his hurting wife in a strange hospital. He stepped up to a pulpit and assured an enthusiastic audience that there were no troubles or disappointments in this life, that their faith could not overcome every time. Deep inside he was hoping this to be true.

The little community hospital staff was so kind as to let Sam and both moms slip into see Pat well after visiting hours had ended As Mom Royer held her distraught daughter in her arms, a not so smart, and not so brave son found solace in the arms of his own mother outside the door of that room. Sam had one question for Opal, the preacher's daughter:

"Mom, where do we go from here?"

"Son, God never takes anything to himself that he will not give back twice as much and more." For the first time in about fourteen hours Sam took a full, deep breath.

****

The first little church pastor experience would only last about six months for Sam and Pat. Conditions were meager, to say the least. He would be the church pianist, and she would learn her way around the keys of an organ. On the morning of their candidacy they were shown the small and poorly conditioned little house, owned by a member and provided as their residence in the blue collar, lower middle class neighborhood of a notorious district called Drexel gardens. What they did not know was the only reason the city did not condemn the house was because the young clergy couple would be living in it. They were also made to understand that if all the church's bills were paid each week, they would receive whatever money was left over from the collections as their personal income. There would never be a week that any money was left over for them. In fact, they would need to find employment just to help pay some of the church obligations that the collections could not cover. Sam's lack of professional training, technical schooling, trades skills, and college education limited his employability to a construction site general laborer at a $2.00 per hour income. Because of Pat's miscarriage and the anemic condition which may have led to it, her doctor would not release her to work. That coupled with the broken foot Sam sustained while dropping a hot water heater through his sweaty arms at the construction site, meant no source of income. The little church had grown, but primarily with the neighborhood kids Pat would pack into the beltless seat of their little car every Sunday Morning.

Sam's grandmother Martha was the beneficiary of a large block of cheese, and boxes of rice from the government as a senior widow. She knew Sam and Pat's income now consisted of the bottles they could garner along the ditches at night and turn in for refund. Grandma Martha sent so much of her government provisions to them they often said they could write a book on a thousand ways to cook cheese and rice.

The fact that kerosene oil was only about nineteen cents a gallon made it possible to get heating oil for the little heater in the decaying house. On occasion, they ran out of coins and oil. In the sub-freezing temperatures of winter they would dress at the church building which was heated, come home and wrap in blankets, while watching their little black and white TV, and eating another form of Grandma's government rations. Then they would return to church to dress in the heat, and prepare for the evening service. Most of Sam's sermon topics were centered on how wonderful the Christian life was, and how God would meet every need of his children. His closing prayers at night were words of gratitude for a roof over their head, food to eat, and the most wonderful woman any man could ever have. Secretly, he hoped his life would get better, and his beautiful wife would not grow impatient waiting for the good times he had promised her if only she would be his wife.

The couple decided to return to their evangelistic travels, where at least food would be more plentiful. And owing to an insurance settlement to cover the little American Rambler totaled in an accident from which Sam miraculously walked away, they were able to acquire a new Ford 150 Pickup truck and a matching, blue and white 21 foot Conestoga

Travel Trailer. Sailing down the highways of America were some of their happiest moments.

"ZephyrHills, now that is an interesting name for a town. Wonder if they have a lot of Zephyrs here?" Sam was really talking to himself as Pat was sound asleep beside him on the bench seat of the pretty blue truck, taking them across several states for the past number of months. He continued his conversation as if she was listening. "Just a few more miles and we will be in Plant City, but I better stop at this station and gas up now." As he stepped down from the truck to the station drive he could not believe what he was feeling. "Pat, Pat. Hey babe, you have to wake up and get out of the truck, and feel this."

After slowly pushing the heavy leopard spotted winter coat onto the floor of the truck she slowly sat up, rubbed her eyes, brushed her disheveled hair back, and in a grumpy tone inquired, "What? What is going on?"

Sam hurried around the vehicle and reached for her hand. "Feel this. Just feel this; it is summer here." Then half-pulling her from the cab he even more enthusiastically said, "We left sixteen inches of snow and twenty degree weather, and it was even snowing when we crossed Mont Eagle. I let you sleep all night, and I didn't even get out of the truck when I stopped for gas." A fact not unusual when gas pump jockeys still came out to your vehicle and filled it for you.

As she began to understand his excitement she responded in kind. "This is amazing! What is the temperature? Look! There are leaves on the trees, and smell that? It smells like oranges."

"You know what this is?" He questioned and then answered his own rhetoric. "This is Florida! No, this is Florida in the winter."

They woke the next morning in the small efficiency apartment, which had been provided by the welcoming church where they would be conducting services. Sam discovered his first grapefruit tree just outside the door of the apartment.

"I wonder if it is legal to take those grapefruit off the tree." Sam pondered. "Well I could always claim ignorance of the law." He pulled till the large yellow ball of citrus snapped from its holding branch."

After taking it inside, washing the exterior, cutting it in half, and spooning each section to release the fruit from the wedge shaped dividers, he sprinkled some sugar lightly across each half as he had seen his dad do often at the breakfast table of his childhood. If ever a winter pale skinned Yankee boy had experienced what the local Florida natives called, "getting some sand in your shoes," Sam was fully infused.

"I never really even knew such a place existed anywhere in the world, and particularly at this time of the year. Did you?" Sam quizzed Pat as they pulled the truck off of the road known as the Clearwater Causeway, and prepared to try the waters of Tampa Bay.

"I guess I knew, but just could never have imagined without being here." She followed with her own question. "I wonder why no one is swimming out here today?"

Their shock was beyond words when they took their first plunge in the warm water and came up spitting and sputtering and declaring the same response, "Oh, that is nasty! Salt! It tastes like salt!" With burning eyes and repeated spitting they displayed their total lack of knowledge about the oceans they had never experienced. All they had ever known was Lake Michigan, or nearby Pine, or Stone Lake. From time to time they swam in the lake at their church campground. It took some getting used to, but soon they realized they were swimming in the month of February in weather that would have felt like June back home. They also began to notice the cars on the causeway slowing down, and the people inside pointing and laughing at the two obvious, Yankee, snow birds. Swimming in that cold water at that time of the year, the water was only about the same temperature as the air, 75 degrees. That was too chilly for the Floridians.

They completed their speaking engagements and started to make the long trip back to the north. He finally got up the nerve to pose a question to his wife.

"Could you ever see yourself living in a paradise like this?"

That question, and the "sand in Sam's shoes" found them relocating, like his brother Manson had done, to the Sunshine State a short five months later. They found a little seasonal cottage to rent, and he took some employment in a men's clothing store, knowing it would take a little time to network with the church world in a new area.

This Florida experience was a bit different than the previous winter amazement. The weather was a combination of heat and humidity as new to them as the winter balminess had been in February. To complicate matters, the income was more than a challenge. Sam worked sixty hours per week and brought home an $88.22 paycheck. For some reason, perhaps the heat, Pat was sick everyday, and could not hold anything on her stomach. After a month, her condition became so severe that Sam found a doctor and took her to be examined. When he returned to the doctor's office to pick her up, he was very concerned when he noticed her head was dropped, and she appeared to be wiping tears as she headed for the pickup truck.

"Are you alright?" Sam asked as she opened the door and slid on to the seat. He continued, "What did the doctor say? What does he think?"

Pat turned her face toward his and burst into tears. Every kind of horrible scenario began to rush through his mind when almost panicked he pressed again. "What, what is going on?" in a heartbreaking tone she cried out the words,

"The rabbit died."

He hollered back, "The rabbit died? The rabbit died?"

She began to laugh through her tears, and suddenly the light of comprehension exploded in Sam's brain. He understood she was referring to the procedure that some laboratories used in that time, whereby injecting a woman's urine into a laboratory rabbit, the result of the rabbit dying would be a positive proof that the subject of the test was pregnant.

"You're pregnant! You're going to have a baby!" He repeated the phrase several times, letting it sink in. He extended his arms and pulled her across the seat until she was fully engulfed in his caress. After a moment of silence, knowing their minds had both moved to the disappointment they had known previously, Pat moved her mouth from Sam's neck to his ear and whispered,

"Let's go home."

The next week was Pat's twenty-second birthday, July 16, 1969. As the truck pulled out of the driveway of the little bungalow and headed back to the northland, Sam dialed in a strong radio signal and listened to the launch of an Apollo Rocket from a location some one hundred miles to the east called The Kennedy Space Center. The fact that this launch for the first man in history to walk on the moon would begin from an Island called Merritt Island, held no particular importance to the young couple heading home. Little could they imagine the important role that island and that new life within Pat's body would come to play in their future.

****

"Hello, Hello?" Sam softly answered into the unique pink and blue telephone as his eyes scanned across the room at the four other men staring at him. "Yes, yes. I am Mr. Pawlak. Ok, straight down the hall, to my right? Yes, I am coming now."
He announced to the others in the room, "This one is for me fellas."

As his shoe heels clicked noisily on the tile hallway and the sound echoed upward to the arched, high plastered ceilings above, he could see the white clothed nurse and the black clad nun both vigorously waving him to proceed to their location. The old St. Vincent Catholic Hospital was located on Fall Creek Parkway near downtown Indianapolis. It was here that Sam and Pat moved after the holidays, living in the actual apartment complex that he had worked as a laborer over two years earlier. Pat's inability to travel at the latter stages of her pregnancy led them to accept an invitation from his Uncle Fred to serve as the church's youth pastor. The same church he had held his first Easter service had moved from their previous location, and built a new facility in the town of Speedway, the home of the famous 500 mile race. Even though the church could only provide fifteen dollars a week for their help, Sam's primary responsibilities were to meet with the group of teens in a small room each Sunday morning, and put together a monthly activity. This meant again that Sam would have to find gainful employment for his expanding little family. After a few different factory jobs he finally landed a good position running a screw machine in the FMC Link Belt factory. His work even paid enough money for him and Pat to go on a date night each week to a little drive-in called The Mug & Bun. They could share a hamburger, onion rings, and one milk shake.

As Sam moved toward the hospital workers at the end of the hall he was feeling a bit of guilt. They would not have let him in the delivery room in those days anyway, but he still felt bad, even though he had been with her in the labor room from early morning. When it appeared she was no closer to delivery, his Uncle Fred who had come to wait with him offered a suggestion.

"Hey Sam, have you eaten anything today?"

He had not for two reasons: he did not want to leave Pat's side in the labor room, and he actually did not have one red cent on him as payday was not for two more days.

Uncle Fred continued his thought. "Since nothing has happened yet, and does not look like it will for awhile, why don't we slip on down to the cafeteria, and I will buy the daddy to be a sandwich."

Pat assured Sam that she was fine, and he should go get a bite. As would be the case, Sam and Uncle Fred had no sooner left her side than the nurse came in and announced,

"Young lady, it is time for you to get to that delivery room and let's get this baby here."

When he returned to the labor room, it was empty. She was gone.

"Where did you take my wife?"

"Oh, she is in delivery." The firm talking nurse took him by the arm, pulling him from the room and ordered, "You go down there to the room where the dads wait. When the pink and blue phone rings, one of you men pick it up, and we will tell you when you can come back down here." She then, with the softness of a prison guard further barked out, "And don't come down here till we call for you. Understand?"

He stood staring through the huge glass window, scanning all those little bodies wrapped and displayed before him. A kind looking face on a small framed catholic nun motioned for Sam to move to the far end of the window. She moved between the beds, softly gathered up the little bundle, and carried it to display the little life through the windows. She mouthed the words,

"Meet your son, Daddy."

"A boy, it's a boy." He smiled back to the nun. Then he thought, "Another boy in this family of so many boys."

The nurse came and stood beside the new father, and explained that the Nun would place the baby back in the maternity ward bed and move it close to the window so they could have a little time together.

"Thank you so much." Sam said and then questioned, "How is my wife?"

"She is just fine. You will be able to see her soon and maybe tomorrow you will be able to actually hold the baby. You will have to robe, mask, and glove, but we have a new policy that the fathers can hold their baby the second day if all is well." She added an additional piece of information. "Your wife did wonderfully. This one might be a singer someday, because the doctor and nurse sang to each other the whole time he was being born."

"What did they sing?" He quickly asked.

"Oh, that new love song from Romeo and Juliet movie that is out now, 'A Time For Us.'" She waved her hand as if it had all been foolishness, and walked away with a little chuckle.

He stared down into the bassinet on the other side of the window as a sober impression swept across his face and unblinking eyes. "Wow, that is a real baby. A real live baby. Oh Man, that is a life." Then he remembered that since Pat had always loved the names Sam and Steve they had already agreed it would be fitting to name him Samuel Paul Jr. The new father then spoke to the little squirming life. "Well, Sammy boy, I am your dad. So glad you're finally here." No more words came as a thought grabbed his throat. "He is so helpless. He will never make it without you, and it's up to you and what you do that will determine what he becomes." That choking feeling never fully let up till Sam went to the nearest payphone and called Mom Royer. He told her she was now a grandmother. After a few details he was surprised when she said,

"Here is Lloyd. Tell him."

"Hey there, Grandpa." Sam greeted his father-in-law. He tried to sound manly by saying, "I'm sure you and my dad will have him fishing before long."

The son-in-law was taken back a bit when the tough ole steel man cleared his throat and softly said, "Let's just make him a fisher of men."

After getting to spend a few minutes with the beautiful mother of his child, Sam was shooed from the hospital. They were bringing the baby to his mommy within a few minutes, and in those days dads were unnecessary at this point. As he drove alone back across the large city that night, the lights of the streets seemed to all be a little brighter, and the sound of tires on the spring rain that March evening sounded like applause of congratulations for a job well done by a young man still a month shy of his twenty-second birthday.

****

Frank and Opal stepped from their new station wagon and began their trek toward the front door of the stately old hospital. Sam met them and began to cautiously prepare his parents for what had been a concerning impression from his observations at first seeing his new son the day before.

"Listen. I wanted to let you guys know before you go in and see the baby and Pat... and maybe it's nothing, but I am not sure if everything is really alright with this kid."

"Well what do you mean?" Opal asked with as little alarm in her voice as possible.

"It is just this one thing that has kind of bothered me all night."
He explained with a little twist of his head to one side. "It is the shape of his head." He continued as they slowly entered the front doors of the hospital. "His head is sort of lop-sided and comes out to a point at the top and side of his head, and both sides of his face are pretty beat up. Like he had already gone a couple of rounds." The young father now displayed a small shadow boxing posture and feigned a fake punch toward Frank.

Opal went on a little fact finding mission of her own when she asked, "Didn't you say he was an instrument baby?" Sam felt again the awkwardness of his elementary knowledge into what actually went on in the delivery room. Opal quickly interjected, "That means they use these forceps to assist in getting the baby out." She continued, "They are like long hot dog tongs you would use on a grill. They grasp the baby on each side of the head and help pull it through the birth canal." She waited for him to let this sink in. "They actually twist and turn the baby's head, and it can be pretty rough at times. That is why the little face gets bruised and beat up."

The new father raised the greater question as the elevator operator closed the door in front of them. "But why is the head so lopsided and pointed?" He declared further, "I think there is something wrong with that kid. It just does not look right to me. His head is more of a football shape that a basketball shape."

At this, Opal did something that she seldom did, she literally began to laugh out loud. Not just a little laugh, but one that seemed to continue much longer than Sam found comfortable.

"What? What is so funny about a crooked headed baby?" When Opal recognized the terse tone in his question she gathered herself and with a comforting reach for his arm she consoled him.

"Listen. When a baby is first born, their head is very soft and not really hardened to the degree it will. I am sure the doctor just got a little aggressive with the instruments, and what is a little misshapen head now will become perfectly round in a few days. You just keep softly rubbing it with a massaging motion and the little head will be as round as a pumpkin."

In the weeks, months, and years to come, one of Sam's favorite pastimes was to disrupt Sammy's run through the house by reaching that large paw that could hold a basketball firmly with one hand, and vigorously rub it through Sammy's thick black hair. As he firmly massaged that perfectly round head, he would often snicker a bit at the accuracy of his mother's previous prediction.

****

"I need to talk to you kids for a few minutes."

The soft but serious declaration from the old gentleman who played such a tremendous role in the lives of this young couple made them pay attention.

The young couple had lost count of how many times they had conducted Revivals for Pastor Melvin Plank. Every few months they would get a call from this dear and kind man, asking them to come for another week or two, and perform their music and preach. This one elderly pastor probably opened more doors of invitations for Sam and Pat than anyone else they knew. The invitations really began to grow exponentially when at a State gathering of ministers, Pastor Melvin gave the endorsement.

"I have invited to my pulpit a great number of speakers, singers, educators, and revivalists. It has been my experience that every speaker will have some messages, lectures, or sermons that will be better than others. We call it 'ringing the bell' in our preaching business. I have also become accustomed that some nights they will 'ring the bell,' and some nights they will simply be adequate to the task." Taking on the tone of a true campaign politician performing the preverbal stump speech with excessive volume and arm waving gesture, he declared forthright, "Every time I have ever invited Sam Pawlak to stand before my congregation, and that has been more numerous than I can count, this young man has never failed to 'ring the bell.' Not one time has he been average or even adequate. He shakes the house with knowledge, passion, and truth."

Sam could feel the heat of eyes, and hear the twist of cranial spines, and for a moment had to physically resist the desire to, if not run from the glaring spotlight, at least slide down in his seat in hope of disappearing behind the twisted characters in front of him. It only got worse when Pastor Melvin barked out the following order to those gathered,

"Get this couple to your church as fast as you can. He has his date book with him, and you will miss God completely if you don't book them before they leave this conference."

Knowing that correcting or demanding anything from your peers is never a good practice to follow, Sam just whispered to Pat, "I don't know if we will ever get any more meetings."

To his surprise, when the meeting ended, Sam and Pat could not even get out of the pew they were sitting, in hopes to hide from the uncomfortable attention. Pastor after pastor stood in the aisle and simply had one comment,

"Well, get out that datebook. We better get this set, when can you come?"

Sam's profession coupled with the general attitude of that day meant that there were no agents to go through, no contracts to sign, and certainly no discussion of costs or honorarium. Just the simple understanding that you would come on the dates decided, preach and sing, stay wherever the Pastor decided to house you, eat whatever food was provided, and on the closing night of the crusade, the Pastor would shake your hand and you could firmly feel some cash or check within the shake of thanks. The last thing you would have done was to look and see how much had been given. You simply thanked them, slipped the funds into your pocket, and drove off to the next series of meetings. What others would never know was how the recipients of this kindness could not wait to get far enough down the road and out of sight of the previous caregivers, to pull the wad of paper from their pocket. They would be so excited when it was at least $50 or $75 dollars that would cover the budget and get the youth faithfuls to the next location. On a few occasions the pay that week would be $100.

Sam jokingly said, "Look out Billy Graham, here I come."

Pat rolled her eyes.

Their great respect for Pastor Melvin went far beyond his ability to help them in their evangelistic career. They had watched him take upon himself the sole responsibility of caring for his beloved wife after her second stroke, some sixteen years earlier. Their hearts often went out to him when they would see him lift the paralyzed and dead weight of her body from the wheelchair to the bed, or anywhere else necessary to her existence. What impressed them more was the fact that this care happened twenty four hours a day, day after day, year after year, in a small attached apartment at the back of the church building. The long and often interrupted nights would only be followed with the responsibilities of Pastor Melvin's daily ministry chores. All this he did without a single complaint.

He was a hero in the truest sense of the word. So when they heard him call them to attention, they were all ears to hear whatever possible counsel or guidance he had to share. And they were ready to heed whatever he had to say.

"I know you two are about the best young evangelists out there. At least that is my opinion, but I feel like I need to talk to you about something."

"Anything, Pastor. Please, feel free to share your heart." Sam immediately responded.

The wise older man pointed to the little playpen in the middle of the room. "Well, with this little guy over here, crawling and standing already, and with that second baby coming in the spring, I'm thinking that this road life is only going to get harder and harder. You might need to be thinking about settling down a little, getting off the road, and finding a church to pastor that can provide some security for this growing family."

Sam resisted the temptation to remind Pastor Melvin that his promotion and proclamations about their ability was a great part of the reason they were still on the road. He simply said,

"Go on."

Then the dear man brought an even more clear picture into focus when he clarified his intention.

"Last week I was invited to speak at a church up in Gary. One of their board members and his wife were a young couple in my church when I pastored in East Chicago years ago." He brought a few more details. "The elderly pastor of the church has just retired and returned to his home in Arkansas. They need some new, younger blood in there. Now, I loved when I was in that area. All those steel mills, petroleum plants and factories were exciting. Good work, people make good money, and being right next to Chicago, you would fit in so well, being Polish and all that." Then he ran off on a rabbit trail of stories of the wonderful Polish people and good food he so enjoyed during those years. Coming back to the subject at hand, he continued, "They have a nice group of people there. They are able to support a Pastor with a full salary, and they even have a nice two bedroom apartment in the back upstairs that they provide for the Pastor's family. They'll cover all the utilities as well."

The young couple tried to resist having an interest in the securities this might afford, still wanting to project a humble position that believed material things had no real concern for those wanting to simply be used by God. Then Pastor Mel threw down the real gauntlet.

"Listen, kids. I can call my friend Al today. He is looked upon as the real one they follow on the board. I know with just a word they would have you there, and I am confident they would vote for you to be their Pastor. It would really be good for you two and little Sammy over there, and this other little guy or gal you're expecting in the spring."

"Give us a few minutes." Sam said while he reached for Pat's hand. "We are going to slip into the church for a little bit and pray over this matter, and maybe we will hear something from the Lord about this." Sam knew that using this kind of jargon was meant to signify one's level of spiritual maturity and insight.

Pat suggested, "I will put Sammy down for a little nap, and I will pray in the bedroom while you go to the church." Her statement indicated two things clearly to her husband: first, "I need to think about this quietly by myself," and secondly, "you need to know that this is the right thing for us to do."

After a little time alone, he slipped into the guest bedroom and asked her, "Well, what do you think?"

"Well, what do you think?" She echoed.

He sat down on the side of the bed. Keeping a low voice so as to not wake the napping baby he voiced, "You know, I love the road. I love the new places each week, and I really love not having to answer to many people." Then a humorous thought struck him. "You know, some churches never look better than in the rear view mirror." When she didn't laugh, he collected his serious tone. "It would be a little closer to home and family. Better yet, only about twenty minutes from Comiskey Park and my White Sox, and only an hour to Wrigley. Monday nights I could be playing basketball with my brothers out at the old Coolspring School. The Bears, the Bulls and…"

"The church, Sam. What about the church? Gary is a pretty rough town, lot's of crime, and the pollution from the mills is really bad, and the apartment is upstairs. Two babies with stairs…"

"Yeah, I hadn't thought of all that." Sam gathered himself a bit and said, "…but it would be full-time ministry. Paid salary, we would know what to expect each week, and housing. When I came back from the sanctuary Pastor said he found out they pay $125.00 a week, and would give us health insurance. I don't know Pat, maybe I should pray a little more about this."

As he rose to exit the room and return to the front of the church to kneel again at the wooden prayer benches, she grabbed his hand and said,

"$125 every week? Housing and utilities? Insurance? Near my Mom? You go pray, I'll start packing."

Two weeks later, the little sign in front of the red-bricked church had newly painted lettering at the bottom that read

Pastor Samuel P. Pawlak

****

"I know your Dad's truck is not too smooth, but it is still probably better than the bucket seats in my Mustang." Sam consoled as he helped Pat make the very difficult step into the small pickup truck. They drove down the same familiar road that led to Sam's memorable collision with the farm truck, a little less than three years earlier. This time they made a much slower and more cautious trek toward Saint Anthony Hospital in Michigan City. It was the same hospital his uncle Eddie had been carried to with that broken arm, and the same Hospital of his own birth, now just eighteen days short of his twenty-third birthday.

"Honey, I just realized something." Pat inserted between uncomfortable groans and increased early stages of labor pains.

"I hope it is not that you don't want any more children." Sam replied with one of his facetious quips.

"No. I just realized we have not settled on a name in case it is a girl."

Since boys were so prominent in the Pawlak family they had discussed several possibilities of male first and middle names, but only a few times had they considered the remote possibility of needing a girl's name.

"Mariah is a pretty name." Pat reasoned, "I have always thought it had a wonderful western sound to it, and I always loved that song 'They call the wind Mariah from Paint Your Wagon."

"Yeah, but then everybody that remembers that song will probably end up calling her Windy."

They laughed a moment before Pat clutched both sides of her fully distended stomach. Groaning with another pain she pleaded, "Can you miss a few of the potholes, Sam?"

This was not so easy a task on a spring evening in the dark, following the normal midwest winter siege. Sam returned to the topic of girl names.

"It is the month of April, you know. April is sure a pretty name, flowers and all that stuff?"

The discussion was abruptly set aside for more important things to be discussed, like how close the pains were coming and whether they could get to the hospital in time. They had been told that most often the second child takes less time in labor than the first.

"Well folks, I think we will have a little while before the baby will be here." Then the doctor added, "I would say the way things are looking, you should have another baby somewhere near dawn."

This being already after the midnight hour gave both of them a sigh of relief, which was only interrupted by Pat's eyes widening to full circumference and her sudden declaration,

"April Dawn. Yes, April Dawn. That is it! That is what her name should be. It is April, and she will be here near dawn. That is a sign, maybe even a word from God." then she lowered her voice and remembered, "That is, if it is a girl. Otherwise, we will stick with the Grandpa's names Lloyd and Frank."

"April Dawn." Sam voiced softly and very contemplatively, "Yes, that is pretty, and sure would sound good for a girl."

That particular April dawn would come and go. Sunrise would shoot through the windows of the fairly new wing of the hospital, but things had stalled. It looked like it could still be some time before a baby arrived. It was the day before Easter and yet, no baby. The lunch hour was nearing when Sam's mother, Opal, came to the hospital. After assessing the status of the slow delivery she asked,

"Have you eaten anything since supper last night?"

"Not a bite. It's been seventeen or eighteen hours now."

"Since nothing is happening yet, why don't we run down to the cafeteria and get a quick sandwich?" a suggestion that required only a quick kiss on Pat's forehead, a promise to be back quickly, and an almost running movement to the hall, in the direction of the nearest elevator.

The elevator bell softly rang at the maternity floor. Sam was quite startled when he stepped out only to see a nurse coming toward him with a small bundle cradled in her arm and a rather stern question being fired in his direction.

"Do you want to see your new baby, or not? Where have you been?" We have been looking for you everywhere."

The nurse, closing in on Sam, thrust the little creature in his direction, leaving him no time to even react to her questions.

"Say hello to your beautiful new daughter, Daddy."

"A girl. Oh wow, it is a little girl."

He stood studying her features, being a bit taken back by how different the restrictions were compared to when Sammy had been born just thirteen months before. No glass separation, no gown, gloves, mask and hat, just standing in a hospital with this beautiful little girl in his arms. His first statement to his mother was, "These must be more modern Catholics at this Hospital."

They were still laughing when the nurse said, "Ok, that is all for now. Give her back. She and I have lots of work to do yet. Your wife is in that little recovery room over there waiting for you."

As Sam entered the room, he first approached the bed from Pat's head; he touched her head and moved around to the side of the bed to say, "She is beautiful, Pat. So beautiful." She simply responded,

"A little girl. A little girl, Sammy has a sister."

He made a declaration about their future, especially considering that he had gone to eat both times that Pat had gone from labor to delivery.

"The next time we do this, I am going to get you admitted to the hospital, just go directly to the cafeteria for something to eat, so you can have the baby without such a long wait."

She weakly smiled and feigned a little snicker. With little consideration that this would turn out to be their last child.

He noticed that she was really exhausted and what should have been less labor with the second child had actually taken nearly twice as long. He touched her hair noticing something white on her head. He realized quickly there was no foreign substance there, but some of Pat's dark strands had amazingly turned to pure white. He didn't say anything at the time, but would learn that this was an occasional phenomenon that could transpire through stress or trauma. He found that after he'd gone for lunch, Pat went into hard labor so quickly that there was no time to administer any normal pain reduction treatments. The delivery was traumatic enough to bring on the sudden hair color changes.

Lloyd Royer playfully suggested, inasmuch as his first granddaughter had been born the day before Easter, her name should be Easter Eve. Sam's hearing impaired Grandma Martha was appalled they were going to name her April Showers. The baby's parents were in full agreement that her name had been given to them from a higher source on that drive from the country the night before. April Dawn rolled off their lips like the sweetest lyric of an angel's song. The fact she was not born till the middle of the day never led them to even consider something as bizarre as April Noon.

Older brother Fred may have said it best when he arrived to visit the new addition.

"Wow! A boy and a girl! Now, that is a million dollar family."

Sam, never being without a timely response, quickly returned with a simple response. "Yeah. Can you find me the million dollars to raise them?"

****

The next two years would serve as a true bootcamp for becoming a pastor. It was in Gary that Sam would learn the time and discipline required for the multifaceted personality of administration, organization, promotion, salesman, confidant, psychologist, pragmatist, revolutionary, instructor, motivator, socialite, communicator, community leader, marriage and family counselor, and close friend. To become adept at all this between the ages of twenty three and twenty five was not only unrealistic, but constituted the factors that drive over fifty percent of ministers from their chosen profession within the first five years of their ordination. Place on top of that the responsibility of fostering and improving a young marriage, and spending the time for the care and nurture of two infant children. Sam's level of immaturity and experience often led him to spend too much time at his beloved White Sox games, and when no Chicago South-side friend was looking, at the beautiful and friendly confines known as Wrigley Field. Then there were the Bears, Bulls, and Blackhawks, Notre Dame, Purdue, Indiana, Northwestern, and a plethora of high school athletics to be attended. There would be Monday night basketball games with his brothers, the fast pitch softball leagues, and TV games to be watched with the younger set of church friends. The strain on a young bride, church needs, and limited budget made for a less that glorious experience for all involved.

Pat's life consisted of constant care for two babies, both in diapers at the same time. And this being still before the common use of disposable diapers. One of the greatest blessings that came her way followed a visit to the hectic little apartment above the church. Uncle Eddie and Aunt Mary presented Pat with the gift of mobile diaper service at just the time she was feeling as if she was about to explode from overload of a young mom.

Since Sam was responsible to plan and lead two services each Sunday, and one during the middle of the week, it meant that Pat would often hear many of Sam's sermons after putting the babies to bed, sitting on the steps between the upstairs apartment and the church sanctuary. She kept one ear tuned to the apartment for the cry of a baby in need, and the other ear to the voice of that young preaching machine beyond the church doors.

It did give her a sense of fulfilled motherhood and a pride in the man she loved. He may not have been the most mature pastor or even yet father, but she loved his passion for preaching and their church family. More important to her was that she knew he loved her and very nearly worshipped their beautiful children.

****

"Wait! Stop! Just a minute. Sam, we have to go back." Opal announced, firmly grasping her son's forearm, turning him suddenly and even pulling him back in the steps they had just covered.

Confused, he walked again down the long corridor of the massive hospital. He had often heard of Edward Hines Jr. Veterans
Administration Hospital in the suburb that carried the same name just north of Chicago, but he was overwhelmed at the size of the aging facilities.

"What is it, Mom? Why did we turn around?" Sam asked Opal while feeling their adjoined pace increase. He was just about to say, "With this being a government facility I really expected it would be a lot nicer, or at least more modern." But in the very institutional, colorless, and dimly lit hallways he began to realize that this mass gathering of world-saving heroes may not have provided for them the comforts and extra care that private money or personal wealth could supply.

"There, there that's my brother Lowell." She pointed in the direction of a nearly bald and frail old man, attempting to get into some pajama bottoms with one hand while holding the other trembling hand to the metal footboard of the hospital bed from another era of medical care. She spoke with a tear-filled voice, "I walked right by him. I saw him but it wasn't till we got way down the hall that I realized it was Lowell."

Sam squinted to bring the pitiful figure into focus. He could actually not recognize anything about this person that resembled one of his favorite Uncles. Then the old fella lifted his head, saw Opal at the doorway, and in a voice Sam recognized over any other voice he knew, he said,

"Hey Sis. Come on into my castle." The welcome was followed by a weak, wheezing laugh.

It was he, James and Martha's oldest boy. He was the writer, the storyteller, and to a young nephew, the legend. After the usual hugs, the uncle was again reclined in his bed. Lowell began to expound about his present circumstances.

"I was going to make a trip to Alaska. Always wanted to get to Alaska."

Sam was surprised he had not been there. This uncle was famous to the younger kids for his wandering and roaming exploits. They understood most of those journeys were the product of a challenged and, at times troubled life. Opal would often say of Lowell, "My brother was never the same after the war, and being wounded in France." But this was just the closing shadow of the man who could write with Shakespearean fluency. Sam's dad used to say he always loved getting a letter from Lowell, because it read like a Zane Grey Novel.

"See that tile right there in the corner, Sam?" His uncle pointed his large but thin hand toward a darkened portion of the room. "Well boy, that is my altar. Yep, I have made that my altar." He used the term Sam understood to mean the kneeling benches that sat at the front of their church. He then continued to explain, "I have talked it all over with God. We worked it out, and I made my peace right there in that tile, my altar."

Opal's handkerchief was pressed firmly against both eyes. She understood her brother was telling her he knew death was imminent. His life of struggle and trial was soon to be at peace. Then he turned to Sam with a rather urgent sounding request.

"Listen, Sammy. I need you to do me a favor. I need to get out of here. I can't stay in here like a caged animal anymore. You got to get me out of here, boy."

Looking for a calming answer to his uncle's panic at immobility and confinement, Sam replied.

"Well, what I will do is go talk to the staff and doctors, and see what they say about you getting out of here." He quickly left the room and when approached the nearest nurse's station.

"Hey, my uncle is asking me to take him out of here. I don't want to do that, but I told him I would check with you." The doctor in charge pushed his seat back from the counter a bit, removed his reading glasses, and said matter-of-factly,

"Look, he checked himself in here, and he can sign himself out anytime he wants. But you won't get him across that parking lot before he dies." The nephew nodded at his under-standing and returned to his uncle and gave the doctor's response.

Lowell seemed to gather one more morsel of his wandering and unconfined spirit, and begged, "Then take me out there and let me die in that parking lot, please."

"Uncle Lowell, you know I love you, but that's a responsibility I'm just not prepared for." the young man reasoned.

"I know you can't, Son. Thanks for trying."

Mother and son soon said their farewells and left, knowing it would most likely be the last visit. Within a few days the family would again gather at that cemetery that held so many loved ones from the past.

"Sammy, stop just a minute, will you?" came the soft and trembling words from his only living grandmother, Martha Rice.

He and Pat stopped immediately and he asked, "What is it, Grandmaw?" using a pronun-ciation of the word assigned only to Grandmother Martha, and his mother's side of the family.

"I need you children to pray for me?" She took each of their arms on either side for her and they supported her across the uneven grave sites.

"Of course, Grandmaw. What can we pray for?"

The tall and stately lady whom Pastor James had so often called his Kentucky Thorough-bred began to openly weep as she spoke. "Would you pray that the Lord will take me home to Heaven?" She expounded, "I am old, I've lived a long life." She lifted her head to gaze across the cemetery, and stretched out her long arm. She slowly waved her white gloved hand back and forth in a horizontal sweep as she spoke. "I followed that hearse carrying my Estella's body out here, and I followed those five hearses carrying my Junior and his wife and their three little girls. I followed that hearse carrying your Grandpa, the only man I ever loved, and so, so many more over these years. Today, I followed my son and buried him. I don't want to follow one more of my children or grandchildren out here ever again. Then turning and tenderly patting the young couples' cheeks, she said again, "Please pray that the Lord will take me home, so I won't follow another one here."

Unsure exactly how to honor this request, and furthermore, not knowing if being a pastor gave him any more rights or authority with God, or even if a prayer of this nature was proper or theologically correct, Sam simply held his dear Grandmother in his arms. He audibly offered a petition to the Eternal God of the Universe who he was confident knew all things.

"Dear God, you have heard the request of your child. She has served you in every way she knows possible. You, Dear Father, have sustained her through every tragedy and painful loss represented by this place in which we now stand. We join with her heart's desire today, and ask that she never have to come to this place again."

After patting away the tears, Sam and Pat escorted her to her son's awaiting car. As it pulled away, they just held each other for a few moments, and silently wondered if their prayer would be answered.

****

"Hey, Mom. It's me." Sam called through the front door.

"How are you feeling today?" He continued his greeting. He was growing accustomed to seeing her in her reclining chair with an afghan cover over her legs. Her five year battle with Leukemia had slowed her some, and even though she was still pretty active selling a few items, the big Tupperware parties she loved to host had to cease. Sam came to sit down in front of her.

"I sure love being this close to you guys. Pat and the kids would have come today, but Pat's got a lot to do. But with Gary being so close we can get back over often. I guess Dad is enjoying this new Maintenance Manager job in the apartment complex, since leaving the factory. Huh?"

Opal seemed to ignore his monologue, and began an interesting little story.

"I had a very unusual dream last night." He suddenly knew he'd better listen up. He had learned long ago when Opal had a dream or a feeling about something or someone, you better pay attention.

"Ok, what did you dream about? Hope it involved me and a lot of money." Sam wise-cracked with a chuckle.

"No, it was really kind of strange."

He could hear the serious tone in her voice and moved a little closer to her. "Hmm, well go ahead, Mom. tell me about it."

"I dreamed that I had gone to Heaven. Somehow, I just knew it was Heaven." she then clarified, "I did not see a bright light, or mansions, or angels, or even Jesus, but I was walk-ing along the banks of a beautiful river. I came across a man sort of squatted down near the water, picking some grass at his feet." She readjusted her body in the chair to reach for the foot release handle on the side of her recliner. As she released it, she sat up fully straight in the chair. "Then, I saw my Mom, your Grandmaw Martha walking down the bank in the direction of the man. The man suddenly stood and turned toward my moth-er, and I realized it was my dad, your Grandpaw."

Sam was trying to picture a scene with his grandmother Martha and grandfather, Pastor James. He heard his mother's voice gather a mixture of sweetness and sentimentality when she excitedly explained,

"My dad said, "Oh Martha, you're finally here. I watched them throw their arms around each other, and by now, in my dream, I was crying and saying, 'Oh, they're together at last, at last." Then Opal's demeanor seemed to change as she told more of the dream, "While I was so excited to see them together, I saw my Dad, still in my mother's arms, lift up his eyes and look up the bank of the river. I was aware that he was looking in my direc-tion, and then he pulled away a little from my mother, and a big smile came across his lips. He said, 'Why Opal, you've come too.'" She stared for a moment, then came back from reliving her dream, and said to Sam, "Then I woke up, and that was it. I was in this chair where I had fallen asleep late last night."

Sam was not quite sure what to make of his mom's dream. "Wow, that is quite a dream." The last hum on the end of the word dream was still vibrating on Sam's lips when Opal's wall phone in the kitchen disturbed the deep contemplation about the dream.

"Can you grab that, Sam? I won't get there in time."

"Sure, I got it mom." Sam assured her as he rapidly stepped to the kitchen, snatched the receiver off the hook, and announced, "Pawlak residence, can I help you?"

"Sam, is that you?" came the voice across the phone line.

"Yes, Levi? What are you doing?" Sam asked.

"Well, I am so glad I caught you at your Mom's." Then with a rather serious and softer pace, Uncle Freddie's eldest began to explain to his cousin. "I am just calling to let you all know that Grandmaw Martha just passed away in her sleep. When I went in to check on her this morning she was gone." Sam quickly responded,

"Just a minute, Levi. Hang on a second." Sam requested, placed his hand over the mouthpiece of the phone and turned to meet his mother's inquisitive eyes, and softly said across the room, "Your dad and mom are together today." He returned to Levi and asked again, "Just went in her sleep, you say?"

Levi gave a little more information, "I knew she was usually up by now, so I went to her room and called but there was no answer. I slowly came to her bed, and she actually had her hands folded palm to palm, placed under the side of her face. Not a blanket was moved, she actually had a little smile on her face, and the peppermint she had placed in her mouth was sitting on the pillow undisturbed. It was so pleasant."

It had been only a year since Sam and Pat prayed with her in the cemetery, and now as they drove back to their church responsibilities in Gary, she reminded him,

"You know, Sam, Grandmaw Martha has been the only grandmother I actually knew in my life. Honey, God has answered our prayer. She will never follow another hearse."

He could not speak in response at that moment. But as he pondered what she said, he had two thoughts circling about in his head. First, he was for the first time in his life without any grandparents. Secondly, he couldn't shake the other part of his mother's dream.

"Why Opal, you've come too."

****

What Sam, Pat, Sammy, and April would in later years recount as their "adventures in moving" seemed more akin to a military family's life. Every two to three years on average, a certain restlessness would seem to pursue Sam. He had an inner desire to see what was over the next hill. This wanderlust led to a series of new towns, new churches, new friends, new schools, and yet there always seemed to be a new excitement that each relocation was an improvement over the previous locale. It was either their willingness or Sam's persuasive salesmanship which had the whole family convinced each move was exactly what God had ordained for them.

They moved from Gary back to Speedway to serve again as Uncle Freddie's youth pastor, but this time with a full salary, housing allowance, and equally shared preaching time.

Sam's passion for sports would be satisfied each spring when the month of May in Indianapolis meant nothing less than what was known as "The Greatest Spectacle in Sports," the Indianapolis 500 mile auto race. Each afternoon found Sam watching the practice sessions, and then he would join over one hundred thousand people at the Time Trials, two weeks before the race. Finally, the Memorial Day holiday would witness the run of the thirty-three fastest vehicles to race five hundred miles on a two-and-a-half-mile oval track to the delight of a quarter million, or more, crazed race fans. There would be higher speeds, and more color and pageantry than any other event in the world. Sam was riveted by the whole affair. He even had in prized possession from the 1970 event, a little article from the Indianapolis Star Newspaper that read, "Perhaps the youngest visitor to the famed track in 1970 has been seven-week-old, Sammy Pawlak."

Returning to Speedway and the famous yearly event certainly had deep meaning to the young preacher and his family. It was here he would finish his studies and be fully ordained by his denomination. And since his folks had moved to a nearby town for work, it meant he could be close enough to look in on Opal as her health deteriorated.

****

The door swung open briskly as Sam entered the apartment.

"Hey, you made it! Look who's here." The exclamations were brought down suddenly by a drastic look of concern.

"What's wrong? Are you alright, Mom?" Even though he did not want to add shock and alarm to where his eyes were fixed, he was utterly stunned as he studied the face and eyes of his Mother.

"She is really sick, Sam." came the first words from his Dad's mouth.

There was that head shake, and the familiar scene of Frank's tongue being protruded from the side of his mouth; the kind of bite that he had seen his dad produce so often in the past. Mostly, it was an expression of stress when Frank would saw a piece of wood, or twist one of Opal's Mason jar canned goods from her garden. But as his dad attempted to help Opal through the narrow apartment door Sam positioned himself on his mother's opposite side realizing she could hardly stand in her own strength.

It was not just her near fainting condition, or even her eyes appearing as if they could not focus, seeming to want to roll upward as would be described as "into her head." What startled Sam the most was the awful color of her face. It was a deep yellow, even more severe than a usual jaundiced infection.

To make matters worse, the little apartment, which Sam had actually helped to build seven years earlier during their first stent in Indianapolis had both bedrooms located upstairs. With all the strength that Frank and his son could muster, they were able to get Opal upstairs, and into the master bed.

"She was not feeling well this morning, and we almost stayed home, but your mom really wanted to spend Easter Sunday with you."

"Yeah, the last time we were together on Easter was seven years ago when I did that first meeting for Uncle Fred." Then the questions began, "Do you think it is her medicine? Did she eat something? Did she get car sick? I know that often happens to her."

Frank shrugged his shoulders, bit his lower lip and said, "Man, I don't know, but I haven't seen her like this."

"Do you think we should try to get her to a hospital and have them take a look?"

"I asked her that, but she said if she can just lay down a little while she thinks it will pass."

Opal stayed in bed the rest of the evening, and took in a little tea and toast late in the night, but they were amazed that by morning she said,

"With a little help, I want to get ready and go to church this morning. I am going to go to Easter Sunday service."

When Opal set her mind to something, the entire family long knew it would take an act of God to stop her. And in spite of her obvious critical condition, she made it to church. The same shock Sam felt at the door the day before was now written on the faces of her brother, Uncle Freddie, as she slowly made it to his church that morning. The questions Sam fielded after the service were all the same,

"Are you sure your mom is okay? Do you think your Mom should have tried to do this today?" and the general consensus of diagnostic opinion, "She doesn't look good, are you sure she is alright?"

She quickly returned to Sam and Pat's bed once home from church and told Frank, "I don't think I can make that hour trip home. Let's just spend the night and then you can get me back, and perhaps to the doctor tomorrow."

Sam, Pat or Frank slept little, if any, that night as Opal's familiar moans seemed as consistent as the spring wind outside each window.

"Do you need us to follow you, Dad?" Sam asked as his Frank guided Opal into the back seat of the station wagon where she could lay down on the pillows Pat had prepared.

"No, I think we can make it." He affirmed. "Her stomach is a little more settled." Then added with a little whisper as to not let Opal hear, "I am going to take her directly to the Hospital when we get back."

Sam nodded and gave a thumbs up in relief.

Over the next month, the family began to digest the entire situation. The Leukemia had elevated to a chronic and terminal diagnosis. Opal returned to her home for only a short time. Opal's only daughter Valery was newly engaged to Dave Dierdorf. He gathered Opal in his muscular arms and carried her to her bed. It would be the last time she slept in her own bed before the ambulance workers negotiated their stretcher down the narrow stairway of the small apartment.

"Hey, Sam. I hate to bother you now with you being at the Hospital and helping with all the family coming by to see Ma, but my wife's grandmother just passed away here in Michigan City last night, and the family was wondering if you could come up long enough to do her funeral service." Older brother, Bud spoke softly on the other end of the phone.

"Yeah. I think so, Bud. Pat is here and she has had some time with Mom. I will take her and the kids back to Indy, and I can drive up tonight, and do the service tomorrow. Then I will get back here with Dad and Mom."

****

"Let's stop at Tamenko's and get us some supper before we head out." Suggested Sam's big brother.

After the funeral service Sam had suggested that his big brother Bud just ride back with him to be with their mother, as it appeared her time was short. They stopped to eat at the truck stop then, Bud assumed one of his favorite after dinner positions. His back to the closed end of the restaurant booth, his long legs and feet stretched the full length of the seat, a fresh cup of coffee in hand, and his newly lighted cigarette in the other.

Sam could not help but think, "Boy he sure is getting awfully comfortable and acting like he is in no particular hurry to get on down the road." The younger brother never liked to sit anywhere for long, and having heard that his mother was comatose and no longer communicating added to his antsy desire to get on down the road. He loved anytime spent with his brother Bud. The stories, the memories, the humor and the philosophies made any session a delight, but he was growing a little impatient that just fifty miles down the road Bud wanted to stop at another old haunt in Monon. Another bite, more coffee, relaxed booth position, and those long, slow and satisfying draws on yet another cigarette made the trip feel even more delayed. It wasn't till after at least two or three more of these unplanned stops that Sam began to see a clear picture of what was going on. "I think I get it. Bud may just be dreading what lay ahead and even the purpose of this journey." With newfound empathy for Bud, he settled down a bit, and decided not to press the issue.

It was well after dark by the time they arrived. Bud and Sam entered their mother's room. Brothers Fred and Dick, and sister Valery were already there, and Manson was just a few miles behind. Bud approached Opal's bedside and observed her eyes now closed, her breathing more strained, and her apparent inability to regain any form of consciousness. Just then, an amazing thing took place.

"Mom, it's me. I'm here." Came the tender words from the strong man with the powerful voice to match. Suddenly Opal's breathing began a rapid increase. Her upper body began to move as her back slightly made an attempt to lift her shoulders. A deep inward moan began to come from somewhere deep in her chest.

"Look. Look, she knows I'm here. She heard me." Bud announced to all in the room, then again softly, and more to himself, with a few tears dropping onto the bed sheet he repeated, "She knows I'm here. She hears me." He turned the words toward her. "I'm here, Mom. I made it. It's alright now."

Valery moved to the side of her big brother, whom she esteemed so highly, and softly laid her head against his shoulder. The tough boys that this strong woman had raised each turned aside toward a different section of the room in an attempt to restrain their own tears and breaking hearts, with a sense that each must stay strong for each other.

Later in the night as the siblings came in and out of the room in a rotation of needed relief, Sam found himself alone at his mother's side. She was always a fighter and even now she was fighting with every breath. Being at the proverbial "death's door" was not an unfamiliar location for her. In her fifty-six years of life, she'd given birth to six children and endured fifty-six surgeries, a major heart attack, and now leukemia. Death had made more than one attempt, only to be set back, and sometimes with no other explanation than "It's a miracle."

"Mom, I don't know if you can still hear me or not, but if you can't I know the God you showed me is listening, and that is why I have to say something." Sam paused to take a deep breath deterring the tears and sobs that were begging to explode from his chest. Recovering that control he made a declaration to both his mother and her God. "Mom, I am your preacher boy. You knew this is what I was made to do, and I promise you Mom, with God hearing, that is what I will be for the rest of my life." Holding her hand to his chest hovered over her, he continued as he surrendered to the onslaught of tears. "I will preach with all I have, and all I am, and anywhere and everywhere that he has a work for me to do." then he added what he thought were rather strange words, "I don't care where this takes me. I promise Mom, I will preach with my last available breath."

The next morning the kind nurse shared the awaited words with the family, "Your Mother has expired."

When Sam heard these words he could not help but think, Pastor James' and Martha's daughter, Kaz' and Mary's daughter-in-law, and the mother of six amazing kids, just one year from her own mother's passing heard her father say,

"Why, Opal. You have come too."

CHAPTER 9 - 1973-1983

From Indianapolis Sam and Pat, with toddlers in tow, returned to the position of Lead Pastor, but this time out of state. They went south to the state of his maternal heritage, and the very county where Pastor James and Martha, his grandparents had first met and married.

Sammy started Kindergarten, and April began to blossom from the shy little girl to a rather outspoken bundle of delightful opinion. On their first Sunday as new pastors, sweet little April, was approached by the elderly former Mayor of the city.

"Well, hello little girl." the southern statesman said kindly.

He was met with a sudden kick directly to an awaiting shin, and a defiant shout, "NO." The old gentleman tried to make the best of it by saying, "Well I bet a big old man like me is a bit scary."

The humiliated parents of this little darling were sure their stay in this church might be their shortest yet.

Daddy took Sammy everyday to the drugstore counter and gave him a nutritionally questionable breakfast of glazed donut and hot chocolate, before walking him to kindergarten. Sam then turned the sugar-loaded package of tyranny over to the unsuspected teacher. There was no ADHD syndrome in those days, just a highly energetic five your old on full sugar overload. To compensate for what April Dawn considered partisan neglect, Sam would often take Sammy for his fix, walk him to the school, and then return to proudly take his little beauty back to the drugstore counter for her own donut of choice and hot chocolate.

Kentucky boasted a tremendous economy from coal and tobacco, and before clean air laws those food counters had as its most notable aura a thick cloud of cigarette smoke.

"Here, April. You sit right up here on this stool, and I will sit beside you. You be sure to say good morning to that nice lady beside you." Sam had no more given her the amiable assignment especially taught and appreciated from children in a place that could be as proper as the Commonwealth of Kentucky, when the rather grandmotherly lady greeted April.

"Good morning, Darling. What brings such a beauty as you out here on this fine morning, may I ask?"

Before April could properly respond, the lady commenced to light up her cigarette, blowing the deeply inhaled cloud in a straightforward and slightly upward direction, as to not blow it down on the pretty little maiden at her side.

"That cigarette stinks." April said, judging the woman.

Before Sam could chide her disrespectful proclamation the dear lady quickly responded, "Well, sweetie, I bet that thing does stink a bit too much." and she quickly began to crush the newly lighted Pall-Mall into the nearest ash tray on the counter.

"My grandpa doesn't smoke." The little girl asserted, though this seemed like an unnecessary editorial to Sam's already visual apology for the verbal spontaneity mixing in the swirl of smoky ambiance.

"Well, you sweet little thing. I am so glad your grandpa don't smoke." came the reply from the assailed victim of the moment.

There was a quiet moment where father, daughter, and lady just stared straight forward not knowing exactly what to say next. April broke the awkward silence, but that with little relief to the moment.

"He's got more sense than that."

The entire food counter of proud Kentucky tobacco-growing entrepreneurs, eavesdropping intently to the encounter burst into uproarious laughter, as the newly educated lady announced,

"Well, that is the first time I have had a four year old preach to me about the evils of smoking."

Little could Sam or Pat know then this little challenger would become, in later years, the epitome of grace, kindness, diplomacy, and tact.

Sam was fully engaged in his responsibilities as the pastor of a historical and prominent church. The city, dominated by a huge courthouse in the center of the town, served as the County seat.

The state of Kentucky had been settled primarily by the Irish and Scottish, so following suit with their former heritage, the county you hailed from was much more important than the city of your birth. Just as an Irishman might proclaim himself from County Cork back in Ireland, so a Kentuckian would much faster let you know he was from Laurel County before he would identify London or Corbin. He might claim Pike County more than Pikeville. So with great pride in not only his Polish heritage, but his mother's ancestry, it was much more of an honor when he was elected the County President of the Ministerial Association. He thought it better than that of a local city government.

The young father spent the best of fun days watching Sammy and April roll down the grassy hills of the local Levi Jackson State Park, and feeling the excitement of his children at their first glimpse of the roaring Cumberland Falls. This was the land of Daniel Boone, the Cumberland Gap, Kentucky thoroughbreds, and Kentucky Fried Chicken.

"Good day, Mr. Magistrate." Sam ascended the large steps at the front of the old and ornate Courthouse.

"Morning, Preacher." responded the long time member of the church, and well known business proprietor of the city.

"What finds you before these beautiful and massive doors of the halls of our County's justice system today?" Sam inquired with what he thought was all the dignity and articulation befitting a true Kentucky Colonel. This term, Colonel was perhaps the most distinguished honorary title that could be bequeathed to a Native Kentuckian whose character and life bespoke citizenship and servitude."

"Well," the answer came quickly, "The sun is shining, the sky is a cloudless blue and it is a beautiful day for a suing."

The old Magistrate, a position somewhat equal to a modern day Justice of the Peace, was simply stating that he had been inside the Courthouse to register and file some documents pertaining to his business dealings. After a good laugh, a hearty handshake, and a mutual pat on the top of each other's shoulder, Sam continued to enter the Courthouse to attend to a little business matter of his own, a speeding ticket the new pastor desperately wanted to keep out of the local eye. It didn't hurt to have a friendship with the influential old gentlemen, who happened to be one of the thirty-three people in the county who personally claimed to have coined the phrase "finger licking good" for Harland Sanders, and his famous recipe of chicken in the State of Kentucky.

****

"I believe that God wants us in Florida by this time next year."

Pat thought for a moment this was another one of Sam's attempts to crack a humorous line in the midst of a challenging circumstance. Then he pulled the ski mask and cap up from his face and she saw a frightening expression. Once the coat, scarf, gloves, and boots were shed in the little breezeway situated between the church parsonage and the back passage way to the attached church facilities and offices, Sam welcomed the hot cup of coffee. He dropped into his large recliner chair to listen to the agony of the approaching weather front being broadcast as an emergency interrupting the normal program of that time-slot.

"That is the third time I have shoveled those sidewalks today, and it is not even 3:30 in the afternoon. Maybe another foot of snow tonight, that could put us over three feet of depth." His tone was becoming more frustrated, and growing to the verge of anger as he verbalized the negatives of another record-breaking Northern Indiana winter storm since having left Kentucky. "That old school bus we use for the church route is now completely covered in snow drifts. Look, you can't even see the bus. That other drift is all the way up to that basketball rim in the parking lot. Man, that is at least ten feet right there.

Pat chimed in. "I tried to take the kids to Sheri's house this afternoon but just walking between the houses we kept falling nearly to our waists in the drifts, and I knew we better turn around and try to get back to the house. I hated it because now we will be stuck in this house for who knows how long?"

"No plow will be able to clean that parking lot, and the News is saying they are closing all roads and streets. They will serve a fine to anyone they catch on the road."

"You're not serious about that thing you said about Florida are you?"

"Right now, this minute, in all this mess, I could not be more serious." Then like the attorney he once aspired to be, he presented another list of undesirable challenges, as if he were giving a closing argument to a jury in the murder trial of the century. "Pat, Last week we couldn't even walk these kids two blocks to Bingham Elementary school, without putting them in so many layers of shirts, pants, sweaters, coats, caps, hoods, gloves, and boots. They could hardly move." Then in a fit of melodrama he shouted, "If they would have fallen down we would not have found their frozen bodies till summer." He expounded on the handcrafted piece of clothing Sammy and April would remember all their days. "And what about those crazy hooded masks you made out of those Gold Medal flour bags? You cut holes in those bags for eye openings and took our kids to school with itchy flour bags over their heads." He even made an attempt at guilt for living in such a horrid place. "It will probably cost us a fortune in psychological therapy to ever get them normal again."

There was a stunned silence for a moment, and after only the sound of the furious howling wind could be heard, the room suddenly exploded with laughter. Sammy and April soon thundered down the stairs to see what all the hilarity was. After their parents could finally control themselves enough to speak again, they assured the kids it was just their dad being dad. They were shooed back upstairs to continue their play.

A few more laughs lingered, then smiles and touches of consolation. The tenor of the room took on a heavy and solemn feel. As they each looked searchingly into each other's eyes it happened. At the exact moment this couple, beginning the third decade of their lives, watched as the other's eyes filled with tears.

"It's not this weather. Is it, Sam?"

They both sat for some time without a word. He cleared his throat, used the heel of each hand to wipe the tears from the corner of his eyes, and began to remove an emotional masking that held even more layers than the previous weather protection laid on the cold cement floor of the breezeway.

"Maybe I should have stayed in Kentucky, but when the committee called and asked if I would consider coming back up here to Mishawaka, I think my heart, my family, and home blinded my reality."

She moved to the large ottoman in front of Sam's chair. As she sat before him, she softly cradled his still cold and red skinned hand in hers.

"I have never been so disappointed with anything in my life." He whispered. Then his real feelings began to open up. "I know even my Superintendent in Kentucky called me when he heard, and begged me not to leave. He said they needed new young blood like mine, and that he saw a great future there for me. He even tried to warn me about coming here. He knew a previous pastor, and told me this was a board controlled church. He even used the words "preacher killer."

Admitting any flawed thinking was always a deep personal challenge to Sam. He saw a disagreement with his view as an assault on his intelligence, or at least on his limited level of education. He began to explain his former reasoning to this faithful partner who he had already uprooted to follow his wandering spirit more than once.

"This church held so much history to me. It was the church that my Grandpaw James launched from, even to the chagrin of my Grandmaw Martha, and my mom. He went from this very church to found and be the first pastor of the church where I grew up. This was the church that held the five caskets for Uncle James' family. This was the church that had the services for Aunt Estelle when she was killed. Uncle Lowell, and Grandpaw, and Grandmaw as well." Then he drilled down to his own personal feelings. "I loved to come here as a kid. It seemed like a big church with that large stage and balcony at the back. Knowing it was the church of my Mother, I knew this church had known greater days and larger membership, but I was sure I was just the guy who could take it back to those days, and even further.

"Honey, you have done great here, and you have done all you could have possibly done." She consoled.

"What more could they have wanted? What more could I have possibly done? What are they thinking? Are they crazy, or what?"
Sam pronounced a listed litany of change, effort, improvement, and growth they had both seen during their tenure as Pastor.
"The attendance has tripled. We have started a preschool that has made money, and we have produced a weekly television program that has paid for itself. We have purchased five homes surrounding the church, and have faithful renters that are paying more than the loans. We have bought over ten prime acres of land on a major thoroughfare for future building, and relocation. We procured a concession stand at the Notre Dame Football Stadium where our youth have used the profits to provide vehicles and equipment for several missionaries around the world, and this has produced a large youth choir of young

people that promise this church another generation of growth and success. And what have I gotten from this leadership council?"

Sam pulled his hand from hers and lifted himself from his chair, pacing from one side of the room to the other as he expressed the broken heart beneath his large heaving chest.

"They have fought me and every new vision I have tried to create for this church. They have run off a great young couple who had directed our preschool and led our youth. Now they want to close the school because it is, according to them, too damaging to our facilities, and not worth the profit margin. They want to stop the television program because, in spite of the fact it pays for itself through donations of friends and viewers, they are afraid that if the money did not come in, the obligation would be 'too unnerving.' Their words, not mine. They want to keep the houses because they see the possibility of making good money there. They said they are sure the church would never grow enough to need that other property, but since we bought it at such a great price we should hang on to it, and they could probably make a 'windfall in time.' Again, their words not mine. They finished the last meeting with their requirements for me. They expect me to begin to downsize all our interests and programs and the main reason is, there are so many new people coming here, and we are growing way too fast. They feel they are losing control of their rightful places of leadership, and they would rather return to the small family atmosphere they had before we came." Sam then said emphatically, "Their words, not mine!"

"Then, what do we do?" Pat softly asked."

"Your pastor wants me to join his organization and start a new church across town, but I just don't think that is my style. I know that a couple of my detractors are gone already, but I don't know if I have enough heart or strength left to fight these powers any further."

She spoke what she felt was the next obvious question. "Do you think you will contact the Headquarters, and see if they might have another church available at this time?" Little did she expect the answer she received as Sam fell back into his original position in the chair and with more anger than hurt said,

"Listen, I can dig ditches to feed my family. I don't need any more of this church stuff."

Pat did not respond but looked out the glass front door into the darkness of the late January afternoon. She flipped the porch light and sadly announced, "Well, your clean sidewalks are all covered again with snow."

While moving toward the kitchen to prepare her family a warm pot of chili, she heard Sam's voice fade off into the air with the words, "I think we will make a little trip to Orlando when the kids get their spring break from school. Disney World would be a good way to finish this rotten winter."

****

"Hello, is this Sam Pawlak I'm talking to?"

The caller on the other end of the line asked, as Sam quickly sat down on the side of one of the large queen-sized beds on the third floor of the large Day's Inn Motel. The voice was so clear and familiar. Like a voice of someone he had heard from childhood up. Distinct, proper, clear, warm, yet businesslike would have been just a few of the adjectives applicable to the setting, yet Sam's brain scrambled through his encyclopedia of thought and memory to recognize the voice in time to assure that he obviously had no idea to whom he was admitting his identity.

"This is an old voice from your past." Without starting one of those aggravating guess who contests, Sam was extremely relieved when the party on the other end of the line announced, "This is Clayton, your old New Buffalo friend."

In absolute amazement, Sam stood to his feet, partly because of the unexpected surprise and somewhat, unconsciously as an act of respect, as if he had been actually standing in front of the great man himself.

"My goodness!" he almost yelled into the mouthpiece of the phone he was squeezing. "Clayton Mulvaney, you might be the last person on Earth I would have expected to get a call from today." He asked. "How did you even know I was here?" and the second part came as fast, "Where are you?" Before the surprise caller could even respond, in an attempt to clarify his inquisition, Sam continued, "I haven't heard from you for years. I really lost track of you, other than I heard that you were somewhere in Florida, but that was a few years ago, at that."

Sam reseated himself on the bed and motioned for the kids to turn down the motel TV. Pat stepped from the restroom having been the last of the foursome to dress herself after their trip to the motel swimming pool. Holding his hand over the speaker of the phone, he whispered to an inquisitive Pat.

"It is Clayton. Remember, from Michigan?" He nodded for her to pull tight the room door as the heavy noise of traffic was producing an early rush hour roar along Orlando's crosstown expressway. This area of the fast growing Central Florida town known as The City Beautiful intersected along a multi-lane street best known infamously as "OBT." This stretch of road had become popular at that time for the multiple, small to large business enterprises that openly and loudly promoted block after block of adult entertainment and fully nude strip dancers. Unfortunately, for Sam and his little family, this was about the only area they could find lodging that would accommodate the budget of a soon to be unemployed minister, and their Spring Break Florida vacation.

Clayton explained to Sam how he had located him.

"Have you ever heard that it is a small world after all? We now live in the area, and I saw a small upholstery shop on Silver Star road this morning, and needed a price for a chair at home. I stopped in and somehow, while talking to the young man who owns the shop, I mentioned we were originally from Michigan, and he asked where." Sam, immediately knowing that his nephew Rocky had moved to Orlando and started an upholstery business began to put a few pieces together When Clayton laid out the rest of the story. "I mentioned we had been in New Buffalo a few years ago and the young man said he was from Michigan City, himself. I told him I knew some families from Michigan City and asked his name and he said, Pawlak. Well, I told him I knew a Frank and Opal Pawlak, and a Manson and a Fred, and a Sam Pawlak. That is when he told me, 'Frank and Opal are my Grandparents, and Manson is my dad, and Sam is my uncle.' I remembered Manson had a little boy named Rocky and I said, 'Surely you're not Rocky, are you?' He assured me he was and added, 'As a matter of fact, my Uncle Sam is in Orlando right now on vacation with his wife and kids.'"

The excited elder preacher finished the mystery by saying,

"I asked him where you were, and he gave me this motel name, and here I am talking to you after all these years!"

Sam figured it had been well over a decade since he had been with the Mulvaney family. He also recalled that the very first service he and Pat had ever conducted just days after their marriage was a youth service for Clayton in the little town of Three Rivers, Michigan. But the family's relationship went much further back than even those days. It was that snowy night, the first winter after Frank and Opal had moved from the Coolspring place to the old farm house on Highway 39, when Clayton and his young son Mike came to meet the Pawlaks for the first time. That night some twenty years earlier was the beginning of these two families starting a new church in the little town of New Buffalo. Clayton was the family's pastor in the little, storefront church in the winter of 1958.

"Why don't we get together while you are in Orlando? I would love to take you to lunch, and both of us could catch up on where we have been over these past years." Clayton suggested.

Knowing that Sammy and April would much rather spend their time in the swimming pool than listening to their parents drone on with some stranger from the past, and knowing Pat would never be comfortable with anyone else attending her young children while in a pool, she recommended that he could meet with the former pastor and old friend by himself.

The socio-economic disparity found in most cities was evident to Sam as he drove from the grungy Orange Blossom Trail to the exquisite sidewalk café in the heart of the neighboring township known as Winter Park.

"So, you have spent the last ten years working as an Evangelist, Youth Pastor, and Lead Pastor, and you are not sure you want to keep doing this type of work?"

The question sounded much more brazen when Clayton summarized and repeated it to Sam. It had taken him the better part of an hour to open up and share from his personal frustration with this old friend, former Pastor, and assured confidant.

The bite of the gourmet sandwich, so elegantly served in a manner the young preacher was unaccustomed to, suddenly became so dry in his mouth he had to quickly reach for the glass of Perrier and wash it down to avoid choking. When he could respond to Clayton's analysis of his unburdened soul he said with a conciliatory tone,

"I feel like I gave it my best, I gave it my all. I worked tirelessly, and not for myself but for their church and their family. And all I got in return was a power hungry, controlling, group of visionless, self-centered characters that would pull a rug out from under me, and only want to downsize or eliminate every successful thing I had accomplished." Then slowing his pace and his rage a bit Sam explained, "So yes, I am going to move my family out of that frozen wasteland and I figure the way Orlando is growing, with Disney and all, I want to be in a place that is progressive, has a future, and is sunny and warm all year long."

"What will you do when you get here?" was the fatherly question from the kind and seasoned voice.

"I am not sure but like I told Pat, I can dig ditches and be happier than this." He continued while wanting to sound more prepared than he was sounding. "Don't misunderstand, I will get the family in a good church and we will get involved, and maybe even be able to help in some areas. I just need to go to church and not have to worry about anything going on, and certainly not have to make the success of the church depend on me."

Clayton said, "You know, Sam I might be able to make a good suggestion about that part of your plan."

"Oh, what is that?"

"I don't know if you know anything about the church I am working at now, but I really want you to visit right away. Maybe even this Sunday, if you're still in town."

"What time is your service?"

"Well, that is hard to say." Clayton said with a little chuckle. "We actually have five services on Sunday."

"Five?" Sam asked incredulously.

"You see, our chapel only seats about 1,400 and we have around 5,000 attendees each Sunday, so we have to have multiple services to get everyone in."

Only at sizable sporting events or music concerts had Sam followed such a line of automobiles into a massive parking lot. He was being directed by a series of parking attendants in orderly guidance to a parking place yet a good distance from the church building.

"This is really big." Pat commented.

"What kind of church is this, Dad?" Sammy questioned while excitedly trying to release his seatbelt and get the car door opened.

"Kids, this is what they are now calling a Mega Church." The father explained. "They run about 5, 000 people every Sunday."

April, already being a little more intimidated by new things than her big brother, softly asked, "Will we be able to stay together, or will they take us kids somewhere else?"

Pat answered in a bit of a calming voice, "We will see when we get up there, but if they have something different for the kids I bet it won't be something you would want to miss."

Before they could get across the property to the church building they were met by smiling greeters and volunteers enticing the kids to come to the children's services in another building. By the time they described the first few planned activities neither Sammy nor April wanted to go to a regular service with their parents.

"There are still some seats available on the main floor, unless you prefer the balcony." said the kind usher with the smart jacket and name tag.

"The balcony will be fine." Sam quickly blurted, but by then Pat was already pulling his arm toward the awaiting door leading into the center Isle of the vast auditorium. To his discomfort, he found himself assertively greeted by another usher.

"Hey folks, I have two great seats right down toward the front. Please come this way."

In spite of his plan to slip in unnoticed from a distance, survey the facilities, and see if this would be a place to consider attending when they made the move that summer, he found himself four rows back on a middle aisle. He was overwhelmed with excited regular attendees extending their welcoming hands and pressing them with everything from visitor gift packets to hugs, and questions like,

"Are you visiting us for the first time today? Do you live in the area?" After each question would come the affirmative declarations, "You're going to love our service; whichever Pastor speaks it will be sensational, the music is the best this side of heaven."

The members of this vibrant church could always spot the first time visitors. They would say, "The visitors are the ones with their mouths hanging open."

Sam felt a little more comfort when the line of pastors marched from a side door to take their places on the stage. He quickly spotted Clayton among them. They were close enough to the front for Clayton to quickly see him, make eye contact, and signal a big thumbs up for the fact they had visited. Although Sam and Pat leaned closely to each other during the service, they could not have been further apart in their reactions to all they saw and heard. Pat was enthralled with the massive choir and excellent orchestra, and she loved congregational singing. She was equally impressed with the liveliness of the service, yet everything had a wonderful structure and carefully planned use of time. While she was totally inspired by the main pastor's preaching ability, Sam's experience was nothing less than a pain filled hour and twenty minutes.

With every presentation of excellence and excitement that swept across the congregation, Sam would voice inwardly an unexpected emotion. "Look at this building. This is what we could have had." These thoughts were followed by, "Our choir was on its way to that. They would have been that someday. Look at this crowd, and they will do this four more times today. The way we were growing, this could have happened as well."
The barrage of comparisons in full assault. "Those big TV cameras right here, broadcasting live from the service. That could have been our next step on Television." Then the combination of mournfulness, anger, and self pity settled somewhere between Sam's gritted teeth. "If it hadn't been for those loggerheads, those small-minded blunder heads, those self-appointed nincompoops."

He remembered every aggravating board meeting. He thought about how many times those committee members had come in from their jobs, shoveled down a sandwich, and vocalized how they hoped the meeting would not last too long, because they had things at home that needed to be taken care of, and still acted like they knew what God would have wanted for their church. After all, he the Pastor had spent hours working, studying, researching, and getting counsel from proven sources about the way to make a church progress.

His mental journey of frustration was pulled back to the present when he heard the name, Clayton. The charismatic and sharply dressed pastor spoke with a sophisticated British accent, and he was doing a teaching new to the young Indiana couple, about the biblical structure of church government and authority. Clayton was hailed to the pulpit to stand by the lead pastor and share a little of his own recent experience of having been limited in his pastoral authority by non clergy members. Sam was suddenly interested in the topic at hand. He also felt a bit of shame that he had bemoaned to Clayton how badly he had been treated by a previous church. He just sat there, hearing Clayton tell how after many more years than Sam had experienced, he was suddenly and without warning fired from his position as Pastor without consideration, consultation or any form of severance. The elder preacher testified that he was now serving as a valuable asset, and gifted pastor where his calling could be appreciated by a church with a visionary leadership.

"I sure hope you enjoyed our service. I see that visitor ribbon on this beautiful lady accompanying you today, and I hope you will come back." The tall handsome, truly southern gentleman soon identified himself as Pastor Jack. Sam did not know he was a pastor on staff, but he did recognize him as the extraordinary organist, who played like no one he'd ever heard before.

"This was a sensational, and much needed experience for us today." Pat softly said while shaking Pastor Jack's large but kind hand.

The smiling broad face turned to Sam again and stated, "Well then, you did enjoy the service."

Sam unconsciously blurted, "I don't know if I mostly enjoyed it or endured it." Just as quickly as the word endured popped from his mouth he saw the startled look on Jack's face. Without a breath, he apologetically injected, "Oh, wait. No, I did not mean that to come out like that. No, no, that is not what I meant. It was great! Wow, you got quite a place here, and yeah, we really were impressed with everything."

Sam did not know if it was Pat's demeanor or just his own quality speaking voice or an unusual sensitivity on the part of a welcoming pastor, but his flow of words were suddenly cut off when Jack placed a hand on his shoulder and asked,

"You're a preacher yourself, aren't you?"

"Well, for at least a couple more months."

Then as if Jack had been reading Sam's personal mail, he came back with one more question, "You're going to be moving here aren't you?" He didn't wait for an answer. "Here is my card. Would you do me a favor? When you get moved in, would you come as my guest to a men's breakfast I have every Tuesday morning in that building right over there? Several hundred businessmen come each week and, if you'll just show my card, your breakfast will be free."

Sam thanked him, and assured him he would come. Jack walked them toward the exit and told Sam, "I want to get to know you, and you will love that breakfast. We have one of the greatest cooks in our kitchen, and her cooking will take your taste buds on a trip to heaven."

The star-dazed couple went to the assigned location to be reunited with their kids. The final deal was sealed as to their new church home when both Sammy and April came running toward them with hands filled with Sunday School material they had received. Both were talking as fast as they could over each other's voice, and begging,

"Can we come here? Can we come back? That was the most fantastic kid's church we have ever been in. Please, please, we want to come here."

As they drove back to the motel Sam finally said. "Well, I guess we found a church, now if we can just find a house to move to."

****

It was a sunny and beautiful day, but there was still a hovering atmosphere of disappointment. Pat cried as she hugged her neighbor who had become such a good friend. Sammy and April said their goodbyes to the neighbor kids and took their seats in the new Chevy Caprice Classic. They fixed their eyes one more time on the back of the familiar U-Haul truck, with what would be another "Adventure in Moving." Sam's anger at the difficult church leaders had slipped down to a simple heartbroken reminder that in life your "dreams come true" can become nightmares you didn't see coming.

The big new apartment was wonderful. The fact that the large swimming pool sat right outside of the master bedroom only added to the excitement of being again in the sandy-shoed paradise that this family loved so dearly.

Getting back to the wonderful church was a spiritual and emotional healing which gave the weary couple a sense of full recovery from past challenges. The only unexpected twist to their happy relocation was finding a job presented for them two distinct challenges. One: the pay scale in the area was nowhere near that of even the most menial employment in the union controlled labor of the industrial midwest. Secondly, in the time before the era of diversity, Sam was considered "too heavy" to even get a grass-cutting job at the largest employer of the area, Walt Disney World. The search for gainful employment was so unsuccessful that the only job he could get with enough income to meet his obligations, and put food on the table was hard, manual, and physical labor, working for an underground company installing heavy water systems and fire hydrant systems. With a mixture of humor and sad truth, he would say to others during that time,

"Be careful what you say you're willing to do or not do. God may be listening, and He has a pretty good sense of humor also. I said I could dig ditches to feed my family."

So as would be the case, Sam found himself everyday, standing waist deep in water in a 97 degree, 97% humidity, burning Florida sunshine, digging ditches from early sunrise until evening for an hourly wage. One additional blessing that came their way when Pat was hired at the church to work with that wonderful cook. She would clean baptismal robes each week, and help serve tables at the daily cafeteria open to the church staff, consisting of seventeen pastors and 130 employees.

After a few weeks of the low-paying ditch digging, Sam thought is best to return to the role of itinerant preaching. Fortunately, opportunities were still available for him to conduct extended services in several churches back in the midwest. The speaking honorariums did provide a better source of income for the family, but the weeks away from Pat and the kids were hard on all of them.

"Pat, with your husband out traveling so much we would really like for you to come be a part of our fellowship group."

The invitation came from the recognizable tall, blond man she'd seen in that last row of the choir every Sunday.

"Tell me a little bit about it." she replied.

Tom brought his wife Charlotte over, and after making introductions explained, "As you have probably heard a lot from our pastor, there is just no way to care for the size congregation we have here without a number of small groups. They meet each week to build relationships and do just that, care for each other. We call these home meetings "Fellowship Groups," and about 2,600 of our 5,000 members meet in one of these groups each week."

Pat explained that Sam was on the road most of the time, but if she could line up someone to watch the kids, it might be something she would really like to join. It became more of just a weekly get-together, but the group helped her really begin to connect with new and wonderful friends who helped her deal with the loneliness while Sam was away.

Sam dreaded each time he had to leave. It hurt when he would return and see how fast his children were growing and changing without him there. Then the unexpected happened.

"Hello. Yes, this is Sam." His response to the lady's voice was with the preconceived notion that it was probably a pastor's secretary inquiring about a future speaking engagement. He was taken back a bit when she identified herself.

"This is Pastor's secretary." In this case the term pastor could mean only one person, the lead pastor of the mega church they were attending. She continued with little fanfare. "Pastor is going to be traveling to Yugoslavia in November, and he would like to ask you to speak at one of the Sunday morning services while he is gone."

He shook his head in disbelief and said, "But he has never heard me speak before. I am honored, but a little surprised with all the wonderful speakers you have there."

"I am sure he has done his research." she quickly said, and added, "He would like you to do Sunday November 12th, and he would like you to speak at the 9:45am service. That is the largest service, and the service that we televise each week. Would that work for you?"

Sam already had his trustworthy pocket calendar opened to November, and was already hoping that it would be the one Sunday he had no prior engagements. "Yes, of course. I would be so honored. Please let me know anything I should for that service."

She laughed a little and said, "The only thing you need to know is you will have from 10:22 am to 10:50 am, and not a second after that, because we have to clear the building and parking lot to get the next crowd in for the 11:30 service."

"Thank you so much, and please thank the Pastor as well. I will be ready." Sam assured as he slowly hung up the phone.

When that Sunday finally came, Pat and the kids were there on the front so the whole family could be introduced. What made the day even more meaningful was that Clayton was the one to introduce them with warm memories of Sam, Pat and his family from the past.

The audience was wonderfully responsive to the speakers, and this day was no different, as he preached with everything he had. And as Pastor Melvin used to say, "Sam rang the bell."

Things started to change for the young Pawlak family. A series of events began to unfold. The wonderful fellowship group saw the strain it was taking on Pat to have her husband away, and they began to pray with her that an opportunity for local work would present itself. One of the group members intervened. He offered Sam a job back in Orlando that would meet their needs and put the family together again. Within a few days, Sam cancelled his speaking engagements, and began to drive a big eighteen wheel propane tanker around the State of Florida. The hours were long, but he was home each night.

"I do appreciate you going to work so early to help us for this time." Sam said lovingly to Pat in the dark Tuesday morning quietness of the church parking lot. Tuesday mornings meant two things at the church, Pastor Jack's men's breakfast, and the Luncheon meeting of the church leadership.

This board consisted of the staff pastors, and was a new approach to church government, in which the pastors were the policy makers for the organization. Any major decision involving bylaw items or large financial issues would be presented to the church membership, as a whole. This new paradigm in corporate structure authorized decisions to add or remove pastors to the leadership team. That particular group was meeting that day.

Sitting in the car, the couple shared some deep feelings about their future from some previously unspoken corners of their hearts.

"I really wish something could happen where you could get off of that dangerous tanker truck, and get back to using your pastor skills. I'd love for it to be here in this great church. I know our fellowship group has made it a matter of prayer. They would love to see you on staff here as well."

Sam made a rather brave and surprising statement when he said, "Honey, from the time I preached here in November I guess I have really wished something like that could happen too. But in a place like this it usually takes years to work your way into that kind of position."

"You know, the board is having their lunch and meeting today. We could always pray and ask God to bring us to someone's attention on that board. Maybe they could see a place where you would be of help here."

He reached across the seat and took her by the hand. She prepared for him to use his logical reasoning to dismiss the small probability of such a thing happening. She was surprised when he just closed his eyes and began to speak.

"Lord, we are your children, and you know our hearts. We are going to ask you to do something beyond ourselves. We ask that while the board meets today, would you please allow our name to come before them? Would you place the idea of bringing us on the staff of this great church as one of their pastors? Amen." When he finished he said, "Well, I hope it is not too presumptuous to ask God to make us one of the pastors of the fastest growing church in America."

She got out of the car and laughed. "You know, Pawlak. You just don't know how to go after anything unimportant, do you?

"Hey, I went after you. Didn't I?" He smiled.

Pat leaned back into the car for one more kiss. "Remember, tonight is the staff Christmas party. I will be working through, but you get to come as my date. My boss is letting me off early to be with you at the party."

Sam entered the hall, so beautifully decorated for the large staff party. The seasonal sounds of music were wonderful and the smell of the food that the kitchen staff had prepared was divine. Suddenly to his surprise, the lead pastor moved quickly to greet him near the door.

"Hey there, Doc." The charming Brit said with a warm smile and a firm handshake. This was a word the pastor loved to use more than Bugs Bunny.

"Hello, Pastor Roy. Merry Christmas!"

"Yes, yes. Merry Christmas. So glad you could be here with us tonight. Say, what are you doing these days, Sam? Are you still driving a truck for Lou?"

"Only about sixty hours a week." They both laughed, and the pastor asked,

"Could we get together for a few minutes after this thing is over tonight?"

"You bet." Sam said without hesitation.

He knew Pat would be cleaning up after the party, and he'd be hanging around waiting anyway.

"Listen, Doc..." The man pulled up a folding chair from the nearest table, and motioned for Sam to do the same. "I need to talk to you about something. The Board met today, and we are in need of expanding our Pastoral Counseling department with three more pastors. Your name came up, and we would like to know if you would consider coming on our staff full time at the first of the year." He then added, "After I heard that tape of your message you preached in November, I also want you to be one of our preaching pastors, filling the pulpit on a rotating basis in my absence."

This all came so fast and so unexpected, but Sam's mind quickly went to the darkness of that very morning, and the simple, yet brazen prayer that he and Pat had prayed together.

"Pastor, let me think about that." He took a short breath, and smiled. "Ok. I've thought about it. Yes. I would be thrilled to serve you in any way."

About the same time. Pat came across the room having finished her tasks in the kitchen.

"Patsy, meet our newest pastor on staff." Pastor Roy announced as she approached. After a hug for them both, he said "...And we can't have one of our Pastor's wives still working in that kitchen, so we are going to take care of you so you are free to be what your husband needs at home and in his ministry."

As the three walked down the hall toward the exit Sam and Pat again expressed their appreciation for this opportunity.

"Pastor, we are so blessed and grateful for this chance you've given us." Sam offered.

"We feel like we are the fortunate ones." The warm gentleman replied. "In fact, we want you so much that I am going to give you your first day off with pay." They all laughed when they remembered no one would be working on New Year's Day 1979.

****

The months to follow were filled with the excitement of long days, and a fresh, dynamic world that made Sam want to pinch himself. Is this really happening to me? Why am I the one who fell from the proverbial pile of fertilizer into this mountain of roses? The summer would be consumed with late night swims where he and Pat could relax in the corner of the lighted pool, and soak in the entertainment of what they called their "little polly-wogs."

Quite often after dinner, they would drive out the few miles to one of the Disney World resort hotels. They would pick up a couple of the Frosty desserts from Wendy's, pay fifty cents for parking, and find themselves sitting in the beach sand along the beautiful man-made Disney lake, and enjoying the lighted water parade. The kids always insisted on staying to see the nightly fireworks display.

In spite of what the Pastor had said to Pat pertaining to her work in the church kitchen, nowhere was she happier than serving others. It also opened an opportunity, as one of the Pastor's wives, to reach out and help, counsel, and pray with many of the staff members and fellow employees. To add to the joy of the busy schedule was a regular cornucopia of programs, productions, and events found only in this sized operation.

Serendipitously, Sam's office was the former office of his old friend, Clayton who would be moved nearer the executive offices. On top of that, the office was right next door to Pastor Jack, the multi-talented man he'd met in the vestibule of the church on their first visit, almost a year before. The offices on the other side of his would be the workshops for two young peers near his age. Sam could never have imagined the day this trio of characters shared their first lunch at a local "greasy spoon" restaurant, they would become dearest friends and confidants. Rick, Larry, and Sam loved each other's humor, talents, and like-mindedness. Their wives became immediate and dear friends, and inasmuch as their children were all close in age, they spent a great deal of time at each other's homes, out on deep sea fishing boats, or playing sandlot football games in their yards, local parks, or beautiful Daytona Beach.

****

"Ok kids, this is where you will be attending school, and this is what is going to happen." Sam reversed the papers so both could look across the kitchen table to their new school plans. Pat explained some more details as they looked over the materials.

"Right out here, in front of the apartment complex, the school bus will pick you up each morning. Now it will be about a half an hour to get you to school and back each day."

"But I thought we would go to the school right up the street here." Sammy queried.

"No, there is a program now in many cities that is referred to as school bussing." Their dad replied.

April interjected, "What does that mean?"

Sam and Pat slowly looked at each other and in an effort to not sound concerned, Pat softly said, "Your dad can explain it better than I can."

He gave her a little smile that said "Thanks a lot, Mom." But he did quickly try to explain. "Well kids, sometimes, as cities grow, people sort of end up with their families and friends mostly living in the same area." He cleared his throat and said, "For example, where I grew up most of my neighborhood were Polish kids whose parents or grandparents had come from Poland. Mom grew up in the country so most of the people that lived there were farmers." Then wanting to be very wise, he began to move the example to a racial understanding, wishing that phrase was more of a reality than it often appeared. "Now, in big cities like Chicago, New York, or Boston, or even Orlando, over time some neighborhoods became predominantly White, or Mexican, or Chinese, or Black." Then he asked, "Do you understand?" They both nodded in the affirmative. "Well," he breathed out slowly. "When one neighborhood, for example has only White kids and another only has Black kids, it makes a problem. See, if the White kids never go to school or church or belong to clubs where there are black kids, then they never make any friends with black kids, and that is really sad. And let me ask you guys, why do you think that would be sad?

For a moment Sam was a little disappointed, and hoped they just did not understand what he was saying when they both, shrugged their shoulders and said,

"I don't know."

But a tremendous relief came when the 8 year old Sammy said, "But we're not really different, are we Dad?"

April quickly chimed in, "It's just our skin, like our color, right? That is the only difference in me and a black kid, isn't it?"

Sam jumped in, "Of course, you're exactly right, but not everybody understands that, and so some people believe if white children and black children would have the opportunity to go to school together, know each other, and play together, people would see it can be, and should be a wonderful experience." He looked to Pat for approvable and reinforcement.

"This neighborhood..." she explained, "is mostly white kids and Spanish kids, so they are going to pick up you white kids and take you to a neighborhood that has mostly black kids. They will also pick up kids from that neighborhood and bring them to this area. It is a big word called Integration. It means putting different people of different races together, so we can all learn from each other, and get over our prejudice toward each other."

"What does that word prejudice mean?" April asked. The nervous mom looked toward her husband to take that one.

"It simply means that somebody thinks they are better than someone else. They think they are smarter, or richer, or better because they have a different color skin."

"Where did that idea start?" Sammy quizzed.

Sam and Pat both looked at each other with grimaced faces. They remembered their own journey, as children of the sixties, watching the battle for American civil rights unfold before their own eyes. Sam quickly flashed back to a vivid memory of that era.

"Hey, Willie! Aren't you making a big trip this week?" came the question from the lead barber at the Spaulding Hotel barber shop.
"Come on Willie, tell us where you going."

Sam slightly allowed his eyes to look toward the left and waited for the friendly young Black man in the corner to respond. The thin figure of the "shoe shine boy," a title meant for the job, but often used to describe the man, never looked up, but just kept rapidly slapping the cloth back and forth across the toe of the freshly polished Oxford shoes, worn by a local municipal judge.

"Naw Sir, rather not say, Sir." was the soft reply.

Sam began to realize the question from his barber was more of a ridiculed challenge than a legitimate question. The words came again.

"Aw, come on Willie. You can tell all of us here. Tell us about that big trip you got planned." The Barber smiled as he chided.

With a bit of an uncomfortable plea, the young man answered back. "Naw sir, I don't believe I care to talk about that right now."

With a sarcastic laugh, the man's tormentor announced to all in earshot, "Willie here has a big plan this weekend. You see, there is this bus coming down from Detroit. Willie is going to take what they call a 'Freedom Ride' all the way down from D.C. to New Orleans with some of his friends, that is his colored friends. Right, Willie? Guess they are going to grab themselves some freedom down there."

Sam was just a thirteen year old boy himself and he really did not understand what they were even talking about. He just knew there was a tremendous discomfort in the room. The room was filled with hilarious laughter, hoots and howls as if some great joke had been told, but He was wondering what was so funny. Willie soon finished with his customer, and having no one next in line he stepped outside for a break from the smoke filled shop. After moving along the large windows that fronted the barber shop, Sam noticed Willie attempting to light a cigarette. He felt troubled deep inside when he saw Willie's hands shaking so severely that he could hardly light his cigarette.

"Thank you, son." Said the barber as Sam placed the fifty cent piece in the man's steady hand and added another dime for a good tip. As the teen exited the door and started the short walk home he said,

"You have a good day, Willie."

As Willie started back to the shop, he looked straight at Sam, deep into his eyes, and never offered even a grunt. The naive teenager thought to himself, "Huh, what's his problem?"

Monday evening the national news telecast, moderated by Opal's favorite newsman, showed pictures and told of an incident that had happened along a stretch of Highway in rural Alabama. The photos displayed a huge Greyhound bus totally ablaze as the results of a fire bomb being thrown by a mob through a window of the non air-conditioned bus.

Sam rode his Montgomery Ward's bicycle on his telegram delivery route that Monday, after school. He felt compelled to stop by the barber shop and check on Willie. Not seeing him, he asked his regular barber,

"When does Willie get back?" His mouth grew dry and he felt like he had just been slugged in his belly when the answer came back,

"Oh, that dumb fool got himself beat up and thrown in jail down there."

"Sam, did you hear what Sammy just asked you?" He was startled back from his memory of the past and tried to gather his thoughts. He spoke rather slowly and softly.

"Well Sammy, unfortunately, that idea has been passed down from the beginning of time, and sadly probably from grandparents, to parents, to kids." Then Sam realized he may have never been asked that question before and he saw an opportunity to hopefully instill a thought to his own children. "You know, if you think about prejudice, what might surprise you is that if it started anywhere it probably started, of all places, at the throne of God."

The kids' stares became blank and Pat turned her head in a way to say,

"What are you saying?"

"Let me explain what I mean by that. You see if you look at what the Bible says, you read that before anything was even created, even before there was an Earth, God was already in Heaven, and there was this big old angel up there. His name was then called Lucifer. He got the idea to overthrow God and take over Heaven. God threw him out of Heaven instead."

"I don't think I understand." April stated.

"OK," Sam searched for words to explain a complicated theological belief so his seven year old could understand. "You see that Angel, Lucifer thought that he was better than God, and he was smarter than God, and he probably thought he was better looking than God, so he should run everything. He even said he would raise himself above God." Seeing understanding in her eyes, he decided to continue. "So here is what happened, this Lucifer guy gets thrown to Earth. Now, we know him by a different name. We know him as Satan, or the Devil. Since he is really mad at God and wants to destroy the best thing God ever made, humans. The way he would like to do that is to convince humans to think like him. In other words, get them to think they are better than someone else because they are richer, or smarter, or better looking, or stronger or even a better color of skin than someone else."

The kids seemed to accept what they were hearing, and quickly changed the subject to the play at hand. Pat encouraged Sam that he'd done a good job with a difficult subject, and they were content for the moment that they were breaking with prejudices of the past to set a new trajectory for their children and their future.

As for the bussing, Sam was never sure if it helped the situation, but he was thankful that this experiment in integration in their city had no significant problems as some of the other cities had experienced. The children did well in school. They made many friends, and did not recognize the ugly behavior that accompanies prejudice from any of the students, staff, or parents.

April came home from her second grade class and told Sam and Pat that her new friend Orangie had informed her that Justice, another little boy of African descent, declared he was going to marry April.

The parents asked April, "Well, what did you tell him?"

"I told him, "I can't marry you. . . I'm not old enough to get married yet."

The couple told her they were very happy that she understood she was not old enough to marry Justice, but in their hearts they were much happier that she knew of no other reason that previous generations would have given her.

****

As the massive church congregation grew, on almost a weekly basis, it required a constant tweaking and readjusting of assignments and responsibilities for the large team of pastors and support leadership.

"How do you feel about your new post today?" Pat asked Sam as they slowly walked across the church campus. She was heading toward the kitchen, and he headed toward the little chapel against the sound barrier wall that divided the property from the busy interstate highway.

"I know it is just a small group of people, and they are rather hidden over there in that little building, but prayer is still one of the most important activities In the life of a church. I am glad that Pastor Jack thought enough of me to ask me to take this part of his portfolio." Then he laughed a bit.

"What? What is funny?"

"Maybe it is because the gathering is primarily older people and senior citizens." Then he laughed again and continued, "Do you think that the leadership just thinks that I appear to be a little more old school and I fit with that group better?" She faced Sam squarely and grasped his large, upper arms.

"No. It is because they know you know how to pray, and inspire others to pray. You always make prayer very personal like you are having a conversation with God." Sam tilted his head, raised his eyes, and cracked a little smile as she said soberly, "What I love about your prayers is that when you pray it feels like you really expect to hear God say something back to you." He gave her a big hug as they parted.

"Have a great day." He said. "See you at lunch. God and I have to go do some talking. Oh, and remember tonight is Wednesday. Pastor wants me on the platform tonight, so I probably won't see you till after church tonight."

Compared to the five thousand who gathered each Sunday, this small group of less than sixty retirees became a highlight in Sam's busy schedule. Each week he would open with a small scripture reading and then turn it over to the group to find a comfortable place for about a half hour of personal prayer. Some would simply sit quietly at their place with their head bowed and perhaps some slight movement of their lips as they communicated to the God they professed. They did not recite memorized words or read scripted prayers, but they held personal conversations with, what they believed was a divine personality who was listening. Others who were physically capable were kneeling at one of the two long wooden benches in the chapel, praying in their unique style. A few of these were at times a bit more vocal, and saw no disrespect in praying at a low but audible volume that produced a mixture of rumbling sounds, not so different from other religions' softly repeated mantras. There were still a few individuals who expressed their intercession in a much more passionate and exterior fashion. This approach took on a bit more of a high school pep rally expression than those enjoying their quiet meditation. It was not uncommon for these persons to walk about the chapel, sometimes with both hands raised upward, and at a much higher level of voice, exuberantly proclaiming the values of the object of their worship. They passionately pleaded with the Most High to respond to a personal crisis or perceived need of the church congregation as a whole.

Following this time of individual prayer Sam called the group to order and began to share from a weekly printed list containing particular requests that they could pray over in a united style. These items ranged from grave illnesses, challenged marriages, financial pressures, major decisions, employment needs, local civic issues, national government issues, protections for family members in the military, missionaries and charity workers throughout the world, prayers for the leadership of the church, and a concluding request for more converts who would become active members of this great church.

When the corporate prayer time was concluded, Sam addressed the faithful group.

"Remember folks, everything we've done today has been directed toward Heaven. Let's take the last ten minutes in quiet meditation to listen to thoughts that might come in a return direction from the Lord."

He walked to one of the two small upholstered chairs on the little stage, and knelt and with folded hands. Quietly he pondered the prayers of the day and listened for an idea, feeling, inspiration, or insight that he could conclude as a small inner voice of the God to whom he prayed. He only wanted to hear God in an inner voice. He was sure if he ever heard an audible voice his next step would be serious therapy.

That particular day Sam ended his listening a little sooner than some others, so he stood from his kneeling position and sat quietly in the small chair. After the last few ended their quiet time, he felt it appropriate to pray the benediction and dismiss those gathered. He lingered a while and looked over the small empty chapel which seated less than a hundred. In this space representing such humble beginnings for the expanding mega ministry. As he perused the small crowd, he could see that all appeared to be finished praying, and they were waiting on him to give the benediction. For a moment he felt like he should not yet move, so he waited quietly, head bowed, hands folded, fingers entwined with index fingers gently placed at his chin.

Then it happened. The small single door at the side of the building, directly to his left, opened suddenly, and the burst of midday Florida tropical beams streamed against the carpeted floor. He quickly studied the opened doorway to see who was coming in but he could see no one. Just as quickly he scanned the awaiting congregation, but no one seemed to notice the startling opening of the door. Within a millisecond of time, what seemed to the bewildered preacher as a rather surreal event unfolded. He heard a voice. To his immediate surprise he noticed several things it was not. It was not a spooky voice. It was not an amplified voice in an echo chamber, not the voice of dynamic actor or orator, but a voice as common and clear as if the Pastor had opened the door and said,

"Are you done in here, Sam?"

Or as if Pat herself would have opened the door to ask,

"Are you ready for lunch yet?"

It could have even been as simple a voice as his Dad, waking him on a Saturday morning to say,

"Hey Sam, want to go to the pier and get a mess of perch this morning?"

It was calm, settled, somewhat peaceful, kind, yet serious. It was not so much the voice that had his attention, but rather what the voice said.

"I have a work for you to do in Poland."

He felt his lungs suck in a short gasp of air. Dropping his head and holding his breath for a moment, he either heard the words again, or he was rehearsing them in his mind. He was not sure which. He lifted his head to see the faces still looking at him for his next move. He slowly turned his eyes to the left to see no sunlight, and the door was tightly closed as it had been since he had entered an hour earlier.

Did I doze off? Did I fall asleep for a moment? Was I having a short dream? Did something just happen in my imagination?

He asked a series of questions in this self-interrogation.

Poland? Poland? What the heck does that mean? Poland...what do you even know about Poland? Then the inner dialogue started answering. My grandfather came from Poland, my ancestry is Polish. Yeah, but that is the story of half of my hometown. I don't know anything about Poland. Seemed like a good place to start a World War, but Poland? What is that all about...Poland?

"I have a work for you to do in Poland." He repeated it very slowly. "I-have-a-work-for-you-to-do-in-Poland. I HAVE A WORK FOR YOU TO DO IN POLAND. I...have...a...work...for...you...to...do...in...Poland."

Sam thought it best to just shake it all off for now, and certainly not tell anybody about this whole event. They would probably have him seeing a psychologist immediately. He gathered himself and quickly prayed a little prayer of dismissal, and decided a little fresh air was due.

"Hey, come on in, Sam. I want you to meet our guest speaker tonight." Pastor Roy sort of pulled him from the office door toward the stranger sitting on the large leather sofa. Before Sam could cross the room, the tall, thin gentleman stood with hand extended as the Pastor made the formal introduction.

"Sam, this is our guest, Pastor Melker Engstrom. He is here from Sweden, where he pastors a marvelous church." Then he turned and said, "Dr. Engstrom, this is one of our fine associate Pastors, Sam Pawak."

Without even as much as a nod or "nice to meet you," the sharply dressed Swede responded, "Pawlak? That is a Polish name, is it not?"

"Yes sir, it is. My Grandfather came from Poland."

The Pastor looked at his watch and announced, "Sam will be helping with the service tonight, giving some announcements and welcoming the visitors. We'd better get out there. Oh, and Dr. Engstrom, you will be sitting on the side next to me until I introduce you to speak."

The music was its usual vibrant and exciting level when the three men walked into the standing room only auditorium. Pastor and his guest arrived at their seats on the stage, and Sam came to his at the far side of the vast platform. As would be the normal pattern of the service, they remained standing in front of the large high back chairs, while the audience also stood and sang with excitement and energy. They clapped their hands to a highly rhythmic selection, as there were not many songs selected from the hymnals, which were in the holding shelf attached to the back of each pew. A huge motorized screen had been lowered from the ceiling at the back of the stage, and lyrics were projected. The congregation was free to clap to the faster songs, and perhaps wave their hands and arms up and back to the swaying rhythm of the slower thought provoking choruses. These were markers of a more contemporary worship form. While this participatory sing-a-long was under way, Sam began to grow a bit uncomfortable and self conscious. This was brought on by the fact that every time he looked in the direction of the Pastor and the guest speaker, he noticed the tall, skinny Swede staring directly at him from across the large stage. With each eye contact it seemed the stare grew stronger. Sam attempted to look away and intensify his singing or hand clapping, as if he had not noticed himself the subject of the good Dr. Engstrom's burning gaze.

It came time for the leaders on the stage and the attendees in the crowd to raise their hands upward and, in concert, vocalize their praises toward the heavens. Sam tried to slip open one eye and see if the Swede was still staring. Sure enough, he was still bearing down on Sam from across the platform. Sam was growing so uncomfortable with this attention that he sent up a little prayer.

"Dear God, please get that weirdo to stop staring at me so I can enjoy this service." And then as if to clarify his request he informed the Almighty, "I don't know what that guy's problem is, but he just can't be right."

The music slowed and the atmosphere became a bit more settled when Sam took the chance of looking one more time to see if that strange man was still glaring at him. He was shocked to see the man had left his seat and was walking in Sam's direction. Worse than that, it was soon obvious that the fixation had elevated far beyond the expected. Engstrom reached Sam, moved within inches of Sam's face, reached up and straightened his own, silver rimmed bifocals. If Sam had felt uncomfortable before, now it was almost unbearable when he felt a not so light pain in his breastbone, the product of a long skinny index finger repeatedly poking his sternum. A heavily Swedish accented voice proclaimed more as an order than a statement, ten words that would change Sam's life forever.

"Gott haas a verk fer you to do in Poland!"

The tall Swede said it only once, turned and walked briskly back across the stage, took his seat and never looked in Sam's direction again.

He could not stand. He was trembling and trying to grasp what had just happened. Those are the same words I heard this morning. What in the world is this all about? What does this even mean?

Every step felt like a slow walk through a deep fog as he somehow performed his assigned duties of the service. Later, he realized he had not really heard one word the guest speaker gave in his sermon that night. He was very relieved when the guest came quickly to him upon the dismissal.

"I have several contacts in Poland, and I can get you many churches where you can preach." The gentleman continued to explain, "With a Polish name, and coming from America people would be excited to hear you. You see, your name is a very common name in Poland; many Pawlak's there. The fact you have this old Polish name and yet you are protestant instead of Catholic, many will want to hear your story. We have a new group of Catholics in Poland, they are called Charismatic Catholics and I could get you with many of these groups." Then he said it again, "Yes, God has a work for you to do in Poland."

The two ministers hugged each other, assured they would continue to communicate. Plans would be made to get Sam to Poland. They parted and Sam stood alone on the stage and wondered what this day was all about.

"Pawlak, this is Engstrom calling from Sweden. How are you?"

"I am fine. Glad to hear from you. I'm so looking forward to getting to Poland."

"Sam, I know it has been better than a year since we started talking about your coming, and I do have some wonderful opportunities for you, but that is what I am calling about."

The delay in the overseas call meant you had to make sure the other person had finished their statement before you responded or you would be stepping all over each other's words, and it would become a difficult conversation. He said nothing but waited for his caller to finish. The Swede continued.

"Have you been watching the news, or at least the BBC?"

After Sam waited for the appropriate pause he then responded, "Yes, I saw something about some problem in Poland, maybe Gdansk or the ship yards or something." He waited again for the voice from the other end.

"Yes, there has been a huge uprising with the union workers in the shipyards of Gdansk, but it is really leading to demonstrations all over the country. It is probably going to get pretty bloody before it gets better."

"What effect does that have on our plans to come that way?" Sam asked and waited what seemed like a long time, and finally asked, "Are you there, Doctor? Are you still there?"

"Yes, yes, brother. I am here. Well, as to your question and coming, I will tell you this, I went down from Sweden to Gdansk a few days ago, and I saw a lot of military. I even saw some Russian tanks on the road. One of the leaders of the city told me that he thinks it will be a real blood bath like the spring uprising in Prague several years ago." After another long pause the man continued to tell Sam, "When I asked the leader and some church officials what they thought about our plans at this time, they had one concern. Your name is Polish, and probably not too difficult to get you into the country. Especially if we do anything with the Catholics. Even the Soviet government doesn't want to deal with the power of the Catholic Church too much in Poland. However," he continued slowly, "Getting you out of the country again could pose a problem if this situation becomes bad."

"Why is that?" Sam inquired.

"For example, if the Russians come in no one will be able to travel till this is settled. Or even if the Prime Minister here, Jaruzelski, were to declare Martial Law, then no one would get in or out." He added, "With you having small children to raise I would just say, if you believe God wants you to come and you might be fine. In all honesty, you better know it is God because you could end up with a prison ministry in Siberia."

They both laughed a little nervous, but thought provoking laugh.
After some more long paused conversation, they agreed that maybe it would be best to watch the events. It was the historic 14th day of August in 1980 when 17,000 workers seized control of the Lenin shipyard in Gdansk, and their burley mustachioed leader Lech Walesa, began a strike that literally changed the world.

One powerful word became the name of a workers union in the Soviet controlled nation, the former home of a little boy named Kaz. That word would cause Sam to lose his contacts with Poland, and he not hear about his coming to Poland again for twelve long years. That one word would hold an almost sacred place in his heart for years to come. SOLIDARITY.

****

Inasmuch as the talk of Poland was put on hold, and the Cold War between the United States and Russia seemed to change in intensity from day to day, Sam and Pat settled into their good and fulfilling life as a young family. It was music that served as the medium which brought the couple together in the first place, and now in their exciting church, new opportunities were presenting themselves, from the massive choir and orchestra performing weekly, to the large-scale seasonal theatrical presentations. For Sam's liking, the latter held the greatest appeal. He had been captivated by what theater performers called "the smell of the greasepaint, and the roar of the crowd." His ability to memorize lengthy portions of script as well as sing in high school led to his being cast in leading roles in church and school. He had even filled the role of professor Harold Hill in "The Music Man."

Now in Orlando, he was selected to fill a small role in the church production about the life of Christ. He portrayed the apostle known as "Doubting Thomas." His powerful voice, near operatic quality, and dramatic stage presence opened an even greater role as the lead character and narrator. The grand production evolved over the next couple of years into an annual event hailed by the entire community. With a full pit orchestra and a cast of over a hundred, it outgrew the church setting and was housed in the largest theater venues in the region, and eventually played in the Queen's Theaters in England.

What was gaining Sam's and Pat's attention during those formative years was not so much their own activities in filled auditoriums, but what they saw unfolding in the lives of their children. The Children's Department in the mammoth church was able to create choirs and musical presentations, for kids at nearly the same level of impressiveness as the adult community. It was not long before Sammy and April were garnering more and more exposure among the young performers. A third generation of familial talent was starting a journey toward their own musical futures. The proud parents stood in awe as applauding crowds would howl and cheer at the excellent gifts of their son and daughter.

This was such a fulfilling time and place for the Pawlak family, which only made the next unusual turn of events seem far beyond bazaar, and stretched their minds to the limits of what is thinkable.

****

"We are just asking if you would be willing to come on out here for a couple days, and look over our situation and talk with us. I mean, you sure know some things about starting up a church and making it grow. That is why we are looking to a place like your church to maybe give us some advice and direction." The young plantation owner and former Vietnam helicopter pilot made the following suggestion, "If you could fly to Memphis, I could fly up there with my eight seater Commander and pick you up, and bring you down to my place. We have our own air strip out here."

The suggestion to consider another church assignment far away from Central Florida had come from some sweet Southern members of their megachurch who were concerned for their grown kids in rural territory with loggerhead turtles, copperhead snakes, and muddy rivers in the Delta of Mississippi.

Sam thought to himself, "What can it hurt? It would be a part of the country we have never seen, the kids would love the flights, and maybe we can help them in their pastoral search and with getting that church up and going." So he quickly responded,

"Sure. We would be honored to spend a few days with you."

"If next weekend sounds good for y'all," Wayne answered quickly, " I will order your flight and be there waiting with my plane. I can show you Mississippi close up."

The stop in Atlanta was typical, knowing you could not fly anywhere out of Florida in those days without a change in Atlanta. As they boarded the sleek private plane of the young plantation owner, the atmosphere was somewhere between exciting and giddy. Their air guide that day very craftily tilted the wings and encouraged Sammy and April to look below and see America's largest waterway, the Mississippi River winding below. Before long he was encouraging Sam and Pat to observe his cotton fields, and soon the little river beneath as he pointed out the Sunnydale River, and the little red building that had become the meeting place for the new Sunnydale Church.

The spring rains fell softly across the barren fields, recently planted with new cotton seed. Acre upon acre, mile upon mile waited in preparation for the hope of the entire population, one more bumper crop of cotton.

"They sure seem like a wonderful group of people." Pat softly voiced while staring at the ceiling above the master bed of the elegant motorhome, which served as their sleeping facility that weekend. As the steady sound of sleepy rain peppered the corrugated metal roof of the shelter above the the motor home, Sam responded,

"Sure is a quiet place, really a different lifestyle out here. I mean, no roar of the interstate, very little traffic compared to Orlando. Just the sound of that rain and a few birds, and that rooster I heard across the field this morning."

She laughed, rolled on her side, and reached up to touch his face. "Hey, city boy. Do you think you could really live in a place like this?"

He did not answer but listened to the sweet breathing of their young boy and girl soundly sleeping in the bed in the middle of the dream vacation vehicle. He was proud of how they awed the small congregation that morning when they provided the additional harmonies to their mother's beautiful voice. For a moment he reasoned, "How could I move them from such an exciting church to such a small and remote location? It would not be fair to them." Then he voiced to his wife a little nagging conversation he had been having with himself since the Sunday morning service, along the banks of the little river.

"Remember the story of Phillip in the New Testament?" Without waiting for an answer he continued, "Phillip was in a similar situation to where we find ourselves right now."

"How is that?" She whispered.

"Well, he was a part of a tremendous church. People by the hundreds were coming to hear him speak, and there seemed to be a deluge of new converts to his cause." She sat up in the bed against the headboard and asked,

"Ok, and where are you going with this?"

"You remember the story. Right at the height of this exciting situation, God told him to leave and take a trip down into the desert to meet one man and share the Gospel with him. Then, in a miraculous moment he was transported miles away and dropped in another city."

"Do you think that is what is happening to you?" She asked.

Sam laughed and clarified, "No, I flew. And it took a few hours in a couple of nice airplanes."

"What are you thinking Sam?" She asked him soberly.

He sat up, and as someone thinking out loud continued, "Do I think I'm too good to go from the big and exciting to the small and smaller?" Before he could muster an answer to his self examination he added, "But there is even a bigger part of Phillip's story I keep thinking about. That one man out in the desert; do you remember who it was?"

Tears began to gather in the corner of Pat's eyes and she shook her head up and down slowly and said, "Yes, an Ethiopian."

"He was an African. A black man." Sam spoke back the words.

Without recounting the rest of the story they both recalled the details. Even from their childhood Sunday school stories, they knew how Phillip was able to explain who Jesus was, how the Ethiopian was converted into Christendom, and even baptized as a new believer. Sam raised the most obvious unanswered question with a passionate sequence of uncomfortable facts.

"This is Mississippi, Pat. This is where James Meredith, only seventeen years ago, became the first African American student to enroll at the University of Mississippi, and this is where Chaney, Goodman, and Schwerner, those three young men trying to help blacks register to vote, were murdered. This is where Medgar Evers was shot and killed in the driveway of his own home just a few miles up the road in Jackson. And this is where Willie, the shoeshine man from my barbershop came on the Freedom Bus, and who knows what ever happened to him? I know much has changed since then, but..." He paused. "Is there a black man, woman, or child that God would bring us here for, or a cause known only to God Himself?"

So Sam celebrated his thirty-second birthday relocating his family into one of the smallest towns in America, and in the Delta of Mississippi. The cultural and traditional learning curve was remarkable, if not understandable. Although the change of pace seemed desirable, the smallness of the community and the repeated repertoire of activity soon began to wear thin.

For the first few weeks it was pleasant to sit on the front porch of the wonderfully built Crocker style home, watch the kids board the bus, leisurely drink another cup or two of coffee, and then try to find enough to do to fill the day. This was a tremendous change from the seventeen hour days working for an enterprise with an endless schedule, surrounded by an explosive, metropolitan lifestyle.

It was the social and cultural constructs that played such an impactful role in the way that this family would live out their daily existence. The bus Sammy and April would board each day carried them outside of the small town to attend the local private academy, suggested by the community. The young parents soon learned that with the adoption of the Civil Rights Bill of the 1960's, the white residents of this area of Mississippi chose to build private academies, rather than integrating their children with the black children, as the law required.

When Sammy was battling his severe allergies while patrolling his area of the outfield on his Little League baseball team, it was perhaps only his parents who recognized fully, there were no children of African descent on the field. The family was invited and treated to Sunday dinner each week, at the local Golf and Country Club restaurant. They soon understood that when the law allowed blacks to dine legally with the white community, the wealthier whites simply built restaurants at the Country Club, where membership was far too expensive for the black, cotton laborers, and poor plantation workers. This was 1980, not 1954. But integration was simply a fact of law on the books, while certainly not being a practice, some sixteen years after the rule of Law provided for its practice.

Even more than the behavior, tradition, culture, or philosophy between the races was the deep seated prejudices that displayed themselves in the practiced discriminations which were the product of the heart and mind.

"Let me tell you something, preacher." Said the aged white haired, and extremely sun weathered plantation owner, as he handed Sam a cold glass of southern sweet tea. This was not the occasional tea Opal would make in the summer to which they would add a teaspoon or two of granulated sugar, stirring till dissolved. No, this was Southern Sweet Tea with the pronounced emphasis on the word Sweet. The sugar was boiled into the tea before it was chilled. Any good southerner knew the difference. "I wish you could have been here, preacher, to see the real Mississippi. No, this ain't Mississippi no more. You should have seen it in the old times." The wealthy retired cotton farmer motioned Sam to join him by sitting in the other high back wooden rocking chair. He had some years ago handed over the operation of the farm to his son. The old man was known as, "Mr. Zack." He told Sam how his son went off to college and "Got him some of that educated farm learning." Even without Mr. Zack's total appreciation of advanced agricultural studies, he seemed most proud of one accomplishment of his son during those college days. "My boy, the one they all call 'Mr. Johnny' was up there at Oxford when that trouble maker Meredith decided he was gonna be the first Neegrah to enroll at Ole Miss." After taking a long draw from the slender tea glass, he smiled a proud and satisfying smile and clarified, "I called my boy on the phone and I told him to get that Browning 12 gauge shotgun I had bought him for his twelfth birthday, and 'you join up with those other proud young Mississippians, and you shoot the first black thing you see step a foot on that campus.'"

For a moment Sam felt his hand tremble a bit till some of the sweet nectar almost splashed out of the cold glass in his hand. Then as a continued afterthought, Mr. Zack laid his head on the heavy wooden top of the chair back and sighed a mournful sound. "Yes Sir, Mr. Preacher Man. I wish you could have seen these fields when they were really beautiful. As the Sun would be setting on a long, hot, summer day, there was no more beauty in the world than to set up here on this porch, sip this good cold tea and listen to my 'darkies' coming up out of those fields whilst a singin' those beautiful old Negro Spirituals. Yep, that was before those northern agitators came down here and got them Yankee jackasses like that Bobby Kennedy and his cronies, sticking their noses where they didn't belong, and destroying a beautiful way of life." He took another long drink and motioned for Sam to take a swig from the glass sweating in the preacher's hand.

Sam held back the waterfall of words waiting to pour out from somewhere deep in his inner man. He strained to maintain his composure, but he was sure he'd lost his fake smile. A geyser of rhetorical questions erupted in his mind.

Late summer evenings? Men, women, and children worked all day in the blistering sun, and finished after nine o'clock, and he calls that beautiful? Darkies? Did he really say that? That's fifteen hours of brutal labor, while he's sipping tea on the porch! I wonder if he could even remember the words of those old beautiful songs? Where am I?

He wished he'd had the fortitude to say aloud the troubling thoughts, whirring in his brain. On his drive back home through long dusty roads, Sam unloaded to the top of his voice everything he had wanted to say to the lost old man.

"Yeah Pal, what you called beautiful was only from your selfish, blinded, soulless, igno-rant, cold, sweet tea slurping position on that porch. Because those poor, stuck, unedu-cated, abused, back aching, leg cramping, finger bleeding souls were singing lyrics you could not even understand. They were singing words like, "I've got a better place to go," and "There will be peace in the valley for me someday," as well as, "Precious Lord take my hand, lead me on help me stand." And most of all they wanted to be free from you, and your misuse, your social bondage, your belittlement, your elitisms, you and your self-ap-pointed superiority and your control. That is why they were coming from those fields singing, "We shall overcome and Free at last, Free at last. Thank God almighty we're free at last."

Sam had tears flowing till it was difficult to see the narrow two lane highway that lay flatly across the mile after mile of white cotton fields. Just then, he espied nearly a football field length ahead of him, the lone figure of a young black man walking from the opposite di-rection. As was the common custom, the African American pedestrian came visibly close enough to see through the front windshield of the big mint-green Cadillac that the driver was a white man, and what may have appeared to him as a successful white man, the young fellow humbly stepped off the side of the road. As he did, he turned his back, not having the customary right to look directly at a white man of importance, until the car was well past his humbled position. Everything in Sam wanted to bring that car to a screeching halt, jump from the driver's seat, run back to the humiliated figure and throw his arms around the victim and weep over him. He'd ask his forgiveness, and assure him he did not ever need to step off a road and turn his eyes off of any other fellow human being another day in his life. But he also knew that such an act would have startled the young man, and caused him to feel threatened by the man in the shiny car coming to do him harm.

"Oh, God…" Sam whispered while drying the last tears from his eyes before he would face his family, "I don't know if I can do this or not."

****

Sammy was lost in his imagination as he played by himself in the vast acre lot dotted with twelve Pecan trees. He tossed the baseball into the air, then swung the wooden bat at the floating object, sending it bouncing through the tall grass of the back yard.

"It's a hard fast grounder to second base...Oh, and it slips through the fielder's glove. It's an easy base hit for the All Star Catcher, Johnny Bench!" He shouted aloud, as he dropped the bat and ran toward an imaginary First Base. His voice hissed as if making the sound of a cheering multitude, then suddenly trailed off self-consciously as his eyes met the eyes of a black child peering through the hedge.

The ten year old preacher's kid stood still for a moment, before realizing the lone voyeur of his private baseball game was, in fact not alone.

"Hi." Sammy waved at the figure hiding in the brush, and the whole hedge shivered with movement and giggles. "Wanna play with me?" He boldly invited, and made a beckoning motion.

Slowly, and timidly a few skinny figures climbed through the brush and cautiously walked toward the friendly white boy. As children are apt to do, play and friendship commenced without a formal introduction or exchange of hands and names. The game was on, and more figures appeared from the hedge until the Pecan treed lot was bursting with over a dozen enthusiastic playmates with dark skin, and one pale boy who knew nothing about the unintentional revolution he had initiated.

"I'll be Johnny Bench!" Sammy announced.

"I'm Willie Mays!" The first interloper shouted.

"I'll be Hank Aaron!" said another.

"I'm Reggie Jackson, and I'm a knock it over dat wall!" shouted the littlest player on the field, and all the boys giggled with delight.

"I beg your pardon Ma'am, but may I have a word with you for a moment?" the rather kind grandfatherly voice asked softly, while approaching the corner of the front porch.

"Well, of course, Sir." came Pat's reply as she rose from the front porch swing and stood almost at the same height as the old gentleman, due to the elevation of the porch. The deep dark skin of the black man was an impressive contrast to the thick and curly white hair, now exposed, as the large brimmed hat was being turned nervously in the thick fingers of the stranger.

"Well here is the thing Ma'am, my name is Green, and I live with my daughter and grand-children beyond that hedge row at the back of your property." He was facing her and ex-tending his long arm and hand in the direction beyond the dozen pecan trees, "Over there on Wilson Street, by the tracks?" and then dropping his head a bit he opened the purpose of his approach. "Your son over here was so kind as to invite my grandchildren to come through the hedges and join him in some ball playing. Now that is a fine young man you have there." Quickly, as with Pat's congenial personality she interrupted Mr. Green to say,

"Well, thank you, Sir. Please know your grandchildren are more than welcome over here anytime."

Just as quickly the man interrupted his friendly hostess and informed, "Well, Ma'am, see that is what I come to talk to you about. You see, as much of a kind gesture as that is to-ward my grandchildren, there is a little something you should know." Now to Pat's sur-prise she did not expect what followed when the old man attempted to explain carefully. "You see, Ma'am; it is really not a good idea for these children to be over here at y'alls place. What I mean is, you see my grandchildren are not good children. They don't have many manners, and they just would not be a good influence on your fine boy there."

"Oh, Mr. Green..." Pat assuredly responded, "Your grandchildren there are beautiful, and they sure look like they are having fun."

Kindly, but a bit more emphatically, the neighbor from the other community and literally on the other side of the tracks quickly declared, "No Ma'am, I just believe it would be better for everybody if my grandchildren just stay over where they belong." He now stammered a bit and talked in concluding tones, "I..I, well I mean it really would be...ah... be best this way Ma'am."

While the words were still kind and very civil he began to move away from the porch, and in the direction of the yard and distant hedge row. Pat could not hear his voice but she knew he was informing the neighbor children, and his own grandchildren they must con-clude their play and return with him to their place.

She watched Sammy's disappointment, as he had really no other boys nearby to play with. The most difficult part for her was she would have to find a way to help her children un-derstand the grandfather knew the truth. It was not that his grandchildren were bad chil-dren, nor was it their becoming a bad influence that sent the man over with the issue. It was the town, the Delta, the attitudes, the history, and the sad reality that if he allowed his grandchildren to come over to the nicer street of white families and be seen playing together with those white preacher's kids, he would be the one with a problem. He would be the one in trouble, and he would be the one to pay the price.

Only a few months before their arrival, when one of the creators of the new church was followed into his own plantation driveway by a couple trucks filled with normally dressed men of the community to inquire if the new church intended to allow blacks to attend. There were no hoods, white robed cross burners, but in that community these men were well known as deeply rooted members of the remaining Ku Klux Klan.

It was also very painful for Pat to walk the sidewalk of the little town square. Often while picking up a few things from the general store, or mailing something at the post office, she was troubled by the reactions of many of the locals. She noticed how often a small group of black men would be conferring along the sidewalk and as soon as they saw the white lady approaching, they would step off the sidewalk into the street, and turn away as to not be looking in her direction until she had passed.

The social life of the black community and the white community of the 1980 Mississippi Delta was in actuality no closer than before the Civil Rights Movement of the 1960's. The Whites still owned it all. The blacks worked for the whites and were mostly still in abject poverty. They lived, ate, schooled, and even worshiped separately. The one exception was in most white churches, the black ladies were still used to care for the babies in the church nurseries on Sunday. Most white mothers were comfortable with this arrangement. Perhaps this took them to a sentimental place in most of their own childhoods, where black women had served as "mammy," the primary caretaker of their early years.

"Miss Pat, can I aks you a question?"

The scene could have been scripted in any famous Hollywood production from Gone with the wind to Pinky, and a vast library of movies that attempted to show the social structure of the early deep south.

"Why, sure you can." Pat answered.

She was the last woman still at the gathering of picnic tables placed next to the church building. The huge trees that shared their name with the state flower, the Magnolia. Just as fluid as the rushing waters of the little Sunnydale River sped by, pretty little Alisha spoke.

"I was just wonderin' if y'all was a plannin' to throw away those leftover foods that y'all be pickin' up there." Then almost without taking a breath she cut to the heart of the matter. "Ifin' you was fixin' to put them there foods in the trash, I would sure be more than willin' to take' em off ya hands. My babies could sure use some fine food like that."

Pat had no idea, at the time that this lovely young woman, who regularly watched the babies for the ladies of the church, knew what she was doing. She had been in ear shot when those departing the picnic all passed on taking home leftovers. They told the pastor's wife, "Just throw that extra food in the trash for now."

It was nothing but the most natural response for Pat when she joyfully responded to the young mother of several little ones at home.

"Most certainly, you can have this food. Wait, let me get some containers from the kitchen, and I can package it all up for you."

"Oh, thank you so much, Miss Pat. Dat'd be wonderful. We will have a party at my house, sure nuff Ma'am."

Then Pat had another idea. "Listen Alisha, could you or your children use some clothes?"

"Oh, yes Ma'am, we sure could use some clothes."

Pat handed her the stack of prepared leftovers and instructed, "You just follow us back to town, to our house and I have several bags of clothes that my children have outgrown. I have some jackets someone might be able to use, and I bet I have a couple dresses that, on you, would make your husband's eyes pop out."

They giggled like a couple school girls divulging a good secret. After a good hour of plowing through bags, closets, and drawers Pat was glowing with such a sense of joy in the knowledge that a young, poverty stricken family, just trying to survive were going to have food and clothes better than they might have ever known.

The knock came firmly at the front door midway through the following week.

"Miss Pat, would you have a few minutes for us ladies today?" There on her front porch was a contingent, made up of the three young wives of the wealthy plantation owners, instrumental in forming the church. Joining the three was the older wife of the well known Mr. Zak. The most wealthy and influential of the four began to present herself as the main voice, which was her custom.

"Miss Pat, we have come to share in kindness and love, of course, a very concerning matter that has come to our attention."

Her mouth went dry as she offered the ladies a comfortable place to sit on the recently reupholstered sofa, or one of the accompanying chairs.

"It was brought to our attention that last Sunday, after the picnic, Alisha, the girl who cares for our baby nursery, may have approached you about obtaining the leftover food you were going to dispose of. We also heard you actually brought her to your house here, and gave her a sizable amount of clothing. Is that true?"

Pat responded without reservation, "Well yes, as a matter of fact, I certainly did just that." The visual response of the self appointed committee was quite demonstrative. By the way each clutched their neckline, took deep breaths, and with raised heads, rolled their eyes, she was sure she was about to hear a unified gasp and combined declaration of, "Well, I neva!"

After all their pulse rates seemed to return to normal and a few waves of their hands prevented a group onslaught of the vapors, the spokeswoman began to enlighten, educate, and explain the deepest dangers entrenched within the foolish and sympathetically emotional misdeed. Pat's misguided attempt at charitable generosity would be wasted on the lesser species of their humanity.

"Miss Pat, we know you meant well, and you were trying to show kindness, but you must understand, these kinds of people you just can't do those kinds of things for." As the heads of the ladies rapidly nodded in dramatic agreement, their leader bequeathed upon the naive pastor's wife the ultimate explanation. "See, these folks are like stray cats or dogs. If you one time give them something to eat or show them kindness, they will come back again and again. You will most likely never be able to get fully rid of them. You do understand and see, we are sure, how this is just a fact about this kind. We just can never allow ourselves to be victimized in this way. You do understand what we are saying, do you not?"

In the very same way that Sam wanted to explode on the blinded bigot that uncomfortable afternoon some days past, Pat had a long list of pointed accusations. She would love to have dressed down this bastion of self-righteous, over privileged gaggle of what one prophet in the Bible called "female dogs." Better reasoning, kinder spirit, and a quick reminder from a heavenly source caused her to quickly say,

"I will admit, I will probably always have a certain weakness. Especially when I have something that someone else does not have, and desperately needs, and I know I could meet that need. But I can assure you ladies today, I have heard you, and this will most assuredly not happen among you again."

The statement was so far over the heads of the bigoted unkindness they had carried into the room, they actually thought they had solved a potential problem. In fact, they had only shown the clergy couple the hopelessness of them being able to stay and raise their children in such a realm, where effective ministry and human progress would be unreachable for generations to come.

Three and a half months from their arrival in the little Delta town, Sam came into the house and asked his small clan to sit down for a family meeting. "I have something important to tell you all." He said seriously.

"You're gonna make me your assistant pastor!" Sammy interrupted to lighten the nervous moment.

The family laughed together, then turned attention back to the father.

"No, though that's a good idea, son." Sam took a deep breath. "We're moving."

The gasp of astonishment was palpable for the other three. April cried. Sammy stood with his mouth agape, and Pat objected, "But I haven't even unpacked all the boxes yet!"

In previous moves, Sam would have rehearsed a convincing sermon for his wife and kids, casting an inspiring vision of a great spiritual conquest to be met. There was no compelling locker room speech. Simply "We're moving."

"Where are we going?" Sammy inquired for more information. His dad's response was as sad as it was humorous.

"I don't know, but we can't stay here."

****

With nothing to return to in Florida, their only recourse was packing a moving truck one more time, declaring across the back of the roll up door "Adventures in Moving." They headed back to the severe winter ahead, on the shores of Lake Michigan, where a little boy named Kaz started it all. While the next eight months seemed a somewhat directionless blur of disconnected activity, it was not without some pleasurable circumstances. Residing on the lake, and this time in a beach home within feet of the beautiful sand dunes of the Great Lakes, provided some great playtime for the family. Sam took employment in his brother Frank's upholstery shop, and Pat returned to teaching school. The weekends were again filled with the four of them reuniting with old pastor friends and conducting Sunday services as guest speakers and musicians.

The entertainment world has a maxim that goes, "Never let a dog or a kid on the stage with you, or you are finished." The obvious indication is that the audience will be so intrigued by the children or the pets that they will pay your efforts little attention. The other side of that idiom says, "If you are flopping on stage, get a dog or a kid out there." The up-front world that Sam and Pat had known so well was changing drastically. The amazing stage presence and talent Sammy was displaying each weekend was already holding audiences spellbound. A ten year old who could sing like a Las Vegas icon, already had the charm of a child actor, and connected with an audience like a hypnotist. April, at nine years of age, had a voice of crystal and such an amazing ear for musical tone. The harmonies she and her brother had learned from their mother during the long hours of dishwashing and house chores, brought an amazing quality to any song they sang. Her grace, beautiful, long flowing hair, and elegant movements only served to radiate from her angelic voice a sincerity that wooed listeners to tears.

Sam could still bring the piano keys to life, and he still knew how to ring the proverbial bell in the pulpit. Pat had never yet lost one strand of her overwhelming alto magic, but now sharing the stage with these two youngsters, who had shown prodigious ability from their earliest childhood, the weekends served as the most fulfilling replacements for all the confusing and unanswered questions that had transpired since their departure from the life they had known back in Orlando. The traveling quartet honed their harmonies in a customized van and logged thousands of icy Indiana miles until the thought of sun and sand began once again to act as a siren call to Sam. When a call came from a fledgling congregation on the Space Coast, it didn't take a lot of prayer to answer the call.

The entire family was so happy to finally be back in the warmth and sunshine of Florida. The couple in their mid-thirties were pastoring again a start up church, living on a canal, and encouraging the blossoming talents of their talented offspring. All of the pieces were finally coming together. Their new task was filled with excitement. Over the next few years they would guide this growing ministry to become their most successful endeavor yet, buying ten acres of land on the same island that housed the nation's Space Center during the launch of the Space Shuttle era. Building a large and impressive church facility made each day a new experience for them. Hundreds of people jammed the gatherings at the new building. The family's fun days were filled with beach time, dinner cruises, and water skiing behind their Carvel speed boat on the Banana River off Merritt Island.

CHAPTER 10 - 1983-1993

For the next several years the Pawlak parents would never know a time when one or both of their children were not filling the stage in leading roles. From school stages, church platforms, Christian rock bands, concert halls, and community theaters a lifestyle had been born. The culmination of their performing years on Florida's Space Coast was when the kids pushed their dad to audition for the role of Tevye in the local community theater's production of Fiddler on the Roof. Sam agreed to try if the other three members of the family came along. They did, and he was cast in the lead, and the rest of the quartet were rewarded with great parts as well. For this family, nothing could have been more rewarding than performing together.

They danced and sang their way into a whole world of fun.

****

Most of the church members on the thriving sub-tropical island were managers, technicians, or engineers at the Kennedy Space Center. Launches were a regular and memorable part of East Coast Florida living. Boats would fill the rivers, traffic would line the causeways, and life would stop as residents scurried outside to watch the impressive smoke trail rocket skyward as the ground shook from the combustion of the twin solid rocket boosters.

The church's pride in the area's most significant industry only made the heartbreaking events of January 28, 1986 more painful for the congregation, as well as the community and nation. It was a cold morning, just seventy-three seconds after Sam and his father Frank, who was spending winter with them in Florida, watched the beautiful blue sky over Cape Canaveral turn into a mixture of fire, smoke, and falling debris. STS-51-L, better known as the Space Shuttle Challenger exploded above them. Sammy and April stood outside the open air Commons area of the high school in stunned silence with the hundreds of classmates who witnessed the disastrous event.

The tragic loss of all seven crew members, consisting of five NASA astronauts, one payload specialist, and a civilian school teacher would go down as one of the darkest days in American history. There was hardly a family in the entire county which was unaffected. America was saddened, and Florida mourned, but Brevard County was devastated. For the next 2 years and 8 months there were lives grieved, jobs lost, contracts cancelled, and hope rebuilt.

The atmosphere would be altogether different on September 29, 1988. Pat had been hired for the contractor who had the software contract for the newest Shuttle launch. She found herself in the actual firing room, and observed several space engineers with heads bowed and lips moving in silent prayer as the Space Shuttle Discovery attempted to return the American Space program to space again. The sighs of relief may have been even louder than the shouts of cheer when the Discovery surpassed the place where the Challenger met its disastrous fate in 1986. That single success meant that space travel would continue. Thousands of workers across America would continue their jobs, and for the Pawlak family this locale was considered home for over ten years.

****

"Hey, Dad! Have I got a story to tell you!" These were not unusual words for Sammy's parents.

Sammy was assessed in high school as having near Echoic Memory, or what is sometimes referred to by a non-clinical term, "audiographic memory." The ability to recount almost everything you hear. This is similar to Eidetic or photographic memory, where one remembers all they see. So his parents jokingly said they saved a lot of money, not having to see movies. Sammy could go, and he could pretty well deliver to them the entire dialogue of the movie script.

"Ok, man. Lay it on me." His dad replied.

"You won't believe this! When we went to All-County today with the choir, the guest conductor asked who would like to try out for the male solo part. So, I signed up, and after lunch a bunch of guys from all the schools in the county auditioned for this director dude. He is a music professor from the University of Florida. When he later announced who the soloist would be, he picked a sophomore over all the Junior and Senior singers!

Sam quickly inserted, "Well, I happen to know a Sophomore that is a pretty good singer."

"Wait! That's not the whole story, because when he announced who the All-County Male Soloist was he said, "Our soloist this year will be Sam Pawlak, from Merritt Island, and he pronounced it perfectly; absolutely perfect Polish pronunciation with the W like a V!"

"He is probably a pretty smart guy if he is a big professor at a big University. Maybe he knew it was a Polish name." Sam Sr. reasoned.

"This is the cool part! Sit down! I'll tell you exactly how it happened."

The dad sat on the sofa and prepared for a full, detailed reenactment.

"So, I asked him 'How did you pronounce my name right? No one ever does that.' He said,

'I knew a family from my childhood with that name.'

I asked, 'Where did you grow up?'

He says 'A small place in Indiana, called Michigan City.'

I'm like, 'Wait! My dad comes from Michigan City. Who did you know there?'

'Oh, I knew a Frank and Opal, and Manson, and Sam and Valery.'

I told him 'Dude, Frank and Opal were my grandparents, and Valery is my Aunt, and Sam is my dad!'"

Sammy continued, and could see his dad's eyes getting bigger.

"'Who are you?' I asked him. He says,

'My dad was the Pastor of your dad's family church.'

I said, 'Wait! Robinson...your dad is Stew Robinson?'"

Sam stood up and exclaimed "Rusty, Rusty Robinson! That is crazy, Sammy. His brother Randy and I were best buddies when we were just kids."

Sammy loved the surprise on his dad's face, and quickly added, "But Dad, he is not Rusty now. He is Dr. Russell Robinson, and he told me I better not call him Rusty." They both laughed. "You will see him at the performance tonight."

An aging Frank Pawlak, hair turned completely white, and coke bottle lens glasses perched on his significant nose, sat next to Sam, Pat, and April, purveying the crowded gymnatorium. They watched the mass choir and concert band perform, and a proud grandfather and parents took delight in the young Pawlak's solo work. It all seemed so surreal that they were watching a conductor of renown, a leading music educator, an arranger for one of the most esteemed music publishers in America, and a man that would grace the stage of the famed Carnegie Hall, leading their own 10th grader. This distinguished virtuoso was just a baby in his mother's arms when the Robinson family first arrived in Michigan City all those years before.

It is often quoted "It's not what you know, but who you know." Sam Sr would more often say to his kids, "It's who you know that gets you in the door. It's what you know that keeps you there." Little could the parents have imagined that through this divine coincidence of reacquaintance, and their children's dedication and talent, the door would open for both Sammy and April to attend the University of Florida, and receive their professional training at the hands of another Michigan City friend.

****

Shortly after Sammy began his second year at the University and April had begun her first, Sam and Pat once again felt the heavenly pull toward another ministerial adventure. They would close out the decade of the 80's, making the pilgrimage across the peninsula from the Space Coast to the SunCoast. They gave themselves again to guiding a small gathering of church members into a future of effectiveness and strength. With both children having left home, the pair in their 40's found themselves comprising the whole ministerial team. This time a little older, a lot wiser, but just as visionary as that young couple in that little storefront church on the west side of Indianapolis, almost a quarter of a century ago. Experience brought wisdom, and wisdom brought maturity. Reflecting on their earlier years the young husband and father of this "million-dollar family" expressed some 20/20 hindsight on their humble beginnings in ministry.

"Honestly Pat," He said as they stood alone on the picturesque property of the little community church on Lake Magdalene, "I sure feel better prepared for the future this time." She looked at him with all the recognition that over twenty years of marriage affords. Even without elaborating, she understood the unspoken references to mistakes and failures of the past. Religious conflicts, marital tensions, financial distress, and personal regrets had a way of beating the early ego out of the once fearless, or blissfully ignorant preaching pioneer. His quick temper had cooled. His humility had deepened like the lines on his forehead, and his tight abs and biceps had fallen to reflect the weight of responsibility he now carried. She didn't even need to speak. The compassion in her eyes couldn't diminish the admiration she still had for the man she chose to follow in pursuit of the plan of God. She could tell he had more to say, and she didn't want to interrupt his self aware resolution.

"I should probably send back every penny that little church in Gary ever paid me. I did not have any idea what I was doing back then. And the only thing that made me the pastor was the sign out front with my name on it."

"Honey," She kindly replied with a knowing smile. "They knew we didn't know what we were doing, but they loved us anyway. And I'm sure they always will."

He acknowledged with a smile that she remembered every disappointment he was speaking of.

"I'm just so grateful God has given us another chance to serve him in this way. There were times, I thought I was done." Sam said seriously. "But hey, if God wants us to love this sweet little group of old folks on this pretty lake, and live out our years to retirement, I guess there are worse places we could be."

No imagination from the mind or the pen of any acclaimed novelist could have created the succession of life changing, dream altering, path directing, and life fulfilling events that awaited this couple, now living and working in a place called Tampa.

****

Sam studied the figure sitting across the yard, and resting on the little chair at the edge of the beautiful little lake, so full of bass, crappie, and sunfish. The silver hair and the rounded shoulders seemed even more pronounced than before. Although Kaz's second son, Frank was the athlete of the family, and his baseball days were long past, he still had those rounded shoulders. Students of the human body would come to identify this figure as an indication of superior upper body strength. This was the best understanding of how, as a very thin young man, Frank was still able to display amazing power when hitting a baseball and launching them often over the heads of the awaiting outfielders. Now approaching his eighth decade of life the most familiar part of the scene was not the hair or the physical frame, but what was being softly yet attentively cradled within those massive hands and fingers. A fishing rod and reel were as comfortable and functional in the hands of Sam's dad, as would be piano keys to Chopin, a violin to Isaac Stern, a basketball to Michael Jordan. As if to pose for the photograph Sam was preparing to snap of his beloved father alongside the lake, Frank suddenly turned his head and the admiring son was able to capture a full facial picture. Sam released a huge sigh and began a conversation with himself in that moment.

"Boy, he has changed a lot. That hair that was so black when I was a boy is so beautifully white, but it is still as thick as it ever was." His lips moved slowly yet without any project- ed sound. "He is really looking thinner, even shorter, and a little more bent over." Sam studied the bright Sun's glow on his dad's moistened face. "There is the biggest change, his nose."

Frank's primary dominant facial feature was not his beautiful baby blue eyes. His identify- ing feature was that rather large Polish nose. Sam felt a distinct sadness suddenly sweep across his psyche as he said the words out loud to himself. "That's sure not my dad's nose is it?"

The famous hump on Frank's nose was no longer there. Instead, the once large breathing feature of character that dominated the space between the blue eyes, which his wife Opal loved so dearly, and the thick lips that had been passed down to him from his mother Mary, was now a rather flattened nose that better would have been the feature of an old bare knuckle boxer. Most of the bone and all of the hump had been surgically removed a few months earlier. The complete redesign of his austere face came at the hands of a drunken driver, who in the late of the night crossed to the wrong side of a country road, colliding head on with the car in which Frank was a passenger. At that moment, the 79 year old sustained over twenty-four bone fractures in his face, and that large, handsome, and humped nose was pulverized into what the doctor would describe as a mass of pow- dered bone.

Frank would not have normally been in Florida at this time of the year. July along the Gulf Coast of Florida brought the most humid and smothering weather of the year. However, nothing would have kept him from missing the wedding of his granddaughter April. Frank always called her "Sweetie," as he did all of his granddaughters, and she so loved this man. The patriarch sat at the beautiful wedding with as much pride and admi- ration as the bride's own parents. He was also very impressed with her new husband, Steve.

As the handsome Airman stood at the front of the church in full dress uniform, the pain of seeing their beautiful April move on to the next stage of her life was tempered by the fact she was marrying a college educated, highly intelligent, military disciplined, and hard working man of character. What pleased grandparent and parents alike was they were fully aware their new son in law, also had strong passions for ministry. Frank was fully supportive of this man marrying his "Sweetie" when he heard that Steve wanted to become a pastor. For April's grandfather this was the true icing on the wedding cake that day.

"Dad, you don't have to do this." Sam encouraged Frank to take a seat in the lobby, while he finished vacuuming the large church lobby of the church sanctuary. "I will take care of it. Besides, we are almost finished anyway."

"Well, Ok. Maybe I will just sit here a little while."

Sam summoned one of the young men from his church helping with the clean up duties. "Hey Joey, do me a favor. While I finish vacuuming just keep an eye on my dad. He is sitting out there in the lobby."

"Is he all right?" Joey questioned.

"Yeah, I think so. He was helping me, but I noticed he was stopping every little bit, and looked like he was taking some deep breaths. It's late and it sure has been a long day, he may just be tired."

"Ok, Pastor. I will go sit with him a bit, and get him to tell me some good fish stories. He will never know I am checking up on him."

He thanked the boy and returned to his chore of cleaning up the borrowed chapel until the only ones left late into the night were he and Frank.

The old man's quick willingness to take a seat in the lobby indicated that something was not quite right. The next day he assured all he was fine, and just a bit tired from the ceremony and heat the day before. Frank was quite happy to board the plane and head back home to the cooler temperatures of Lake Michigan.

"Sure enough, all we have to do is sit down for dinner and that blasted phone starts ringing." Sam quickly grabbed the napkin beside the plate, rose quickly to his feet, and wiped the rigatoni pasta from the edges of his mouth. It was his favorite meal when the kids were still at home.

"Hey Fred, good to hear your voice man. What's happening up home?"

"Well, we are all ok, but I thought I better call you guys right away. We have a little problem here."

Sam put one hand toward Pat in the fashion of a police officer directing an oncoming car to stop and asked, "What, what's going on?"

Fred cleared his throat and spoke softly, "Dad has had a heart attack, and they are transferring him over to Memorial Hospital in South Bend."

Sam called Valery right away, and explained what was happening with their father. They were on the next available flight that following morning. As the plane circled the small airport and they observed the Golden Dome of Sam's favorite University below, a strange and unknown feeling surfaced in his emotions. He softly said to Valery, "Boy, this is strange. Do you realize we have never gone to a hospital to visit our father as a patient?"

They were both somewhat relieved to see him talkative, and still questioning his diagnosis.

"I don't know how in the world I could have had a heart attack. I didn't have the first pain or trouble breathing. I was just sick to my stomach like the flu. I asked these other guys around here, did they have any pain with their heart attacks, and they all say, heck yeah they did, like an elephant sitting on their chest. But I never felt anything like that."

Sam could not pass up on the opportunity for humor. He remembered often when the boys would recall, with exceptional detail, how difficult their lives had been at times in that extreme conditions at the old Coolspring place, Frank would often respond with his own attempt at comfort. "Yeah, but you guys were tough." As if that was to make the conditions tolerable.

"No pain, huh Dad?" He asked

"That's right, not the first pain."

"You probably had lots of pain, but you got to remember Dad, you guys were tough."

The room exploded with laughter as each of Frank's six kids watched him drop his head a little, and that big broad smile spread across his much thinner face.

Sam, Bud, and Fred met with the cardiologist down the hall away from the patient. "Doctor, we need you to be honest with us and with our dad." Sam said. "Do you believe, knowing what you now know and because of his age he should consider the surgery you've talked about?"

"Understand, I can't make that decision. That is up to your Father."

Fred quickly looked for a way to rephrase his question. "Alright, let me ask you this; if this was your father, and he was eighty, would you recommend the surgery?"

The doctor gazed for a moment toward the hall ceiling and said, "As a matter of fact, my father is the same age as your father, and I can't tell you what your father or you should do. As to your question, no I would never recommend my father to do this." He explained. "There is a very small percentage that your father would survive this surgery. The recovery would be filled with numerous challenges, and for at least the next two to three years your father would be considered a heart invalid. If, and that is a big if, he could survive all of that, he might have a few more years."

After thanking the doctor for his professionalism and candor, Frank's children knew that they had no alternative but to share with complete honesty what the doctor had said. None of them were surprised at all when their dad listened to every detail and possibility, and spoke just as they thought he would.

"For the love of Mike, no I am not going to do all that. For me to be in some nursing home, spending the last years of my life looking out some window, and being pushed down some hall is the last dahg gahn thing I would ever want." Then the real Frank Pawlak revealed himself just as they had expected. "Besides, God has healed me plenty of times, like that way he healed my back. And if he still has a reason for me to stay here longer he will do it again. If not, then I am ready. Nope, take me home, and let's just leave it to Him and see what he has in mind."

****

"Sam, it's the phone. The phone there, on your side of the bed, you got to answer the phone." Pat's groggy stupor and scratchy voice brought him up immediately to his feet.

"What the heck time is it anyway?"

"About 3 a.m. according to this clock." She answered as she slowly rose to the side of the bed. Sam made several attempts to clear his throat.

"Hello, this is Sam."

"Hey, Sam this is Bud." The deep rasp and serious tone at the late hour brought a sudden realization that this was not a casual phone call. His brother continued. "You know if it is me calling it's not with good news."

"Oh?" was Sam's one word response.

"We lost Dad tonight, Sam."

Pat had come around the bed and was standing in front of Sam as he quickly sat back down on the side of the bed.

"My dad is gone." He tearfully said to her, then back into the phone he asked, "What happened, Bud?"

"The old man had finished watching the Cubs game on TV, and went into Fred's kitchen to get what he always called 'a slug of water.' You know how he takes his drink to bed with him. Margie went in to help him and she said he grabbed the counter with both hands and just said 'Oh!' and slumped to the floor."

Sam immediately thought of the description of how Kaz had died in a similar way in his daughter's kitchen, forty-seven years earlier. "I will call Manson immediately, and we will head that way tomorrow."

After Sam had notified the eldest son and namesake, Frank Jr, known to the family as Manson, he dressed and walked out to the lake behind the house. The middle of the night darkness and sweltering humid August heat, just one month after Frank's heart attack, and one month before his eightieth birthday, were the backdrop for his sorrow. This youngest son looked out across the little lake and thought, "I am so glad my dad got to fish that lake." As he slowly walked back up the hill to the sound of the air-conditioning system's long night of work, his body began to shake in response to the tears being released. After a few moments he gathered his composure, looked up at the stars and said,

"Well Kaz, your boy has rounded third base, and is coming home to your welcoming arms."

Of all Kaz's and Mary's children, including John, Sophie, Lily, and Eddie, Frank was the first to die. The graveside service ended more like a celebration than a mournful event. At one point, the familiar funeral director leaned over to Sam.

"It always amazes me the joy at your family's funerals. It is almost as if you all believe the person is going somewhere."

Sam smiled and responded. "Yeah, I guess we do."

****

Sam was not really accustomed to the new phone system. It wasn't that it was such new technology, but as he was now in his mid forties, he was beginning to prefer the more comfortable equipment he understood, rather than the learning curve being demanded by a digital age. So when the strange buzz startled him, it took a moment for him to remember his secretary needed him to pick up his phone for something important.

"Yes, Patty. Did I do this right?" He leaned entirely too close to the speaker on the desk.

"Yes, Pastor. You have a call from the District Office, and the voice just asked would Pastor Sam have time to speak with his Bishop."

Sam understood her dither. Although the term Bishop was truly the office held by the gentleman calling, it was not the commonly used title in their particular denomination. So the Bishop of his church organization carried a more common title of District Superintendent. However, it was still a bit concerning when the Bishop, or whatever title used, placed a personal call to a local pastor in a small church. After figuring out that he had to push the blinking button on the desk phone, Sam hesitantly spoke. "Hello, this is Sam Pawlak."

"Hello Sam, this is Gordon. Thanks for taking my call." Sam immediately recognized the strong and extremely identifiable voice on the other end of the line.

"Yeah, like I would really have any other choice when my 'Bishop' calls?" He chided because this voice brought him little trepidation. This was a voice he had known since childhood. This church leader had been a long time acquaintance to Sam's parents. There were pictures, somewhere in the boxes of photos, with the man they knew as Gordon when he was a young pastor in the Chicago area long ago. In some of those pictures he had been baptizing some family relatives in that same old creek of Kaz, Frank, and Sam's childhoods. "To what can I attribute the pleasure of this call?"

"Listen Sam, I have a young couple sitting here in my office, and I am looking to see if I could get a few of our pastors in the Tampa area to have them in as guests in an upcoming service." Not waiting for a response, and knowing he would need to give any pastor a little more information about his request he quickly continued. "They are a delightful young team. He plays the guitar, and they sing wonderfully. He is also an excellent speaker." Again before Sam could even verbalize a response, the requester moved as quickly as the proverbial used car salesman with more. "I know the wife's father and uncle very well, and they have often been in our church speaking and singing when I was a pastor in Tampa. So they come from some wonderful stock"

Sam's mind was in a swirl, knowing the busy schedule he already had on the calendar, and the extra things involved in bringing guest speakers to the church. There would be concerns like housing, meals, transportation, promotion, advertising, and budgetary items like honorariums or special collections. Furthermore, he had learned the hard way to never have a guest speaker or performer that he had not personally heard himself. He would want to be assured they would fit his congregation's needs. Secondly, an even bigger issue, how do you say no to your Bishop, Superintendent, or in actuality your Big boss who has the realistic control of your credential and perhaps your future? While this entire cacophony of thought was intersecting with the explosive interactive wave lengths within Sam's cranium, the voice at the other end uttered seven words that would profoundly change the conversation and to some degree the history of the Pawlak family, forever.

"Oh, by the way, they're from Poland."

POLAND...POLAND...POLAND, screamed across Sam's brain, silencing every other thought he'd just been entertaining. He felt himself stop breathing. Both ears plugged as if he had just exceeded the 16,000 foot level of Mount Everest's 29,000 foot peak.

POLAND... POLAND...POLAND again echoed through his entire body. A pain seemed to thrust itself deeply through Sam's breastbone and with his left hand, the one not holding the receiver, he clutched his chest, and could only describe what felt like a knife through the heart.

It had been twelve long years since he had heard the audible voice say "I have a work for you to do in Poland." Twelve long years of lost contacts, no communication, different starts and stops, hopes and disappointments, fulfillments and frustrations, finishings and failures, wonderings and wanderings, questions unanswered, fullness and emptiness, happiness and sadness, successes and sorrows, but above all else unexplained mystery. In the milliseconds it took the Superintendent to speak those seven words, the cerebral equipment of Sam's brain conducted an entire conversation with itself.

"Did you hear that, Sam? They're from Poland. They want to come to you, meet you, see you, talk with you, speak for your church, and sing to your congregation. From Poland, Sam, from Poland." Then the brain voice spoke even faster and louder. "You know what you heard, Sam. You know the only time you truly heard the voice of God. You know, you remember, you have never forgotten. Poland Sam, it was about Poland. The land of your fathers, it has come, it has come to you."

"Poland. Did you say Poland, sir?" Sam sounded frantic in his voiced response, wiping both sweat and tears from his eyes.

"Yes, Poland. That is why I thought of you. I remembered that your family was Polish. I loved Frank and Opal, and even your Grandpa Kaz. I really thought you might like to meet these folks."

"Yes, yes we will have them tonight for our mid-week service."

To which the orchestrator of this scenario asked, "Are you sure you can do anything that fast?"

Sam was still somewhat out of his mind with emotion. "Yes, Yes. We will get on the phone and tell the people to be here tonight. And we will tell them if they are not here tonight, they will be going to Hell, for sure." Both men burst into laughter at what had just come out of Sam's mouth.

"All right then." said the caller, and Sam sealed the deal with the final arrangement.

"I will be to your office in an hour to pick them up, take them to dinner, and they can stay with us till you arrange their next engagement."

Quickly he hung up the phone, and burst from his office door. He gave his secretary explicit details to notify every member she could that they were to come to the meeting at 7:00 pm as the Pastor had a surprise for them tonight. He literally ran from the church office to the house by the lake, swung open the door and told his startled wife, "Grab your purse. We have to get to Lakeland right now!"

"Why now?" She inquired, as she quickly gathered her purse.

He pulled her toward the door, and yelled to the top of his voice "Because, Poland is waiting for us!"

They were much much younger than he had expected. Sam said to Pat as they pulled up in front of the District Office, seeing the couple awaiting their arrival, "They can't be any older than our kids."

They were indeed close to the ages of their own Sammy and April, and they had been married only one year. But in some ways this made the excitement even greater. Hands shaken turned quickly to comfortable hugs.

"Now give me the proper pronunciation of your name. I am sure Gordon butchered it pretty good." They laughed and the young tall handsome Pole replied,

"Yes, he could never get it right. He would say Mario or Marius, but it is actually Mariusz."

Sam knew already how the sz sound was like the English sh sound. He also knew from the Pawlak name that the a was the long ah sound. So it was not Mary but Mari, and the u sounded like oo.

"I am Lydia." said the beautiful young woman at his side, as she extended her hand, producing a purely angelic smile.

The biggest challenge came when sharing their last name, Muszczynski. Sam was captivated by the name. He thought, "There just could not be a more identifiable Polish name," especially when he recognized that of the eleven letters comprising the name, eight or nine of them were consonants. Depending on whether you use the "sometimes Y" as a rule. Mariusz would explain how to pronounce their last name phonetically.

"Just say moose (like the animal), chin (like at the bottom of your face), and ski (like going down a snowy mountain). See how easy? Moosh-chin-ski."

Mariusz was fluent in English. However, there was still enough of the eastern European touch to remind Sam of so many hometown memories. The th sound is one of the most difficult for the Polish speaker to master. That is what felt like home to the Michigan City native. His own dad could never master the sound. That is why north was always pronounced "nort," and south was spoken as "sout." When Frank Pawlak spoke of work mates at the factory, he often said "dem guys" for "them guys."

Lydia understood English language well, and could certainly converse. Her soft voice and a bit of timidity let Mariusz do most of the talking, and an occasional word translation if necessary. Lydia grew up in a home where her father, Jan and his twin brother Pawl had taught themselves the English language. They became so fluent they both became noted translators for English speakers who visited their churches throughout Poland.

Mariusz's huge smile, tall stature, and lovingly gregarious spirit was only exceeded by Lydia's grace and raving beauty. The Pawlaks commented that she carried herself like a young Jacqueline Kennedy.

The small church sanctuary was filled to capacity that evening. When Mariusz pulled the guitar strap over his head full of thick, tall, standing hair, smiled and joined his voice with that of his lovely young wife, the audience was captivated. It mattered not that the crowd of predominantly southern Floridians could not understand one word the duo lofted across the room that night. Their smiles, exuding love, and sincere message was quickly interpreted by every heart. There were few dry eyes in the place, as Mariusz began to deliver his message in English. He told of his childhood and early years, growing up in a very independent minded country that had suffered through the years of want and need under the forceful hand of Soviet control, and the minds of the Russian Kremlin. He shared the joy of the new found freedoms and improvements that had transpired since the fall of the Soviet Union. He so excitedly told of the new religious freedoms, and then explained how after doing his Seminary training in Canada, He and his young bride were endeavoring to plant a new church in a small industrial village near his home in Poland. Their city leaders had even made a former hotel building, used by the Nazis during the War available to the small church for the purchase price of only a dollar.

"What kind of money do you need for the renovation of your church building?" Sam asked Mariusz as he set the hot tea on the coffee table in front of his guest.

"I have talked to some professional people and also some who know how to do this work, and with what our church people could do also through volunteers it seems we could get it done for about thirty thousand dollars, American."

Sam reached in his pocket and pulled out a folded check representing that evening's collection and said, "Maybe this can be a start. I have several people who told me they were not prepared to give tonight, but they will be bringing more Sunday." Sam thought for a moment how much larger the amount on the check was from that twenty dollar bill that rolled up and stuck on his grandfather Kaz's shoe, ninety nine years earlier on that wet and windy day in Baltimore. "There will be more money coming, and I really will talk to some others and see if I can help get this project moving with you."

Mariusz kindly thanked Sam for the wonderful help and then raised an idea. "Maybe when the weather breaks after this winter, you could think about coming to us, staying with us. You could see the project, preach to our people and some other churches in Poland. I could translate for you, you could take some pictures. It would better show people back here, not only our need, but many other needs as well."

For a moment it felt like déjà vu. He could almost hear the voice again of the Swedish pastor from twelve years ago, "I can bring you to Poland, I can open some churches for you to preach, and with a Polish name you would be very welcomed." He remembered the Solidarity uprising, the declaration of Martial Law, and the silence that followed. "Twelve years...nothing. But the original message rang in his memory. "I have a work for you to do in Poland."

For a long moment, neither man spoke. Sam began to argue with his mind. "I have just come here recently. My focus has to be this church. I have a job to do here. If we grow we will need to build and enlarge ourselves. My heart has to be here. I cannot let it be pulled another direction. I can do some, but not too much. What if I become overwhelmed with the needs I would see there? No, I missed my opportunity. It is too late. The time is not right, Poland did not happen then, I must not let it happen now." With all these issues flooding Sam's mind he felt a bit amazed and shocked when he heard himself suddenly say, "Sure, you name the dates, and we will be there."

"Oh wonderful, wonderful! Super." Came the words out of Mariusz's mouth. Then with a softer and more serious tone he stood, and placed his hand on Sam's shoulder. "I am happy. Thank you so much. We will make plans and so look forward to you coming to Poland. May of next year would be a great time if it would be good for you."

After a little more talk, and telling the ladies of their plans, the two couples said their good nights and headed for their rooms. Mariusz called back across the house, "Dobranoc."

Sam had not heard the word for "good night" spoken in that house since the last night his dad had spoken it. Lying on his back, hands behind his head, and staring through the darkness of the room he thought to himself, "*What a day, what a phone call, what a change in plans, what a church service, what a couple.*" Hot tears began to roll from his eyes and he whispered off to sleep with the words, "What is the work he has for me to do in Poland?"

****

Although it would be almost another decade before airports would require the personal security search and pat down, the fact that more planes and more persons had the freedom to fly into the former Soviet Union satellite countries like Poland, had not yet made the old clearing procedures any faster for the exhaustively slow method of safeguarding passengers, or better stated, dangerous suspects. With passports stamped, and all their paperwork, including Mariusz's invitation letter safely in hand, the young, attractive Polish woman extended her hand toward the breathless grandparents. Their daughter April had given them their first grandchild, Kimberlee only a few months earlier. The young attendant greeted them with a very kind,

"Dobry wieczór." Upon recognizing that the documents were accompanied by U.S. passports, she quickly spoke again. "Good evening." She smiled even more beautifully when Sam and Pat, simultaneously displayed their limited knowledge of Polish greetings.

"Dobry wieczór, Pani."

After a short observation of the papers, and seeing their frazzled appearance, she gave them their first settling words since deplaning in East Elmhurst. "We have a little delay due to the weather, so there is no rush. We will have a little time yet before we begin to board. Welcome to Lot Polish Airlines, I hope you enjoy your experience with us."

"Are you ok?" Sam asked his wife, after placing the carryon luggage above Row 16. The aisle and middle seats were a bit wider than the domestic flight from Tampa to New York. Pat's purse fit under the seat in front of her as required, but Sam's brief case would have to go overhead.

"Yes, I am fine. I think I have settled down a bit."

"Oh really? Can't say I noticed." He teased about her famous high strung personality.

She cradled her arm around his arm, and laid her head against his large, strong shoulder. Kicking her feet forward and back like an excited little girl on a school yard swing she asked, "Can you believe this day has finally come? We are really going to Poland." He swallowed hard the rising lump in his throat, shook his head slowly, and softly chewed his tongue in hopes that the facial gesture, genetically inherited from his dad, would quickly prevent the warm moisture at the corner of each eye from openly flowing down his face. He took a deep breath and gave a slow release from his puckered lips.

"We are going to Poland at last, at last."

Their backs pressed hard against the seats as the large plane defied gravity and pressed upward from the wet and rainy runway. Once above the low cloud cover engulfing the city that never sleeps, the last visage of sunset descended beyond the silhouetted shapes. The familiar skyline could be no other than that city so nice they named it twice, New York, New York.

Between the first serving of drinks and snacks and the arousal announcement that dinner would soon be served, Kazimierz Pawlak's grandson and his beautiful Polish-by-choice wife, fell exhaustively into a necessary sleep over the first depths of the ocean that had carried his grandfather to a land that offered his people a unique invitation.

"Give me your tired, your poor.
Your huddled masses yearning to breathe free.
The wretched refuse of your teeming shore.
Send these, the homeless, tempest-tossed to me.

I lift my lamp beside the golden door!" [4]

After a safe landing and rather chaotic transfer in Frankfurt, Germany, they were boarded, seated, and then greeted by the pleasant flight attendants, consisting of three pretty young Polish women.

"Would you like perhaps a glass of wine, a good Polish beer, or something a little stronger?"

The Pentecostal pastor's wife responded as expected, "Perhaps we could have a Coke or Ginger Ale, please?"

"But of course." came the reply and then the question. "Is this your first time to Poland?"

"Yes it is! We are so excited, but my husband's family is originally from Poland, Poznan in fact." Before Sam could respond the attendant quickly declared,

"Oh, then you are Polish..." As quickly as the words flew from her lovely voice, her right hand quickly replaced the Ginger Ale. Her left hand reached to the lower part of the cart, crossed the right arm, and rather emphatically banged the replacement drink on Sam's awaiting table. "No, no." she said in a commanding and corrective voice. "You are Polish, your first time to Poland, you must have a good Polish beer. Piwo." She demanded.

Sam and Pat looked at each other sheepishly while the second cold can of Zywiec was given to them, as if they had won the prize for being the one millionth flyer of the year. Now there came a dilemma. The clergy couple understood well the kind hospitality that had been shown them. Knowing there was such a light manifest of passengers probably made the generosity a bit more possible, but it did not make the situation less awkward. They had practiced for some time the abstinence policy toward the use of alcoholic beverages as a matter of choice and compliance with the church organization to which they held their credentials. They were also aware, or at least had heard, that this total abstinence policy was not necessarily the position or practice of many of the European churches who were, at least, shirt-tail relatives of the same denomination. This was attributed to the fact that the European culture was much more comfortable with a social participation of drinking than their American counterparts.

---

4 "The New Colossus" a sonnet by Emma Lazarus's 1883

"Oh, thank you, but we really don't drink beer, and would prefer the soft drink." Pat attempted a non offensive way out of the situation.

"Nonsense." The quick reply from the delightfully kind attendant. "You are Polish. Of course you drink beer. In fact, I will be right back with some good red wine for you also; our gift to welcome you home to Poland." As she darted toward the back of the plane, Sam and Pat could not restrain the laugh. He jokingly said,

"Well, when in Rome, do as the Romans do."

"But this is Poland..." She slyly smiled. "...not Rome. So we will be kind, and let them know we are just too full to drink it now. We can take it with us and I will poor it out when we get on the ground."

She already had an escape plan in mind. She had removed her heavy black socks when she got on the plane, and they were still in her purse. She could put a can of beer in each of her socks in order to dispose of the Devil's brew without the crew knowing.

"Here you are." The attendant returned. "Two fine small bottles of excellent German wine. Again, I hope you enjoy our airlines, and maybe later you can have a beautiful glass of wine with your first good Polish meal. Be sure to have some good pierogis, as well."

Sam and Pat graciously thanked her, and stared at the abundant supply of alcohol on each tray. Sam began to voice a partial solution. Referring to the Bishop that had first connected them again to Poland, Sam suggested,

"I remember Gordon telling us that when he visited the churches in Poland, they used real wine for the Lord's Supper ceremony. Perhaps we could give the wine to Mariusz when we get there, and they could use it in their communion meal. Probably would save them a little money too."

"That sounds like a good idea." She happily responded.

Sam secured the two small wine bottles in the corner of his carryon bag, and Pat hid the beer can socks deep in the bottom of her huge purse to be dealt with later. They enjoyed the small dinner served on the plane consisting of tasty sausages, pickled herring, a few strong tasting pieces of cheese, and some of the best poppyseed bread they had eaten since Frank Pawlak was alive and baking his own.

"Ladies and Gentlemen, we welcome you to Warsaw, Poland."

Sam sat silently with his eyes transfixed on the back of the seat in front of him. His trance-like state was quickly broken when he heard Pat say, "Hey, some of your stuff you were working on fell off the seat next to you. There, on the floor."

He looked down to his feet and saw a few papers with his folded calendar. He quickly flipped the calendar closed, gathered the scattered notes, and stuffed them into his attaché. The generous flight attendant walked down the aisle, preparing for the deplaning process. She tapped Sam, and pointed at the floor.

"Is that yours?"

He looked to the floor and saw a form he'd missed.

"Oh, I'm so glad you caught this one." He sighed. He turned to Pat as he stuffed the old paper into the calendar. "I almost lost my grandpa Kaz's immigration form."

"Whew, that would be pretty hard to replace." She admonished.

As they walked down the passageway and into the terminal they stopped long enough to look out the large windows at the still heavy downpour pounding on the plane they had just flown.

"That's it, Babe. That is Poland." He said, and then released a huge breath. The torrential rain became just a blur in his eyes as they began filling with tears.

They moved toward the doors with the green exit sign to the terminal. Sam softly opened his passport and flipped a few pages till he saw it. Stamped in black ink, clear as it could have possibly been displayed, one word - Polska. His feet were standing on the homeland of his fathers. Waiting on the other side of the electric sliding doors was a gathering of excited and happy people, many with the customary bouquet of flowers. The cheers, squeals, and hilarious celebrations for returning family or long awaited friends was a vast contrast to the scene one floor above. The sadness, sorrow, and heartbreak of farewells.

There he was, tall, thin, handsome, smiling with one hand waving far above the crowd, and the other hand securing the pretty flowers to present to Pat.

"So, welcome home." Were the surprising words from this young preacher who had so endeared himself to the Pawlaks on his previous visit to America.

"We can't believe we are finally here." Pat excitedly affirmed to Mariusz while Sam shook hands, hugged, and gripped both shoulders of the thin figure, while waiting for his voice to fight its way through the enormous blockage of emotion embedded just above his larynx.

Sam didn't wish to make a spectacle of himself, but neither could he resist from quickly reaching down to touch the wet grass at his feet, as he reflected on the 8 year old Kaz rolling on the first grass he'd touched in America.

"I cannot believe the cars and the traffic. This is like any major city I have ever visited." Sam vocalized at every new and surprising detail he observed beyond the fogged windows of the smaller and older model car.

"Look, Sam." became an oft repeated phrase from Pat perpetually shifting up and back across the rear seat. "It looks like every balcony in these high-rise apartments has a satellite dish on their balcony."

Mariusz began his personal tour guide dialogue of welcomed information to the giddy newcomers to his land. As fast as their eyes could scan, heads could twist and ears could absorb both the oral and visual panorama they found so engrossing, a regular and rapid-fire infusion of sight and sound dispelled all effects of tiredness, jet lag, or that initial discomfort usually experienced upon one's first time in strange surroundings.

"Look, Sam. Some are even parking on the sidewalks." She narrated as she looked.

"They are not supposed to do that." Mariusz explained. "But with so many cars now, what are you to do? Besides many of them are the small Polski Fiat."

"I think we can park here for now." Mariusz said with a voice of concession and hope. Hoping at least not to return to a citation firmly secured to the wiper blade. He continued the tour when he strained his long Adam's-apple-protruding-neck to gaze with others at the Warsaw Palace of Culture and Science. Its spire reaching 778 ft (almost 80 stories), it was the sixth tallest building in what would become the European Union. At that time, it was the tallest clock tower in the world. Mariusz took them on the elevator ride to the high observation deck, since the rain had now gone. The skies had cleared and the hot sun warmed their faces in spite of the strong breezes high above the capital city. From the north and east corners of the building they looked down on the beautiful Vistula River that served as the Mississippi of Poland. Its power, width, and beauty gave little evidence or memory of the human ashes that had flowed half a century before from the furnaces of Auschwitz and Burkenau, northward to the cold Baltic Sea. To the west they observed the magnificent roofs of the "Old City" of Warsaw, called in Polish "Stare Miasto." This area, completely leveled by the Nazi air and ground forces was rebuilt after the War in the exact same seventeenth century design, using only photos and ancient plans for reference.

"There, Pat." Mariusz pointed. "Right down there, by that blue building is our church headquarters. It is on Sciana Street. The word Sciana means 'Wall.' See, we have our own Wall Street in Poland."

This thoroughfare was named Wall Street, not because of being the financial district of Poland, but because it was there that the city was walled up to create the Warsaw Ghetto, the largest of all the Jewish Ghettos in German-occupied Europe during World War II.

Sam felt the tears well up again in the corner of his tired eyes as he recounted how over 400,000 Jews had been imprisoned there. On average there were nine or more people living in one room with squalor, and daily starvation. It was from this very location they were looking down upon, that Jews were deported to Nazi concentration camps and mass-killing centers. The ghetto was demolished by the German forces in May of 1943 after the heroic and famous Warsaw Ghetto uprisings. The total death toll among the Jewish inhabitants of the ghetto is estimated to be at least 300,000 killed by bullets or gas, combined with 92,000 victims of rampant hunger and hunger-related diseases.

As if to break the heaviness of that moment, Mariusz guided them forward to the west and south view where they could see the vastness of the city that housed some of the strongest and most determined peoples to ever populate a nation, and against centuries of hostile oppression could neither be defeated, diminished, or removed from their rightful place in the land of fields.

"Hey, wait a second guys." Sam called to his guide and to Pat after exiting the tower. "I want to get one more picture of the whole building, but I need to lay down to get it all."

"No Sam." Pat quickly objected. You will get dirty and you have a hard enough time getting back up." But before she could finish he was descending to the sidewalk. Just as she had predicted, it was not an easy task for Sam to get back to his standing position. The two middle-aged and sports-damaged knees were developing more arthritis and less flexibility with each year of the approaching age of 50.

"Can I help you get up, Sam?" Mariusz questioned as he quickly moved toward the struggling figure, extending his hand for assistance.

"No, no, I got this. All I need is a little help from my old friend here, the garbage can."

As he twisted from his sitting position he placed one hand firmly on the top of the concrete and stone receptacle. A pull, followed by a grunt, accompanied with a groan, and bone snapping sound from both knees and the figure, stood in total denial of being anything less than the flexible young figure of his past imagination. With both hands holding the top of the centrically fixed article at just below his waist, he observed atop the refuse within the container, a most unusual and unexpected site.

"What in the world is this?" Bolted from his panting chest. "I don't believe my eyes, how can this be?" He released the balancing grip on the trash container, and to the shock of Mariusz and Pat, thrust his hand directly into the disgusting garbage within. As his hand reappeared from who knows how much germ infestation, he lifted out a perfectly folded copy of the most recent edition of the major Warsaw Newspaper. He quickly thrust the front page view in the direction of the approaching eyes of his two partners. "Look! Look at this headline! What does it mean?" Sam asked frantically.

"Pawlak! Pawlak! Pawlak! Look, it is right there on the top of the paper, the headline, my name, three times, my family name, Pawlak! Why, what the heck does that mean, for the love of Mike? I come to Poland and one of the first things I see is my name on the front page of the paper?"

Mariusz had that sneaky little grin that Sam would come to know as the precursor of a good one line, impromptu response that brings the unexpected and hilarious comedic retort. "Yes, the whole nation heard you were coming, and now it is already in the headlines of the nation's largest newspaper."

Sam responded with a huge sarcastic, "Right! Yeah, I'm sure that is what it is. No, really. Why is it there?"

Mariusz stepped behind one shoulder, while Pat moved closely to Sam's opposite side. He pointed to the cartoon on the page, and the printed story beneath the picture. It reported that the newly elected president, none other than the same Lech Walesa, who had led the Solidarity demonstration movement of the past, was now looking at three different figures. He would have to accept one of them as the new Prime Minister of Poland's democratic, but parliamentary form of Government. The significance of the picture was that the three competing parties were all presenting Walesa with the same choice. This would not have been his choice, since the person being recommended to him was a political opponent to his party platform. The new Prime Minister bore the name Pawlak, Waldemar Pawlak.

"Mariusz, can you help me get a few copies of this paper?" Sam was aware from some previous research that the name Pawlak, with this original spelling, was a fairly common name in Poland. This fact was represented by not only the multiple pages of Pawlaks in the Polish phone books, but even the several pages in the phone books of Chicago, Cleveland, New York, Detroit, and Pittsburgh.

"Sir, I need five copies of this newspaper." He repeated this same sentence several times to the proprietor of the local news kiosk. The more he tried to explain in English, the more the Eastern European entrepreneur misunderstood him. "Sir, I have four brothers and one sister, and I would like to take each of them a copy of this paper to America." He started to speak more slowly and loudly to help the non-English speaking gentleman understand the importance of these multiple copies. "I need five, please." But the frustrated American could not understand the man's passionate gestures, as the paper salesman kept saying,

"Nie. Nie." Pointing his index finger in a poking movement toward his own eyes and then pounding the same finger on Sam's garbage can copy. He began yelling at the loud Yank, as if volume would make either one of them understand the other.

When Sam turned to see if Mariusz perhaps could intervene through some form of translation, he was confused to see Mariusz again laughing uncontrollably, enjoying the entertainment value of this international misunderstanding. It was the kind of exchange that could often lead to misconceptions of both peoples represented at these negotiations.

Sam rather sheepishly asked, "What is going on here? How can I make him understand?"

"He is not Polish. He is probably Romanian, what we call Roma. You say, I think Gypsy but that is a racially offensive word to them." Mariusz tried to explain through intermittent laughter. "I think he is saying you don't need five copies of this paper. You only have two eyes, and you already have a paper. So he doesn't want to sell you more when you can only read one at a time anyway."

Sam laughed at himself, and with an understanding smile sighed and said, "They really haven't quite figured this capitalism thing out yet, have they?"

Never one to give up too easily, Sam thought he would make one more attempt with a little more clarity in spite of the language barrier. He came up with a sure fire solution, meant to clear the air and help the man make a good sale.

"Sir, please, maybe I can make you understand." He stood a little taller, in fact, very erect, pointed his own index finger to his breast bone, followed by a few hardy thumps of his flattened hand to his chest, and for a little more effect, made the hand into a fist, strongly pounding his chest several times while declaring, "My...name...is...Pawlak. See? Just like the headline here, Pawlak. Yes, I am a Pawlak, and I want to take many copies of this paper to America. USA. Understand? Pawlak, my name, in America."

Then as if all the lights of the Palace behind them would have illuminated at the same time, the kiosk salesman put his hand to his mouth, then his head. He motioned for Sam to stay right where he was, and wait just a moment.

"At last, I think he got it." Sam announced to his more than amused traveling companions.

But instead of returning with additional copies, the man returned with a woman, and little girl, rattling on in his native tongue so fast it was a simple blur of noise to Sam. But Sam understood one word very clearly, Pawlak, followed by more foreign words, then again, Pawlak, Pawlak.

Mariusz quickly and seriously said to Sam as he reached for his arm, "I think we better go. I am not sure, but I think that is his wife and daughter, and I believe he is trying to introduce them to the new Prime Minister of Poland. He thinks you are the Pawlak in the newspaper."

With that Sam responded, "Let's get out of here before I get arrested for impersonating an elected official!"

They practically ran in the direction of the questionably parked car. What made the matter even more hilarious was that when they got in the car Mariusz simply handed him the five copies of the paper he so vigorously had sought. The foreign tourist with the Polish name had not noticed that during the height of the stalemated negotiations, Mariusz had quietly taken five newspapers off the rack and laid the money on the glass counter. Neither the seller nor the failed buyer even noticed.

As the trio enjoyed the drive out of the impressive city, the real Poland began to open before them. Mile after mile of colorful and productive fields were only interrupted by occasional tall, thick and glorious sections of woodlands. But the sight that caught Sam the most was the elegantly displayed forest of white barked birch trees. Every section of woods made him think of his father, Frank. The wonderful days of squirrel, rabbit, pheasant, and quail hunting alongside the proficient man with the double barrel, 16 gauge shotgun. So fantastic were his hunting skills that the family nicknamed him "Eagle Eye," Then came a sigh and a whisper, "O Dad, I so wish you could be here with us."

Soon the modern scenes were nowhere to be viewed. Old farmhouses, horse drawn equipment, and wagon drivers who all looked like Tevye the milkman from the little village of Anatevka, in the settlement of Imperial Russia in 1905. Each next village and town painted a picture, and gave Sam awareness of his roots, heritage, and legacy. The new world was suddenly being overtaken by something so familiar and so real. Not new, but known deep somewhere in his heart, in his thoughts, in his ways, and in his blood. Each town and village name was pronounced for Pat. Nadarzyn, Radziejowice, Tomaszow, Radomsko, Częstochowa, Klobuck, Olesno, Chudoba, Zawada, Opole, Krapkowice, Krempna, and finally, their destination Zdzieszowice.

"Over there, I just saw my Uncle John." Sam announced to Pat who was scanning landscape, building designs, and all those strange words with their overabundance of consonants. "Oh my." became a repetitive and breathy expression as he continued. "That lady, coming out of that shop, that could have been my Aunt Sophie, and that one on the bus stop bench, the way she has wrapped that scarf around her head and face, looks everything in the world like my dad's Aunt Celia. Man, this is uncanny."

They were both startled when Mariusz abruptly applied the brake, bringing the car to a sudden stop. It took only a moment for them to see the reason for the sudden halt. A sizable group of students had burst across the small town street, right in front of their vehicle. Just normal inattentive behavior of middle school age youth, scrambling their way from another boring day of school to play the world's most popular sport, futbol. The identification resemblances turned to an entire new generation in Sam's vision, while the roll call of family members peeled softly from his tongue. "That big blond kid there, is exactly what Manson looked like when playing basketball for Jim Grott out at Coolspring School. And the boy over there, with the glasses, that is for sure my brother Dick, hump on his nose and all." Now a melancholy little crack in Sam's voice would require a quick throat clearing and a fast shake of his head as he whispered "Oh, for love of Mike, that looks like almost every kid I grew up with in Michigan City, at least all the Polish kids."

Once again under way, he remained quiet and reflective until they finally exited the Polish countryside, crossed a single track rail line, passed the big smokestacks of the factory and were introduced to the little village they had so longed to see since hearing Mariusz and Lydia's first descriptions. The plain, grey, eight to ten story apartment buildings were still, for the most part, the expressionless, simple, and identical structures so common to the Russian, Communist controlled architectural design of the post war Socialism. Those who lived in a building with eight or more stories of height most likely had a small elevator. The abundance of satellite dishes affixed to balconies meant the secluded, and often travel-prohibited citizenry were no longer cut off from the actions, behaviors, lifestyles, fashions, and political philosophy of the democratic, capitalistic and opportunistic free world.

"Hey Mariusz," Pat hesitantly called for their host to come to the little room that had been prepared for their stay. While Lydia prepared the main daily dinner meal, known in Polish as Obiat, Pat held behind her back the items she had planned to present to Mariusz. Not a gift from America, that would come later at the meal, but the resolution to their airplane dilemma. As Mariusz entered the room, Pat began to explain, with a playful smile. "We need you to help us with something."

"Sure, what do you need?"

"Well the flight attendants on the Polish airline were so kind to us, and when they found out my husband's family came from Poland they bequeathed us with some lovely presents."

She slowly pulled her hands from behind her back, and stood there holding four sporty tube socks. It was obvious that there was some item in each sock, and they appeared to be a bit heavy. She then pulled from two of the socks the small bottles of red wine they had smuggled off the plane. "Since we could not drink these we thought perhaps you could use them for your communion service at church."

"Oh, thank you very much. Yes, this will be very good, and since money is very little with our new church of young adults, this is much appreciated."

Feeling full approval of her resolution to the uncomfortable situation, she continued to the next two socks. Thinking she might be even more spiritually effective, she pulled out two empty cans of Zywiec Polish beer. She explained to Mariusz how she had, upon arriving at their apartment, quickly gone to the restroom and poured the contents out, but did not know how to dispose of the empty cans. Mariusz, using his amazing and humorous timing, held each can. Looking deep into the hollow containers, he said with a serious tone,

"You know Pat, it probably would have looked much better and more convincing of your obedience to your church, if you had left the beer inside the cans. How do I really know you poured it out?"

The seldom speechless Patricia stood with her mouth gaped open. It was not till Mariusz spread that warm and mischievous smile across his face, and Sam burst into laughter that she fully grasped the folly of her, not so ingenious master plan.

Still holding the cans, he announced back in the direction of the little kitchen, "Lydia, we almost had good Polish beer for dinner tonight." After the funny exchange, he excused himself to help Lydia prepare the traditional Polish meal.

Lydia insisted that Pat get a little rest rather than help in the kitchen. The jet lag and time difference did not allow Pat to sleep, but she did lie down for a little time on the day bed which was opened in their guest quarters. Sam stood gazing out the front window, relating to her all he was observing from his lofty station, high up in the apartment building. She responded with an occasional "Hum" or "Oh," but she was intently wondering what was really going on in the active mind of this man. She was sure he had questions about his purpose in this compelling place.

Sam continued to voice his observations. "Pat, there is not one blade of grass in that courtyard down there. Really reminds me of the old Coolspring place. Aunt Sophie tried a few times, but she could never get a yard started there, not with our bikes running over it and the boys' cars pulling up. There was just too much traffic, the same here." He persisted in his sentimental journey. "There is a little garden beyond those buildings. Kind of reminds me of the gardens in Snake Town, along the track by Aunt Hattie's house." Then he said with a little more excitement in his voice. "Hear that? Those little whistles in the distance. That is a train. Sure a different sound than the old Night Owl."

Pat asked "What's the old Night Owl?"

"Oh, that is what my dad always called the train whistle on the Monon train when it crossed at Earl Road. In the evening it always had a rather lonesome sound to me as a kid." He was thinking out loud. "I wonder how many box cars carried people to Auschwitz along that line?" It was perhaps that thought that moved him to reflect to her what he was really feeling. "Honey, this probably sounds pretty odd, but standing here by this window, with this visual explosion before my eyes, I almost feel like I have travelled way back to somewhere deep inside of me. It's a place that I never knew existed."

"I think I know what you mean." She sat up to face him. "I feel something really significant happening here. I know you, Sam Pawlak, more than anyone else alive. I've been sharing this adventure with you since we were teenagers on a front porch, and I'm going where you're going, whether it's a field in Indiana, or a field in Poland." Then she soberly said, "Tell me. What is God showing you?"

He took a deep breath, and shuttered as he looked back out the window. "This is me. That grassless yard, those running kids, those older people on the porches, that garden in the distance, trains whistling in the dark, that smell coming from Lydia's kitchen, smelling so much like Grandma Pawlak's kitchen. An apartment up stairs, I am home. I know who I am today. This is not just familiar, this is right. I have been a wanderer searching for 'The Place,' my place. I belong. This is it!"

Mid-phrase he was interrupted.

"Hey, you two. Can I come in a moment?" Were the soft words of their host. Pat stood up quickly and Sam spun out of his near trancelike state.

"Sure, Sure, come on in, no problem, enter." They barraged him with welcome.

"Your good Polish dinner is just about ready, but I wanted to check with you about tomorrow. Maybe we can make a few plans. We could take you to see the museum at

Auschwitz, or our amazing salt mines near Krakow, or perhaps the mountains in Wisla for some mushroom hunting. You might also prefer to just rest from your trip and see the village tomorrow.

Always looking to make a funny reply before a serious answer, Sam quipped, "Well, let me get my calendar out and see how many important meetings I have with the government officials and rich people tomorrow."

All three laughed as Pat lightly slapped his arm as if to say, "Don't be so silly."

Sam reached over his head where he had placed his attaché case on a shelf provided for some of their smaller items. But as he touched the case, the large photo calendar came sliding out first. It hit Sam squarely in the face, and it changed directions when he swatted at it like he would have been back-handing a line drive baseball from the bat of an opposing team member. The calendar fluttered to the floor of the little room. Slowly, Sam bent at the knees, and reached with both hands to gather the calendar when the most unexpected revelation presented itself. Holding it firmly with both hands, he seemed to be removed, isolated, in a silent cone of time. He stared intently for a moment at the top half of the folding calendar and seemed transfixed by the beautiful artistic rendering of an old battered ship on smooth surf, with just a small image of a shoreline and perhaps civilization beyond the shore. Then he saw it for the first time. He had not even thought, or considered the possibility of such an extremely significant destiny. His mind replayed a vision of changing scenes faster than any modern camera could project on any cinematic screen. There appeared suddenly picture after picture, photo after photo, person after person.

A little boy, rolling in the wet grass, and suddenly he heard the voice saying, "Mama, Mama it's true! Money grows on the streets of America!"

Then just as quickly a lady on a bed, with a bottle in hand, weeping the words, "Poznan, Poznan, Poznan."

The scene changed to a Band Shell, an orchestra, and long beautiful hair wafting over the back of a park bench.

And then a voice in panic, "Eddie is missing in action, Oh no! God, Please!"

The flashes came faster.

"Pearl Harbor, sounds like a pretty place."

"Dem Dahg Gahn kids!"

"Mom, it's so hot up here. I can't breathe."

Interspersed between this menagerie of sights and sounds were the oft repeated phrases from no other voice than his dad.

"Oh Sure."

"That's swell."

"For love of Mike."

Sam saw the inside of the little Orlando chapel. The vision of the side door opening, and the voice like he had never heard nor may never hear again.

"I have a work for you to do in Poland".

Just as quickly as he was mentally, visionally, and emotionally transported from the present, he was returned. He placed the calendar on the little day bed, reached his hand to Pat's arm, and said,

"Look at this! Grandpa's immigration form. See the date? I never saw this, or even realized it till now. 8th of May, 1893!" He flipped the calendar open to the current date. His finger firmly pressed on the number of the day printed in heavy black ink."

Pat read aloud. "May 8, 1993!" Then as tears filled her eyes, she reached for her husband's hand. "Oh, Sam!"

He tearfully affirmed, "One hundred years."

The End

EPILOGUE

In the quarter century since the reunification of the nation of Poland and the Pawlak family of Michigan City miraculous adventures have continued, the details of which may be written perhaps by a future grandchild or great-grandchild and revealed to the public of their day. Needless to say this journey of one hundred years did not come to an ultimate conclusion in that little apartment bedroom in the village of Zdzieszowice.

All of Kaz's children, John, Frank, Sopie, Lilly, and Ed have passed, but Michigan City is still full of their legacy and memories.

Frank and Opal's other kids, Manson (Frank Jr), Bud (John), Fred, Dick, and Valery have all experienced their own novel's worth of challenges, blessings, and miracles.
Within three years of that first visit, Sam and Pat stepped down from their church pastor position in Tampa to become fully-appointed missionaries residing fully entrenched in the language, life, and culture of Jan and Anna Pawlak's beloved Poland. They spent their days encouraging young pastors, loving the dear people, hosting visiting tour groups from America, and sharing their remarkable stories of miraculous events in their own lives.

Sam and Pat's children and grandchildren have all returned to Poland, and are regularly involved in the continuation of and support of national church planting.
Three years after Sam and Pat's discovery trip to Poland, Pat was diagnosed with bilateral breast cancer. She underwent massive surgery, months of radical chemotherapy and radiation. She not only survived the terrible experience but remained in complete remission and cancer free for the next ten years. On the ten year anniversary of her initial diagnosis the disease metastasized in her bones, this time primarily in the spine. She received a prognosis of 3-18 months to live, but with faith and fight she again overcame the monster and shocked all her doctors with another 16 years of vibrant life, and a testimony of God's grace which she shared with anyone who would listen. On August 26, 2020, with Sam at her side, Pat left a final instruction, "Rejoice," and she journeyed to Heaven.

Sammy and April became professional musicians, married wonderful mates, and continued their parents' life of planting and pastoring wonderful churches.
Sam retired from the work of a Pastor after several years in Southern California, and now resides near his children. He loves his time with his five grandchildren and three great grandchildren. He still takes speaking invitations and writes. As this work of twenty years

goes to print, this author is looking forward to doing more fishing like his father Frank loved so much.

The most pressing issue on Sam's future agenda is always the question, "How quickly can I return to the land, the churches, and the people of Poland?"

Mary & Kaz Pawlak

Eddie, Kaz, Frank Pawlak

Frank, John (Bud), Frank Jr. (Manson)

Richard (Dick), Fred,

Valery, Opal, Sam

Patricia & Sam Pawlak

Sammy, Sam, Pat, April

Made in the USA
Columbia, SC
13 June 2021

39918668R20280